Movie Minorities

Movie Minorities

Transnational Rights Advocacy and South Korean Cinema

HYE SEUNG CHUNG AND DAVID SCOTT DIFFRIENT

Rutgers University Press

New Brunswick, Camden, and Newark, New Jersey, and London

Library of Congress Cataloging-in-Publication Data

Names: Chung, Hye Seung, 1971– author. | Diffrient, David Scott, 1972– author.
Title: Movie minorities : transnational rights advocacy and South Korean cinema / Hye Seung Chung and David Scott Diffrient.
Description: New Brunswick : Rutgers University Press, 2021. | Includes bibliographical references and index.
Identifiers: LCCN 2020050464 | ISBN 9781978809642 (paperback) | ISBN 9781978809659 (hardcover) | ISBN 9781978809666 (epub) | ISBN 9781978809673 (mobi) | ISBN 9781978809680 (pdf)
Subjects: LCSH: Motion pictures—Korea (South)—History—20th century. | Motion pictures—Korea (South)—History—21st century. | Human rights in motion pictures. | Minorities in motion pictures.
Classification: LCC PN1993.5.K6 C5453 2021 | DDC 791.43095195—dc23
LC record available at https://lccn.loc.gov/2020050464

A British Cataloging-in-Publication record for this book is available from the British Library.

∞ The paper used in this publication meets the requirements of the American National Standard for Information Sciences—Permanence of Paper for Printed Library Materials, ANSI Z39.48-1992.

www.rutgersuniversitypress.org

Manufactured in the United States of America

This book is dedicated to the memory of Nancy Abelmann, a scholar of tremendous generosity whose passing in 2016 left a hole in the field of Korean studies and in our hearts

Contents

A Note on the Text

The romanization of Korean names in this book follows the McCune-Reischauer system, which is the academic standard endorsed by the Library of Congress. Exceptions to this rule are names of filmmakers, actors, political leaders, and geographical locations whose spellings are well-known to English-speaking readers, such as Bong Joon-ho, Chun Doo-hwan, Park Chan-wook, Park Chung-hee, Moon Jae-in, Jeju, and Seoul. Whenever Korean authors' works that have been published in English are cited, their names are presented in the way that they are printed in the source materials. Korean and other East Asian names appear in their native standard order, with surname first (except for names printed otherwise in English-language publications).

Movie Minorities

Introduction

"I Am a Human Being"

The Question of Rights in South Korean Cinema

On April 12, 2019, the ACT Human Rights Film Festival, an annual celebration of international social justice films held in Fort Collins, Colorado, hosted the Vancouver-based Chinese Canadian filmmaker Leon Lee, whose most recent documentary, *Letter from Masanjia* (2018), was part of that year's programming. The film, which concerns the brutal conditions faced by prisoners inside one of China's most notorious labor camps, features black-and-white animated sequences that depict in excruciating detail the various forms of torture that a soft-spoken engineer named Sun Yi suffered during his nearly three-year-long incarceration. As members of the festival's programming committee, we had already witnessed this moving testament to Yi's indominable spirit, which is conveyed not only through animation but also through talking-head interviews conducted after his release. However, we were unprepared for the affective spell that this film would cast over its audience at the Lyric (Fort Collins's only art-house theater and cohost of the festival since its launch in 2016). Throughout the first half of that screening, our fellow festival attendees gasped, sobbed, and shook their heads in disbelief, particularly during animated sequences that illustrated otherwise unrepresentable moments when Yi was mentally and physical punished for his earlier practice of Falung Gong (a meditation exercise outlawed in China). Midway through *Letter from Masanjia*, we stepped outside the darkened auditorium into the lobby of the theater to check on the film's director, who was

FIGURE I.1 One of the highest-grossing local films in South Korea, *A Taxi Driver* (*T'aeksi unjŏnsa*, 2017) presents a dramatic portrayal of events leading up to the Kwangju Uprising of May 1980. Its box-office success attests to the commercial viability of ostensibly difficult subjects and the readiness of present-day audiences to address human rights abuses of the nation's authoritarian past. Here, West German journalist Jürgen "Peter" Hinzpeter (Thomas Kretschmann), one of the main characters in the film, interviews a group of protestors in the midst of civil unrest.

casually chatting with festival organizers and volunteers prior to the post-screening Q&A session. The conversation that ensued, segueing from small talk about the local culture of northern Colorado to shared thoughts about human rights cinema as a global phenomenon, unexpectedly took us to the subject of South Korean filmmaking.

Specifically, we talked about the relative ease—at least from Lee's standpoint—with which commercial artists working within the South Korean film industry are able to inject social consciousness into high-profile, commercially viable motion pictures. To our surprise, the Chinese Canadian documentarian expressed admiration for recent Korean-language productions such as *The Attorney* (*Pyŏnhoin*, 2013), the story of a tax lawyer who becomes a legal representative for tortured victims of the government (based on an actual legal case taken by the human rights lawyer–turned–former president Roh Moo-hyun [No Mu-hyŏn]); *A Taxi Driver* (*T'aeksi unjŏnsa*, 2017; see figure I.1), a dramatized depiction of the events surrounding the Kwangju Uprising of May 1980 (as seen through the eyes of two outsiders, the German journalist Jürgen Hinzpeter and a cabbie in Seoul whom he hires to take him to Kwangju); and *1987: When the Day Comes* (2017), a political thriller about the June Uprising of that titular year, which resulted in the fall of a decades-long military dictatorship (after Pak

Chong-ch'ŏl, Yi Han-yŏl, and other innocent college student activists were killed at the hands of police). Near the end of our conversation, Lee mused, "When can China make a similar film about the June Fourth Incident?"—alluding to the Tiananmen Square Massacre of 1989 and putting a rhetorical spin on the transnational valences of human rights cinema as a means of bringing traumatic histories and painful memories to the screen. Ultimately, the director appeared to be skeptical about any such prospect in his place of birth. And he let a note of envy seep into his praise of South Korean filmmakers, whose artistic and political freedoms have made it possible for them to openly expose and critique their government's past atrocities within contemporary mainstream cinema in addition to independently produced 16mm or video documentaries shot during the 1980s (an "age of reform" that gave rise to the Youth Film Study Group [Ch'ŏngnyŏnyŏngsang yŏnguhoe]'s *South River* [*Kangŭi namjjok*, 1980], the Seoul Film Collective [Sŏul yŏngsang chipdan]'s *Water Utilization Tax* [*Surisae*, 1984], and Kim Dong-won [Kim Tong-wŏn]'s *Sanggye-dong Olympics* [1988], among other important forerunners of today's human rights films).[1]

Our brief encounter with Lee left an indelible impression and has prompted us to rethink the meaning of rights-based cinematic advocacy—or what is sometimes colloquially referred to as the human rights film—in the context of twenty-first-century South Korean cultural production. Generating tremendous returns on their investments at the box office (with 12.2 million and 11.4 million admissions, respectively), *A Taxi Driver* and *The Attorney* currently rank as the eleventh and fourteenth highest-grossing Korean films of all time. As Ryu Chae-hyŏng points out, these films are examples of "Korean national cinema" embraced by individuals across the demographic spectrum, cutting across the ideological divide between conservatives and liberals and demonstrating a collective desire to rectify past atrocities and heal historical traumas.[2] The ways in which rights violations of the authoritarian past are depicted in these recent films differ considerably from how they were obliquely alluded to or poetically allegorized in Korean New Wave films of the 1980s and 1990s, such as *Black Republic* (*Kŭdŭldo urich'ŏrŏm*, 1990), by Park Kwang-su, and *A Petal* (*Kkotnip*, 1996), by Jang Sun-woo (Chang Sŏn-u). Rights advocacy is no longer just a marginal subplot embedded within a larger heroic (or antiheroic) narrative, like the dark, expressionistic Kwangju sequence that flares up in *Peppermint Candy* (*Pakha sat'ang*, 2000), by the writer-director Lee Chang-dong (Yi Ch'ang-dong). In this critically acclaimed film, the indiscriminate killing of hundreds of citizen protesters and innocent bystanders by paratroopers is displaced by the injured, disoriented protagonist's accidental shooting of a high-school girl. Today, thanks to several sociopolitical factors, human rights advocacy is a popular theme of contemporary South Korean cinema, one that has increasingly been employed as a narrative in its own right.[3] It is an all-encompassing yet reductive "grand narrative," organically integrated into commercial motion pictures produced for mass consumption in multiplexes rather than in alternative venues such as universities, cinema clubs, and film festivals (where the abovementioned collectivist documentaries from the 1980s were first shown).

In this book, we pinpoint some of those sociopolitical factors and explain how, through a combination of "institutionalization" and "diffusion" (to borrow the conceptualization of Paul Y. Chang and Gi-Wook Shin),[4] the medium of motion pictures has played an important role in solidifying social movements within discrete, identity-based categories while universalizing the experiences of different activist communities and transnationalizing uniquely Korean sentiments about such issues as undocumented workers' rights and political prisoners' rights. The rise of rights-based advocacy in recent years, literally magnified through camera lenses and projected onto movie screens around the world, runs alongside an affective turn not only within the discipline of film studies (and related academic fields) but also within the local film industry, where filmmakers such as Hwang Tong-hyŏk, Chang Hun, Yang U-sŏk, Chang Chun-hwan, and Bong Joon-ho (Pong Chun-ho) have learned how to wring pathos from potentially risky or controversial subjects and build empathy for the most vulnerable members of society. This shared commitment to what might be termed "political affect" underlines the need to unite theory and practice in pursuit of a cross-disciplinary language equal to yet critical of the moralistic vocabulary of human rights as a politics of feeling. Rhetorically framed in such a way, South Korean cinema proves to be an especially powerful vehicle with which to transport international audiences—including filmmakers like Leon Lee—to distant locales and not-so-distant times when the fight for democracy alone was sufficient in bringing different activist communities together around a common cause. As a medium that is often mobilized to make viewers feel something (such as sadness, elation, pride, resentment, or guilt), movies indeed move us and might even prompt people to take action through such emotional appeals. This is particularly true of those cultural productions in which once-peripheralized minority groups (for example, people with disabilities, immigrants, and members of the LGBTQ community) take center stage and forge an empathetic relationship with mainstream audiences—something that South Korean cinema is doing with increasing frequency.

Structure and Scope of the Book

Ranging across several related topics, this book consists of eleven chapters and a coda. The chapters are paired thematically into six parts, in the following order: "Institutional Foundations and Formal Structures," "Movie Minors and Minor Cinemas," "Disability Rights in Mainstream and Minoritarian Filmmaking," "Representing Prisoners of the North and South," "Migrant Worker Rights in Hybrid Documentaries," and "Nonhuman Rights in a Posthuman World." Chapter 1, "The Rise of Rights-Advocacy Cinema in Postauthoritarian South Korea," charts the origins of rights-advocacy cinema in South Korea from the underground independent films (*tonip yŏnghwa*) of the 1980s to the human rights films (*ingwŏn yŏnghwa*) of the 1990s and beyond. The latter term began to circulate in public discourse during the government of Kim Young-sam (Kim Yŏng-sam), particularly after the launch of the Seoul Human Rights Film Festival (SHRFF) in 1996, but it was not until after the 1998 presidential inauguration of Kim Dae-jung (Kim Tae-jung), a former political prisoner and victim of rights abuses, that rights advocacy became a prominent facet of fiction and nonfiction films.

One of the top agendas of Kim's administration was the formation of the National Human Rights Commission of Korea (NHRCK; Kukka ingwŏn wiwŏnhoe), which was created in November 2001 after three years of intense deliberations and demonstrations. The contentious public debates surrounding the birth of this first national organization for human rights (independent of the government's three branches, yet dependent on the state's budget and bureaucratic appointments) speak to both the growing influence of a flourishing civil society (with bottom-up initiatives undertaken to correct the wrongs of the past and usher in a more egalitarian future) and the limitations of that society's power to make institutional changes. Drawing upon interviews with representatives of the NHRCK and the SHRFF, we introduce both inclusive and exclusive definitions of rights-advocacy cinema, an institutional genre reliant upon the support of governmental and nongovernmental organizations. Ultimately, we define the genre as a category of cultural production whose affective sway in provoking tears, raising awareness, and altering the mind-sets of demographically and geographically dispersed moviegoers (at home and abroad) is what matters most, the very thing that might actually yield consequential social changes.

Adopting transnational and cross-cultural perspectives, chapter 2, "*If You Were Me*: Transnational Crossings and South Korean Omnibus Films," takes as its main case study a multidirector omnibus film (a feature-length film divided up into distinct episodes) produced by the NHRCK. Bearing a title that hints at the spectatorial solicitations that are often directed toward audiences of human rights cinema, *If You Were Me* (*Yŏsŏt kaeŭi sisŏn*, 2003) foregrounds both the aesthetic and ethical dimensions of contemporary social problem films that might be accused of creating false equivalencies among a range of unrelated grievances, discriminatory situations, or rights claims. But the film also points toward the metaphorical bridge building or need to cross over that is bound up not only within the omnibus form but also within human rights cinema—an institutional genre underwritten by governmental and nongovernmental organizations that frequently asks audiences (both near and far) to imagine the pain or vulnerability of those situated on the other side of the screen. As the first in a series of seven similarly titled motion pictures concerning civil liberties and social justice, *If You Were Me* is noteworthy for several reasons. It is especially foundational to the chapters that follow, for it brings together the contributions of six widely recognized filmmakers of different generations and genders—Park Kwang-su,

Yŏ Kyun-dong, Im Sun-rye, Park Chan-wook (Pak Ch'an-uk), Pak Chin-p'yo, and Chŏng Chae-ŭn—whose backgrounds, affiliations, personal drives, artistic motivations, and professional commitments to minority rights vary considerably and thus highlight the wide assortment of topics that are brought together under the umbrella term "human rights cinema," an empathy-building genre of almost unparalleled inclusivity at both the institutional and structural levels. By delving into the production background, critical reception, and narrative operations of this particular film, which covers various types of embodied discrimination related to gender, physical disability, class status, past criminal record, and country of birth, we gesture toward some of the fundamental paradoxes undergirding this and other examples of human rights cinema—especially those that seek to reach mass audiences beyond school classrooms, both inside and outside South Korea.

Speaking of school classrooms, there are few spaces (with the possible exception of courtrooms) in which the fight for one's inalienable rights is as prominently featured in contemporary South Korean cinema. In chapter 3, we venture into that seemingly safe but most treacherous of locations, turning our attention to the increasingly prevalent theme of school violence (*hakkyo p'ongnyŏk*), which is discernible within low-budget independent films such as *Bleak Night* (*P'asukkun*, 2010) and *Night Flight* (*Yagan pihaeng*, 2014) and mainstream coming-of-age dramas such as *Once Upon a Time in High School* (*Maljukgŏri chanhoksa*, 2004) and *Bullies* (*Il-jin*, 2018). Titled "Hell Is Other High Schoolers: Bigots, Bullies, and Teenage 'Villainy' in South Korean Cinema," this chapter sets out to problematize the simplistic delineation between bullies and their victims. We argue that the young people who subject their peers to physical and/or verbal attacks are sometimes just acting out a deeper, systemic level of violence that has been part of South Korea's educational system for decades. That is, the bully—a stereotypical construct of villainy that motion pictures and other forms of popular culture (including K-dramas, or Korean television and internet dramas) have begun to foreground in recent years—is symptomatic of the institutional failings and widespread social dilemmas (such as homophobia, classism, conformity, and cutthroat competitiveness) that are paradoxically both concealed and revealed in the person of a preternaturally adult juvenile delinquent or "problem child." We present our textual analysis of the above case studies within a contextualizing discussion of the public debates surrounding the 2004 Act on the Prevention of and Countermeasures against Violence in Schools. We also incorporate data that serve as the basis for a transhistorical reading of texts whose meanings are necessarily multiple, shifting according to the place and time in which they are consumed. Although *Once Upon a Time in High School* is a nostalgically imbued action film set during the 1970s, a 2011 focus-group study of 278 college students who attended high school in the 2000s reveals that a majority of respondents were able to see themselves in its cinematic depiction of school violence and social discrimination, despite the passage of over three decades. This information about the film's reception—combined with images of bullies being victimized themselves by educators, administrators, and parents in *Bleak Night*, *Night Flight*, and other productions—indicates a disturbing trend in the cyclical revisitation of school violence upon the bodies and minds of young people whose only way out of such an oppressive environment is death. This sad reality is most apparent in those films in which students resort to suicide by throwing themselves from rooftops—a setting that, like the classroom, is conspicuous in writer-director Leesong Hee-il (Yisong Hŭ-il)'s *Night Flight*.

Chapter 4, "Indie Filmmaking and Queer Advocacy: Converging Identities in Leesong Hee-il's Films and Writings," extends some of the arguments from the previous chapter by highlighting other motion pictures made by *Night Flight*'s writer-director. One of South Korea's few openly gay filmmakers, Leesong is also a prolific generator of film and cultural criticism, and his provocative writings—as much as his cinematic output—are the focus of this chapter. Following Leesong's lead in his August 2000 article on "minority cinema" (*sosuja yŏngwha*) published in the *Independent Film Magazine*, we conceptualize his unique brand of minoritarian cinema as a site of generic and identity-based convergence, where multiple sets of dichotomous pairs (homosexuality and heterosexuality, indie filmmaking and genre filmmaking, melodrama and human rights cinema, and so on) are undermined through a strategic blurring of lines. After discussing Leesong's double advocacy for independent filmmaking and queer cinema in his writing and activism, we analyze his breakthrough production *No Regret* (*Huhoehaji ana*, 2006), an interclass love story between a rich man and a gay bar worker that has been compared to softcore "hostess films" of the 1970s and early 1980s (for example, *Yŏng-ja's Heyday* [*Yŏng-ja-ŭi chŏnsŏng sidae*, 1975], *Women's Street* [*Yŏjadŭlman sanŭn kŏri*, 1976], *The Woman I Threw Away* [*Naega pŏrin yŏja*, 1977], and *Winter Woman* [*Kyŏul yŏja*, 1977]). Applying Gilles Deleuze and Félix Guattari's concept of "minor literature," we redefine *No Regret* as a "minor film" that deterritorializes the language of melodrama (a dominant mode of cinematic discourse in South Korea) through a strategy of double queering: first, by foregrounding a gay couple in place of a heterosexual couple; and second, through the incorporation of anomalous thriller elements, which further defamiliarize the melodramatic aspects of the story.[5] As the first Korean queer film directed and produced by openly gay activists (Leesong Hee-il and Kimjo Gwangju), *No Regret* is a prime example of what Deleuze and Guattari call a "minor" text, for it is based on collective identity, political solidarity, and community building within a long-marginalized population. Despite the individualistic tendencies of its loner protagonists and its overly melodramatic premise, Leesong's gay romance (which abruptly morphs into a murder thriller during its final twenty minutes) is indeed subversive in its challenges to both heteronormative patriarchy and the dominant storytelling conventions of the South Korean film industry.

Chapter 5, "*Always*, *Blind*, and *Silenced*: Disability Discourses in Contemporary South Korean Cinema," moves away from minoritarian filmmaking to examine emerging trends in mainstream cultural productions. In this chapter, we explain how three disability-themed genre films theatrically released in 2011—the romantic drama *Always* (*Ojik kŭtaeman*), the crime thriller *Blind* (*Bŭllaindŭ*), and the social problem film *Silenced* (*Dogani*)—together highlight a problematic tendency in contemporary cinema. These otherwise well-intended productions reflect a propensity within the culture at large to infantilize people with disabilities, using their supposed helplessness as an opportunity to applaud the benevolence or selfless intervention of able-bodied defenders of their rights (including, in the case of *Silenced*, representatives of humanitarian nongovernmental organizations). Not only do these motion pictures treat perceived deficits in a character's mental or physical performance as an individual, rather than a societal, problem, but they also—to paraphrase the English-language title of the above case study—"silence" those for whom such courageous activism is performed by nondisabled protagonists. Despite creating greater public awareness and paving the way for positive legislative changes related to the issue of child abuse, director Hwang Tong-hyŏk's *Silenced* pushes a trio of abused deaf kids to the background once one of their teachers (assisted by a human rights defender) takes center stage, becoming a hero in the process of exposing a disturbing pattern of sexual violence committed against the disabled children by other educators and administrators at the tellingly named Benevolence Academy (a fictional stand-in for Inhwa School, where actual underage molestation occurred during the 2000s).

Chapter 6 takes a very different film as its main case study, one that restores cinematic agency to individuals whose disabilities are put into a social framework that is largely missing from the abovementioned genre productions, even as it devotes considerable time to the main characters' domestic lives (in quiet, seemingly uneventful scenes devoid of traditional heroism). Titled "Barrier-Free Cinema: Caring for People with Disabilities and Touching the Other in *Planet of Snail*," this chapter moves beyond mainstream productions to examine an important independent documentary by the South Korean director Yi Sŭng-jun. Years before he was selected to direct the official film about the 2018 Winter Olympics (held in P'yŏngch'ang) and having his 2019 short *In the Absence* (*Pujaeŭi kiŏk*) nominated for an Academy Award, the documentarian began to attract international attention with his 2011 production *Planet of Snail* (*Talp'aengiŭi pyŏl*), which—like its spiritual successor, *Wind on the Moon* (*Talae punŭn param*, 2015)—adopts a sensitive approach to a largely underrepresented or misrepresented community: that of deafblind individuals. Specifically, *Planet of Snail* focuses on Cho Yŏng-ch'an, a young man who interfaces with the world around him primarily through his sense of touch. Like the deafblind protagonist's relationship to raindrops, tree bark, beach sand, and other natural elements that might be haptically perceived by seeing audiences, human rights and the human sensorium are intimately linked in this film. Thus, a textual as well as textural approach to film analysis is encouraged by *Planet of Snail*, one of several motion pictures to be integrated into a "Barrier-Free" platform that, as we will explain in chapter 6, has fundamentally altered the experience of theatrical exhibition for audiences with hearing or visual impairments. By alluding to that alternative means of experiencing films (one that guarantees descriptive audio and subtitle services in addition to other accommodations), we seek to enhance the reader's phenomenological understanding of disability rights as a physically felt subject that, in the right hands (those of directors like Yi Sŭng-jun), is conducive to poetic cinematic expression.

An equally sensitive approach is taken by another documentarian, Kim Dong-won, who directed the 2004 film *Repatriation* (*Songhwan*). The film concerns the daily struggles of long-term political prisoners who have been released from the brutal South Korean carceral system into a civilian population that looks considerably different from the world they had been forced to leave behind. That production, which took Kim a dozen years to complete (shooting and then editing eight hundred hours of footage on five hundred tapes), is the main case study of chapter 7. Titled "Beyond Torture Epistephilia: The Ethics of Encounter and Separation in Kim Dong-won's *Repatriation*," this chapter investigates the ethical dimensions of cinematic rights advocacy and looks specifically at a pioneering work by the first president of the Association for Korean Independent Film and Video (Han'guk tongnipyŏnghwa hyŏphoe), who has been called the "godfather of Korean independent documentaries." As the winner of the 2004 Freedom of Expression Award at the Sundance Film Festival (an honor that had never before been given to a Korean-language film), *Repatriation* garnered critical accolades for the way that Kim humanized his subjects, with whom he had developed an almost familial connection. Those include "unconverted" (*pijŏnhyang*) prisoners—captured North Korean spies and agents—who had remained faithful to their communist beliefs in the face of a torturous "ideological conversion system" (*sasang chŏnhyangjedo*) practiced in the authoritarian South Korean prisons from the 1960s through the 1980s. One former prisoner in particular, "Grandpa" Cho Ch'ang-sŏn, is singled out as a kindhearted soul, someone who becomes a surrogate father of sorts for the director-narrator. In 2001, Cho and sixty-two other unconverted prisoners were voluntarily repatriated to North Korea (thanks to Kim Dae-jung's Sunshine Policy in the wake of the 2000 inter-Korea summit). Kim's film closes with a deeply personal voice-over ("I miss Grandpa Cho"), which drew the ire of some leftist commentators for its perceived lack of political commitment. Nevertheless, *Repatriation* is an ethically responsible text that eschews the tendency (apparent in other prison-themed films) to reduce its subjects to passive victims or informers. Unlike American "torture documentaries" embodying Julia Lesage's concept of "torture epistephilia" (such as Alex Gibney's *Taxi to the Dark Side* [2007] and Errol Morris's *Standard Operating Procedure* [2008]), Kim's film is an extension of the director's decade-long personal commitment to his subjects, who are portrayed as dignified witnesses to South Korea's anticommunist policies and the power of the human will to triumph over unspeakable acts of state violence and cruelty.[6]

Chapter 8 directs the reader's attention to North Korea, specifically to the widely reported cases of prisoner abuse that have been documented and dramatized in a number of nonfiction and fiction films. Titled "Story as Freedom or Prison? Narrative Invention and Human Rights Interventions in *Camp 14: Total Control Zone*," this chapter takes as its main case study an unusual German–South Korean coproduction released in 2012 and based on the *New York Times* best seller *Escape from Camp 14* (written by the American journalist Blaine Harden, first published in 2012, and reprinted with a new foreword three years later).[7] Subtitled "One Man's Remarkable Odyssey from North Korea to Freedom in the West," Harden's book profiles a former North Korean prisoner, Shin Dong-hyuk (Sin Tong-hyŏk), whose harrowing escape from a Soviet-style gulag drew the attention of international human rights organizations as well as the German documentarian Marc Wiese. In combining talking-head interviews shot in color and black-and-white animated sequences (showing the life that Shin allegedly led in the world's harshest penal colony), the filmmaker harnessed a hybridized form of storytelling in which the line between history and fiction is blurred. Such an approach is fitting, given the controversies that have circulated around Shin's recounting of past traumas and that are referred to in the second edition of Harden's book. It now appears that Shin stretched the truth and misrepresented his actual experiences as the only person known to have escaped from Camp 14, and this recent revelation further illustrates the documentarian's literally illustrative approach—in which animation (an increasingly prominent device in contemporary nonfiction films) becomes an appropriately imaginative vehicle to render what was not recorded and could not be seen (or verified) by witnesses to North Korean rights violations. It is not uncommon for someone in Shin's position to embellish, exaggerate, and even distort his testimony about his experiences as a prisoner in the North. Many defectors suffer from discrimination, unemployment, and financial hardships while trying to survive in the South, forcing them to capitulate to the market demand for shocking, salable stories about their homeland for media outlets and the national security lecture circuit. Whether or not one chooses to believe Shin's story, what is depicted in this transnational film is fundamentally true as a creative interpretation of something that has been experienced by many others like him who were routinely abused by guards and who, unlike him, remain voiceless and nameless objects of the West's humanitarian gaze.

A similarly hybridized or mixed approach to nonfiction storytelling is visible in the 2013 film *Scenery* (*P'unggyŏng*), by the Korean-Chinese filmmaker Zhang Lu (Chang Ryul). As the main case study of chapter 9, titled "Between *Scenery* and Scenario: Landscape, Narrative, and Structured Absence in a Korean Migrant Workers Documentary," this important yet understudied documentary focuses on the lives of fourteen migrant workers (*oegukin iju nodongja*) living in

South Korea. It adopts a fragmented, episodic approach that recalls the structure of *If You Were Me* and other omnibus films that present a series of "small" stories in piecemeal fashion. The workers who populate Zhang's film hail from such places as Bangladesh, Cambodia, the Philippines, Thailand, and Uzbekistan, but, speaking directly to the camera, they express common hopes and dreams as foreigners who long to return home to their families. Zhang juxtaposes conventional talking-head interviews with experimental interludes and beautifully framed exterior shots (of factories, building sites, and agricultural zones), implicitly putting these intimate tales of loneliness and loss within a larger societal and industrial context. In this chapter, we further contextualize the plight of migrant workers in relation to the South Korean government's neoliberal labor importation policies (including the Industrial Trainee System of the 1990s and the Employment Permit System that replaced it in 2004). Although allusions to exploitative working conditions are made in some episodes (such as the one centering on a Chinese butcher), for the most part the tellingly titled *Scenery* maintains an ethical distance from its subjects and evokes identity politics subtly, as evidenced by a final point-of-view shot from the vantage of an invisible migrant worker (presumably on the run to evade an immigration crackdown) who is unable to escape the labyrinth of passages and collapses to the ground, leaving the fate of this and other unseen objects of human rights discourse undecided.

The entanglement of fact and fiction, slyly gestured toward by the documentarians responsible for *Camp 14: Total Control Zone* and *Scenery*, is a major theme in director Mun Sŭng-uk's *The City of Cranes* (*Sit'i obŭ k'ŭrein*, 2010). In chapter 10, titled "'Powers of the False' and 'Real Fiction': Migrant Workers in *The City of Cranes* and Other Mockumentaries," we examine this production's mock documentary aesthetics and its complex representation of migrant workers and other immigrants. Drawing upon Deleuze's theory of the "powers of the false," we explore the film's subversive potential in creating a relatively new type of cinematic praxis through the experimental blending of real characters (such as Mahbub Alam, a Bangladeshi immigrant who is now a naturalized Korean citizen, and who plays a fictionalized version of himself), documentary images, and staged scenes.[8] Falling short of the director's goal of honestly depicting Koreans' discriminatory attitudes toward immigrants and the various hardships experienced by migrant workers, *The City of Cranes* is a fascinating multicultural text whose picturesque landscape shots of Incheon (which appear to have been mandated by the film's state sponsor, South Korea's Ministry of Sports, Culture, and Tourism) only partly undermine its underlying subtext. Ultimately, we judge the film's "powers of the false" approach to be compelling in its rejection of not only the authenticity of documentary images but also the constructed notion of Koreanness as a national identity.

We wrap up our book with a focus on nonhuman rights, drawing attention to the peculiar salience of animals and robots (or artificial intelligence) in the

South Korean cultural context. Chapter 11, "Animal Rights Advocacy, Holocaustal Imagery, and Interspecies Empathy in *An Omnivorous Family's Dilemma* and *Okja*," starts with the premise that motion pictures, even those that depict the harsh realities and unequal power structures of a classist society or that seek to dismantle various discriminatory practices (such as racism and sexism) in an ethically responsible way, leave unexamined the framework of speciesism that undergirds most representations. That framework, the cultural theorist Cary Wolfe claims, has made it nearly impossible to reverse the "fundamental repression" of nonhuman subjectivity "that underlies most ethical and political discourse"[9]—especially human rights advocacy, with its emphasis on humanity as the basis for personhood. After discussing a few classic and contemporary literary texts that foreground nonhuman characters, including two novels for children by Hwang Sŏn-mi (the 2000 *The Hen Who Dreamed She Could Fly* [*Madangŭl naon amt'ak*] and the 2012 *The Dog Who Dared to Dream* [*P'urŭn kae changbal*]), we turn our attention to a couple of films that, despite their outward differences, each encapsulate the challenges involved in fighting for animals' rights in a country that has only begrudgingly begun to implement legislation concerning the welfare of nonhuman creatures. Specifically, director Hwang Yun's low-budget documentary *An Omnivorous Family's Dilemma* (*Chapsik kajokŭi tilema*, 2014) and director Bong Joon-ho's transnational coproduction *Okja* (2017) stand out as exemplary, porcine-focused texts through which to problematize the speciesism that informs most narratives about animal-human relationships. Notably, both films include scenes that rhetorically evoke the horrors of the Jewish Holocaust, thereby gesturing toward a history that is not only beyond their narrative scope but also arguably unrepresentable. *Okja* in particular, as a fantastical allegory about a young girl striving to save the eponymous "super pig" from being exploited by a multinational corporation and killed in a slaughterhouse, provides a litmus test through which to measure audiences' willingness to swallow a premise that, in Bong's hands, is made simultaneously serious and comic (or absurd). Featuring grossly caricatured representatives of the Animal Liberation Front (played with campy, flamboyant hamminess by an international roster of stars, including Tilda Swinton, Paul Dano, and Jake Gyllenhaal), this globally distributed Netflix release is—like so many other mainstream productions steeped in rights advocacy—a contradictory text, ultimately privileging one form of agency (that of humans) over another (that of nonhumans), whose malleability as a metaphor for what ails the nation is apparent in even the most well-intentioned of documentaries (such as *An Omnivorous Family's Dilemma*).

Akira Mizuta Lippit, the author of *Electric Animal: Toward a Rhetoric of Wildlife*, draws attention to cultural representations that trade on the transversality of animal and metaphor. As he states, "the animal is already a metaphor, the metaphor an animal. Together they transport to language, breathe into language, the vitality of another life."[10] The ease with which animals are shaped into allegorical figures in Korean films underscores the need to be ever vigilant, as spectators ethically attuned to their largely unheard calls. It also means that more inclusive definitions of human rights are needed if we are to successfully resist the temptation to reproduce an asymmetrical power dynamic discernible within society at large, through the inherently biased privileging of human beings over nonhuman beings. Along those lines, and inspired by the writings of Rosi Braidotti and other contemporary philosophers, we bring our book to a close with a short coda, presented as a series of speculative observations about the proposed personhood of robots and other programmable machines. Although not biologically human, the various forms of artificial intelligence that appear in several South Korean cultural productions (including K-dramas such as *Borg Mom* [Munhwa Broadcasting Corporation, 2017], *I'm Not a Robot* [*Roboti aniya*; Munhwa Broadcasting Corporation, 2017–2018], and *My Absolute Boyfriend* [*Chŏldae kŭi*; Seoul Broadcasting System, 2019]) are humanoids capable of expressing varying degrees of self-awareness, and the storylines in which they appear (although far-fetched) pose provocative questions about the moral obligations that we have toward individuals generally perceived as things rather than as people. Although brief, we hope that this coda—in which we refer to two particularly noteworthy motion pictures, the science fiction–themed omnibus film *Doomsday Book* (*Illyu myŏlmang pogosŏ*, 2012) and Park Chan-wook's *I'm a Cyborg, But That's OK* (*Ssaibogŭjiman kwaench'ana*, 2006)—will stimulate additional inquiries into the priority that humans have historically given to their own species while pointing toward a future when potentially sentient machines might achieve a level of respect and/or "enlightenment" that their nonrobotic brethren can only aspire to reach today. Indeed, it might be that our uniqueness as human beings resides partially in our species' capacity to imagine a moral community or lifeworld beyond ourselves, one that is not limited to human consciousness or being. This capacity for ethical reflection on the very concept of personhood, which lies at the center of South Korea's cinematic rights advocacy, could very well serve as the starting point for a new chapter in the nation's (and the world's) march toward an even more inclusive form of social justice.

Before sketching the origins and institutional foundations of human rights cinema in postauthoritarian South Korea and then embarking on individual case studies that eventually lead us to the concept of nonhuman rights, we wish to make a couple of caveats. First, it should first be noted that, while this book aims to provide an expansive overview of cinematic rights advocacy inclusive of several marginalized groups' experiences, it is far from exhaustive. Indeed, much work remains to be done on the many forms of discrimination and victimization that have already been broached in the field's existing literature but that are not covered in the following pages, including those related to the enduring pain of former "comfort women" (who were forcibly drafted into military sex slavery before and during World War II); the alienation felt by many North Korean refugees and defectors who are not political prisoners; and the ordeals of survivors of domestic abuse, whose voices are finally being amplified by mainstream and independent films ranging from the upbeat *Punch Lady* (*P'ŏnch'i leidi*, 2007) to the downbeat *A Girl at My Door* (*To-hŭi-ya*, 2014). While any critical account of the sweeping social and political changes that have made such cultural productions possible is necessarily hamstrung by the authors' tastes and biases as well as the built-in constraints of academic research (itself a precarious yet privileged form of labor), we are sensitive to the need of these and other vulnerable groups to have their stories heard alongside the ones that we ultimately selected as representative case studies. Stated simply, it is inadvisable, if not impossible (in theory), to cover all of the historical bases and to discuss each and every form of rights-based advocacy in a single volume. In fact, the prospect of such a study ever being written (much less published) shrinks with each year that scholarly resources diminish as a result of university- and archive-based budget cuts. It is our hope, however, that the present work will spark subsequent investigations into the role of cinema—not only in uniting disparate people in shared observance of their commonalities and differences, but also in dismantling prejudicial systems of oppression that predate the medium's origins as a potentially democratizing form of mass communication at the beginning of the twentieth century.

In lieu of writing a more comprehensive study twice the length of this book, we have endeavored to pinpoint the intersections where various social movements in modern Korean history converge and possibly cross paths. And in an effort to identify the most salient forms of rights advocacy in South Korea today, we have scoured countless articles across multiple disciplines (from art history and performance studies to political science and sociology) as well as archival documents from the NHRCK. But we have also consulted unconventional sources of information such as the DVD box sets and their often lengthy and detailed liner notes produced by the Korean Film Archive. For instance, in 2018 and 2019, the archive released two sets of independently produced films on home video, as part of the Movements on Screen DVD collection, which gives viewers a clue as to what counts as canonical texts in the still to be-written history of cinematic rights advocacy. Included in the first box set are three documentaries from the 1980s that we mentioned at the beginning of this introduction—*South River*, *Water Utilization Tax*, and *Sanggye-dong Olympics*—as well as high-profile works like *The Night before the Strike* (*P'aŏp chŏnya*, 1990) and *My Own Breathing* (*Sumgyŏl*, 2000). The second box set showcases four motion pictures directed by talented filmmakers who are little known outside South Korea: Kim Ŭng-su's *The Past Is a Strange Country* (*Kwagŏnŭn natsŏn narada*, 2008), Kim Mi-re's *Stayed Out Overnight* (*Waebak*, 2009), Kim Il-ran and Hong Chi-yu's *Two Doors* (*Tugaeŭi mun*, 2012), and Yi Yŏng's *Troublers* (*Pulonhan tangsin*, 2015). This quartet of feature-length films explores a wide range of topics, including (1) the long history of U.S. cultural imperialism in South Korea and the resulting anti-Americanism that led two twenty-year-old protesters to immolate themselves in

1986, (2) nonstandard workers' rights and the 510-day strike led by middle-aged female employees of the Homever superstore following massive layoffs in 2007, (3) the human costs of urban renewal projects and the tragic loss of life resulting from the 2009 Yongsan fire, and (4) the structural forms of oppression imposed on South Korea's sexual minorities and the efforts of an older generation of lesbians to combat heteronormativity in their country of birth.

Broadly speaking, those subjects (bundled together in a lavishly packaged DVD box set that encourages the viewer to look for thematic parallels across the four titles) have found cultural expression through other documentaries as well, as anyone who has attended the Seoul Human Rights Film Festival over the past twenty-five years can attest. In addition to attending the festival and witnessing firsthand the effect that a public screening of politically charged films can have on fellow audience members, we have examined the SHRFF's past programs (printed or published online) in the hope of determining which social movements have been privileged by its organizers since its launch in 1996. As with most human rights–themed festivals, this event (first annual but now biennial) brings together an assortment of topics, rhetorical modes, and cinematic styles and strives to balance local productions made by Koreans alongside international submissions from the likes of respected auteurs known to many in the world of documentary filmmaking. However, perusing the festival's past programs, we saw that certain themes stand out as perennial concerns that have been revisited over the years. Though largely associated with the *minjung* (people's) era of workers' protests during the late 1970s and early 1980s (giving rise to films like the abovementioned *The Night before the Strike*), labor issues continue to be foregrounded in contemporary productions such as *A Letter from the Street* (*Kŏlisŏon p'yŏnji*, 2015), *I Need You* (*Niga p'ilyohae*, 2015), and *Play On* (*P'ŭlleion*, 2017). The twentieth and twenty-second editions of the film festival showcased those and other documentaries concerning job insecurity, subcontractors, and temporary employees who stood up to large companies like GM Daewoo, Kiryung Electronics, SK Broadband, SsangYong Motor, and Star Chemical. The idea that South Korea is a beckoning but often heartbreaking destination for immigrant workers is a topic that was highlighted through festival screenings of Yi Ko-un's *Host Nation* (*Hosŭt'ŭ neisyŏn*, 2016) and Shekh Almanun's *Journey into the Dream* (2017), and recent editions of the SHRFF indicate a gravitation toward subjects such as denuclearization (*Stopless Hope* [*Oraedoen hŭimang*, 2015]), the status of people with disabilities (*Ding-Dong*, 2018), LGBTQ rights (*Queer Room* [*K'wiŏŭi pang*, 2018]), and widespread protests against both presidential corruption and the misogynistic culture of South Korea (*Candlewave Feminists* [*Sigugp'emi*, 2017]).

Although we do not examine any of these latter cultural productions in the chapters that follow, we have used the SHRFF programs and similar materials from other organizations as a guide throughout the process of narrowing our focus on specific themes while trying to mimic the festival's inclusive approach to social justice as a matter of concern to various civic groups and cultural institutions. But we have also tried to refrain from uniformly exalting human rights discourse as a salve for what ails the nation, adopting instead a more circumspect approach to the sometimes empty rhetoric of government officials who claim to be on the side of the disenfranchised but who implement policies that reinforce existing power structures. As several commentators have pointed out, liberalism frequently masks neoliberalism when human rights are offered up as a means of protecting "the freedom of individuals to act in a competitive and unequal society,"[11] and this is especially true in South Korea (which has witnessed a long history of capitalistic collusion among state, military, and industry leaders backed by hegemonic Western powers apathetic to people's rights). To quote Michalinos Zembylas and Vivienne Bozalek (who are themselves paraphrasing the political theorist Joe Hoover), human rights often "construct political subjects that are dependent and vulnerable who must seek out the state to provide for their well-being," and in doing so they can be said to perpetuate structural inequalities and actually "limit social, economic and political possibilities for change."[12] While such critiques may be just as unnuanced as the facile celebration of human rights as a universal standard of moral decency, we maintain that the freedom that many Koreans have collectively yearned and fought for can be achieved only once the inherent limitations of that metaphysical discourse (and the vague, abstract, transcendental ideal it is based on) are finally recognized. Only after acknowledging human rights' historical shortcomings yet vast potential (for sparking social change and holding elected officials accountable) can the actual legal, juridical, and physical work of dismantling the structures of exploitation and oppression begin in earnest.

Part 1

Institutional Foundations and Formal Structures

1

The Rise of Rights-Advocacy Cinema in Postauthoritarian South Korea

According to the sociologist Cho Hyo-je, the imported neologism "rights" (*kwŏlli*) was first used in Korea in the late 1880s and became popularized in the 1890s (coincidentally around the same time that the first experiments in moving-image technologies were undertaken in France, the United States, and other countries). As an example, Cho alludes to Korea's first elementary school textbook (*Kukmin sohakdokbon*), published by the royal government in 1895, which includes the passage, "Although titles may be different, there is no difference in the rights of all individuals."[1] In 1950—five years after Korea's liberation from Japanese rule, which had suppressed colonial subjects' political and economic rights—Syngman Rhee (Yi Sŭng-man)'s newly installed Republic of Korea (ROK) regime promoted human rights as a means of "winning international recognition" from the United Nations and declared December 10 as the Memorial Day of Human Rights.[2] Such outward compliance, however, belied the reality of a divided nation where civil rights were wantonly violated by the National Security Law (Kukka poanbŏp), a draconian system that empowered politicians to quell leftist dissent in the name of security. The subsequent military dictatorships of Park Chung-hee (Pak Chŏng-hŭi [1961–1979]) and Chun Doo-hwan (Chŏn Tu-hwan [1980–1988]) cracked down on labor movement and student protests while employing violent interrogation and conversion techniques against political prisoners. As Paul Chang notes, human rights "became part of South Korean civil society for the first time when antigovernment dissidents made it an integral part of the larger democracy movement in the 1970s," particularly after the formation of such advocacy organizations as the Amnesty Korean Committee (AKC), which was founded in 1972.[3]

Five years after the restoration of civil rule in 1993, a sea change occurred, when Kim Dae-jung (Kim Tae-jung), a longtime political dissident, was inaugurated as president. Originally from Chŏlla Province (an area that includes Kwangju, where a civil uprising was brutally put down by government paratroopers in May 1980), Kim had lived a portion of his life on death row and then in forced exile in the early to mid-1980s. With the installation of the National Human Rights Commission of Korea (NHRCK; Kukka ingwŏn wiwŏnhoe) during his presidency, human rights became an openly pursued policy of the ROK government, which had been a violator of civil liberties only a decade earlier and was still far from where it could and should have been, especially with a former political prisoner and future winner of the Nobel Peace Prize sitting in the presidential Blue House. Much of the progress made during the two liberal administrations of Kim and his successor Roh Moo-hyun (No Mu-hyŏn), a former human rights lawyer, was undone by the two conservative administrations of Lee Myong-bak (Yi Myŏng-bak) and Park Geun-hye (Pak Kŭn-hye), Park Chung-hee's daughter, that followed. After the latter's impeachment in 2017, the new government of Moon Jae-in (Mun Chae-in) publicly announced that the two previous administrations had put 8,931 artists and cultural producers (including internationally acclaimed directors such as Lee Chang-dong [Yi Ch'ang-dong], Park Chan-wook [Pak Ch'an-uk], and Bong Joon-ho [Pong Jun-ho]), as well as 342 organizations on a government blacklist to suppress what officials had perceived as subversive cultural activities. As shown by our interview with the director of the Seoul Human Rights Film Festival (SHRFF), cited below in this chapter, the present relationship between the nation-state and cultural activists is still plagued with suspicions, miscommunications, conflicts, and hostilities (as is often the case in other civil societies, including Western democracies).

As if reflecting the monumental societal changes summarized above, there was a major shift in cinematic rights advocacy from the 1980s (when democracy, antiauthoritarianism, and the labor movement together constituted a kind of master narrative in underground films) to more recent times (when a diverse cross section of disenfranchised groups, including homosexuals, migrant workers, people with disabilities, North Korean defectors, and political prisoners, came to the fore in both low-budget festival selections and big-budget commercial films). Balancing multiple perspectives on human rights cinema in South Korea with input from such institutions as the NHRCK and the SHRFF, we attempt to corral this ornery concept, which has yet to be defined through critical consensus and therefore could be taken to mean any number of things. Indeed, depending on one's evaluative criteria, a heartrending biopic such as Park

Kwang-su's *A Single Spark* (*Arŭmdaun ch'ongnyŏn Chŏn T'ae-il*, 1995), which recounts events leading to the union activist Chŏn T'ae-il's self-immolation protest in 1970 and which was partly funded by donations from 7,700 citizens, might (or might not) qualify as an example of human rights cinema. How flexible does this category of cultural production need to be to accommodate a big-budget, action-filled blockbuster such as director Chang Hun's *A Taxi Driver* (*T'aesi unjŏngsa*, 2017), which is set during the time of the May 1980 Kwangju Uprising? Backed by Showbox, one of South Korea's big three film companies, it is among the highest-grossing motion pictures in the country's history. The few readers who might be familiar with such recent shorts as *Santa in Wonderland* (*Isangha naraŭi Sant'a*, 2013), *Paki* (2013), and *Day by Day* (*Haru tto haru*, 2016), all of which are independently produced autobiographical films made by migrant workers and rarely screened outside of the region's small festival circuit, would likely cite these and other politically engaged works as exemplars of cinematic rights advocacy, although their cultural imprint is necessarily smaller than that of the motion pictures mentioned above, which have been distributed around the world and honored with regional and international film awards. Is a film that fails to resonate with audiences or that simply does not find its audience (owing to limited distribution) automatically ruled out as an example of human rights cinema if the latter is predicated on emotional affect or the ability to inspire people to take action? While we do not attempt to answer these questions, we seek to lay the groundwork for a supple conceptualization that is located at the nexus of filmmakers/artists, films/texts, and audiences/publics, in the hope that future scholars might benefit from or build upon the foundation that is laid in the following pages.

From Independent Cinema to Human Rights Cinema

Most scholars agree that South Korea's independent cinema (*tonip yŏnghwa*) of the 1980s shares some of the themes and characteristics of contemporary human rights cinema.[4] Similar to works in Latin America's revolutionary "imperfect cinema"—which during the 1960s and 1970s, under the leadership of the Cuban polemicist Julio Garcia Espinosa, posed an alternative to dominant modes of motion picture production and reception in the Global North—many of the Korean independent films made over three decades ago were raw, low-budget efforts on the part of politically activated members of the *minjung* (people's) movement that circulated through underground and noncommercial networks, such as university film clubs and activist labor organizations. For the most part, those films—including Kim Tae-yŏng's short film *The Announcement of Mr. Kant* (*K'antŭ ssiŭi palpy'ohoe*, 1987) and the Changsanggotmae Collective's *O Dreamland!* (or *Oh! Dream Country* [*O kkum ŭi nara!*], 1988), both of which concern the Kwangju Uprising of May 1980—were positioned on the opposite end of the ideological spectrum from the nondemocratic state under authoritarian military governance, which not only outlawed subversive texts but also prosecuted their makers. For example, the forty-minute documentary *Blue Bird* (*P'arangsae*, 1986) by the Seoul Visual Collective (Sŏul yŏngsang chipdan), shot on 8mm film stock and coproduced with the Catholic Farmers' Collective, presents an exposé of the harsh realities of sustaining farming communities in the face of the government's free market policy, which allowed the importation of foreign agricultural products. President Chun Doo-hwan's military regime arrested the film's producers (Hong Ki-sŏn and Yi Hyo-in) on charges of illegally exhibiting *Blue Bird* without a permit from the censor. Similarly, South Korea's first independent feature, *O Dreamland!*, was shot in a film gauge (16mm) befitting its status as a rough-hewn alternative to the comparatively polished look of commercial (35mm) cinema. It tells the story of Chong-su (Kwŏn In-ch'an), a fugitive student activist from Kwangju who takes shelter in Tongduch'on, a U.S. camptown near Seoul. Chong-su suffers from post-traumatic stress disorder, prompting flashbacks to the massacre he witnessed in his native city. T'ae-ho (Pak Ch'ung-sŏn), Chong-su's friend and a black marketeer, is double-crossed by Steve (Kurt Reinken), an undercover American investigator who flees to the United States after robbing the Korean (operating behind the ruse of a big smuggling deal). By drawing parallels between the betrayal of state power (the military and law enforcement) in Kwangju and Tongduch'on, the film indicts not only the South Korean government but also the United States for its failure to uphold the human rights principles of the outgoing administration of President Jimmy Carter, as it did not intervene to stop mass civilian killings (and symbolically endorsed the murderous dictator Chun by inviting him to the White House as the first foreign head of state to visit Ronald Reagan, the new president). The government fined a representative of Changsanggotmae—an emerging indie film consortium that united "several college film clubs" and that, as Nam Lee notes, would soon be dismantled after the release of its last feature, *Opening the Closed School Gates* (*Tach'in kyomunŭl yŏlmyŏ*, 1992)—as well as the owner of Hanmadang theater for producing and exhibiting *O Dreamland!* without a permit from the censor.[5]

In her study of Korean independent filmmakers' networks, Young-a Park points out that, as the tide of "political radicalism" began to subside "in the context of the post-Cold War global order and the post-authoritarian Korean civilian state" in the early the 1990s, South Korea's independent cinema assumed new roles and purposes, departing from its earlier antistate incarnations such as that of producer of *undong yŏnghwa* (activist films) and *minjung yŏnghwa* (people's films).[6] By the mid-1990s, the neologism *tonip yŏnghwa* (independent film) had emerged as an umbrella term that designated noncommercial productions made outside of the mainstream Ch'ungmuro film industry's financial control and star system. In the mid- to late 1990s, there were concerted efforts to organize independent filmmakers, showcase their work, and create a new group identity. In December 1995, the first Seoul International Independent Film Festival was launched. The following year saw the founding of the Indie Forum, a noncompetitive independent film festival programmed and organized by a community of creative artists. Their first filmmakers' festival was held at Yonsei University between May 21 and 26, 1996, and sixty-three films were screened. In 1998, small and dispersed independent film groups were finally united under a central trade organization, the Association for Korean Independent Film and Video (KIFV; Han'guk tongnipyŏnghwa hyŏphoe), with the documentarist Kim Dong-won (Kim Tong-wŏn) adding to his growing reputation as an activist filmmaker by serving as its first president. Kim's twelve-year project *Repatriation* (*Songhwan*, 2003), a documentary about the everyday lives of newly released, long-term political prisoners of conscience (former North Korean spies or communist sympathizers) is an exemplary human rights film from that period, laying the groundwork for subsequent attempts to generate solidarity-building sympathy for the plight of individuals who, just a few years earlier, had largely been demonized as two-dimensional villains in mainstream, anticommunist cultural productions.

Of particular significance to the present study is how the concept of rights advocacy in South Korean cinema has shifted over the past four decades, transforming from a unifying master narrative (celebrating democracy, antiauthoritarianism, the labor movement, and so on) in 1980s underground films (such as *Blue Bird*, *O Dreamland!*, and *The Night before the Strike* [*P'aŏp chŏnya*, 1990]) to a set of disparate minoritarian stories of disenfranchised groups in both mainstream and independent films made after 2000. In this book, we do not limit the playing field of rights-based cinema to independent productions or documentaries. Rather than draw a hard line between mainstream and independent cultural productions, and in lieu of separating discussions of narrative fiction filmmaking from those of documentary filmmaking, this book links different modes of production and meaning-making under common themes and identities, including (but not limited to): gender and sexuality, disability rights, prisoner rights, migrant workers' rights, and animal rights. Such an approach makes it possible to indicate how a number of selected case studies—chosen for their representativeness as well as their distinctiveness—reinforce similar messages of acceptance, inclusion, and respect for one's fellow humans (as well as compassionate and ethical treatment of their animal companions), despite facing different limitations and obstacles (such as underfunding, censorship, genre conventions, and diluted or displaced politics).

While adopting a more fluid, inclusive approach to the human rights film as a unique mode of production and reception, we acknowledge that this institutional genre has relied upon the support of governmental and nongovernmental organizations (NGOs) such as the NHRCK, the SHRFF, and the KIFV. It is not a coincidence that rights advocacy has become a prominent facet of fiction and nonfiction films (as well as of the nation's recent literary output) following the presidential inauguration of Kim Dae-jung, a former political prisoner and victim of rights abuses who received the Nobel Peace Prize in 2000 for "his work for democracy and human rights in South Korea and in East Asia in general."[7] The human rights film is part of a larger cultural phenomenon that reflects shifting social values and growing civic awareness of the rights and dignity of oppressed, silenced members of South Korean society. In other words, it represents the ethos of "post-authoritarianism," which, as Young-a Park notes, is rooted in the Kim Dae-jung and Roh Moo-hyun administrations' "conscious efforts [to redeem] the oppressed."[8]

While the term "human rights film" (*ingwŏn yŏngwha*) began to circulate discursively in the mid-1990s, during the administration of President Kim Young-sam (Kim Yŏng-sam) (particularly after the launch of the SHRFF in 1996), it was not until Kim Dae-jung assumed leadership of the country (1998–2003) that this and broader civil liberties discourses emerged as key elements within political debate and public deliberation. As Jeong-Woo Koo, Suk-Ki Kong, and Chisung Chung state, "Korea experienced a dramatic improvement in human rights in the late 1990s and early 2000s when the two reform-oriented administrations with a strong commitment to rights-promoting policies were in power. Civil and political rights barely improved in the early and mid-1990s, yet they began to flourish from 1998, the inaugural year of Kim Dae Jung's presidency, and underwent an uninterrupted period of improvement throughout the 2000s."[9] Of course, the cultural spread of human rights discourses during the second half of the 1990s can be attributed to several factors, and it would be foolish to detach Korean social and political developments from the larger international regime of human rights that, since the 1940s, has been incrementally pieced together through an extensive series of U.N. "conventions, councils, courts, tribunals, and related regional institutions."[10] Indeed, the seeds for that growth were planted well before the ROK was granted U.N. membership in August 1991, and the country's apparently newfound commitment to institutional reforms and to the idea of a flourishing civil society seems to have resulted from the prodemocracy movement of the 1970s and 1980s.

During those years, several key events helped inject the sentimental rhetoric of a still-nascent human rights discourse into the widespread call for democracy bubbling up in South Korea. In *Protest Dialectics*, Paul Chang presents a meticulous account of those historical moments from the 1970s, referring to Amnesty International's approval of the creation of the AKC—which was led by religious spokespeople (including Pastor Kim Chae-jun, who was appointed as the first AKC chairman), and which "worked to make human rights an important part of the anti-Yusin movement."[11] One year after the 1972 establishment of the AKC, the U.S. government's revised Foreign Assistance Act was passed, and then a year later a Congressional Committee on International Relations opened hearings on the ROK government's widely publicized rights violations (in particular, those pertaining to political prisoners).[12] Thus, a new relational dynamic was brought to bear on the long-standing ties between the two countries, with the

United States exerting its questionable authority over the ROK in a way that sums up the main complaint leveled against human rights as "a set of universal moral principles" that, according to some critics, ironically "ends up legitimating the power structures and social inequalities of Western imperialism and neo-colonialism."[13] Indeed, the shifting U.S. foreign policy agenda during that period, when the country was as concerned with protecting its own interests as it was with encouraging the spread of democracy, included threats to withdraw troops from South Korea if the ROK did not comply with the universal norms of human rights as a symbolic if not globally enforceable ideal.

To be clear, while criticism that human rights are "vague" and "abstract"—or, worse, tools through which hegemonic governments reinforce "existing power structures"[14]—is valid, they remain worthy ideas so long as their sentimentalism is grounded in pragmatism, as Richard Rorty, Michael Ignatieff, and other liberal thinkers have maintained. According to Michalinos Zembylas, they are valuable precisely because they carry such an emotionally resonant and affective charge: they are "sentimental stories of cruelty and suffering" capable of motivating ordinary people (if not always their elected officials or policy makers) to take action against torture, rape, and killings.[15] In fact, were it not for the 1979 summit meeting between President Carter (the first U.S. "human rights president") and President Park (whose administration's record of abuse had been under intense scrutiny by Amnesty International since the early 1960s), it is unlikely that the 108 political prisoners released in the aftermath of those talks would have seen the light of day.[16] Nor would the many social movements that made up the prodemocracy movement of the 1980s have been as effective in achieving their goals were it not for the material and educational support provided by external NGOs and transnational advocacy networks.

As Paul Chang and Gi-Wook Shin state, "one significant effect of democratization on social movements in Korea was the increasing diversification of issues pursued by activist communities," a diffusion linked to the rise in identity politics that also contributed to the emergence of an ungainly yet institutionally defined type of cinematic praxis (the human rights film) that would serve a compensatory function through its consolidating power—that is, as a way to bring the nation together, this time around not one but a host of social justice issues. While the motivating factor behind the production of several precursors to the contemporary human rights film in South Korea (the *undong yŏnghwa*, *minjung yŏnghwa*, and so on) was "the common goal of replacing authoritarianism with a democratic government,"[17] the transition to civil rule in the early 1990s (followed by the inauguration of Kim Dae-jung in the late 1990s) set the stage for cultural producers, including filmmakers, to take on a variety of projects that dealt with everything from gay and lesbian rights and reproductive rights to environmental issues and the sexual harassment experienced by women. But that diffusion, as Chang and Shin remind us, ran parallel to an "institutionalization of social movements,"[18] meaning that they were integrated "into the state body" partly through the medium of motion pictures—the social and political value of which was understood by representatives of the NHRCK and other governmental (as well as nongovernmental) organizations during the early 2000s.[19]

Civic Activism and the National Human Rights Commission

Scholarly consensus points to the fact that, within the South Korean cultural context, the term "human rights cinema" can be traced back to November 1996, when the inaugural SHRFF was held with the support of a hundred human rights organizations and six hundred citizens and screened thirty-two films free of charge.[20] The slogan of this momentous event was "Human Rights in Cinema and Cinema in Human Rights." Although there is general agreement that the SHRFF was the first major South Korean venue where an explicit connection between human rights and cinema was made, a major stimulus for rights advocacy took place three years earlier at the Vienna World Conference on Human Rights, a two-week international event hosted by the United Nations and attended by an unprecedented seven thousand participants hailing from academia, government institutions, or one of eight hundred NGOs. Delegates from 171 states jointly adopted the Vienna Declaration and Plan of Action, "a new 'framework of planning, dialogue and cooperation'" that would, in theory, "enable a holistic approach to promoting human rights and involve actors at all levels—international, national and local."[21] Article 36 of the declaration states,

> The World Conference on Human Rights reaffirms the important and constructive role played by national institutions for the promotion and protection of human rights, in particular in their advisory capacity to the competent authorities, their role in remedying human rights violations, in the dissemination of human rights information, and education in human rights.
>
> The World Conference on Human Rights encourages the establishment and strengthening of national institutions, having regard to the 'Principles relating to the status of national institutions' and recognizing that it is the right of each State to choose the framework which is best suited to its particular needs at the national level.[22]

Prompted by this international call to action, Korean participants at the conference—grassroots NGO representatives—demanded that the Kim Young-sam government enact a human rights law and establish a national institution for human rights. Although Kim's administration was largely nonresponsive, there was continued civil pressure throughout the 1990s to affirm the U.N. Paris Principles (which are related to the status of national institutions and were adopted in December 1993) and to found a national human rights institution.

This bottom-up activism of Korean civic groups secured a political platform in Kim Dae-jung's presidential campaign, whose main agendas included guaranteeing human rights. In February 1998, the Kim Dae-jung administration included the enactment of a human rights law and the formation of a national human rights institution among the top "100 tasks of the new government," thus making the issue a central feature of South Korean political discourse for the first time in the nation's history. The initial proposal of the Ministry of Justice (Pŏmmubu) to establish the new institution as a private, advisory watchdog body with no jurisdiction over law enforcement agencies was fiercely opposed by civic groups, representatives of which demanded a more powerful state institution with investigative and prosecutorial powers. Following three years of deliberations, demonstrations, and public debates, the NHRCK was launched in November 2001 as a "national advocacy institution" for human rights protection and promotion.[23] As defined by Article 1 of the National Human Rights Commission Act (promulgated in May 2001), "the purpose of this Act is to contribute to the embodiment of human dignity and worth as well as to the safeguard[ing] of the basic order of democracy, by establishing the National Human Rights Commission to ensure that inviolable, fundamental human rights of all individuals are protected and the standards of human rights are improved."[24]

While in principle the NHRCK is a noncorporate private body that is independent of all three branches (executive, legislative, and judicial) of the government, the facts that the organization receives all its funding from the state and its eleven commissioners are appointed by the president of the ROK (four), the National Assembly (four), or the chief justice of the Supreme Court (three) compromise its presumed independence and freedom from partisan politics.[25] For many activists, the NHRCK's ultimate form represented a major setback, not a fulfillment of Kim Dae-jung's human rights policy. Despite such disappointments and the feelings of disillusionment that were already becoming apparent at the time of the organization's launch, as Paek Un-jo points out, the National Human Rights Commission Act represents the first burst of legislative activity in which citizens participated in the deliberative process of lawmaking.[26] Although it may not have lived up to the original vision of social justice nurtured by the Korean activists who attended the Vienna World Conference on Human Rights, the NHRCK stands as an important legacy of the emerging aspirations of civil society for equality, rights guarantees, and redress of wrongs committed in the not-so-distant authoritarian past.

The NHRCK Film Series and Inclusive Definitions of Rights-Advocacy Films

On December 22, 2015, we visited the NHRCK and sat down for a chat with Kim Min-a, a section manager in charge of the commission's film production. At the time of this interview, the NHRCK had produced fifty films (four feature-length productions and forty-six shorts, which together make up nine multidirector omnibus films) as part of the much-lauded If You Were Me (*sisŏn*) series. Kim explained how the NHRCK became involved in cinematic productions, indicating that, after the organization's launch in 2001, its staff members were "at a loss in the beginning in terms of how to promote human rights." "Public awareness of the concept was relatively low," and the NHRCK was faced with the challenge of altering people's perception of human rights as "a difficult, boring subject," Kim said. "We were searching for a medium that could reach wide audiences and showcase the fact that human rights are about everyday lives. For our purposes, film was a natural choice."[27] The NHRCK's motion picture program was launched in 2002 to fulfill one of the organization's core missions, "education and awareness" (the other three such missions are "policy recommendations," "investigations and remedial actions," and "domestic and international cooperation").[28] Kim told us that the NHRCK ultimately chose the omnibus format primarily because its films are intended for pedagogical purposes, and films of 20–30 minutes in length have proved to be conducive to curriculum adoption in schools (especially since classes in middle and high schools are 45–50 minutes long). A short film is therefore just long enough to raise awareness of or promote an issue, yet also of an appropriate length to leave time for a discussion after the screening. Although all of the NHRCK-backed films have been theatrically released and made commercially available in different formats (including video on demand), their primary targets of distribution are educational institutions (including elementary schools, high schools, and universities) and civic groups whose members can request complimentary DVDs of the works.

Table 1.1, which shows some of the NHRCK's statistics concerning the If You Were Me series that were prepared for a National Assembly [Kukhoe] audit, indicates that the first eight films have not reached mass audiences, with theatrical admissions ranging from 3,100 to 31,171. The film program's budget needed to be renewed and approved by the National Assembly every year, and given these low box-office receipts, political lobbying has not been easy. Kim acknowledged how challenging it has been to counteract the negative public perception of the NHRCK's film program as government-funded propaganda. However, steady funding and the relatively low commercial pressure placed on the If You Were Me series has allowed her team to guarantee creative freedom to filmmakers who are not required to follow any policy guidelines or set definitions of human rights. Kim said, "We do not define what is or what is not human rights for directors or audiences."[29] Instead, NHRCK films are placed before the public as starting points or stepping-stones for political debates and consciousness-raising vis-à-vis a broad assortment of rights issues covered by the series, including rights for people with disabilities, children, LGBTQ people, migrants, temporary workers, single mothers, and athletes—as well as privacy rights.

As evidence of the organization's broadly conceived notion of human rights, the first entry in the series, *If You Were Me* (*Yŏsŏt kaeŭi sisŏn*, 2003), challenges the conventional wisdom of rights advocacy and expands the concept by

Table 1.1
The NHRCK's Film Budget and Admissions between 2002 and 2011

Production date	Film title	Budget	Release date	Screens	Admissions
2002	*If You Were Me 1* 여섯 개의 시선 (6 episodes)	358 million won	Nov. 14, 2003	57	31,171
2003	*If You Were Me: Anima Vision* 별별이야기1 (6 episodes)	519 million won	Sep. 23, 2005	16	7,232
2004	*If You Were Me 2* 다섯 개의 시선 (5 episodes)	489 million won	Jan. 12, 2006	18	12, 621
2005	*If You Were Me 3* 세번째 시선 (6 episodes)	546 million won	Nov. 23, 2006	8	3,811
2006	*If You Were Me: Anima Vision 2* 별별이야기2 (6 episodes)	430 million won	Apr. 24, 2008	11	4,205
2007	*If You Were Me 4* 시선1318 (5 episodes)	405 million won	Jun. 11, 2009	13	5,748
2008	*Fly, Penguin* 날아라 펭귄 (feature)	254 million won	Sep. 24, 2009	30	21,648
2009–2010	*If You Were Me 5* 시선 너머 (5 episodes)	351 million won	Apr. 28, 2011	11	3,100

NOTE: One million won is equal to approximately $890 as of March 2021. Admissions are shown in numbers of people who attended the theatrical screenings. Numbers of commercial screens that played these films are also noted above.

tackling such issues as a physically attractive woman's right not to be judged (positively or negatively) by her outward appearance (Park Kwang-su's "Face Value") and a sex offender's right to privacy (Chŏng Chae-ŭn's "The Man with an Affair"). The latter episode in particular drew the ire of the Commission on Youth Protection, a government agency, for distorting the constitutional sex offender registration system through exaggerated images of a Scarlet Letter–like oversize fingerprint on the door of an apartment unit, the panopticon-like surveillance structures of the building's architecture, and provocative graffiti on the wall. The NHRCK defended its film for advocating an individual's right, rather than questioning the legitimacy of the sex offender registration system, and refused to discontinue its public screenings of the film.[30]

We asked Kim Min-a her opinion about big-budget rights-advocacy films backed by media conglomerate CJ Entertainment, like *Silenced* (*Dogani*, 2011), the cost of whose production and marketing reached 4.5 billion won ($4 million), or roughly ten times more than one of NHRCK's films. As we discuss in greater detail in chapter 5, this film is based on the 2009 best seller of the same title by the popular novelist Gong Ji-young (Kong Chi-yŏng) and presents a fictionalized account of rape and sexual harassment of hearing-impaired minors that took place in Kwangju Inhwa School, a state-subsidized special education institution, from 2000 to 2005 (until a newly appointed teacher reported to local authorities shocking details of sexual offenses by teachers and administrators that involved at least nine victims who came forward). After the indictment of two members of the school staff (a teacher and an administrator, who received two- and one-year prison sentences but would serve only eight and six months, respectively), the NHRCK's follow-up investigation in 2016 revealed that four additional culprits, including the school headmaster, were responsible for molesting children. Two of the newly accused were cleared of charges immediately on the ground that the statute of limitations (seven years) had expired. The headmaster—who had raped a young girl in his office in the presence of another student—initially received a five-year sentence in a local court, but an appellate court reduced the penalty to probation and a fine due to the settlement between the victims' parents and school management. The school survived the scandal and continued to receive state funding until *Silenced* enraged audiences around the country. Seen by one million theatergoers within five days of its September 22, 2011, release, the film prompted fifty thousand citizens to sign an online petition to reopen the case and another eighty thousand to demand a lifting of the statute of limitations for sexual crimes within the first week. Politicians and bureaucrats responded swiftly to the public outrage, reopening the case, shutting down the school, and passing the Dogani Law (which abolished the statute of limitations for sex crimes committed against children and the disabled and strengthened the punishment for institutional sexual violence) on October 29, 2011, a mere two months after the film's release.

The NHRCK had investigated the case and in August 2006 (six years before the release of *Silenced*) had recommended to the city of Kwangju that school board members be dismissed and a new board convened. However, the subject was beyond the scope of a film program that focused on everyday subject matter that could be contained within its omnibus format. Reflecting on the power and mass appeal of commercial cinema and its impact on rights advocacy, Kim stated: "Mainstream film has become a major vehicle through which to promote human rights in South Korea, as evidenced by *Silenced* or *The Attorney* [*Pyŏnhoin*, 2013]. It's almost unprecedented in the world." She admitted to being cautiously optimistic about the phenomenon, which she found "encouraging."[31] On the surface, productions like *Silenced* (which was seen by 4.7 million theatergoers) and those like the NHRCK's films (which have been seen by no more than a few thousand people in commercial venues, prior to their nonprofit public distribution) appear to be completely different, belonging to separate cultural categories and institutional contexts. However, they all fulfill—or seek to fulfill—the mission of rights-advocacy cinema, insofar as they serve to enlighten the public, raise awareness, and spark social change. Inclusivity is key to understanding both the form and content of rights-advocacy cinema.

"'Dark' Subject Matter in Broad Daylight": The Seoul Human Rights Film Festival

On July 11, 2019, we met with the director of the SHRFF, Lego Hyun Park. Unlike the highly visible NHRCK headquarters—located in a fifteen-story renovated office complex in Ŭljiro (the heart of downtown Seoul), with a bus stop in front of the building named after the organization—the makeshift office of the SHRFF was, as Park had warned us, quite hard to find: it was in an alley in a nondescript residential district near Independence Gate. Balancing her duties as a graduate student pursuing a degree in gender studies and as human rights activist committed to equality and other issues, Park had taken on the considerable task of festival programming seven years before our meeting. At the onset of our interview, a hint of pride was discernible in her voice as she pointed out that the SHRFF was as old as the Busan International Film Festival (BIFF), the largest and most influential film festival in South Korea. Both festivals had their inaugural season in 1996, but the two would go down radically different paths: the BIFF organizers pursued regional and eventually global recognition for an event that combines artistic and commercial agendas, while Park's predecessors aimed for the more noble goal of changing the hearts and minds of local audiences through socially relevant film and video programming. Facing financial struggles and political pressures every step of the way, the SHRFF has managed to uphold three principles since its launch over two decades ago: (1) free screenings, (2) no government or corporate sponsorship, and (3) the rejection of the rating system. The festival is wholly funded through the individual donations of roughly three hundred citizen sponsors. At the time of our meeting, Park was being assisted by twenty volunteer activists who were involved in every facet of festival operations, from planning and programming to grounds management and facilitation of question-and-answer sessions. The festival is accessible to the hearing and visually impaired: all of its screenings are accompanied by sign language translation, and some are equipped with audio descriptions.

Throughout its history, the SHRFF has concentrated on the issues of freedom of expression and resistance to censorship. The festival first ran into trouble with state authorities during its second year, when police officers raided Hongik University, where a film screening was taking place. The documentary that caused that alarm, *Red Hunt* (*Redŭhŏnt'ŭ*, 1997), a look back at the Jeju Uprising of 1948 (which led to a brutal massacre of 10 percent of the island's

FIGURE 1.1 Concerning the killing of thousands of alleged communist sympathizers on Jeju Island in 1948, the documentary *Red Hunt* (*Redŭhŏnt'ŭ*, 1997) was one of two dozen films screened at the second Seoul Human Rights Film Festival (held at Hongik University and in other cities in September–December 1997). In the weeks that followed the November arrest of the festival chairperson Sŏ Chun-sik, several U.S. filmmakers (including Jonathan Demme, Norman Jewison, Barbara Kopple, Albert Maysles, Arthur Penn, John Sayles, Paul Schrader, and Oliver Stone), as well as nongovernmental organizations such as Amnesty International and Human Rights Watch, rallied to support Sŏ's cause, sending passionately worded letters to President Kim Young-sam and bringing international attention to Korea's long history of rights violations.

population by government security forces), was confiscated, as was the projection equipment used during that September 27, 1997, screening (see figure 1.1). The police maintained that the film screening was a violation of the National Security Law's prohibition of antistate images or print materials (*ijŏk p'yohyŏnmul*). The SHRFF defiantly continued its screenings of the film in other venues (such as Myŏngdong Cathedral) until its director, Sŏ Chun-sik, was arrested. The bad blood between the government and the SHRFF reached its peak in 2008, when the new conservative government of President Lee Myung-bak strengthened the Motion Picture and Video Promotion Law and imposed a de facto ban on the theatrical distribution of unrated films by dangling the threat of a three-year prison time or a fine of thirty million won (approximately $27,000) over theater owners who exhibit films without their being classified by the Korea Media Rating Board (Yŏngsangmul tŭnggŭbwiwŏnhoe).[32]

There are two ways to circumvent this prohibition: (1) hosting a one-time preview to which underage audiences are not admitted; and (2) acquiring a recommendation of the state-funded Korean Film Council (KOFIC; Yŏnghwa chinhŭngwiwŏnhoe) for special festival screenings—which, according to Park, is another form of censorship due to the state-subsidized agency's political disadvantaging of non-approved events. The revision of the Motion Picture and

Video Promotion Law forced the SHRFF to move its festival outdoors in 2008, and since that time it has held public screenings of unrated films in Marronnier Park. Although SHRFF representatives believe that the current Korean rating system is unconstitutional and have openly discussed the prospect of taking legal action against government officials, outdoor screenings have brought unexpected benefits. As Park puts it, the space of the park "fits the subject and mission of our festival. If audiences want to focus on every shot and listen to every word on screen, they should go to a regular theater. If they want to have open conversations about controversial issues—such as a woman's right to have an abortion, LGBT rights, abusive forms of state power—in the public arena, they can come to us. Many directors have found the experience liberating and appreciated having opportunities to publicly discuss 'dark' subject matter in broad daylight."[33]

When we asked Park about her festival's relationship with the NHRCK, she explained that many human rights groups have boycotted the commission since 2006 (the final year of President Roh Moo-hyun's liberal administration), mainly for appointing An Kyŏng-hwan, a Seoul National University law professor with few human rights credentials, as its chairperson. Over the years, through the successive conservative administrations of Presidents Lee Myung-bak and Park Geun-hye (during which the NHRCK's operations and personnel were downsized), antagonism between the commission and grassroots NGOs has become enflamed. After the launch of President Moon Jae-in's liberal administration following Park's impeachment, human rights groups noticed signs of change in the NHRCK, but they have not yet taken a collective stance on the commission. Not surprisingly, Lego Hyun Park did not have very many positive things to say about the NHRCK's film program and confirmed Kim Min-a's comment about the negative perception of her program among activists as a government-initiated project.

Unlike the NHRCK film manager, the SHRFF director was also skeptical about counting mainstream films such as *The Attorney*, *A Taxi Driver*, and *1987: When the Day Comes* (2017) as examples of rights-based cinematic advocacy. She elaborated by saying, "In the process of programming, we always ask ourselves whether or not narrative fiction film is the right medium for human rights." She and her fellow programmers tend to "scrutinize them [narrative fiction films] more closely than [they do] documentaries or avant-garde films." Films like *The Attorney* and *A Taxi Driver*, she argued, "are commercial works that exploit the subject of rights advocacy for dramatic purposes. We do not view them as human rights films." Expanding on this point, Park stated that *A Taxi Driver* "may simply be a cultural response to political changes that occurred at that time [the installation of the new Moon Jae-in government]," and that it was "the kind of film that *must* be made and which *could* be made at that particular time." "However," she continued, "this so-called liberal film is still silent about more timely human rights issues concerning the Kwangju Uprising, such as rape and sexual assaults on female protesters by troops and interrogators." *A Taxi Driver* is, in her final analysis, "just another 'feel-good' commercial film."[34]

Park's view of rights-advocacy cinema is filtered through the traditional antistate, anticapitalist lens that has characterized South Korea's democratization movement (*minjuhwa undong*) throughout the authoritarian period. The fact that the SHRFF was put on the KOFIC's blacklist during the administrations of President Lee and Park (because of its organizers' participation in peaceful candlelight demonstrations against the government's trade policy in 2008) and was denied the state-funded organization's cultural subsidy demonstrates that many of the political struggles of the past continue to plague today's activists in the so-called postauthoritarian era. Despite the SHRFF's severe fiscal shortages over the years, which have led to a decision to reduce the frequency of the festival to every other year (skipping 2019 as a result), many of its organizers remain cautious about receiving the NHRCK's financial support (viewing it as government money), which has been offered several times. The festival's dogged commitment to independence from corporate interests and government funding can serve as an inspirational reminder to future activists who might likewise hold cultural productions to higher standards for them to qualify as examples of rights-based cinematic advocacy—that is, as human rights films capable of contributing to social change. In a way, the SHRFF can be viewed as an idealized variation on Jürgen Habermas's notion of the public sphere, an egalitarian space that is "open in principle to all citizens" and where "private persons come together to form a public . . . acting neither as business or professional people . . . nor as legal consociates."[35] According to Habermas, the political public sphere is a counterpoint to—and cannot be a part of—state power, which the SHRFF has consistently framed as being oppositional to its interests in matters of social justice.

1987: Moon Jae-in's Tears and Political Affect

In "A Semantic/Syntactic Approach to Film Genre," Rick Altman distinguishes between inclusive and exclusive approaches to genre delineations. To illustrate his point, Altman proposes a "typical conversation" between an "exclusivist" ("I mean what do you do with Elvis Presley? You can hardly call them musicals. . . . *Fun in Acapulco* [is] surely no *Singin' in the Rain*") and an "inclusivist" ("Why not? They are loaded with songs and they've got a narrative that ties numbers together, don't they?"). He then puts forth a rhetorical question of his own, asking, "When is a musical not a musical? When it has Elvis Presley in it."[36] We would like to twist Altman's inquiry and pose our own: When is a rights-advocacy film not a rights-advocacy film? When it is produced and distributed by CJ Entertainment or another media conglomerate? When it is exhibited in multiplexes and seen by tens of millions of people? When it has recognizable generic traits of narrative fiction cinema? When it is funded by the government and produced by the NHRCK? We do not believe that the motives of the production company or the source of financing automatically qualifies or disqualifies a film as rights-advocacy cinema. Nor do we believe that there is an overall system of textual or generic traits that determines what is or is not a rights-advocacy film. A more fruitful way to conceptually frame the rights-advocacy film is to examine its affective power as a "body genre,"[37] one that is conducive to "connecting the social and the somatic," to borrow the subtitle of John Protevi's 2009 book *Political Affect*.[38] Indeed, human rights cinema exerts phenomenological sway as an institutional category of cultural production uniquely capable of provoking tears and potentially altering mind-sets, something that we explore over the course of several case studies in the chapters that follow.

On January 7, 2018, President Moon Jae-in, a former human rights lawyer, and his wife, Kim Chŏng-suk, made a surprise visit to a CGV movie theater in Yongsan to watch a morning screening of *1987: When the Day Comes* along with a crowd of moviegoers. At the screening's conclusion, the tearful leader of the nation participated in an impromptu conversation with fellow audience members. He opened up in a forthright fashion, telling them that the most emotionally resonant dialogue was spoken by the apolitical college student, Yŏn-hŭi, who at one point asks her activist love interest if the world can be changed through the act of political demonstration. Moon is reported to have elaborated on this point, telling the crowd that "in fact, during the June Uprising and throughout the democratic movement era before that," variations on Yŏn-hŭi's question were posed by the parents and relatives of prodemocracy activists, who—just as Yi Han-yŏl does in *1987*—stood strong against an authoritarian government and despite pressure from their own family members. "A lot of you probably heard the same question from your own parents or those close to you when you participated in candlelight vigils [for the impeachment of Park Geun-hye] last winter," the president told the audience, and he concluded, "I believe today's movie is the answer to that question." Although Moon acknowledged that "the world doesn't change overnight," and that demonstrations alone will not make much of a difference if they are not followed by substantive talks about the actual implementation of rights-protection policies among lawmakers and other government officials, he also reminded the audience that the military dictatorship on view in recent commercial films such as *A Taxi Driver* "was put to an end by the June Uprising of 1987. . . . When we all put our efforts together and when someone like Yŏn-hŭi participates, then we can change the world. I believe that this is [*1987*'s] message."[39]

Moon's singling out of Yŏn-hŭi (Kim T'ae-ri), a fictional character, is relevant as she represents a cynical, apathetic citizenry whose defeatist attitude (she initially believes that resistance to power is useless) must be replaced with youthful optimism if the struggle—writ large in the form of other protesters like her—is to gain momentum. The college student has to be bribed to do "the right thing" on behalf of her uncle, a prison guard, who risks his safety to deliver a dissident

FIGURE 1.2 Yŏn-hŭi (Kim T'ae-ri), a formerly apolitical college student in *1987: When the Day Comes* (2017), is overwhelmed by the sight of thousands of protesters taking part in that year's June Uprising against the authoritarian Chun Doo-hwan presidency. Unable to hold back her tears, she functions as an onscreen surrogate for viewers of this mainstream human rights film, many of whom might feel prompted to cry during this heavy-handed yet affectively powerful final scene.

prisoner's message to the outside world, using his niece as a cover. She also makes a discouraging remark—the passage paraphrased above by Moon—before her boyfriend, Yi Han-yŏl (Kang Tong-wŏn), a real-life student activist from Yonsei University who will be fatally injured by a tear-gas canister thrown by riot police in the penultimate scene, heads out to protest against the torture and murder of another activist, Park Chong-ch'ŏl (Yŏ Chin-gu). Yŏn-hŭi's transformation achieves full expression in the film's final scene, after she has seen a newspaper image of Yi's bloody, unconscious face. In a tracking shot, the camera follows the movement of Yŏn-hŭi, who navigates past injured protesters along a street on her way to City Hall square, where tens of thousands of young men and women are gathered, singing the national anthem. One of the protesters offers his hand to the college student and lifts her to the roof of a nonoperational bus. The camera shows a frontal medium shot of a tearful Yŏn-hŭi, who is apparently overwhelmed by the offscreen sight (which has thus far remained concealed from the audience; see figure 1.2). As an offscreen female voice leads people in chanting protest slogans ("abolish the current constitution [which disallows direct presidential elections]" and "down with dictatorship"), the camera slowly circles to expose the size of the gathered crowd from a high angle (Yŏn-hŭi's elevated perspective vis-à-vis those on the ground). As the camera retreats from Yŏn-hŭi's position, it shows an extreme long shot of the full view of City Hall and the throng of demonstrators who, chanting as one, are united in their political aims and under banners, including an oversize portrait of Park Chong-ch'ŏl (whose

FIGURE 1.3 The camera, now positioned behind Yŏn-hŭi, shows her to be part of a collective struggle for democracy and direct presidential elections involving what might be called a mass protagonist (the faceless thousands situated below her). Ending in this way, with the now-enlightened female character standing on high moral ground, *1987: When the Day Comes* literally elevates previous decades' fight for social justice and rights protections to a matter of present-day concern.

death sparked the uprising; see figure 1.3). Prompted by her fellow human rights advocates and moved by the sight, Yŏn-hŭi lifts her fist in a sign of combined defiance and compliance and joins the movement.

Protevi sees "political affect" as having two aspects: "political physiology" and "political feeling." The author defines the former as "the direct interaction of the social and the somatic, skipping the subjective level"[40]—as evidenced by Yŏn-hŭi's relationship to the mass body of protesters in the final scene of *1987*, which shows the formerly apolitical character involuntarily reacting to the overpowering spectacle of the social. Perhaps what rights-advocacy cinema provokes is what Protevi terms "political feeling," which is "the conscious, subjective registration of that interaction"[41] between the social and the somatic that we witness as film spectators. In this light, the human rights film can be said to function in a way that is similar to that of diegetic newspaper images and the spectacle of demonstrating masses in *1987*. They are mobilized in the hope of inspiring a change in the mind-set of the spectator (diegetically inscribed as Yŏn-hŭi, an onscreen surrogate for the audience) and prompting action. To return once again to a sentiment expressed by President Moon, when something like that happens—when even the most cynical or apathetic members of society can be made to feel or are moved—then the power of political affect is especially palpable and perhaps even global in its reach.

2

If You Were Me

Transnational Crossings and South Korean Omnibus Films

> How often do we show a film or read a testimonial in human rights classes (whether social science oriented or humanities based) where only the plot and themes are discussed? What are we missing when such texts are taught with little or no attention to the *forms* of their expression?
>
> —Sophia A. McClennen and Joseph R. Slaughter, "Introducing Human Rights and Literary Forms"

In their introduction to a special issue of *Comparative Literature Studies* devoted to the subject of human rights, Sophia McClennen and Joseph Slaughter pose a series of provocative questions about the role that cultural representations play in both strengthening and weakening global humanitarian discourses. After ruminating on the paradoxical vilification or denigration of human rights advocacy in the age of muscular, U.S.-led military interventions and then suggesting that oppressive political regimes throughout the world have increasingly appropriated humanitarian discourses "in the service of domination," the authors turn their attention to films, novels, paintings, and other types of cultural production, asking, "What happens to those texts . . . when they outlive their urgent utility? Do they become artifactual repositories of memory, cultural souvenirs of a struggle? Or does the very endurance of the work mean that the struggle continues in a less urgent form?"[1] These questions, like the ones in the epigraph above, invite critical reflection on the manner in which signifying practices are employed by artists, experienced by audiences, and studied by historians and other scholars with a vested interest in the social conditions of the oppressed—individuals and groups that are frequently positioned outside legal and juridical frameworks and rendered as the phantasmatic protagonists of allegorical narratives. One of the central claims made by McClennen and Slaughter is that "we cannot talk about human rights without talking about the *forms* in which we talk about human rights." And they maintain that it is at the level of form "where much of the social work and political potential of cultural production lies."[2]

McClennen and Slaughter's questions about the ways in which "innovative cultural forms have given us new human rights vocabularies" can be fruitfully directed toward those modes of audiovisual expression that most decisively highlight the "paradoxes and contradictions" of contemporary humanitarian discourses.[3] Following these authors' lead, this chapter focuses on a unique mode of cinematic production and reception—the omnibus film, a feature-length episodic work that brings together two or more filmmakers who, in certain cases, may serve as national representatives and who contribute short works to a larger whole that can encompass a range of directorial styles, narrative modes, and genres—and highlights how central this oft-ignored and marginalized type of cultural expression is to the experiential process of projecting oneself into the real and imagined spaces of others. We make the case that the omnibus film, owing to its heterogeneous array of thematic material and its fragmented form, is well suited to address some of the social ills that still plague various parts of the world while structurally highlighting the economic chasms or material obstacles that continue to separate people despite their best efforts to generate consensus across national borders. Owing to its own troubled corporeality (as a text both vulnerably positioned on the periphery of film history and often dismissed by critics because of its visible differences from traditional cinematic storytelling), the omnibus film is an appropriate, if also problematic, vehicle for bringing embodied human rights discourses to light. Moreover, when deployed for the purposes of highlighting issues related to the subject of human rights, this frequently overlooked meta-genre reveals that, behind many altruistic acts on the part of well-intentioned individuals, a politics of pity rather than compassion threatens to increase rather than diminish the distance between subject and object, self and other, and the protected and the vulnerable. That is, the textual proximity of stories in omnibus films, besides generating false equivalencies by linking discrete sites of suffering, relies upon a form of narrative "wounding" in which the gaps between episodes might serve as metaphorical reminders of our spectatorial remove from that suffering.

Derived from the Latin word *vulnus*, meaning "wound," the concept of vulnerability has itself been susceptible to institutional precariousness, according to the sociologist Bryan Turner. In *Vulnerability and Human Rights*, Turner argues that the evolution of human rights legislation has been driven by "the instability of global financial markets" and "the insecurity of orderly civil society through the globalization of slavery, organized crime, and the narcotics trade," among other things.[4] One unavoidable outcome of vulnerability, Turner states, is "the experience of suffering," a universal yet variable experience that connects people from different parts of the world. We contend that suffering can be rendered palpable—experientially felt, at least to some degree—when delivered in omnibus form, a form that metatextually lays bare, rather than masks, the wounds associated with the "violence" of narrativity. If cinematic narrativity can be construed as a signifying process that reductively aestheticizes or essentializes the pain of others, turning the cultural and/or historical particularities of people's experiences into a series of universalizing tropes or moments of temporary contemplation for the comparatively privileged viewer, then the omnibus film—as a gap-filled text consisting of two or more episodes (each supplied by a different director)—can serve to remind audiences of the challenges involved in linking discrete sites of embodied suffering while acknowledging the twin commitments bound up in the idea of human rights: universality and equality.[5]

Just how central those two commitments are in the many filmic texts that are brought together under the banner of human rights cinema is a question that demands consideration. Indeed, most examples of human rights cinema tend to emphasize, through a limited array of presentational and representational means, the underlying humanity of all individuals (be they fictional characters or real people, which is the case more often than not) whose entitlement to inalienable rights has been ignored. Such films frequently foster spectatorial attachment to or allegiance with those individuals, although the lens through which we access and bear witness to the violation of their rights is sometimes figuratively smeared or darkened by a politics not of intersubjectivity but of essentializing pity. The latter, according to the French sociologist and philosopher Luc Boltanski (channeling the spirit of Hannah Arendt), has an eloquence lacking in the comparatively mute form of direct, interpersonal engagement that we call compassion, and moreover pity "generalizes and integrates the dimension of distance"—something that has to be overcome or bridged if these films are to have any real and lasting impact on viewers.[6]

Defined as a feature-length motion picture consisting of two or more discrete narrative sketches or vignettes, each separated from the others by way of interstitial gaps (the "wounds" of the text alluded to above), the omnibus film is a decidedly undecided form, one whose dialogic capacity to combine multiple voices and visions makes it both especially difficult to pin down and conducive to a rethinking of narrative formulas and spectatorial solicitations. After elaborating that definition with an eye to the omnibus film's historical roots, we examine the intersection of humanitarian discourses and visual media in the South Korean context, where human rights covenants and debates surrounding the idea of civil society have become an increasingly conspicuous part of the post–Cold War political climate. In particular, we look at a series of multidirector features that are thematically organized around issues relevant to the study of minority cultures and human rights. Adopting a transnational and comparative perspective, we shed light on the production background, critical reception, and narrative operations of *If You Were Me* (*Yŏsŏt kaeŭi sisŏn*, 2003). This is the first of six live-action motion pictures that (together with two animated features) currently constitute the If You Were Me series, an ever-growing collection of episodic works that address pressing social and political concerns related to, among other rights, those of people with disabilities, children, LGBTQ people, migrants, temporary workers, and single mothers—as well as privacy rights. Financially supported by the National Human Rights Commission of Korea (NHRCK; Kukka ingwŏn wiwŏnhoe), this series was officially launched in April of 2003, when the first entry kicked off the fourth Jeonju International Film Festival.

Before the film's November theatrical release in Seoul, a number of prestigious venues—including the Vancouver Film Festival (where it won the Dragons and Tigers Award), the Vladivostok Film Festival, the Fukuoka International Film Festival, and the London Film Festival—had asked to screen *If You Were Me*. Its success at those and other events ensured that subsequent entries in the series would be produced and distributed overseas at a time when South Korean cinema was receiving unprecedented coverage in English- and French-language film periodicals. Indeed, apart from its focus on human rights issues, the series is noteworthy as a showcasing of local talent, spotlighting some of the country's most gifted and prominent directors, each of whom contributed episodes ranging in length from thirteen to twenty-one minutes. The first film alone, which deals with various types of embodied discrimination and human rights violations related to gender, physical disability, class status, past criminal record, and country of birth, brings together contributions from Park Kwang-su, Yŏ Kyun-dong, Im Sun-rye, Park Chan-wook (Pak Ch'an-uk), Pak Chin-p'yo, and Chŏng Chae-ŭn. Its characters range from an overweight high-school girl who struggles to find a job (in the opening segment, Im Sun-rye's "The Weight of Her") and a young boy forced by his parents to undergo a grueling orthodontic operation known as frenectomy so he can speak English more fluently (Pak Chin-p'yo's "Tongue-Tie") to an immigrant woman from Nepal named Chandra Kumari Gurung who physically resembles Koreans and—because she does not understand the language—is misdiagnosed as having schizophrenia and subsequently put in a psychiatric hospital in Seoul (Park Chan-wook's concluding episode, "NEPAL: Never-Ending Peace and Love"). Although limited space prevents us from completely unpacking the themes and directorial styles of each of the eight motion pictures in the If You Were Me series, we will gesture toward satellite sites of intertextual and extratextual signification, including a multidirector work that is said to have inspired the making of the Korean film series: a French-language motion picture titled *Lest We Forget* (*Contre l'oubli*, 1991).

Omnibus Cinema, Political Participation, and Human Rights Film Festivals

While a longer project than this chapter would take into consideration the full range of intertextual allusions and thematic motifs found in all eight of the feature-length films in the If You Were Me series, we have chosen to draw attention to the participatory imperative evident within human rights documentaries as well as narrative works that inhabit a transnational imaginary in relation to both the directors' intentions and the films' global reception (at film festivals, in academic institutions, and through home video or DVD rentals and sales). Indeed, no discussion of human rights cinema would be complete without at least a passing reference to the distribution networks and exhibition venues that make it possible to view such films. Moreover, because so many human rights films are institutionally linked to humanitarian organizations as well as government bodies, it is important that future studies consider the roles played by Amnesty International, Asia Watch, and Human Rights Watch, which not only have promoted democracy, good governance, and conflict resolution but have also commissioned, endorsed, and/or partially funded omnibus projects featuring the contributions of several directors whose involvement recalls the spirit of politically motivated participation in multi-episode films made throughout the twentieth century.

There is a long if understudied tradition of generating dissent and attempting to mobilize the masses through the inclusive, participatory format of the omnibus film. Beginning with the agitprop vehicle *Life Belongs to Us* (*La vie est à nous*, 1936), a series of narrative sketches and newsreels produced by the French Communist Party and supervised by Jean Renoir that today is recognized as an early forerunner of "film collectives" such as *Return to Life* (*Retour à la vie*, 1949), *Far from Vietnam* (*Loin du Viêtnam*, 1967), *Germany in Autumn* (*Deutschland im Herbst*, 1978), *After the Gulf War* (*Harbu al-Khallij wa B'ad*, 1991), and *The Only Country in the World* (*L'unico paese al mondo*, 1994), the politically charged omnibus feature has proven to be a perennial means of both challenging official policies or prejudicial attitudes and solidifying public consensus while mining the many economic and material resources made available through Europe's common market. Such collectively conceived cultural productions were thought to be the perfect vehicles for rallying support around a common goal and articulating the spirit of protest. Although released less than two decades ago in an East Asian, rather than a European, nation, *If You Were Me* and its live-action and animated sequels can be seen as the postmillennial culmination of that view.

Although omnibus productions have long been a part of film history, the format did not become a prominent fixture in European and Asian contexts until the 1960s. Since that turbulent decade, omnibus films have increasingly lent themselves to collaborative efforts to shore up a sense of solidarity in the face of historical, political, and social changes. For instance, there was an unprecedented outpouring of multi-episode films in Czechoslovakia shortly before and immediately after the 1968 Soviet invasion of Prague, including *A Place in the Crowd* (*Místo v houfu*, 1964), *Pearls of the Deep* (*Perlicky na dne*, 1965), *Crime in the Girls' School* (*Zlocin v dívcí skole*, 1965), *Dialog 20-40-60* (1968), *Prague Nights* (*Prazské noci*, 1968), and *The Deserter and the Nomads* (*Zbehovia a pútnici*, 1969). Such examples attest to the importance of episodic works in capturing a wide assortment of perspectives on contemporaneous moments of political contestation, social unrest, and/or industrial transformation, as evidenced in subsequent productions like *In Our Time* (*Guang yin de gu shi*, 1982) and *The Sandwich Man* (*Er zi de da wan ou*, 1983), two films that jump-started Taiwan's New Wave of the early 1980s; and *Echoes of Conflict* (1989), a collection of three short films (directed by Gur Heller, Jorge Johanan Weller, and Amit Goren) about the Israeli-Palestinian conflict.

Indeed, the textually transformative and multiple dimensions of the omnibus film meta-genre make it appropriate for addressing calamity or crisis. Examples include *Spotlights on a Massacre* (1998), a ten-episode collection of shorts from different parts of the world that highlights the destructive power of land mines, with contributions from an international roster of directors (Youssef Chahine, Pierre Jolivet, Mathieu Kassovitz, Pavel Lounguine, Rithy Panh, Volker Schlondorff, Coline Serreau, Bertrand Tavernier, Fernando Trueba, and Jaco Van Dormael); and *18-j* (2004), an Argentinean film combining ten shorts about the July 18, 1994, bombing of a Jewish community center in Buenos Aires. An even more ambitious example is the 2008 collective project *Stories of Human Rights*, which—under the guidance of the producer Adelina von Fürstenberg—brings together short films from twenty-five directors (including Jia Zhangke from China, Idrissa Ouedraogo from Burkina Faso, and Walter Salles from Brazil), thus consolidating multiple languages, ethnic identities, and regional settings into a commemorative celebration of the historical significance of the Universal Declaration of Human Rights (UDHR), the first U.N. statement committed to upholding the basic civil and political rights of all people regardless of nationality. Initiated at the behest of the Office of the High Commissioner for Human Rights (a U.N. agency established in 1993) and launched by the nonprofit organization ART for the World, this project was designed to promote international cooperation and the rule of law in countries where it would be theatrically exhibited. Consisting of over two dozen three-minute episodes (each directed by a different filmmaker), *Stories of Human Rights* succeeds in ushering forth a multitude of themes.

However, like the omnibus films in the If You Were Me series, *Stories of Human Rights* paradoxically waters down the language of human rights (and perhaps even undermines the rights' legal foundations) by suggesting that chauvinism, narrow-mindedness, and a general disrespect of other people's feelings are sufficient to satisfy the requirements for humanitarian intervention. As McClennen and Slaughter state, "The increasing appearance of rights-associated discourse outside of specific legal-juridical frameworks has brought with it a scaled-down conception of human rights. This transformation of the discourse of human rights into a language of desire and indulgence threatens to undermine 'their position as central principles of political and legal organization'; that is, human rights begin to lose their institutional force as the founding ideals of a polity when they become a free-floating discourse of social satisfaction and goodwill."[7] This concern about the definitional discursivity of human rights as a broadly applied marker of authoritative entitlements—of justified, high-priority claims for decent and respectful treatment—characterizes much philosophical work in this area, with the question of which protections and benefits should be extended to people continuing to divide critics and historians. As the political scholar Jiwei Ci argues, "Human rights discourse is vitiated by its tendency to reification, a tendency manifest in an ideologically motivated failure to take the reasons for human rights seriously."[8]

In recent years, several human rights organizations have played pivotal roles in distributing films for both theatrical release and home video consumption. Those organizations include the United Nations Center for Human Rights, the Human Rights Cinema Society, the International Gay and Lesbian Human Rights Commission, and the New York City Commission on Human Rights. As mentioned in Cindy Hing-Yuk Wong's study of film festivals, Movies That Matter (a Dutch-based initiative of Amnesty International) provided monetary support in 2009 to various human rights groups in Africa, Asia, Latin America, and Eastern Europe. That money facilitated the creation of "various types of human rights film events," including "mobile cinema programmes, . . . small-scale screenings for specific target groups, rotation within a network of film houses, school and university screenings, and distribution through multimedia platforms."[9] As a "harbinger of the future of generalized film distribution," one that accords with Wong's suggestion that an emerging type of "transnational public sphere" can be conceptualized "through a more concrete transnational public power," such diversified film events—occurring within and between different countries and regions of the world and engaging a variety of "subaltern counterpublics" within "parallel discursive arenas"—are what mark human rights festivals as uniquely porous spaces conducive to the formation of "alternative public spheres."[10]

As alternatives to the traditional Habermasian model of the public sphere, human rights film festivals shed light on "sensitive issues that more mainstream cinema tends to overlook because of perceived controversies."[11] In doing so, they celebrate the work of established auteurs, such as Amos Gitai (whose 2008 film about the Holocaust, *One Day You'll Understand*, opened that year's Toronto

Human Rights Festival) and Michael Winterbottom (whose 2006 drama *The Road to Guantanamo* was among the featured films at that year's Human Rights Watch Film Festival, held in New York). Furthermore, they also often illuminate "unknown audiovisual texts, their directors and their country of origin," as Elena Di Giovanni observes. Looking at the annual Human Rights Night event held in Bologna, Di Giovanni states that the idea of "bringing to light" is "built into the very essence of festivals," never more so than in those gatherings that "focus on the discussion of human rights, where audiences are involved in an experience of violations, abuses and forced obscurity," and where a plethora of topics (ranging from freedom of expression to indigenous and minority rights, slavery, and the plague of AIDS in Africa) are lent an omnibus-like quality of situated relatedness.[12]

As an example, the summer of 2009 marked the twentieth anniversary of the Human Rights Watch Film Festival in New York, where audiences had the opportunity to watch feature-length motion pictures that dealt with a range of topics, including an Italian aid organization's efforts to bring medical care to two children hospitalized as a result of the ongoing conflicts in Darfur and Afghanistan (*Back Home Tomorrow* [*Domani torno a casa*, 2008]), the practice of female genital mutilation in various parts of West Africa (*Mrs. Goundo's Daughter* [2009]), a Greek immigrant's quixotic quest to realize his personal and professional dreams in Paris (*Eden Is West* [*Eden à l'ouest*, 2009]), and a group of villagers' desperate struggles to survive in war-torn Bosnia (*Snow* [*Snijeg*, 2008]). In a way, the heterogeneous, mixed-bag nature of film festivals, which bring together disparate subjects as well as different representational modes and directorial styles within single venues, is reflected in miniature in the omnibus film, a feature-length assortment of topics and tropes that often leaves spectators feeling spent from having witnessed so many emotionally moving stories (abbreviated though they may be, since they appear as brief sketches or episodes lasting only a few minutes).

For example, the 2007 production *Invisibles*, an omnibus film made to support the Spanish branch of Médecins sans Frontières (Doctors without Borders), presents five vastly different stories over the course of its 105-minute running time. Although ostensibly tied together by a thematic emphasis on invisibility as a metaphor for moral disregard, and although each was shot on high-definition video (bringing some degree of visual cohesiveness to the project), the five episodes—directed by Isabel Coixet, Fernando León de Aranoa, Wim Wenders, Mariano Barroso, and Javier Corcuera—range so widely across a seemingly borderless world that spectators might feel like transnational travelers, or perhaps emotionally invested yet materially detached tourists who merely dip their toes into a series of different regional pools from the safety and comfort of their own film-viewing environments. The film focuses first on a Bolivian girl working in Barcelona, shifts to rape victims in the Democratic Republic of Congo, and then introduces a group of child soldiers in Uganda. From there it segues to an episode about multinational pharmaceutical companies and culminates with a story about impoverished farmers in Colombia. A miniature "festival" of internationalized differences in its own right, *Invisibles* reveals the impetus to squeeze many potentially moving stories into a single feature. This is a tactic that, perhaps not coincidentally, is similar to the one adopted by the drafters of the UDHR, an omnibus document that includes thirty short articles in addition to a seven-paragraph preamble.

Today, over seventy years after the U.N. General Assembly adopted the UDHR in December 1948, dozens of North American cities have played host to the Human Rights Watch Travelling Film Festival or similar, politically themed programs presented by Amnesty International (which began showcasing films in 1992). The Human Rights Watch Film Festival, which was officially launched in 1988 (to celebrate the nonprofit organization's tenth anniversary), is the oldest of these, and it has been instrumental in promoting widespread awareness of human rights issues. As Kenneth Roth, the former executive director of Human Rights Watch, stated in an interview, "There is an immediacy to film that allows the viewer to more readily identify with the victim and thus makes it more likely that someone sitting in the movie theater will be moved to action on behalf of the victims."[13] Although no empirical data have yet been presented to substantiate Roth's claim that people are more likely to participate in humanitarian initiatives or political activities after watching a particularly provocative film, one can certainly make the conjectural leap that the visceral impact of moving images is such that audiences might be shocked out of their complacency and moved to act in ways that that extend beyond monetary donations. Human rights films might indeed have the capacity to emotionally affect audiences in ways that other types of cultural production often fail to do.

In her study of film festivals, Wong hints at this idea when she states, "Because of cinema's mimetic power, concrete individuals replace statistics and make actions and situations real."[14] Speaking specifically about the Human Rights Watch Film Festival, she explains that its programmers are "invested in using cinema to 'uncover the truth and make justice possible.'" That goal—an attempt to transform the medium of motion pictures into "an agent of dialogue and change," one that "has the power to do good in society"—was shared by the producer and distributor of *If You Were Me* and was promoted when they and the contributing filmmakers were interviewed after its theatrical release.

If You Were Me: Production Background and Political Resonances

As indicated above, the origins of *If You Were Me* date back to 1991, when the human rights–themed omnibus feature *Lest We Forget* was produced. This earlier, more politically charged French-language production for Amnesty International consists of thirty short films—each approximately three minutes long—made by internationally famous directors and actors, including Chantal Akerman, Claire Denis, Jean-Luc Godard, and Alain Resnais. Each filmmaker examined the life of a different person from around the world who had been imprisoned and/or tortured. Originally, each of the episodes was shown individually on all but one of the French television channels (TF1) throughout the last quarter of 1991 as part of Amnesty International's "Ecrire contre l'oublie" campaign, coordinated and launched by Béatrice Soulé in recognition of the thirtieth anniversary of the international nongovernmental organization (NGO). Individual segments were subsequently assembled into a feature-length film in mid-December of that year and shown in Paris theaters, bringing to light the many human rights violations faced by prisoners whose civil liberties had been denied and whose freedom of speech had been suppressed. One of the thirty episodes in this omnibus film concerns the plight of the Korean political dissident Kim Sŏng-man, a former student at Western Illinois University who had come into contact with North Korean diplomatic representatives during his travels through Europe in 1983 and 1984 and who was eventually imprisoned in South Korea because of his suspected communist sympathies.

As someone who had talked idealistically about reunification with his friends and colleagues in the Korean American community, and as an increasingly outspoken critic of U.S. foreign policy and military presence in South Korea, Kim attracted the attention of government officials, who falsely accused him of being a North Korean spy. Because Kim had met with staff members of the North Korean embassies in Budapest and East Berlin, he was arrested not long after his return to South Korea. In June 1985, he was detained on charges that he had violated South Korea's National Security Law, which was essentially an anticommunism law designed to suppress antistate activities. At Taejŏn Prison, where Kim was one of over forty detainees suspected of conducting espionage activities on behalf of North Korea, interrogators working for the Agency for National Security Planning tortured him physically and mentally while denying him adequate medical care. Although his death sentence was eventually changed to life in prison, Kim continued to suffer beatings at the hands of Korean Central Intelligence Agency operatives.[15] In 1989, Amnesty International selected him as one of the thirty subjects to be featured in *Lest We Forget*, a film that would soon bring international attention to his case. Directed by Constantin Costa-Gavras, a filmmaker long associated with politically engaged cinema and human rights issues (as evident in such works as *Z* [1969] and *Missing* [1982]), the short episode "For Kim Song-Man" features the French rap star MC Solaar repeating the chant "Release Kim Song-man" (see figure 2.1). Eventually, the rapper's plea was heard by South Korean officials, who released Kim in 1998, thirteen years into his life sentence.

During the 1990s, videotapes of *Lest We Forget* were sent to several NGOs and various national councils throughout the world, including the Mingahyŏp Human Rights Group, based in Seoul. *Mingahyŏp* is a shortened form of *minjuhwa silch'ŏn kajok undong hyŏpŭihoe*, and it stands for the Association for

FIGURE 2.1 Produced in 1991 as part of Amnesty International's "Ecrire contre l'oublie" campaign, the omnibus film *Lest We Forget* features an episode titled "For Kim Song-Man." Directed by the Greek-born filmmaker Constantin Costa-Gavras, this music video–style short features a performance by French rap stars (one of whom holds up a photo of Kim) who plead for the release of a man sentenced to life imprisonment under South Korea's National Security Law.

Families in Support of Democratic Movements. Established in 1985 by the mothers of young men who were being tortured as political prisoners, this group generated support for democratization during the repressive regime of President Chun Doo-hwan (Chŏn Tu-hwan; 1980–1988). When Nam Kyu-sŏn (who was then secretary of Mingahyŏp) received a videotape of *Lest We Forget*, she began thinking about the prospects of making a similar human rights omnibus film project in South Korea. However, it would take another ten years before such a project was launched. Before leaving Mingahyŏp to work for the NHRCK (established in April 2001), Nam had collaborated with the director Yŏ Kyun-dong on human rights shorts as *The Outer Coat* (*Oet'u*, 1996) and *My Computer* (*Nae k'ŏmp'yut'ŏ*, 1999). Supported by Yŏ, Nam began to spread the word of their desire to spearhead a more ambitious production, one that would combine several shorts into a single feature and that would eventually be given the English title *If You Were Me*. Before turning to this film's textual features, let us step back a moment to assess some of the contextual issues related to its production background and distribution, as well as the political changes that led up to its release.

Limited space prevents us from providing anything more than a cursory overview of the enormous changes that occurred prior to and in the wake of the Asian financial crisis of 1997 and South Korea's presidential election in December of that year—won by the former political dissident and future Nobel Prize winner Kim Dae-jung (Kim Tae-jung). However, it should be noted that after the election, the Kim Dae-jung government not only set out to adopt the democratic reforms and suggestions for economic restructuring provided by the International Monetary Fund, as well as seeking to engage the leaders of North Korea as part of the new administration's Sunshine Policy, but also attempted to rectify the long history of human rights abuses that had occurred throughout the authoritarian regimes of President Park Chung-hee (Pak Chŏng-hŭi) and Chun Doo-hwan. Throughout much of his adult life, Kim had seen firsthand how adept political and military officials could be in sidestepping diplomatic agreements with foreign powers and legal constraints related to human rights. Kim had been kidnapped, beaten, and placed under house arrest by members of the Korean Central Intelligence Agency in 1973, and six years later he was arrested and sentenced to death on sedition charges (leveled against him by General Chun Doo-hwan, head of the Army Security Command who seized power in a 1979 coup). Thus, the new president understood how necessary political change was to the social and spiritual well-being of a nation torn apart from within, a nation whose citizens increasingly took to the streets and demanded democratic elections.[16] Throughout the tense 1980s, two Washington-based groups—the Korean Institute for Human Rights and the North American Coalition for Humans Rights in Korea—as well as a few NGOs in South Korea tracked the increases in the number of abuses occurring on Chun's watch, drawing attention to the imprisonment of over 1,500 student and labor activists in 1986 and to the May 23, 1987, illegal detainment of Han Hwa-gup (then an aide to Kim Dae-jung). Facing increased U.S. scrutiny, and leading up to the 1988 Summer Olympics held in Seoul, the ruling party—headed by Roh Tae-woo (No T'ae-u), the new president—was forced "to make significant political concessions" related to civil liberties and human rights.[17]

Despite these and other events (including the 1992 election of the human rights activist Kim Young-sam [Kim Yŏng-sam] as president), a national advocacy institution for human rights protection would not be set up until 2001, three years after Kim Dae-jung's election. Established in November of that year by the new government, the NHRCK fulfilled South Korea's signatory role as a supporter of the Paris Principles (adopted by the U.N. General Assembly in 1993). The new organization's stated objective was to safeguard "the basic order of democracy" and "to ensure that inviolable, fundamental human rights of all individuals are protected".[18] Six weeks after its launch, the NHRCK heard complaints from individuals at the Daegu Correctional Institution as well as the Chŏngsŏng Custody Office, and, according to a press release, it "investigated an unnatural death case at Ulsan Detention Center." Besides looking into instances of human rights violations requiring legal action, the NHRCK expanded its objectives into the cultural arena, seeking novel ways to publicize and promote its mission of "creating a society where all members are treated equally."[19]

In early 2003, Nam Kyu-sŏn—the former press secretary of Mingahyŏp, who had become the publicity spokesperson for the NHRCK—initiated the omnibus film project *If You Were Me*. After getting approval from commission chairman Yi Chŏng-gik, Nam began searching for filmmakers who might be interested in contributing short works that dealt with the general theme of discrimination (*ch'abyŏl*). One of her biggest challenges was convincing directors to shoot a short on a budget of only fifty million won (approximately $44,000). Nevertheless, she managed to convince established filmmakers such as Park Kwang-su as well as up-and-coming talents like Park Chan-wook to participate in the project. Park Kwang-su, once a leading figure in the Korean New Wave cinema movement of the 1980s and 1990s, signed on to the project immediately, opting to cut his shooting hours short to save money (ensuring that each day of work would end before sunset). Park Chan-wook, an iconoclastic auteur of the new millennium who is celebrated for his unique brand of "extreme cinema," likewise sought to cut back on spending after agreeing to supply an episode that would be partially filmed in Nepal.[20] A female contributor to the film, Im Soon-rye, initially declined to participate in the project, as she was busy producing a feature-length melodrama titled *A Smile* (*Miso*, 2003). However, at the cajoling of another director (Yŏ Kyun-dong, one of Nam's close associates), and because she had been discriminated against because of her size, Im decided to pitch in.

During an interview with a reporter for the magazine *Cine 21*, Nam was asked how she had been able to bring this project to fruition and then commence production on two subsequent projects—which, several years later, resulted in *If You Were Me 2* (*Tasŏt kaeŭi sisŏn*, 2005) and *If You Were Me: Anima Vision* (*Pyŏlbyŏl iyagi*, 2006). She replied: "It's not easy to invite directors and staff because it requires voluntary service. I can't force that. But a professional distributor and good directors made it feasible. I think the recent growth and newly gained power of Korean cinema made our project possible."[21] Nam's comment effectively synthesizes two particular subcategories of cinematic transnationalism described by Mette Hjort, who argues that both an "auteurist transnationalism" and a "modernizing transnationalism" are evident in the institutional frameworks of or discourses surrounding omnibus films. Whereas the former type emerges when established filmmakers embrace "a particular kind of collaboration beyond national borders" (as the celebrated auteurs Park Chan-wook and Bong Joon-ho [Pong Jun-ho] have done through their contributions to the multicountry omnibus films *Three . . . Extremes* [2004] and *Tokyo!* [2008], respectively), the latter arises when a "significantly transnationalized film culture becomes a means of fueling, but also signifying, the mechanisms of modernization within a given society."[22] The result of government-based initiatives, South Korea's uniquely hybrid brand of auteurist modernizing transnationalism was highlighted in the creation and launch of the Jeonju International Film Festival, which, as Bérénice Reynaud has pointed out, was designed to promote the host country as "the cutting edge of international film culture."[23] Significantly,

Jeonju's "omnibus film initiative" (a yearly project launched in 2000, when Park Kwang-su and Kim Yun-t'ae, along with the Chinese director Zhang Yuan, contributed digital shorts to a feature-length production) moved from a strongly "trans-Asian dimension" during its first year to a more globally dispersed assemblage of allegorical stories (provided by Jia Zhangke, John Akomfrah, and Tsai Ming-liang) for its 2001 incarnation—a production that simultaneously highlighted and forged transnational connections while singling out South Korea as a dynamic site of multicultural convergence.[24]

The distributor alluded to by Nam in the quote above from the interview is Ch'ŏngŏram Film, an investment company that, only a few months earlier, had handled such commercial successes as *Singles* (2003), *A Tale of Two Sisters* (*Changhwa Hongryŏn*, 2003), and *A Good Lawyer's Wife* (*Param nan kajok*, 2003), and would go on to produce one of the highest grossing Korean films of all time, *The Host* (*K'oemul*, 2006). Agreeing to take care of any publicity and marketing costs not already covered by the NHRCK, Ch'ŏngŏram strove to highlight connections between this unusual omnibus venture and some of the other, less commercial, motion pictures that it had distributed not long after its founding in 2001, including the low-budget indies *Too Young to Die* (*Chugŏdo choa*, 2002), *Road Movie* (*Rodŭ mubi*, 2002), and *The Road Taken* (*Sŏnt'aek*, 2003), which similarly focus on socially marginalized individuals, ranging from sexually active septuagenarians to political prisoners, homeless homosexuals, and frazzled prostitutes. The company also forged a link between *If You Were Me* and another episodic feature that it had distributed in 2002, the multidirector comedy *No Comment* (*Mutjima p'aemilli*), which chains together three blackout sketches dealing with the overarching theme of hatred.

The CEO of Ch'ŏngŏram, Ch'oe Yong-bae, not only sought to position *If You Were Me* as a wholesome and entertaining yet educational film (in the process minimizing its ties to the South Korean government) but also had final say over the order in which the six episodes would be presented to spectators. Believing that the segmental sequencing of the episodes was vitally important to the film's commercial appeal, Ch'oe knew that he needed a strong opener, one that would hook viewers and hopefully dispel any prejudice they might have against a human rights film. For the first slot he selected Im Sun-rye's comically inflected story of a plump high-school student named Sun-kyŭn (Yi Sŏl-hŭi), who is persistently harassed by teachers and teased by classmates because of her failure to lose weight and her pitiful attempts to create the illusion that she has Western-style *ssanggap'ul* (eye folds). This episode, while humorous, carries autobiographical elements, providing the spectator with a glimpse into the life of a girl who is not so different from the director—one of the relatively few female filmmakers in South Korea at the time of the film's production, and someone who has been discriminated against not only because of her gender but also due to her plus-size proportions. In an interview, Im stressed that she had long been interested "in the worsening degree of appearance-worshiping trends" and that she saw the short-film format as an opportunity to release some of her pent-up frustrations about living in a society that puts a person's physical looks before his or her intelligence.[25]

This convergence of the private and the public, the personal and the political, is literalized in the final scene of Im's episode. After the downhearted main character exits a café (where she has been turned down, once again, for a job), the camera pulls back to reveal the film crew on the street, where a male passerby, obviously confused, asks, "Who is the director?" When members of the crew point toward Im, situated to the right side of the frame, the man exclaims, "What, that fat *ajumma* (old auntie)? No way!" This obviously staged, yet documentary-like rupture at the end of the episode is strategically placed, coinciding with the interstitial break between the first two narrative segments of the film. Such breaks are an intrinsic part of the omnibus experience for audiences, who are asked to realign their sympathies toward a different set of characters with each introduction of a new episode and, in doing so, are reminded of their status as distant observers of the action. However, this spectatorial realignment can occur only if the viewer is willing to figuratively cross over, to make the intersubjective leap or effort required of those who—in their literal distance (from both the screen and the people depicted on it)—might otherwise feel detached from the array of discriminatory experiences being presented one after the other.

Significantly, Ch'oe Yong-bae chose to position Park Chan-wook's episode about a female Nepali migrant worker in the final slot of the film so as to leave the audience sufficiently moved at the end. Briefly, this episode concerns a woman named Chandra, who was "arrested for non-payment of a restaurant bill [and] referred to a mental hospital by the police on account of her impoverished appearance and inability to speak Korean."[26] As explained in Kevin Gray's article about the emergence of a migrant workers' union movement in South Korea, Chandra's "constant protests that she was Nepalese were ignored and she was force-fed medicine and confined for six years before anybody noticed (or was willing to notice) that she might in fact be telling the truth."[27] In shots that once again inject a meta-reflexive perspective into the proceedings, Park's offscreen voice can be heard throughout the opening scene, set in Nepal. A succession of women—each answering "no" to the question, "Are you Chandra?"—is capped by an image of Chandra herself responding "yes" (see figure 2.2). What follows that face-to-face meeting between an old Nepalese woman and a younger, border-crossing Korean man is a series of black-and-white scenes designed to put the viewer in Chandra's shoes, giving audience members the opportunity to see events in the past and the indifference of police officers and hospital workers from her point of view, but with the effect of turning her into a kind of invisible presence: someone who is there but not there.

Only in the episode's coda, which returns the film to color, does Chandra address the cinematic apparatus, partially revealed to us in a shot of the boom-mic's operator walking with her toward the camera. Finally allowed to speak her

FIGURE 2.2 In this segment of the six-episode omnibus film *If You Were Me* (*Yŏsŏt kaeŭi sisŏn*, 2003), a Nepalese woman faces the camera directly and answers affirmatively to filmmaker Park Chan-wook's question, "Are you Chandra?"

native language in a medium shot that emphasizes her dignity as a human being, she reveals herself to be a forgiving and patient person. According to the director, she expressed gratitude to those Koreans "who did fundraising for her lawsuits after the incident was publicly exposed." As these examples suggest, privileged sections tend to come either first or last in the chain of miniature narratives that make up omnibus films. Producers and programmers may feel that such an arrangement either immediately captures the attention of audiences, making them more likely to immerse themselves in subsequent episodes after the first segment has cast its spell, or engenders spectatorial anticipation for the final episode.

Although not as broadly international in scope as *Stories of Human Rights* and *Lest We Forget*, this first entry in the If You Were Me omnibus film series is similarly discursive at the textual level and prone to genre hybridity, taking the viewer from a coming-of-age dramedy to a dystopian science fiction parable about a convicted pedophile, a video diary, a tale about a medical procedure, a ghost story, and an ethnic mockumentary over the course of its ninety-minute running time. Taken as a whole, these six discrete yet thematically linked episodes—many of which are based on true stories involving actual people—prove to be significant not only for their consecutive foregrounding of distinct genres or subgenres, but also for their unflinching look at often ignored yet institutionalized forms of prejudice. However, while *If You Were Me* introduces the spectator to a wide range of issues and individuals whose stories are relevant to the study of social inequalities and minority cultures in South Korea, its contributors—much like former President Kim Dae-jung, and despite their good intentions—could be accused of failing to "distinguish 'human rights' from and in relation to other rights."[28] Just as Kim Dae-jung—in a paper written in 1994, before his election to the presidency, and in a speech that he delivered in 1999 at an international conference titled "Democracy, Market Economy and Development" that was hosted by his government and the World Bank—"did not explicitly define or otherwise indicate a generic, categorical notion of 'human rights,'"[29] so the film occasionally muddies the waters with its emphasis on marginalized outsiders who are simply trying to fit in.

In a way, this all-encompassing approach was Nam Kyu-sŏn's original intention, given her stated desire to have the contributing filmmakers deal broadly with the theme of discrimination rather than the often-contested legal or juridical frameworks of human rights. In South Korea, *ch'abyŏl* (discrimination) is an inclusive, omnibus-like concept that brings eighteen protected categories into the purview of the NHRCK: sex, religion, disability, age, social status, region, nationality, ethnicity, physical appearance, marital status, pregnancy or maternity, family status, race, skin color, ideological or political persuasion, criminal record, sexual orientation, and medical history.[30] A violation of rights is thus any infringement on a person's individual character and/or social status based on those categories. It should be noted, though, that while *If You Were Me* may obfuscate or obscure the specificities or contingencies related to particular subjects (including pedophilia, the subject of the film's second episode), its gap-filled structure makes it possible for audiences to fill in missing information and forge connections between seemingly disparate people, a maneuver that has ethical implications. Because of the combined span and brevity of its form (a feature-length motion picture composed of several shorts), the omnibus film paradoxically facilitates the spectatorial act of "crossing over" by withholding information, sketching in only a few details, and providing open spaces in which viewers might dwell (if only momentarily) as active participants. Indeed, the omnibus film's interepisodic juxtapositions reveal a perverse logic at play in this most contradictory of genres, with unseemly connections being forged and with the concept of depth being altered in the process.

Depth, traditionally conceived of as a kind of vertical plunging into profundity or an almost geological search for meaning below the surface, is thus made horizontal or geographical in the context of omnibus features. Although the act of extracting hermeneutic significance through sustained engagement (with a single group of people or a solitary protagonist) is one way of acknowledging the relative depth of a cultural production, this attempt to dig below the surface of texts is offset by a new model of profundity in films such as *If You Were Me*. What this and other omnibus films do is move beyond the temporal or historical markers of vertical depth to point toward the spatial and textual coordinates specific to what we call horizontal depth, which extends signification across an array of different environments or milieus that are segmentally plotted and transtextually linked. In the case of *If You Were Me*, those spaces include institutional and professional settings (such as a high school and a physician's office) as well as heterotopic nonplaces or liminal zones (such as an apartment complex and a parking garage). In transitioning from one setting to another, the viewer not only engages in a kind of intersubjective cosmopolitanism, increasing his or her capacity to see similarities among the text's visible differences, but also metaphorically enacts at the "local" level the kind of border-crossing movement inscribed in transnational flows. Indeed, the omnibus film is the most "trans" of all transpositional forms related to cinematic culture, collapsing transmedial, translinguistic, transgeneric, translocal, and transnational modes in the space of a single feature that unites multiple voices and visions.

Marketing *If You Were Me* and "Crossing Over" to the Other Side

Once postproduction had been completed and the order of the episodes decided, *If You Were Me* was released in thirty theaters nationwide throughout the fall of 2003. Tellingly, the theatrical release of the film was marketed in ways that downplayed its human rights angle. Rather than feature some of the film's characters (many of whom literally embody the theme of alterity or physical difference), the posters designed by Ch'ŏngŏram's publicity team trumpeted the buffet-like bounty and variety of stories supplied by its six visionary directors. Indeed, vision itself is foregrounded, not only in the original Korean title (which is more accurately translated as "Six Gazes") but also in the subtitle of the poster that appears just above the heads of those tuxedoed auteurs, which reads, "A Brave Gaze Rejects Discrimination" (see figure 2.3). The lower half of the poster is festooned with red and white captions, proclaiming, "We shot as we pleased! You watch as you please! Variety movie party!!!" In other words, *If You Were Me* was promoted and sold to the public as a fun, multi-story celebration hosted by fearless auteurs rather than as a serious "enlightenment" project or propaganda piece backed by the government.

Despite the distributor's attempts to frame this feature as a celebratory assortment of short films sure to please even the most apathetic viewers, the NHRCK positioned it as an instructional means of solidifying public and prosecutorial support for legal enforcement of human rights policies. At the NHRCK's suggestion, the South Korean Ministry of Justice (Pŏmmubu) arranged mandatory work-hour screenings of *If You Were Me* for Supreme and District Court public prosecutors during the 2003 Human Rights Week (December 7–13). As reported in a *Cine 21* article, a ministry representative explained the rationale behind the screenings this way: "We sought cooperation from the distributor through the NHRCK to make public prosecutors think about human rights issues through this film, since they are responsible for protecting such rights."[31] Regardless of whether or not this goal was met, it is significant that the omnibus film—a site of internal difference and structural ruptures (at the textual level)—could be so easily situated within different reception contexts that its underlying purpose (to call for social change) might be seen in a different light. It is even possible

FIGURE 2.3 The Korean-language movie poster for *If You Were Me* (or "Six Gazes") foregrounds the tuxedo-clad filmmakers—an auteurist rather than advocacy-based promotional strategy that dissociates the film from state-sponsored "enlightenment" projects.

that the antidiscrimination attitudes that permeate the text might be offset by the many solicitations extended from the distributor to viewers: invitations to select a favorite episode and/or filmmaker during their pleasurable consumption of the film as a whole. This unavoidable part of the omnibus film experience is allegorically conveyed in the first episode of *If You Were Me*, when a panel of middle-age men is shown rating the appearances of much younger female job applicants, including the plus-size protagonist.

Although not a commercial hit, *If You Were Me* attracted the attention of international audiences after being shown in the film festival circuit in 2003 and 2004, and it has spawned five live-action sequels (in addition to two "Anima Vision" films). Its first live-action sequel, the five-episode omnibus *If You Were Me 2*, foregrounds, among other things, the difficulties faced by North Korean defector refugees ("A Boy with the Knapsack") and Chinese-Korean laborers ("Jongno, Winter"), whose lives of quiet desperation are lent a therapeutic degree of dignity by the directors Chŏng Chi-u and Kim Dong-won (Kim Tong-wŏn), respectively. Although these two episodes adopt radically different storytelling modes (the former is a black-and-white narrative fiction short, and the latter is a cinema verité–style color documentary), their main characters—a nineteen-year-old defector delivery boy and a forty-five-year-old ethnic Korean laborer from China, respectively—function similarly as representatives of a larger, collective identity. In "A Boy with the Knapsack," Hyŏn-i (O T'ae-kyŏng), an alienated young defector whose backpack holds gifts for his parents in P'ungsan, North Korea and who is eager to return home (to an enemy state, where defectors are not allowed to redefect), dies in a motorcycle accident. In preparation for this episode, Chŏng interviewed several teenage defectors, most of whom faced prejudice as a result of their northern accents and worked in gas stations or at delivery service jobs (lines of work that do not require refined speech skills). During a question-and-answer session following a 2013 NHRCK-sponsored public screening of the episode in Daegu (where it was paired with an episode from *If You Were Me 5*—"Two Teeth," which focuses on an awkward situation in which a defector accidentally breaks the teeth of her classmate), Chŏng explained: "When they deliver, they ride motorcycles and sometimes they become aggressive to release stress. There are actual defector teenagers who died in traffic accidents. Defector youths go to school, too, but it is hard for them to follow this [South Korean] curriculum. . . . This situation made one boy speed his motorcycle and he was killed. I wanted to make a film about the story."[32]

Just as Hyŏn-i's story represents the shared experiences of defector minors (as of 2018, 3,100 teenagers living in South Korea came from North Korea), Kim Dong-won's episode ("Jongno, Winter")—which consists primarily of talking-head interviews, archival news footage, and dramatic reenactments—exposes the broader discriminatory conditions faced by low-wage Chinese-Korean migrant workers through the story of Kim Wŏn-sŏp, who froze to death on Hyehwa Street in the Jongno neighborhood of Seoul in December 2003. The Chinese-Korean migrant (who had overstayed his work visa at the time of his death) had come to the South Korean capital from Heilongjiang in China to earn money to support his family. After laboring in a construction field and being laid off without receiving his back wages, he joined other Chinese Koreans for extended sit-in demonstrations to protest the deportation of undocumented migrants in the Korean Church Centennial Memorial Building (which had served as a temporary shelter for protesters since mid-November). On December 8, Kim left the center to visit his former employer and attempted to collect his back pay. On the way back to the shelter, he took the wrong bus and got lost. Having starved for two days, Kim—too fearful of deportation to approach strangers for help—was left stranded, exhausted, alone, and shivering in the freezing cold. When he finally called 119 (the Korean equivalent of 911) and 112 (to reach the police) to try to get an ambulance, his inability to articulate his request in standard Korean was mistaken as a drunken man's babble, and all twelve of his phone calls were ignored. Kim's body was found by a street cleaner near a police station, one hour after his final emergency call. Kim Dong-won's documentary short ends with a caption, revealing the alarming fact that a hundred Chinese Koreans are found dead or commit suicide each year. As Ko Pu-ŭng observes, the *t'albukja* (defectors from North Korea) and *Chosŏnjok* (ethnic Koreans from China) in these episodes are both stateless "diasporic communities" that are opposed to the South Korean state (which prohibits repatriation for the former and fails to provide equal protection for the latter) but open to the idea of forming alliances with fellow members of the diaspora and other supporters within South Korea.[33] This is evident in Hyŏn-i's narrativized friendship with a neighbor defector girl named Chin-sŏn (Yi Chin-sŏn), as well as in documentary interviews with *Chosŏnjok* laborers, organizers, and South Korean activists who speak for Kim Wŏn-sŏp after his death.

The six-episode *If You Were Me: Anima Vision* covers similar terrain, albeit with the added distinction of being a completely animated examination of institutional biases and injustices (concerning disabilities, psychical appearance, nationality or citizenship, and educational status). Ostensibly made to educate children and young adults about the pervasiveness of discrimination and the problems endured by everyone from migrant workers to physically challenged Koreans, this animated omnibus production supplements its pedagogical pedigree with poetic reveries about human interconnectedness. One episode in particular, "Animal Farm," allegorizes the idea of discrimination through a fable in which a herd of farm sheep ostracize a lone goat who goes so far as disguising himself in a sheep's skin and cutting off his horn to gain acceptance within the group. When all of his efforts fail, the goat attempts suicide by hanging himself from a tree branch. Seconds before that fatal act, however, he spots the arrival of new animals (a cow, pig, chicken, and goose) who quickly make themselves at home. Regaining hope at that sight, the goat reintegrates himself into a newly diverse farmyard. Notably, Yun Il-su's 2010 reception study of 127 college students reveals that 86 percent of the respondents expressed a positive view of the animation's optimistic ending, which calls for the recognition of diversity and peaceful coexistence with others. When asked to compare Korean society to the eponymous farm, 42 percent of the respondents labeled the former as "a society where the weak are discriminated against." As for the objects of such discrimination (one of the other questions in the study), 56 percent named "migrant workers," 34 percent named "persons with disabilities," 5 percent named women, and another 5 percent named socially excluded (*wangtta*) students. Yun concludes that a rights-advocacy text such as *If You Were Me: Anima Vision* can serve as a potent form of cinematic "therapy," eliciting respect for others from audiences young and old alike while raising awareness for individual accountability for "building an ideal society" (that is, one that "integrates all people").[34]

In closing, we wish to turn to the third segment of *If You Were Me*: "Crossing," directed by Yŏ Kyun-dong. This episode is itself episodic, sprinkled with individually titled video diary entries of Kim Mun-ju, a thirty-year-old social outcast with cerebral palsy who candidly records his day-to-day activities from the confines of his small apartment.[35] At one point, Kim momentarily turns his camera away from the daily indignities he is forced to endure, focusing instead on his leg and foot. Framed in such a way, the disfigured limb could be said to symbolize his entire body, in a manner not unlike the way this fragmented episode (which is composed of smaller parts) represents the film as a whole. Toward the end of this self-reflexive episode, the paralytic man makes his first outing in eighteen years, attempting to cross a busy intersection at Kwanghwamun in the heart of Seoul. Aided only by crutches and a fearless determination, the man wills himself across the boulevard as cars speed by, an action that would appear to be suicidal but that is, in fact, necessary (see figure 2.4). Since the underground passageway at Kwanghwamun is steep and has not been retrofitted for wheelchair access, Kim and other disabled Koreans must contend with the countless hazards aboveground if they are to cross over to the other side.

This scene in *If You Were Me* is significant on many levels, not only because it marks the midpoint of the film and culminates with two cops stopping Kim halfway across, but also because it provides a diegetical allegory of our own spectatorial involvement with omnibus narratives and human rights documentaries—both of which require members of international audiences to make a concerted effort to "cross over" if we are to grasp the underlying meanings fully. As noted above, omnibus films demand a willingness on the part of audience members to move from one episode to another, often with no effective means of "transport" (such as interstitial segues that smooth out the narrative bumps). Reminiscent of a similar scene of crossing a street that occurs midway through the Iranian director Mohsen Makhmalbaf's three-episode film *The Peddler* (*Dastforoush*, 1987), this small yet significant moment in *If You Were Me* illustrates how the automobile has affected the lives of pedestrians and become a prominent fixture of the modern cityscape. However, what gives this scene a deeper layer of meaning is the way that it allegorically encapsulates the often epistemologically shaky relationship between

FIGURE 2.4 The lack of wheelchair access to underground passages forces Kim Mun-ju, a man with physical disabilities, to attempt to cross the busy intersection at Kwanghwamun—an act of everyday heroism featured in *If You Were Me* that carries allegorical implications in the larger context of human rights cinema.

Western spectators and non-Western texts, particularly those coming from nations with long histories of human rights violations, gender discrimination, ethnic skirmishes, and racial inequalities.

Just as Makhmalbaf's *The Peddler* thrusts the spectator into an uncomfortable proximity to physical deformities, so the South Korean film forges an often painful relationship between onscreen bodies and those of the spectators, who are asked to watch an extended sequence of a tongue operation and, in "Crossing," video diary footage of the disfigured leg of Kim Mun-ju. If one is to gain insight into the lives of these marginalized people, it becomes necessary to move to their side and witness sometimes shocking displays of their troubled corporeality. This is precisely what films such as *If You Were Me* demand of Western audiences, who generally remain physically and materially, if not emotionally, distant from the social issues and health problems specific to East Asian regions despite their most altruistic intentions. Although confrontational, the extreme close-ups of Kim's gnarled appendage, like the leering faces of mentally challenged and physically handicapped children in the first episode of Makhmalbaf's film, are meant to promote personal reflection as well as political activism. They invite spectators to think about human rights violations in their own country and strive to improve living conditions at home and abroad. Such intersubjective cosmopolitanism—though hampered by a watered-down conception of human rights (or an overly general emphasis on antidiscrimination)—is an integral part of the tellingly titled If You Were Me series, which explicitly asks audiences to replace their myopic worldviews with a more transnationally informed understanding of social marginality and injustice, as well as to imagine a life beyond their own.

Part 2

Movie Minors and Minor Cinemas

3

Hell Is Other High Schoolers

Bigots, Bullies, and Teenage "Villainy" in South Korean Cinema

In recent years, the much-discussed issue of school violence (*hakkyo p'ongnyŏk*) has become an increasingly visible element in South Korean cinema, which reflects the widespread concern for students' well-being among disparate groups (for example, parents, educators, government officials, and human rights organizations) while milking that provocative subject for all of its inherently dramatic potential. Feature-length narrative films such as *Once Upon a Time in High School* (*Maljukgŏri chanhoksa*, 2004), *The Art of Fighting* (*Ssaum kisul*, 2006), *Gangster High* (*P'ongnyŏk ssŏk'ŭl*, 2006), *The King of Pigs* (*Twaejiŭi wang*, 2011; see figure 3.1), *Pluto* (*Myŏngwangsŏng*, 2012), *Days of Wrath* (*Ŭngjingja*, 2013), *Eighteen Noir* (*18: Uridŭl ŭi sŏngjang nŭwarŭ*, 2014), *Wretches* (*Koemuldŭl*, 2018), *Bullies* (*Il-jin*, 2018), *Bullies 2* (*Il-jin 2*, 2018), and *Bullies 3* (*Il-jin 3*, 2019) tend to favor exploitation over edification, offering up emotionally gripping if necessarily reductive images of adolescent gang activity, physical violence, and other forms of antisocial behavior for the sake of our own questionable spectatorial pleasure. These and other contemporary motion pictures hinge thematically upon the dialectical interplay between victims and victimizers, the latter group generically encoded as being stereotypically villainous in the most melodramatic

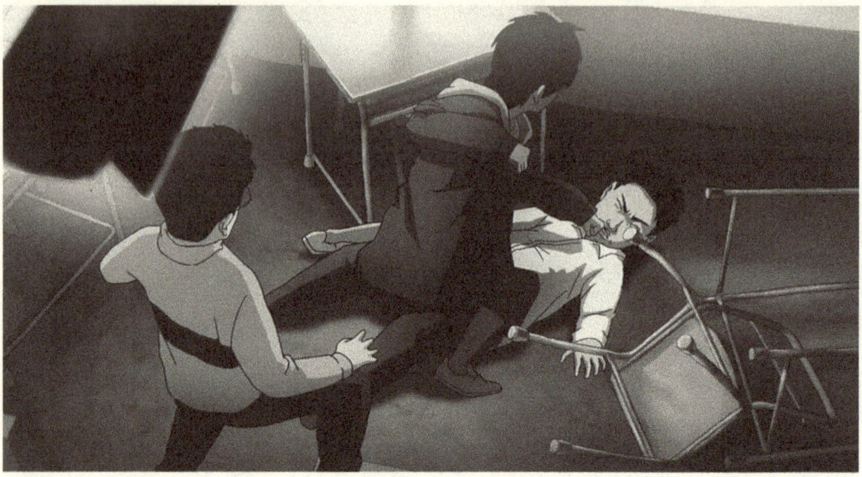

FIGURE 3.1 Writer-director Yŏn Sang-ho's animated film *The King of Pigs* (*Twaejiŭi wang*, 2011) is one of several recent Korean productions to tackle the subject of school violence. Here, Kim Ch'ŏnl (Kim Hye-na), a middle school student who had earlier been beaten up by a group of boys called "The Dogs," resorts to violence himself in the classroom, illustrating how young people who have been bullied might likewise transform into bullies.

of senses. Broadly caricatured as swaggering, swearing, uniform-wearing juvenile delinquents lacking emotional maturity or interiority, high-school bullies are thus symptomatic of social problems that go beyond academic settings, as well as institutional failings on the part of an educational system that continues to breed resentment for its hierarchical structures, authoritarian disciplining, and cutthroat competitiveness—specifically, South Korea's examination-based college-preparatory culture—that merely magnifies disparities across social classes. Rarely, however, does the question of state responsibility and societal culpability enter the picture in cinematic treatments of *hakkyo p'ongnyŏk*, which is generally shown as the result of individual teenagers' maladjustment vis-à-vis their teachers and peers.

In this chapter, we focus on a few representative yet unusual case studies—including the writer-director Yun Sŏng-hyŏn's *Bleak Night* (*P'asukkun*, 2010) and Leeson Hee-il (Yisong Hŭ-il)'s *Night Flight* (*Yagan pihaeng*, 2014)—which conform to yet challenge traditional representations of bullying on the big screen. To varying degrees, each of these explorations of *hakkyo p'ongnyŏk* adopts a melodramatic mode of representation, showcasing characters who are excessively obvious recipients of our sympathy or scorn. But they also expand the visual syntax and thematic undertow of this still-nascent genre to accommodate images and ideas related to familial dysfunction, parental separation, queer desire, and entrenched homophobia, in the process giving us both empathetic and epistemological access to the hearts and minds of victims and victimizers alike. What these and a few other Korean films demonstrate is that the bully is as much as a social and cultural construct as it is a state of mind or a marker of identity for individuals who, in their own ways, can be said to suffer from the same institutional limitations or relative lack of governmental support that their victims have been forced to endure. Although this idea is not revolutionary and applies to other national cinemas besides that of South Korea, *Bleak Night*, *Night Flight*, and other bullying films effectively highlight a system of oppression and educational indoctrination in which abuse trickles down from the teachers to the tyrannical students who are simply mimicking what they have witnessed schools' top administrators doing to young people. Thus, if we may use a hackneyed expression, violence begets violence. But because cinematic high-school settings and exclusionary social groupings are presented as a microcosm of the larger society, as the cultural historian Sung-ae Lee has argued, audiences are confronted with the fact that "violence is rife in Korean society" as a whole[1]—an existential condition that, to quote from the English-language title of one of our case studies, is indeed "bleak."

Before we turn our attention to *Bleak Night*, *Night Flight*, and a few other notable films, it will be useful to consider the representational modes that they either adhere to or go beyond, paying attention to the character archetypes, narrative structures, visual tropes, and other conventions of the genre as a whole. Indeed, if the bullying film can be thought of as a hybridized genre or subgenre (combining elements of the coming-of-age drama, the teenpic, and the social problem film), then a more general overview of the past decade and a half of thematically relevant cultural productions, dating back to the 2004 commercial hit *Once Upon a Time in High School*, is in order. Not coincidentally, the latter film undertakes a retroactive move similar to our own, pointing viewers back to an even earlier era when rights violations were a fact of life for a populace growing weary of presidential abuses of power. Thus, two historical contexts—one specific to the narrative's period setting (the late 1970s) and the other the film's time of production (the mid-2000s)—will be layered in this chapter to show how diachronic and synchronic temporalities influence the critical marking off of particular genres as well as the differently situated publics whose members make up those genres' target audiences. Aimed ostensibly at people in their teens and twenties at the time of its theatrical release, *Once Upon a Time in High School* actually engages older viewers who might bear the literal or figurative scars of its represented time period—an era when a fiercely independent yet consumer-driven youth culture (*ch'ŏngnyŏn munhwa*) emerged simultaneously with a rise in political dissidence at the moment when a rejuvenation of the nation was being transformed from rhetorical slogan to government program through President Park Chung-hee [Pak Chŏng-hŭi]'s Yushin Constitution (Yusin hŏnpŏp). Signaling the beginning of the Fourth Republic (1972–1979), the Yushin system of governance enabled Park and other high-ranking officials to bypass political elections, exert unprecedented command, and scale back civil liberties in a manner that eerily resembles what our selected case studies show school administrators and teachers doing (albeit on a smaller scale). Therefore, these films' representational modes and adherence to genre conventions bear palimpsest-like traces of the past, reminding us that previous decades' rhetorical privileging of national restoration (indicating economic and industrial growth) coincided with the emergence of South Korea's first full-blown youth culture (that of the Hangŭl Generation, a postwar baby boom whose members "came of age" during the authoritarian Park years).[2]

According to the film researcher Kye Un-gyŏng, *Once Upon a Time in High School*—a deeply contradictory teen drama/romance that features hostility toward previous decades' authoritarian rule yet is drenched in nostalgia for that bygone era—is an extension of the "educational films" (*kyouk yŏnghwa*) that were produced in South Korea during the 1970s, a heyday of escapist youth comedies such as *Yalgae: A Joker in High School* (*Kokyo yalgae*, 1977) and its sequel, *Mischief's Marching Song* (*Yalgae hangjingok*, 1977).[3] Since the 1990s, this so-called educational genre has abandoned its comedic roots in favor of a more serious, yet action-filled, mode of discourse attuned to contemporary social ills, as exemplified by *Our Twisted Hero* (*Uridŭl ŭi ilkŭrŏjin yŏng'ung*, 1992), *Whispering Corridors* (*Yŏgogoedam*, 1998), and other films that are at least moderately focused on students' rights. Even in lighter fare—such as *Dasepo Naughty Girls* (*Tasep'o sonyŏ*, 2006), from the director E. J-yong (Yi Chae-yong), which takes place in the hallways and classrooms of "Mussŭlmo High School" (literally translated as "Useless High School")—viewers can discern how the genre enables filmmakers to satirize the rampant "uniformity and conformity imposed in high school and in Korean society at large," as Jinhee Choi has noted in her study of cinematic youth culture.[4] Following Kye's lead, we explore the political resonances of the bullying film as a genre that—like the "educational film" and the teenpic—caters to adolescent and young adult audiences yet opens up a space of societal critique within mainstream popular culture by exposing the consequences of an abusive disciplinary system, class discrimination, gender oppression, and the decades-long exclusion of nonconforming identities in educational settings.

Although the teenpic has traditionally focused on members of the opposite sex developing romantic relationships and dealing with often-unrequited sexual yearnings, there is a growing tendency in South Korean youth films—from mainstream commercial productions such as *Bungee Jumping of Their Own* (*Pŏnjijŏmpŭ'rŭl hada*, 2001) to low-budget critics' darlings such as *Night Flight*—to showcase long-repressed forms of queer desire and to challenge the country's homophobic bullying culture within high-school settings. If venturing into a discussion of ostensibly straight films (that is, those privileging cisnormative subject positions and heterosexual networks of romance and desire) appears to take us far from the themes associated with youth-oriented queer cinema (of which Leesong's low-budget *Night Flight* is an important yet understudied example), this might be because of a perception that the latter has nothing to do with the former, which is simply not the case. Indeed, just as more work needs to be done to place mainstream and independent cultural productions in conversation with one another, so too should the histories of LGTBQ films and non-LGTBQ films—as well as the encodings and decodings that attend their production and reception, respectively—be entangled. Situated on a slippery continuum rather than being crammed into different pigeonholes, such seemingly disparate motion pictures as *Once Upon a Time in High School* and *Night Flight* (both of which each mired in the semantic world of South Korean high schools) share more than just a few iconographic elements (such as narrow hallways, overpopulated classrooms, and rooftops offering a vantage on the world below). In emphasizing social stratification and toxic forms of hypermasculinity—and by demonstrating, if sometimes unwittingly, how normative gender roles are learned, rehearsed, performed, and sometimes overturned (rather than inscribed at birth)—they transcend their own modes of production and genre categories as films about bullying. With this in mind, let us go back to 2004, when the scene was being set for many of the abovementioned factors and films to take shape.

Once Upon a Time: 2004, a Year of Advocacy and Reform

Although at first blush 2004 appears to be an arbitrary historical marker with which to begin contextualizing and thematizing cinematic bullying and the homophobic bigotry that sometimes accompanies it, that year is significant for several reasons. First, three years after President Kim Dae-jung (Kim Tae-jung) launched a rhetorical war on *hakkyo p'ongnryŏk* in 2001, a law was finally put in place to counter this escalating problem.[5] Established by the Ministry of Education (Kyoyukpu) early in the regime of Kim's successor, President Roh Moo-hyun (No Mu-hyŏn), and enacted on January 24, 2004, the Act on the Prevention of and Countermeasures against Violence in Schools would, among other things, "make it mandatory for K–12 schools to carry out a 'Prevention Education Program' on a yearly basis," as Trent Bax explains in *Bullying and Violence in South Korea*.[6] Additionally, professional counseling services had been recommended by spokespeople for the Kim administration as one way to support students who were being verbally intimidated or physically harmed by their peers. This approach was strengthened and augmented by additional requirements initiated by Roh's administration, which called for the establishment of a violence task force.

Not surprisingly, since Roh had been a center-left "activist lawyer of human rights" before assuming leadership of the country, the 2004 act against school violence incorporates rights language in the first of its twenty-two articles.[7] Furthermore, it establishes a dyadic relationship between victims and aggressors and grafts such discourse onto a call for the government to intervene whenever reports of students being victimized by their peers can be verified. Specifically, Article 1 states: "The purpose of this Act is to protect the human rights of students and raise students as healthy members of society through the protection of victim students, the guidance and education of aggressor students, and mediation between victim students and aggressor students, by providing for matters necessary for the prevention of and countermeasures against violence in schools."[8] Besides its framing of victims of school violence as individuals whose basic human rights have been violated, the law (which went through seven subsequent amendments over the next several years), provided a definition that, while including many forms of abuse, has been criticized for being "vague and abstract" from a legal perspective.[9] It states that school violence encompasses any activities involving "injury, assault, confinement, threat, kidnap, defamation, insult, coercion, sexual abuse, outcast [status], or providing violence information that causes any physical, mental, or property damages to students within and outside of school."[10] From this, one might conclude that the law, wrapped in the rhetorical cloak of human rights advocacy, focuses on the victim. But in fact it "does not present fundamental solutions" to the problem of school violence beyond recommending punitive measures aimed at offenders. And punishment, in the eyes of many rights advocates who call for greater educational reforms, is seen as a solution that too closely resembles the problem of school violence—which flows not only horizontally between students but also vertically, as a disciplinarian tactic of abusive faculty members enacting their own top-down punitive approach to *hakkyo p'ongnryŏk*.

Of additional significance is the fact that in 2005, one year after the enactment of this law, in partnership with over half a dozen governmental bodies (the Administration of Government Administration and Home Affairs, the Ministry of Culture and Tourism, the Ministry of Information and Communication, the Ministry of Gender Equality, the Commission on Youth Protection, the Supreme Prosecutors' Office, and the National Police Agency), South Korea's Ministry of Education established a five-year plan whose goal was to reduce the rate of school violence by 5 percent each year. The plan fell short of that goal, with the number of victims actually increasing over the first five-year period. After the failure of that top-down governmental plan, responsibility shifted to the autonomous committees in charge of mediating conflicts among students and investigating reported cases of school violence that all schools have been required to create since the 2011 revision of the Act on the Prevention of and Countermeasures against Violence in Schools. At least half of the committee seats must be filled by parents and the other half by third-party mediators, such as lawyers, judges, doctors, or police officers. According to statistics provided by the Ministry of Education, 17,749 cases of school violence were submitted to the committees in 2013, which increased in 2017 to 31,240.[11] Fifteen years after the original enactment of the law against school violence, all major players—students, parents, school administrators, autonomous committees, and so on—are still struggling to solve the problem of bullying and have tended to shift the blame to one another. Many parents and students (including both victims and perpetrators—the distinction between which can sometimes be blurry, as we demonstrate below) believe that the committees' rulings are either too light or too harsh, and this has led them to apply for retrials or even take their cases to court.

Cinema, in the form of scripted narrative, provides another way to transform words into actions. As alluded to at the beginning of this chapter, throughout the early 2000s the subject of bullying was being addressed not only by lawmakers and human rights activists but also by filmmakers and other cultural producers. And as stated above, 2004 was a pivotal year in many respects, giving rise to a handful of notable motion pictures set in high schools—including *Temptation of Wolves* (or *Romance of Their Own* [*Nŭkdaeŭi yuhok*, 2004]) and *My Little Bride* (*Ŏrin sinbu*, 2004). The film that sparked this trend in South Korea's cinematic output is *Once Upon a Time in High School*, a nostalgically imbued coming-of-age drama (set during the waning days of Park Chung-hee's administration) about a teenager named Hyŏn-su (Kwŏn Sang-su), who must resort to different survival techniques if he is to graduate from a notoriously brutal educational environment, a place that breeds conformity and stokes interclass animosity.

This box-office hit, which drizzles a few moments of social commentary atop copious scenes of teacher-on-student and student-on-student abuse (in addition to romantic interludes between Hyŏn-su and the elusive object of his desire, a student named Ŭn-ju [Han Ka-in]), sparked public debates about *hakkyo p'ongnyŏk* following its theatrical release in January 2004 (notably, one week before the Act on the Prevention of and Countermeasures against Violence in Schools was enacted). Written and directed by the poet-turned-filmmaker Yu Ha, a genre specialist who has dabbled in everything from erotic romance (*Marriage Is a Crazy Thing* [*Kyŏlhonŭn mich'in chisida*, 2002]) and historical epic (*A Frozen Flower* [*Ssanghwajŏm*, 2008]) to gangster film (*A Dirty Carnival* [*Piyŏlhan kŏri*, 2006]) and horror-tinged detective thriller (*Howling* [*Hauling*, 2012]), this high-school drama contains many of the elements that would define cinematic bullying for years to come. Iconographic touchstones—such as high-school students wearing militaristic uniforms in various states of dishevelment, crowded hallways leading to even more congested classrooms, stashes of contraband (including girlie magazines and cigarettes), and weapons of all kinds (sticks, baseball bats, nunchaku, and so on) at the ready whenever a fight breaks out—are abundantly displayed. *Once Upon a Time in High School* would be noteworthy for these alone, but they would not make it integral to the spate of South Korean bullying films that followed its theatrical release. Bearing a title that can more accurately be translated as "The Cruel History of Maljuk Street,"[12] the film's most significant contribution to the present discussion is its visceral and sometimes shocking depiction of the cruelties experienced by students in the past (the film is set in 1978), which are only slightly more brutal than the kinds of abuse that will be doled out by offscreen and onscreen adult educators and teenage bullies following this film's 2004 release and continuing well into the second decade of the new millennium.

The sundry forms of physical and verbal abuse that will erupt over the course of the narrative, inside the not-so-hallowed halls of Chungmun High (a school located on Maljuk Street in the now-flourishing Gangnam district of Yangjae-dong, as the protagonist's voice-over informs us), are intimated in one of the film's first scenes. Following an opening sequence that shows a much younger Hyŏn-su sitting in a packed movie theater, his eyes glued to the screen while watching Bruce Lee in *Fist of Fury* (*Jing mou moon*, 1972), the story picks up a few years later with his transfer to the new school as a teenager. He and dozens of other uniformed students—male and female—jam into a bus and clamor for seats. Their bodies are so tightly packed inside that one boy, pushing up against a girl, says he "might get a hard-on" if anyone else bumps into him (a remark that visibly disgusts her). After she and the other female passengers get off the bus at the Ŭnmyŏng Girls' High School stop, Hyŏn-su and the other male passengers are taken to their destination. Once he steps off the bus, it is immediately clear that an authoritarian style of disciplining will define his forthcoming interactions with the school's teaching staff. A phalanx of guards outside the gate inspect the uniforms of the newly arrived students, and one of them calls Hyŏn-su over to berate him about the state of his clothing: his collar is missing because a senior stole it from him on the bus. The officer informs the dumbstruck protagonist that a lesson must be learned and nods in the direction of a group of other rule breakers. With their hands on the ground and their backsides in the air, they are being beaten, one by one, by an administrator wielding a baseball bat—an image that anticipates a similar act of top-down school violence in director Chang Kŏn-jae's *Eighteen* (or *Whirlwind* [*Hwiori param*, 2009]), although in that case a stick is used rather than a bat. This is the first of several such actions taken by the staff against their young wards, who will come to adopt similarly vicious approaches to perceived infractions or deviations from the normal state of affairs, both inside and outside the classroom.

In her discussion of *Once Upon a Time in High School*, cultural historian Sung-ae Lee notes that the hierarchical chain of command in which "violence begets violence" is visible not only within the educational setting but also within Korean society as a whole. The punitive measures on view in the film, she argues, are an extension of the outdated Confucian principles that undergird social relations even today, including the belief "that someone older has natural dominance" over someone younger.[13] This is true not only when it comes to adults' asymmetrical relationship to children, but also in the case of senior students' imagined superiority over freshman, sophomores, and juniors. This power differential, Lee observes, "generates a leader/subaltern structure that is nothing more than physical and psychological bullying."[14] Notably, she refers to the beatings that we witness near the beginning of the film, as well as throughout its increasingly dark story of authoritarian disciplining, as "severe abuses of human rights." While some critics might question the soundness of her argument that the school's "regime of punishment . . . is tantamount to torture,"[15] there is enough support for it within the film to at least acknowledge the insidiousness with which human rights abuses, masked as the relatively innocuous form of harm that we call bullying, become commonplace from an early age in the everyday lives of students.

Hyŏn-su is thoroughly immersed in a world of male violence, not only as a transfer student at Chungmun High but also as the son of a tae kwon do instructor who, besides physically intimidating the teenager, demands academic excellence from him on a daily basis, reminding him of the importance of ranking among the top five students in his class. Moreover, the patriarchal control that Hyŏn-su endures at home is aligned with another type of masculine power, that wielded by members of South Korea's military (soldiers and generals, as well as government inspectors, show up at the high school from time to time and whip the boys not into shape but into bloody pulp). Parents, teachers, and representatives of the armed forces all appear to be conspiring against Hyŏn-su and his fellow teenagers, leaving little doubt as to why they might adopt a defensive yet aggressive stance in regard to their so-called superiors.

Jinhee Choi, who offers one of the most sustained and substantial critiques of high-school films in *The South Korean Film Renaissance: Local Hitmakers, Global Provocateurs*, notes that the male protagonists of such works "often turn to violence as a means to self-defense and empowerment."[16] This is discernible not only in *Once Upon a Time in High School* but also in other motion pictures produced before and after its 2004 release, including *Volcano High* (*Hwasango*, 2001) and *Gangster High* (*P'ongnyŏk Ssŏkŭl*, 2006). However, Choi claims that Yu Ha's film has a palpable "critical/reflexive dimension" not found in these latter productions, and she supports this claim by drawing attention to the manner in which embedded representations of Asian masculinity—specifically, globally circulated images of the Hong Kong–Chinese American action star Bruce Lee—lead the protagonist down a perilous path in which imitation bleeds into "near self-destruction."[17] Not coincidentally, this film's subtitle is *The Spirit of Jeet Kune Do*, a reference to the philosophy and style of martial arts popularized by Lee in motion pictures made during the early 1970s, such as the abovementioned *Fist of Fury* (extracts from which appear in the opening sequence of *Once Upon a Time in High School*).

Those first minutes of *Once Upon a Time in High School* are significant for two reasons. First, they show a large group of Korean boys basking in the glow of their cinematic hero, whose naked torso and rippling muscles—in addition to the almost comically charismatic flourishes that accompany his defeat of Japanese antagonists (the colonial culprits in *Fist of Fury*)—constitute an eroticized visual spectacle as well as a transnational symbol of subaltern resistance. And second, those early minutes also hint at the way that adoration sometimes leads to imitation, a theme that might be applied to *Once Upon a Time in High School* and other feature-length or televised treatments of bullying (including the

2012 K-drama *School 2013*), which some critics claim (albeit without providing any supporting evidence) have inspired young people in the real world to emulate the kinds of glamorized antisocial behavior contained within those fictional worlds. Complicating matters is the fact that the self-esteem that Hyŏn-su has attained through his mastery of Jeet Kune Do, which gives him the confidence to test his own fighting skills against high-school oppressors (including a bully named Chong-hun, whom he bests in a rooftop battle), ultimately "provides a false sense of empowerment," according to Choi.[18] Not above fighting dirty, the main character—consumed with rage and hardened by the loss of his one true love (Ŭn-ju, a senior student from a nearby school who has run away with his only real confidante, U-sik [Yi Chŏng-jin])—emerges less as a victor than as a victim of institutionalized violence. Having been run through a gauntlet that leaves him bloodied and practically friendless near the end, Hyŏn-su has little recourse other than to shout impotently at the school officials who will soon remove him from the premises. Yet the unbridled defiance of his exclamation—"Fuck all the schools in Korea!"—should not be underestimated as a rallying cry that continues to resound today, even if that moment of spoken insolence is immediately undermined by the director's staging of the scene—which concludes with a shot of Hyŏn-su walking away from school with the now-meaningless slogan "Promoting Restoration Education" emblazoned across its façade.[19]

Misogyny, Homophobic Bullying, and the Tragic Costs of *Wang-tta* Culture

A 2011 focus-group study of 278 college students who attended high schools in the late 2000s reveals that *Once Upon a Time in High School* resonates with a majority of Korean millennials who identify with cinematic depictions of school violence, college exam pressure, and discrimination based on parental social status. After watching the film, 140 respondents noted that Korean students are just as deprived of their inalienable rights now as their peers were in the 1970s, when the film was set. Despite the fact that, in the words of one student, school violence today is "more internalized and hidden" compared to the rampant brutality depicted in *Once Upon a Time in High School*, it remains "equally horrific and terrifying." Only 75 students responded that the conditions are better than they were in the past. Fifty-six students felt that the rights of teachers, more so than those of students, are in need of protection today. What is especially noteworthy about the study is that a considerably greater number of female students (86 as opposed to 56 male students) found their current situation to be no better than the abusive environment in the 1970s. It can be inferred that this gender discrepancy in student views is a reflection of women's disempowerment in society and more pressing calls for change among those who are discriminated against because of their gender (regardless of the institutional context in which that victimization occurs).[20]

Notably, director Min Pyŏng-hun's psychological drama *Love Never Fails* (*Sarangi iginda*, 2015) highlights the extraordinary stress placed on high-school girls, not only by educators but also by the girls' parents. In this film, a teenager named Su-a (O Yu-jin) is forced to endure ceaseless parental pressure to achieve academically, so that she might rise to the top of her class and go to a prestigious university. Even when the girl does succeed, after a grueling series of problem-solving drills at home, her mother slaps her, furious that Su-a had not done so earlier in the school year. Ultimately, all this domestic abuse, which prompts Su-a to complain that she does not want to "live like a monster" anymore, has dire consequences for the female protagonist, who begins behaving like a kleptomaniac, cutting her thigh with a razor at school, and eventually taking more drastic steps toward self-harm. Significantly, Su-a's father, separated from her mother for months and thus an infrequent observer of the girl's pain, is an academic who has been slapped with a sexual harassment charge by his research assistant, and his being found guilty further implicates the failings of the family in the tragic downfall of a high-school girl for whom emotional support is in short supply.

It should be pointed out that 2004 is notable not only for the theatrical release of *Once Upon a Time in High School* but also for another, more important historical milestone. Specifically, we are referring to several tragic, interrelated events that took place in the southeastern city of Miryang over an eleven-month period, beginning in January 2004. Widely reported throughout South Korea at that time and recently brought back into the country's collective consciousness by the theatrical release of the writer-director Yi Su-jin's feature-length film *Han Gong-ju* (2014), the incidents to which we are referring involved several middle-school and high-school girls who were sexually assaulted by boys their own age or slightly older. In part because of the violators' adolescent status, but also in response to police officers' blaming the victims and general mishandling of the case, the initial wave of shock and dismay that swept through Miryang and the nearby cities of Ulsan and Ch'angwŏn (where many of the students' families had come from) was soon transformed into outright hostility toward local law enforcement, publicly elected officials, and school administrators—all of whom were castigated by outraged citizens for failing to protect the most vulnerable members of society. Hundreds of protesters took to the streets, holding candlelight vigils and calling for greater organizational oversight in the carrying out of justice. Ultimately, though, none of the forty-one suspects in the case were convicted of criminal charges, and "only five were sent to a juvenile correctional center," according to *JoongAng Ilbo* and other Korean newspapers whose reporting fanned the flames of discontent among those who have grown increasingly concerned about the safety of young people over the past decade and a half.[21]

As illustrated in director Kim Yong-han's *Don't Cry Mommy* (*Ton k'ŭrai Mami*, 2012)—another film that, like *Han Gong-ju* after it, was inspired by what some commentators have referred to as the "Miryang gang rape" case—female

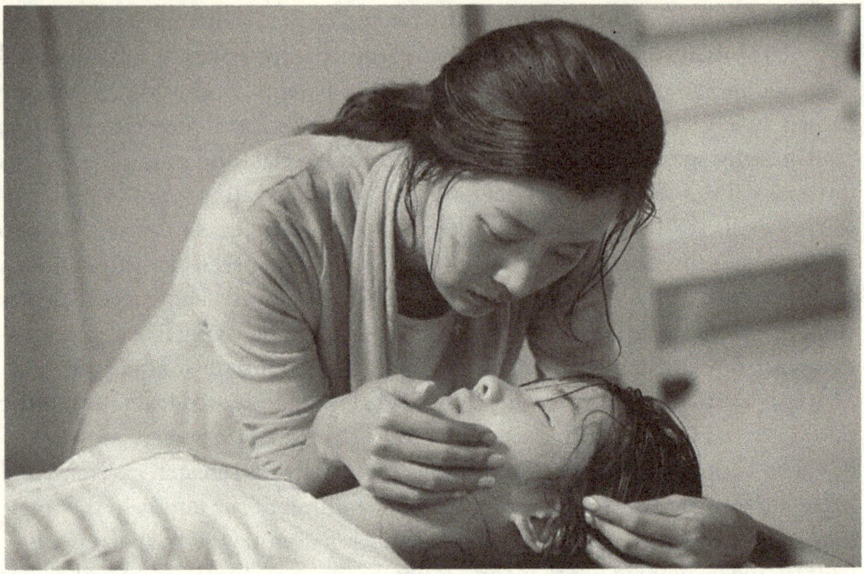

FIGURE 3.2 Director Kim Yong-han's *Don't Cry Mommy* (*Ton k'ŭrai Mami*, 2012) is one of several recent Korean productions to explore the effects of physical and emotional abuse on teenage girls. Drawing from real-life instances of sexualized bullying and violence (including the 2004 Miryang gang rape case), the film makes a connection between female victimhood and the virulent spread of toxic masculinity in South Korea (where the #MeToo movement has found cultural traction). Here, the mother of a teenage girl who committed suicide (after being bullied and raped by her male classmates) mourns the loss of her daughter.

students frequently experience bullying before being subjected to outright sexual violence, and that the incremental movement from one form of male aggression to another is what many parents fear when they hear of relational power imbalances among high schoolers (see figure 3.2). Additionally, because some of the rape victims in that case (as well as in other well-documented instances of adolescent abuse) are known to have attempted suicide (a somewhat problematic plot element in *Don't Cry Mommy*, *Han Gong-ju*, and an earlier film that takes poetic license in dramatizing that subject—the tellingly titled *Poetry* [*Si*, 2010], by the writer-director Lee Chang-dong [Yi Ch'ang-dong]), a feeling of combined anger and hopelessness has settled over the country as it copes with a social problem that demands both clear-eyed pragmatism and misty-eyed optimism if it is to ever be solved. With suicide now being the "most common cause of death" among Koreans ages 15–24,[22] onscreen representations of young girls jumping to their deaths from great heights (something that occurs, for instance, in *Poetry* as well as the 2014 *Compassion* [*Ch'ŏnbŏnŭl pullŏdo*]) carry an affective charge beyond their narrative or diegetic worlds and in the social or extradiegetic contexts in which such acts of quiet desperation are all too real and frequent occurrences. In other words, films like these might exacerbate our feelings of desperation as we passively consume one image of school violence or sexual abuse after another, sitting idly by while watching scores of teenagers take their lives.

In "Stories of Cruel Youth," Peter Y. Paik refers to *Poetry* and a few other motion pictures as "anti-youth" films.[23] Although Lee Chang-dong's critically lauded work, like Kim Ki-duk (Kim Ki-dŏk)'s *Samaritan Girl* (*Samaria*, 2004) and Park Ch'an-ok's *P'aju* (2009), dwells on "the destructive behavior and anti-social actions" of young people (including a group of juvenile delinquents who "drive a female classmate to suicide by blackmailing her for sex"), according to Paik it ultimately "take[s] the side" of older characters who suffer untold degrees of anguish in the face of their teenage adversaries.[24] All three of these widely distributed cultural productions thus present adult protagonists as "more moral, more compassionate, and even more *innocent* than their teen counterparts,"[25] who—in their callousness and lack of empathy for others—come to embody a kind of underage villainy that, if not unique to Korean cinema, accrues unsettling salience within it.

In the years that have elapsed since the first reports about the above incidents were published, a slew of articles about the increasingly pervasive and more generalized problem of school bullying has fueled interest in the subject, not only among national and international readers but also within the sphere of South Korean cultural production (of which cinema is only one part). Bearing titles such as "Korea Struggles to Save Students from Bullying" and "South Korean Parents Hire Thugs To Stop School Bullies," these articles play up the desperation that drives some educators and politicians as well as parents and other guardians of children's safety to think outside the box and adopt unorthodox ways of handling a situation that has reached a crisis level unprecedented in modern history.[26] Such alarmist discourse runs the risk not of overstating the problem but rather of oversimplifying a complex issue and treating teenage victimization in black-and-white terms. In a manner that one might expect to encounter in a mainstream film or television series, newspaper and magazine articles like the ones cited above in fact ironically lack the nuance of some popular entertainments, with one side (the "helpless" young victim) being divested of any agency and presented as someone in need of saving or adult supervision, while the other side (the victimizing bully) is presented as a dehumanized force of nature, an abstract "evil" against which even the most preposterous of defense measures begin to sound reasonable. Without the subtle shades of gray that might come from lengthier, more thorough, and more carefully researched investigations (academic or otherwise), such journalistic accounts frequently fall back on rhetorical maneuvers that elide any question about the rights of the bully, the individual whose own humanity has been conveniently cast aside so as to make him a "monster" or "villain" in the most melodramatic of senses.[27]

Notably, the English word "monster" is a more accurate translation of the title of the 2018 bullying film *Koemuldŭl*, which was called *Wretches* when it had its international release. Inspired by a real incident in 2011, during which the tables were turned on a high-school bully who was hospitalized after an attempted murder, *Wretches* adds a twist to the now-familiar tropes of the genre by showing that victims of adolescent aggression can resort to violent behavior themselves if pushed too far. This includes Chae-yŏng (Yi Wŏn-gŭn), a high schooler who is forced to go on missions or "shuttle" runs—for bread, girls' underwear, and so on—at the behest of a boy seeking mastery over him. However, Chae-yŏng is transformed into the thing that he hates after learning of the bully's rape of a disabled girl, something that the guilt-ridden protagonist had unwittingly abetted. This film, by showing one character turning another person into a thing through a form of humiliating enslavement, corresponds with the general tendency (visible across multiple texts) to treat bullies as irredeemable villains (essentially reducing them to things). But *Wretches*, like Yŏn Sang-ho's 2011 animated feature *The King of Pigs* (which includes several references to students behaving like monsters), also acknowledges that such figures are products of their environment: the social milieu in which cutthroat competition—a central component of South Korea's capitalist economy and the culture of materialism that has filtered down from its financial sectors to its educational system—is perceived as necessary to get ahead of one's peers on the path toward college.

Wretches is one of the latest additions to a growing body of films that focus on *il-jin*, a slang term that has various connotations but basically refers to the violent gang culture that gives rise to bullies and other juvenile delinquents who instill fear in their classmates and project the image of being number one (that is, people on the top rungs of society). This expression has gained traction as a catchall signifier thanks in part to the release of *Bullies*, a film that has already spawned two sequels despite its recent vintage (as a 2018 production). But there are many other linguistic signifiers that lend cultural specificity to Korean representations of this social phenomenon. For instance, according to Keumjoo Kwak and Seung-ha Lee, the slang term *wang-tta* (an abbreviation of *wang-ttadolim* [exclusion], equivalent to the Japanese *ijime*) began to enter general parlance—especially among high-school pupils—following a series of highly publicized accounts of teenage suicide in the late 1990s and early 2000s.[28] Although the South Korean government has recommended the use of alternative expressions (such as *jipdan ttadolim* [group isolation]) to denote the kind of verbal harassment or physical abuse that sometimes leads particularly vulnerable students to take their own lives, *wang-tta* gets to the heart of the severity of the situation. However, this informal term, which Jun-mo Kwon defined as a socially harmful behavior that reflects "an imbalance of power . . . between aggressor(s) and victim(s),"[29] might lead to a further stigmatization of the isolated individual, whose very being is ignored even as he or she is publicly labeled as "less than" his or her fellow students. While it has been officially reported that 6–16 percent of Korean adolescents experienced organized peer isolation or rejection (with another 10–20 percent reporting that they had excluded their peers), as Hee Jeong Yoo points out, official statistics might not fully capture the prevalence of school violence due to underreporting and the possible collusion of an entire class or school in which a majority of students passively participate in bullying as silent bystanders.[30]

Negative labeling, often through the spreading of rumors, is just one aspect of the larger problem of antisocial behavior that we encounter in bullying films, which typically showcase a range of actions from name-calling, slander, and the telling of sexual jokes to exclusion, intimidation, and outright physical violence.[31] Although in the words of one researcher "there is no universal agreement on a singular definition,"[32] the concept of bullying generally encompasses four specific elements:

1. Physical, verbal, or psychological attack or intimidation that is intended to cause distress, fear, or harm to the victim
2. An imbalance of power, with a more powerful person oppressing a less powerful one
3. Absence of provocation by the victim
4. Repeated incidents between the same people over a prolonged period of time[33]

All four of those elements are on view in the 2010 film *Bleak Night*, an accomplished first feature written and directed by Yun Sŏng-hyŏn when he was twenty-nine, as part of his graduation project at the Korean Academy of Film Arts. Winner of multiple awards following its theatrical release (including the prize of Best New Director for Yun at the Grand Bell Awards and the Busan Film Critics Awards), this relatively low-key indie drama anticipates *Wretches* in its depiction of the circumstances that might lead emotionally troubled people to do something drastic, either to themselves or to others. In this case, audiences learn why Ki-t'ae (Yi Che-hun), the nominal bully of *Bleak Night*, took his own life after seeing his friendships—tenuous though they were—crumble as a result of his violent and antisocial behavior. Using flashbacks and a nonlinear narrative structure—which encourages spectators to piece together the puzzle of Ki-t'ae's death along with his bereaved, guilt-ridden father, who is shown searching for answers in scenes set in the present—and shifting our sympathies from the victims of his abuse to the victimizer, the film provokes both questioning and an empathetic response from viewers who might otherwise blanch at the idea of trying to fathom the mind or understand the motives of a bully. But it does so while keeping the audience at a distance and in the dark, both through cinematographic means (the use of shallow focus shots, low-level lighting, handheld cameras, blurry whip pans, lens flares, and other ways to literally obscure the image) and through a storytelling approach that embraces ambiguity rather than clarity (see figure 3.3).

Kye Un-gyŏng offers a novel interpretation of *Bleak Night*, hypothesizing that Ki-t'ae represents the son's generation for Hyŏn-su and his peers (in *Once Upon*

FIGURE 3.3 Yun Sŏng-hyŏn's *Bleak Night* (*P'asukkun*, 2010) features several tight close-ups and over-the-shoulder shots in partially obstructed frames that—along with a cold, almost monochromatic, mise-en-scène—heighten the main characters' feelings of claustrophobia and isolation from others.

a Time in High School), who attended high school in the 1970s and therefore would be in their fifties within *Bleak Night*'s narrative timeframe. Kye points out that the excessive displays of hitting and kicking that pepper Yu Ha's mainstream action flick are absent in Yun's more introspective indie film. However, a subtler, less conspicuous form of symbolic violence in the latter film turns members of the school's student body into silent accomplices whose complicity is a prerequisite for sustaining and reproducing the culture of cruelty, exclusion, and psychological (if not physical) torture—treatment whose visceral effects on victims are as real as those of the corporeal punishment habitually implemented during the authoritarian military rule of the past.[34] The increased pressure of exams and academic competition within a neoliberal economy is what pushes an underachieving student like Ki-t'ae into delinquency and bullying as the only means of garnering respect from his peers—the loss of which augurs a kind of foregone calamity and ultimately brings about his own (anticipated) demise. If anything, *Bleak Night* intimates that the internalized violence of the current generation is even more repressive and unbearable than the physically externalized violence of the generation three decades earlier. This is demonstrated by Ki-t'ae's debilitating depression and eventual suicide, which contrasts with Hyŏn-su's defiance in the face of an unjust educational system and his heroic escape from that hostile environment. Using all of the tools of his chosen medium, director Yun lends cinematic texture to such allegorical readings, filling *Bleak Night*'s monochromatic mise-en-scène with cold, concrete edifices (school buildings and apartment complexes) that make the urban environment seem more claustrophobic than inviting—a visual motif he accentuates through tight close-ups and over-the-shoulder shots that figuratively trap characters inside overcrowded or partly obstructed frames (see figure 3.3).[35]

Yun's unorthodox approach to the subject of school bullying has been applauded by many critics around the world. As one *Hollywood Reporter* critic stated in his review of *Bleak Night* after its successful showing at the Rotterdam International Film Festival, "If nothing else, it's intriguing to find a tale of bullying and teen suicide where it's the *bully*, rather than the bullied, who emerges as the real victim."[36] Although it would be incorrect to say that the filmmaker endorses any of Ki-t'ae's violent behavior—which includes slapping and snidely undermining his closest friends, Hŭi-jun (Pak Chŏng-min) and Tong-yun (Sŏ Chun-yŏng)—Yun does provide clues as to why the angsty teenager might resort to such conduct. For example, there are references to the broken home that left Ki-t'ae motherless (after his mother died) and, to a certain degree, fatherless (after the older man abandoned his son). But such information, coming in dribs and drabs throughout the flashback-laden narrative, merely supplements what audiences must infer about Ki-t'ae's relationship to Hŭi-jun and Tong-yun. Some online reviewers and bloggers have suggested that this relationship has a homoerotic subtext that lies just below the homosocial surface. For example, a reviewer for one website, Gay Asia Films, makes this point in his sensitive exploration of *Bleak Night*'s themes, including the main character's denial of his sexual identity, which exacerbates Ki-t'ae's feeling of disconnect with his friends (whom he paradoxically pushes away for fear of getting "too close").[37]

Although *wang-ttta* is a widespread social phenomenon that targets boys and girls, as well as men and women, of all ages, regardless of their social status, and is prevalent in schools and workplaces through South Korea, LGBTQ youths are especially likely to being subjected to organized cruelty due to the blatantly homophobic culture that has become pernicious in recent years. The current president, Moon Jae-in (Mun Chae-in), a liberal-minded former human rights lawyer, came under fire when he made a controversial statement during a 2017 televised presidential debate that he "opposes" and "doesn't like" homosexuality. Although the Catholic president-elect apologized for his remark in the wake of a public outcry, many of the world's leading human rights organizations have continued to denounce South Korea's lack of antidiscriminatory legislation protecting LGBTQ rights and the criminalization of consensual same-sex relationships in the military.[38]

According to a 2014 report by the National Human Rights Commission of Korea (NHRCK; Kukka ingwŏn wiwŏnhoe) on the status of discrimination based on sexual orientation and gender identity, among 227 LGBTQ youths ages 13–18, 80 percent reported having encountered homophobic comments from their teachers, and 92 percent said that they had heard their fellow students make such remarks. And among the 227 respondents, 20 percent said that they had experienced harassment from teachers, and 54 percent reported experiencing it from fellow students.[39] Of the respondents who experienced peer harassment,

86.5 percent did not report it to their teachers. Of those who did report it, half said that the educators spoke directly to the bullies to warn or counsel them and only 14.3 percent implemented disciplinary responses. Of those who reported peer harassment, 21.4 percent said that no action had been taken, and another 21.4 percent received only promises of action. Over a quarter of the respondents (28.6 percent) were told to forget the incident or not to mind it, while 14.3 percent were scolded for causing a problem. Only 14.3 percent saw their problem solved. No respondent was referred to a human rights organization or counseling services. Given the lack of proper education, discipline, conflict resolution, and counseling policies in Korean public schools (which focus on exam-oriented education), one should not be surprised that an endless cycle of violence and harassment continues. Nor should one wonder why the boundaries between perpetrators and victims are so easily crossed.

Notably, in his September 2014 interview with the entertainment magazine *Ten Asia*, Leesong Hee-il—one of South Korea's few openly gay writer-directors (and the main subject of chapter 4)—describes his oeuvre as "queer melo," observing that melodrama has always prismatically reflected societal ills (albeit in conspicuously heightened form) and thus explaining his attraction to this most affectively charged yet critically disparaged of all cultural categories.[40] His film *Night Flight* opens in the manner of a teen romance, one in which a sociable middle-class honors student, Yong-ju (Kwak Si-yang), pursues a working-class classmate, Ki-ung (Yi Chae-jun), who remains aloof while earning a meager living as a part-time delivery man (see figure 3.4). Due to his father's identity as a union activist who has been sent to prison for arson, Ki-ung grew up as a victim of bullying in middle school, where he first befriended Yong-ju. In high school, though, he has begun to behave violently after joining a gang headed by Sŏng-jin (Kim Ch'ang-hwan), a teenager who is unafraid of any disciplinary actions on the part of school administrators due to his rich family's powerful influence in the community. A frequent target of peer pressure and bullying is Yong-ju's best friend, an overweight, dim-witted student named Ki-t'aek (Ch'oe Chun-ha). When Yong-ju reports Ki-t'aek's harassment at the hands of the gang, the homeroom teacher coldly advises him to focus on his current studies and college-prep work rather than other students' problems.

Night Flight exposes the precarious boundary between perpetuator and victim, especially throughout the second half of the film, following Ki-t'aek's sudden betrayal of Yong-ju after learning about the latter's sexual identity. Not only does Ki-t'aek out Yong-ju to Sŏng-jin's gang (the members of which verbally and physically lash out in horrifying displays of violent machismo), but Ki-t'aek also participates—albeit only as a witness and accomplice—in the criminal act of gang rape, a ritual of violence that is recorded by a camera for the purpose of posting it on YouTube to further humiliate their victim. After learning about the incident, Ki-ung, who has been pushing Yong-ju away and struggling with his own confused sexual identity, rushes to school to beat up the perpetrators and

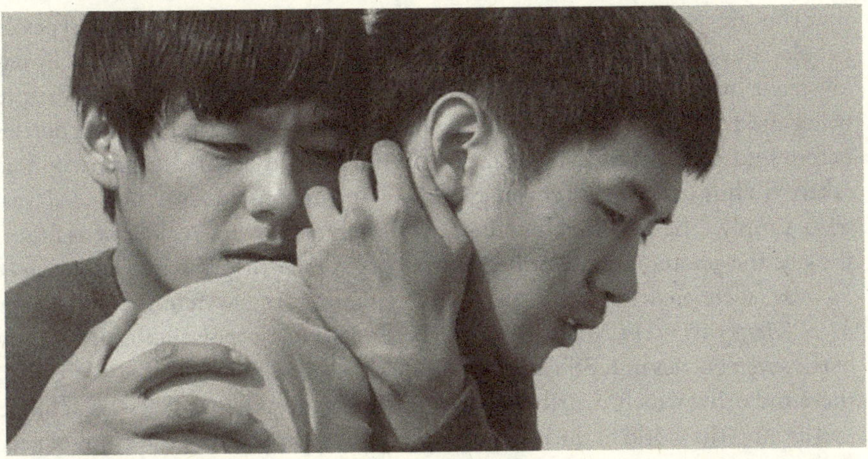

FIGURE 3.4 Besides illustrating how South Korea's deeply entrenched high-school bullying culture is connected to widespread homophobia, Leesong Hee-il's *Night Flight* (*Yagan pihaeng*, 2014) fits into the independent auteur's filmography as an example of queer advocacy. Here, Yong-ju (Kwak Si-yang) and his working-class classmate Ki-ung (Yi Chae-jun) share an intimate moment far away from the disciplinary gaze of school administrators and bullies.

teachers single-handedly and retrieve the camera's memory card that contains the recording. In the abovementioned interview, Leesong attests to the emotional catharsis that LGBTQ audiences are said to have felt when watching this scene of self-appointed justice, aimed against the habitual antagonism of heterosexual students and silent acquiescence of teachers and other school officials. Ultimately, films such as *Bleak Night* and *Night Flight* transcend generic limitations related to the teenpic, queer romance, and coming-of-age melodrama and ask audiences to direct their gazes both inward and outward: toward their own complicity in the problem of bullying but also toward a larger context of social "villainy" that stunts the spiritual and emotional development of adolescents by fostering a destructively competitive culture of one-upmanship and personal achievement at all costs.

Conclusion: They're (Not) Just Bullies

On September 13, 2017, a contributor to the popular culture website SeoulBeats posted an article about the ongoing problem of school bullying and teenage sexual assault, focusing not on feature-length motion pictures but on several locally produced television programs that have devoted episodes to those interrelated subjects.[41] The author begins her short article by alluding to a graphic photograph that had recently circulated on Facebook, one in which a fourteen-year-old Korean girl from Busan is shown "kneeling on the ground covered in blood." "Looking at the photo," the author writes, "you would probably think that this girl was the victim of an attack by gangsters or other similar types of people," but in fact the high-school student had been physically assaulted by fellow teens (who—as revealed in CCTV footage that became a viral video before being aired on JTBC News—beat her with a chair, a metal pipe, and soju bottles before snubbing out their lit cigarettes on her bruised flesh). The girl, who was taken to a hospital soon after being found "lying unconscious on the floor," was, quite simply, "the victim of bullying." Although nothing as explicit or as unsettling as the photograph described above occurs in such TV series as *Boys over Flowers* (*Kkot poda namja*, KBS [Korean Broadcasting System], 2009), *Angry Mom* (*Aenggŭri mam*, MBC [Munhwa Broadcasting Corporation], 2015), or any of the seven entries in KBS's long-running *School* (*Hakgyo*) series (1999–present), these and other widely distributed cultural productions remind viewers at home and around the world of the need to protect young people from the kinds of peer and parental pressure that can lead to tragic endings.

One such fate befell Kwŏn Sŭng-min, a middle-school boy who, on December 20, 2011, committed suicide by jumping from the balcony of his parents' seventh-floor apartment in Daegu. That incident, which is referred to by the author of the *SeoulBeats* piece, garnered national and international attention once details of the thirteen-year-old's torture at the hands of classmates were reported. Kwŏn's suicide note spelled out the circumstances that led him to take his own life, painting a bleak picture of a cutthroat social environment in which school-age kids resort to the kinds of abuse that—though far removed from the relatively safe world of the traditional teenpic—would not be out of place within a gangster film (*chop'ok yŏnghwa*).[42] Tellingly, the online commentator's suggestion that the sometimes deadly effects of bullying can appear to be the work of gangsters rather than teenagers corresponds to the cultural framing of school violence within South Korean genre productions, which cater to audiences presumably drawn to dynamic, action-packed fight scenes and territorial battles involving groups of street-hardened thugs (*kkangp'ae*).[43]

A case in point is *Gangster High*, by the writer-director Park Ki-hyung (Pak Ki-hyŏng). Though produced and theatrically released in 2006, the film—like *Once Upon a Time in High School* before it—is set during an earlier period, prior to the passing of the Juvenile Act of 1995 and the government's attempt to remedy this social problem through passing of the Act on the Prevention of and Countermeasures against Violence in Schools nearly a decade later (during President Roh Moo-hyun's administration). Specifically, *Gangster High*'s narrative unfolds over a four-week period in 1991, beginning with a scene in which the adolescent protagonist, Sang-ho (Chŏng Kyŏng-ho), is informed by a police officer that he has been arrested for the murder of three people. His wide-eyed look of surprise, which leads to an extended flashback that details the events leading up to this opening scene, will likely be mimicked by the film's audience—who, by the time the narrative finally circles back to its beginning, will have been visually assaulted by multiple moments in which Sang-ho and other high schoolers succumb to merciless beatings by rival gang members whose bad behavior goes unchecked by any authority figures until his run-in with the police. Suffering ruptured eyes, fractured skulls, and broken legs, Sang-ho's friends—fellow soccer enthusiasts who form a club (the Tigers) to which he is elected president—had earlier professed an interest only in "booze, smoking, and chicks" before being caught up in a cross-town rivalry with East High students. When one of Sang-ho's pals, Ch'ang-bae (Yi Sŏk), asks why the local authorities do not put these hoodlums behind bars, another friend, Chae-gu (Yi T'ae-sŏng), responds that the East High students are "not really gangsters." "They take money off kids," Chae-gu remarks, before concluding that "they're just bullies." Tellingly, in a press conference held on October 17, 2016, two days before the film's release, its director stated: "Many people asked me how high-school students could fight like this in *Gangster High*. Despite some instances of extreme fictionalization, the film is based on a real-life event that involves not only high schoolers, but also middle-school students."[44] This alarming revelation reaffirms the severity of Korean school violence, whose reality is even more dire than what is dramatized in cinematic fictions.

Throughout this chapter, we have argued that even in crowd-pleasing yet disturbing commercial releases such as *Once Upon a Time in High School* and *Gangster High*, no one—not even the most malicious or maladjusted of teenagers—is ever "just a bully." The latter film in particular, owing to the near-absence of any adult supervision or authority figure older than Sang-ho and his cohort, hints at the idea that bullies are products of their social environment, which in this case is noticeably lacking in institutional forms of support (counseling, violence prevention programs, and so on) that are now part of South Korea's reformed educational system.[45] Scene after bloody scene in *Gangster High* shows the boys acting like men outside the surveillance of teachers and parents. And their performance of hypermasculinity is just that: a showy display of excessive manliness made all the more stylized or artificial through Park's use of slow motion, music-video-style montage sequences, and intertextual allusions to U.S. popular culture (such as the Tom Cruise bartender movie *Cocktail* [1988] and David Lee Roth's rendition of "Just a Gigolo"). Significantly, the film's first fight, which breaks out on the dusty soccer field but spills over into the school gymnasium, culminates with Sang-ho and a rival gang member squaring off against one another inside a chalk circle, drawn on the floor of the gym. Like the "magic-circle" theory of game studies (in which players, young and old alike, are perceived as entering a rule-bound imaginary space of paradoxically boundless possibility), the chalk marking on the gym floor creates a kind of protective bubble, giving the teenage boys license to act out their gangster-mimicking masculinity while figuratively shielding them from the world of adults (including their own physically abusive parents). In anticipation of that moment, their teacher, audible but hidden from the spectator's view (like most of the other invisible adults in this film), flatly informs his all-male class that they "are men and no longer kids"—a comment that further suggests that the untarnished youthfulness of the teenpic genre has been replaced by the mature themes and blood-soaked imagery of adult-filled gangster films.

Less mainstream entries in the growing body of works that we call "bullying films"—from *Bleak Night* to *Night Flight* and similarly low-budget indie productions such as *A Stray Goat* (or *Snowflake* [*Nunbal*, 2017])—go even further in revealing how the victimizers are also victims of a brutal classist society. Largely demonized by the press and reduced to statistical evidence of the spread of juvenile delinquency,[46] bullies often receive as much abuse as they dole out, both from other students and from adults who appear to have inherited their top-down approach to disciplining from South Korea's most consistent violators of human rights—namely, members of the military government whose suppression of civil liberties and personal freedoms during the 1970s and 1980s was actualized on the streets of Seoul, Kwangju, and other cities where baton-wielding troops were sent to crack down on political agitators and peaceful demonstrators. As distant as a film like *Once Upon a Time in High School* might appear to be from the rights violations of decades past, its copious scenes of student-on-student and teacher-on-student violence dredge up painful memories of the country's authoritarian regimes, representatives of which are actually present at various points in this superficially amusing yet ultimately depressing period piece (for example, they are shown giving the teachers and administrators at Chungmun High their marching orders on the school's premises). In the end, this and other examples of the bullying film, though produced in the hopes of turning a profit and entertaining the masses, demand attention for their often-blistering commentaries on social exclusion, class warfare, and the culture of competitiveness that has bred resentment among the nation's young people and driven so many of them to the brink of suicide in recent years.

4

Indie Filmmaking and Queer Advocacy

Converging Identities in Leesong Hee-il's Films and Writings

On August 2, 2007, a relatively obscure indie filmmaker became an overnight internet sensation in his home country when he blogged his derisive take on the veteran comedian-turned-director Sim Hyŏn-rae's science-fiction blockbuster *Dragon Wars: D-War* (*Tiwŏ*, 2007), whose six-year production and massive marketing campaign—culminating with a theatrical premiere the previous day—reportedly cost an unprecedented 70 billion won ($62.6 million).[1] The online post's author was Leesong Hee-il (Yisong Hŭi-il), one of South Korea's few openly gay filmmakers, who had come out of the closet eight years earlier on a nighttime talk show aired by the Seoul Broadcasting System (SBS). "*D-War* is not a movie," declared Leesong, "but . . . a knock-off of a U.S.-brand toaster assembled in [the hardware district of] Ch'ŏnggyech'ŏn in the 1970s." Criticizing the nationalistic fanfare surrounding the Showbox-released film's use of "Hollywood-like advanced CGI [computer-generated imagery]" and its anticipated "wide release in the U.S. market" (it would open on over 2,200 U.S. screens in September 2007), the independent director encouraged his fellow Koreans to "stop talking about [Sim's] passion." "With 70 billion won, I could have shown passion in 350, or at least 100 quality films," Leesong wrote, adding that "plenty of people starve while making movies. Many independent films are made with a tsunami of passion but with no money at all, let alone 70 billion won."[2] Leesong's unfiltered tirade, which would prove to be characteristic of the provocative writing style that he would hone in the following years, rubbed many mainstream movie fans the wrong way, and he shut his blog page down due to a barrage of negative replies from offended users.

We begin this chapter about South Korean independent filmmaking and queer advocacy in this way because Leesong's notoriety as a champion of both causes owes as much to his anti-*D-War* blog, which sparked a national debate about the relative merits of one of the highest-budgeted films in Korean history, as it does to his directorial breakthrough *No Regret* (*Huhoehaji ana*, 2006), a sleeper hit made on a smaller budget (1 billion won, or roughly $895,000) and with a fraction of the blockbuster's production and marketing resources. In this chapter, we build upon and go beyond the economic concerns specific to low-budget filmmaking to highlight the slippery identity politics discernible within both the independently produced motion pictures and the critical writings of Leesong Hee-il, a unique public figure who has expanded the epistemological boundaries of homosexuality and heterosexuality, queer and genre filmmaking, and art cinema and commercial cinema. *No Regret* is an interclass love story between a rich man and a gay bar worker and has been compared to soft-core hostess films of the 1970s and early 1980s (sexually explicit movies about bargirls and prostitutes), despite its politically progressive reinterpretation of that genre's melodramatic narrative formulas. As discussed in chapter 3, Leesong's fourth feature-length film, *Night Flight* (*Yagan pihaeng*, 2014), about the lives of gay teenagers, is as much an anti-bullying film as it is a button-pushing example of queer cinema.

In this chapter, we emphasize the ways in which the fluidity of identity formations in this important writer-director's cinematic output reflects his philosophy, as expressed in many of his critical writings that have been circulated in film and literary magazines such as the *Independent Film Magazine* (*Toknip yŏnghwa*), *Cine 21*, and *Literature Community* (*Munhak tongnae*). In a manner that recalls the early careers of Jean-Luc Godard, François Truffaut, and other French film critics who wrote for the magazine *Cahiers du Cinéma* while nurturing their own nascent directorial careers in the 1950s and 1960s, Leesong is a prolific writer who has used his pen as frequently as his camera in challenging the cultural establishment and deconstructing hegemonic norms related to gender, masculinity, and sexuality. Leesong's activism—he has assumed leadership roles in several advocacy groups such as Ch'ingusai (Between Friends; a gay human rights group), as well as Chŏlmŭn yŏngwha (Young Film) and Indie Forum, two of the many independent filmmakers' collectives to emerge in South Korea in the past two decades—and his published writings in popular magazines attest to a desire to build bridges between different identities and maintain a dialogue with members of mainstream society who might not identify themselves as LGBTQ activists. Leesong has risen to prominence as one of the most outspoken and widely heard cultural commentators in print and visual media, thus serving as a role model for any genderqueer youth who might have experienced the kinds of verbal bullying or physical abuse so viscerally depicted in his unique brand of minoritarian cinema.

"A Certain Tendency in Korean Cinema": Leesong's Theory of Minority Cinema

Although there are other contemporary Korean filmmakers who started their careers as film critics (most notably Park Chan-wook [Pak Ch'an-uk] and Chŏng Sŏng-il), Leesong stands out as someone whose life blurs the boundaries among social activism, cultural criticism, and filmmaking. His earliest writings on cinema (published in the Association for Korean Independent Film and Video [KIFV]'s *Independent Film Magazine*) are not about individual films or filmmakers but about larger conceptual concerns related to minority cinema, the cultural function of film festivals, and the importance of maintaining communication with an audience. Collectively, they constitute a socially engaged form of cinematic theory rather than straightforward film criticism. Leesong's irreverent, provocative essays are united by "the whole spectrum of theoretical, philosophical, and aesthetic *premises*," a phrase Marco Grosoli uses to describe the collectively conceived idea of *la politique des auteurs* put forth over a half-century ago by *Cahiers du Cinéma* critics (including Godard, Truffaut, Claude Chabrol, Jacques Rivette, and Eric Rohmer).[3] In his first piece in the *Independent Film Magazine* ("For Minority Cinema [*Sosuja yŏngwha rŭl wihayŏ*]," published in the August 2000 issue), Leesong comes across as a kind of Korean Truffaut, a Young Turk challenging his native country's cultural establishment just as the French critic had done in his now-canonized essay "A Certain Tendency of the French Cinema" ("Une certaine tendance du cinéma français"), which was originally published in the January 1954 issue of *Cahiers*. Truffaut, who would soon gain international recognition as a director at the forefront of the French New Wave, flatly rejected the then-current status of the French film industry, which was entrenched in the literature-based "Tradition of Quality" and which pumped out "screenwriters' films." Truffaut's piece essentially calls for a radical undoing of mainstream French cinema—which, as he saw it, was incompatible with *cinema d'auteur* (auteur cinema), a form of personal expression guided by the vision and visual language of talented directors that was what he thought filmmaking should be.[4]

Although it gained relatively little notoriety or critical attention compared to what has been lavished on Truffaut's essay, Leesong's "For Minority Cinema" is no less ambitious or philosophical in its conceptualization of a "certain tendency" in Korean cinema. This essay was published along with an interview with Leesong that introduced him not only as an up-and-coming indie director (with two gay-themed short films under his belt: *Everyday Like Sunday* [*Ŏnjena iryoil kach'i*, 1998] and *Sugar Hill* [2000]) but also as an LGBTQ activist. Born in 1971, Leesong nurtured his passion for the cinema in high school, skipping classes to spend his afternoons in movie theaters, where he watched countless Hong Kong martial arts and action films in the 1980s. After entering Chonbuk National University as a sociology major in 1990, Leesong immersed himself in campus activism and boycotted the cinema, which many radical students regarded as a bourgeois medium. It was not until his senior year that the fledging social activist redirected his attention to film, viewing it as a means of studying cultural theory rather than a self-contained artistic form. After agonizing over what to do after college, Leesong chose cultural activism over labor activism and cofounded Young Film in 1995 along with four other aspiring filmmakers. After struggling to launch his career and dealing with deteriorating health, the disillusioned would-be filmmaker returned to his hometown to become a farmer. Following a two-year hiatus in the countryside, he relocated to Seoul and found his calling as a human rights activist, assuming leadership in Ch'ingusai, the first Korean gay male organization whose motto is "men who love other men." According to Phil Ho Kim and C. Collin Singer, this pioneering advocacy group contributed to "the 'normalization' of queerness" by constructing images of gay men as ordinary people through the strategy of "'different but equal' masculinity."[5] In 1998, against all odds, Leesong debuted as a director with a twenty-three-minute 16mm film titled *Everyday Like Sunday*, about a dysfunctional intimate relationship between two gay men. The film was shown at the inaugural Seoul Queer Film Festival, which opened in November 1998 (its slogan was "Different Eyes, Denying Eyes") and was attended by six thousand people. Two years later, Leesong's second 16mm short film, *Sugar Hill* (based on the real-life story of a closeted gay man who marries his lover's sister because of family pressure) won a top award in the short-film section of the prestigious Busan International Film Festival.

This brief biography shows that the consolidation of institutional support networks, such as KIFV and the Seoul Queer Film Festival, was instrumental in advancing Leesong's goal of bringing his brutally honest, critical interrogation of homophobic culture and LGBTQ alienation to the big screen. In the abovementioned 2000 interview with the *Independent Film Magazine*, Leesong was asked what "Korean independent cinema" meant to him. The indie director replied: "I see it as a discourse. It does not necessarily mean a mode of production nor is it a concept defined by the government, but instead is a community of discourse. . . . In that community, diverse attitudes of life and forms of resistance discourse by different filmmakers are transformed into film form. That's independent cinema to me." He went on to state that "the concept of resistance is inclusive and diverse today." "Because independent cinema is a community of discourse," he concluded, "the question of identity continues to matter."[6] Leesong's vision of independent cinema coincides with the version of the concept in KIFV's founding document. The new independent filmmakers' association defines the amorphous term "independence" not as "the rejection of censorship" or "low production capital," but as liberation from the "formulaic film language" and from hegemonic power to protect "an individual's human rights and the freedom of minorities."[7] In other words, both KIFV and at least one of the organization's founding members saw independent cinema as a type of discourse rather than a mode of production, distribution, or exhibition.

In addition to being asked to define independent cinema in the interview, Leesong was commissioned to contribute a piece on minority cinema, discussed above. His essay opens using an epistolary format, ostensibly addressed to his boyfriend in the military. The pretense of writing a letter to an intimate friend justifies the author's irreverent attitude toward and unfiltered candor about his assignment at hand. Leesong confesses, "I was at loss for a while in front of the editor who was requesting the manuscript as if he took it for granted that I was the most appropriate person for the subject. Minority cinema? Does it even exist in South Korea? The editor must have thought I would be able to say a few things because I [had] made two films and they were about minorities."[8] After critiquing the premise of his commissioned essay, Leesong grapples with the concept and asks the seemingly straightforward but provocative question, "Is a woman's film a minority film?" He acknowledges that many critics would hesitate to answer yes because of the presumed equality (both numerical and constitutional) between the genders. He goes on to state that critics, festival programmers, and scholars are apt to label documentaries about the lives of migrant workers "human rights films" rather than "minority films."[9] Ultimately, Leesong defines minority cinema as a "plural antithesis to conventionalized film forms and contents," or "reorganizational efforts to poke holes, scratch and damage, and provide alternatives to dominant mainstream discourse."[10]

The type of cultural production with which he is associated—specifically, queer cinema—seems to lend itself to the label of minority cinema "because there are diverse differences within the category and endless new questions are raised" about those differences. Leesong endorses the distributive decentering of queer cinema in the hope that the "hypocrisy of the homo-hetero binary," which has long plagued onscreen representations of gay and straight relationships, might be exposed and even obliterated.[11] This would not only provide greater opportunities to feminist lesbian filmmakers but would also open up space for transgender storytelling and a Third World queering of binary, Eurocentric sexual politics. After dangling the possibility of consolidating different minoritarian cinemas (for example, queer, woman's, human rights, labor, and environmental film) under the category of minority cinema, Leesong ultimately rejects the concept altogether in a deconstructive way. He declares: "Queer cinema is just queer cinema and a woman's film is just a woman's film. . . . We should leave their differences alone."[12] For him, the all-encompassing label is problematic as it negates differences among a wide range of films with diverse purposes and ghettoizes them as marginalized alternatives to commercial entertainment cinema.

Leesong ultimately calls for "an overthrow of concealed majority power embedded in the concept" and urges readers to do away with minority cinema altogether. In the concluding paragraph, he envisions KIFV's role as a "culture center for bacteria that breeds garden-variety germs" rather than a centrifugal force to combine different films under a single label to counter mainstream cinema.

In *French Minority Cinema*, Cristina Johnston defines the term "minority," stating that groups lumped together under that term are "entities of which full understanding can only be gained in the context of their relationship with either a numerical majority or a culturally or politically dominant societal norm." She goes on to clarify the point:

> This is not to suggest that the minority is permanently in a weakened position, nor that it is necessarily subordinate to the majority/norm. It is rather a question of focusing on the interdependence of the minority/majority or minority/norm relationship. In cultural, political, and linguistic terms, the minority gains much of its sense of identity from its relationship with and divergence from established patterns or norms. It makes little sense to talk of a minority or to refer to, for instance, "minority literatures" or "minority cinema" if there is no norm against which to offer such a categorisation. Equally, however, the majority/norm only exists as such insofar as there are alternatives against which one may establish its status as such. The minority can thus be said to be both constituted by and constitutive of the tandem within which it is placed.[13]

This constitutive relationship between the minority and the majority is precisely what Leesong's essay challenges. He opposes the pigeonholing of people with different identity affiliations in the numeric categorization of minority groups. Leesong's thinking is reminiscent of Jacques Derrida's theory of deconstruction, which can be conceived of as an "irreducible plurality" that, in Nicole Anderson's paraphrasing, "*inhabits* structures (metaphysical, philosophical, etc.) [that] are constantly in the process of deconstructing themselves." Derrida's theory rejects the notion of "a pure presence . . . foundation or origin" and stresses the constitutive relationship between a structure and "a non-structure (which is not opposite to structure, as in de-struction, but can be defined as an alterity, otherness, heteronomy)."[14] Despite its potential to expose structures' dependence on nonstructures—or, to extend the metaphor to the concept in question, the majority's dependence on the minority—and to overturn the normative cultural order, cynical readers might perceive deconstruction without political commitment to be merely an exercise in interpretative postponement, a means of deferring any ultimate meaning or revealing the polysemic potential of texts that speak in the plural.

However, Derridean *différance* (difference/deferment) is conducive to reconstituting the majority-minority binary, as Homi Bhabha demonstrates in his writing on margins and minorities. For Bhabha, "Minority discourse sets the act of emergence in the antagonistic *in-between* of image and sign, the accumulative and the adjunct, presence and proxy. It contests genealogies of 'origin' that lead to claims for cultural supremacy and historical priority. Minority discourse acknowledges the status of national culture—and the people—as a contentious, performative space of the perplexity of the living in the midst of the pedagogical representations of the fullness of life."[15] In applying Bhabha's theory to the context of the New Chinese Cinema of the 1980s, Yingjin Zhang finds the term "minority discourse" more useful than "minority film" or "ethnographic film," since the movement "takes a strategic position of 'marginality'—a reconstructed marginality that questions and challenges the 'centrality' of the state discourse."[16] In the 1950s and 1960s, minority films were appropriated by the socialist state as a means of propagandizing minority people's solidarity with the Chinese nation. Films by Fifth-Generation directors (such as Tian Zhuangzhuang's *Horse Thief* [*Daoma zei*, 1985]) deconstruct such a "pedagogical" (to borrow Bhabha's term) view of minorities and therefore open up a performative space wherein the ambivalent and liminal status of minority culture and identity can be explored. Zhang's understanding of "minority discourse" in New Chinese Cinema is analogous to Leesong's conceptualization of the equally fluid cultural praxis in the Korean minoritarian cinema that emerged in the late 1990s and early 2000s.

From Minority Cinema to Minor Cinema: *No Regret*

Gilles Deleuze and Félix Guattari define "minor literature" not as "the literature of a minor language" but rather "the literature a minority makes in a major language."[17] Unlike "great" literatures, as these theorists note, a minor literature involves the "deterritorialization of the language, the connection between the individual and the political, the collective arrangement of utterance."[18] Deleuze and Guattari's concept of minor literature is applicable to reconceptualizing Leesong's genre-bending queer films as examples of minor, rather than minority, cinema. His first and most commercially successful feature-length film, *No Regret* (which garnered an unprecedented 44,000 admissions, becoming the highest grossing low-budget independent film in South Korea to date) is a productive case study for testing the concept of minor cinema.

Labeled as a "queer melo[drama]" in the promotional and press discourse at the time of its theatrical release, the film revolves around a rocky and nearly fatal interclass romance between Yi Su-min (Yi Yŏng-hun), a factory worker-turned-gay bar "host" (someone who is paid to be a companion for drinks and a provider of sexual services upon request), and Song Chae-min (Kim Nam-gil), an

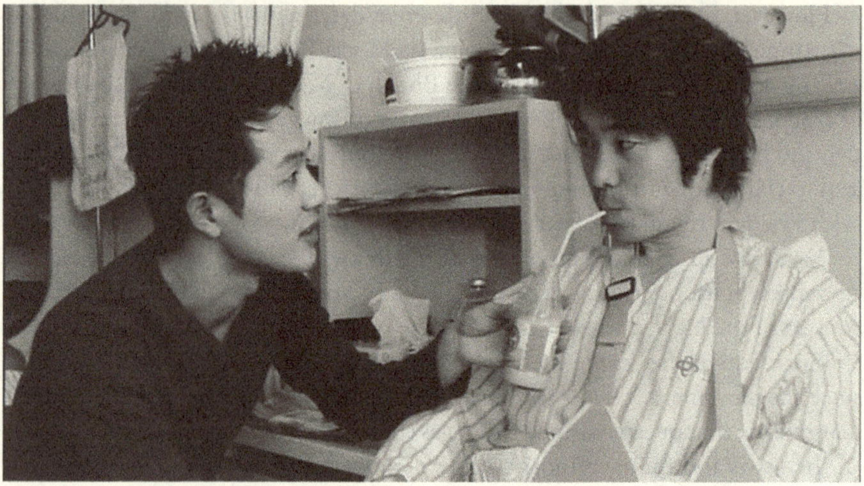

FIGURE 4.1 Su-min (Yi Yŏng-hun; left) and Chae-min (Kim Nam-gil; right) initiate a passionate and tender relationship as a steady couple in Leesong Hee-il's interclass love story *No Regret* (*Huhoehaji ana*, 2006).

executive's son in the factory where Su-min worked before being laid off. Despite being engaged to a woman, Chae-min doggedly pursues Su-min, who resists the rich client's advances and threatens to kill him. Chae-min's desperate declaration of affection in the form of self-mutilation (of his hand) moves Su-min, and the two men begin a passionate yet tender relationship as a steady couple (see figure 4.1). Wishing to keep her son's closeted sex life under wraps and maintain a public display of his heterosexuality, Chae-min's mother notices her son's new passion and rushes to arrange a wedding for him against his will. Pressured by his family, Chae-min screens Su-min's calls and coldly pretends not to recognize him when the latter shows up to confront him in his office with his family and fiancée present. A humiliated and vengeful Su-min plots to kill Chae-min with the help of a disgruntled former coworker at the gay bar, who has been betrayed by his girlfriend and is looking for someone on whom to take out his anger. Unbeknown to his vengeance-seeking lover, Chae-min has come out to his fiancée and called off their engagement immediately after they had an uncomfortable confrontation in public. Without this knowledge, Su-min and his accomplice abduct Chae-min in his office parking lot and take him to the remote mountains to bury him alive in the middle of the night. The plotters then deposit their bound and gagged victim in a shallow open grave. A regretful Su-min has a change of heart before his accomplice is able to fully bury Chae-min and tries to put an end to their absurd plot. This provokes the wrath of his accomplice, who knocks Su-min unconscious with a shovel and threatens to bury the two men together. After venting his anger, Su-min's coworker leaves the two men in the open grave, their bodies exposed to the cold. After narrowly escaping death and finding shelter in Chae-min's stranded car (where they fall asleep out of exhaustion), the lovers silently reconcile and display their affection publicly when a cop finds them on a morning patrol.

Before unexpectedly turning into a dark thriller in the final twenty minutes (starting with the parking lot abduction scene in which Chae-min is stalked and knocked unconscious by an offscreen, unseen attacker), *No Regret* follows the formulaic plot of interclass romance between poor hostesses and rich patrons popularized in the hostess genre throughout the 1970s and 1980s. Examples of such motion pictures include *Hometown of Stars* (*Pyŏldŭlŭi kohyang*, 1974), *Yŏng-ja's Heyday* (*Yŏng-ja-ŭi chŏnsŏng sidae*, 1975), *Winter Woman* (*Kyŏul yŏja*, 1977), and *Miss O's Apartment* (*O-yangŭi Ap'at'ŭ*, 1978). "Hostess" is a cultural neologism of the 1970s, which reflects the rapid rise of sex markets for the nouveaux riches and industrialists in the form of so-called room salons (high-class bars with escort service). The hostess film depicts the tragic fall of innocent, rural girls into a web of urban prostitution due to poverty and the need to meet familial responsibilities. For example, based on the memoir of O Mi-yŏng, *Miss O's Apartment* features a self-sacrificial, filial heroine who becomes a hostess to pay the medical bills for her tuberculosis-afflicted father and support her family.[19] As a representative example of the hostess genre, *Yŏng-ja's Heyday* spotlights a member of the working class: an unskilled, uneducated migrant woman from the countryside mobilized to provide labor for the nation's industrialization. *Yŏng-ja's Heyday* shows what typically happened to these inexperienced and undereducated women and girls after they arrived in the city. First, Yŏng-ja (Yŏm Pok-sun) finds work as a maid in a rich household, only to be fired after she is raped by the son in the family. Then she joins the industrial workforce as a sweatshop laborer. After losing her arm in a traffic accident, she descends into the red-light district. Like other hostess films, *Yŏng-ja's Heyday* exploits the sexual content of rape and prostitution rather than realistically depicting the atrocious working conditions of sweatshops and factories—spaces more frequently seen in the politically conscious New Wave cinema of the late 1980s to the mid-1990s. Nevertheless, *Yŏng-ja's Heyday* is now considered a cult movie among Korean film scholars because of its latent criticism of the dehumanizing effects of modernization, as evidenced in one famous scene in which Yŏng-ja's amputated arm is shown flying up into the sky against the backdrop of an office building. Yŏng-ja represents the members of victimized subaltern classes whose safety and welfare were deemed less important than increasing exports and the gross national product. The so-called Miracle of Han River would not have been possible without their blood, sweat, and tears.

Like Yŏng-ja, *No Regret*'s Su-min (who grew up as an orphan in the countryside) moves to Seoul, innocently dreaming of social mobility through hard work and higher education. He saves his wages and attends night classes to prepare for college. The gay protagonist turns to prostitution only as a last resort after he loses more honest, if less profitable, jobs as a worker on an assembly line and a dishwasher. Comparing his film to *Yŏng-ja's Heyday*, Leesong explains his authorial intention in a 2007 interview with the *Independent Film Magazine*:

> I was curious what effect it would have to replace [the heterosexual storyline] with a story of two gay men. It is really regrettable that I had to cut 20–30 minutes toward the end. Originally, I intended to cut the film in half. I wanted to bend the genre more drastically and turn the text from a melodrama to a fantasy. The first part of the film is conventionally melodramatic, so I wanted to add weight toward the end. In South Korea, people put more emphasis on melodrama and ask me why I covered up the popular genre [toward the end]. Foreign journalists and audiences think differently. They often ask me why I mixed different genres. . . . I intended to bend the genre [of melodrama,] and that's why I accentuated its conventions up front. Perhaps Koreans got curious about that because it's such a familiar cliché of the 1970s–1980s.[20]

Leesong originally intended to conclude his film with images of the entire city being hit by a hurricane, an ending that would have intensified the personal drama by linking it to the collective peril of people coming to terms with a natural disaster. He was forced to give up this grand vision due to budgetary restrictions and, as a result, restored the melodramatic mode at the film's end.

This compromise ironically reaffirms *No Regret*'s status as a form of minor cinema, one with an imbalance of genre elements rather than a more fully developed narrative detour—as seen, for instance, in Jordan Peele's romantic comedy-horror film *Get Out* (2017), which cost $4.5 million to make (a minuscule budget by Hollywood indie standards but more than five times that of *No Regret*). Gobbling up roughly one-fifth of the film's 114-minute running time, the final twenty minutes of *No Regret* radically subvert audience expectations of conventional melodrama, a dominant genre of South Korean cinema and K-dramas (Korean television dramas) that thematizes interclass romance and rewards the virtues of patient, self-sacrificial heroines who deservedly "marry up." Like the "minor literature" defined by Deleuze and Guattari, *No Regret* "deterritorializes" the language of melodrama, a major popular genre in South Korea, through a kind of double queering: first, by replacing a heterosexual couple with a gay one; and second, by defamiliarizing the genre through seemingly out-of-place thriller elements and conflicting aesthetics: the nighttime mountain scene is shot in black-and-white, film noir style, which contrasts with the earlier overexposed, bright interior and exterior scenes that idealize Su-min and Chae-min's budding romance (see figure 4.2).

Deleuze and Guattari argue that "everything in [minor literatures] is political" because they exist "in a narrow space."[21] Of course, this does not mean that only queer melodrama is political. As Thomas Schatz asserts, 1950s family melodramas such as Douglas Sirk's Technicolor, wide-screen weepies *Written on the Wind* (1957) and *Imitation of Life* (1960) can be considered "the most . . . covertly

FIGURE 4.2 Toward the end of *No Regret*, Leesong Hee-il deterritorializes the language of melodrama by incorporating seemingly out-of-place genre elements (related to the thriller and neo-noir) in dark, black-and-white shots, including this image of the two main characters sitting inside an open grave.

'anti-American' films ever made by the Hollywood studios" for their "subtle, self-conscious criticism of American values, attitudes, and behavior."[22] However, by substituting a homosexual couple for a heterosexual one while retaining the same narrative formula, *No Regret* criticizes more than just Korean values, attitudes, and behavior regarding class and gender differences. It directly challenges the homophobia that is not only directed at the LGBTQ community from outside but that also occurs within the community. The male "madam" (Chŏng Sŭng-gil) of X-Large, the gay bar where Su-min is offered a position, confronts the newest recruit about his sexual orientation: "I don't hire fags. Patrons don't like fags, either. I'm a fag, but I despise ambiguity. Which side are you on?" At that point, the camera pans to a profile close-up of Su-min, who refuses to answer the question and changes the subject. This pre-employment conversation between the openly gay operator and his new recruit who is hired to provide sexual services to closeted (and predominantly married) men who "hate fags" exposes the oppression that sometimes is manifested within closeted LGBTQ communities, where poor "non-fag" men cater to the covert sexual desires of affluent "non-fag" men without challenging heteronormative values of marriage and family.

The hypocrisy latent within Korean upper- and middle-class social and familial structures is also hinted at in a later scene: Chae-min confronts his mother (Kim Hwa-yŏng), who has invited all company employees to his wedding to force him to give up the love of his life. Aloof, the older woman looks at the office window with a cigarette in her hand and says: "I'm not so ignorant as to not understand sexuality. I don't care if you screw a guy or not. You don't get him pregnant anyway." Turning around to face her son, the mother issues a nonnegotiable demand, telling him to marry his fiancée, Hyŏn-u (Kim Chŏng-hwa). Likewise, Hyŏn-u reacts by slapping Chae-min and expressing anger at his selfishness when he comes out to her in the elevator by informing her that "the man we've just passed by is the one I love." The jilted woman's reproach is aimed not at his sexuality but at his coming out, which she labels as a shady action on the part of a man who no longer considers the feelings of others—including his parents, who are in the same elevator and witness the couple's argument. This dialogue implies that she would not have been selfish and would have played the role of an understanding wife to the closeted husband as long as he kept up the façade of a happy heterosexual family man (while frequenting an underground gay bar like X-Large to release his pent-up sexual frustrations). Chae-min says thank you to her as if understanding her offer of a marriage of convenience, which he rejects to be true to his identity. Perhaps his near-death experience in the mountains (and his revival and awakening the next morning) is symbolic of the death of a closeted gay man who was engaged to be married to a heterosexual woman and the rebirth of an openly gay individual who is free to pursue his love with another man. Su-min's implausible revenge plot symbolically punishes Chae-min for having betrayed his own identity and community and in the end helps him learn to "be faithful to one's libido," a phrase that Leesong uses to sum up his film's moral.[23] This interpretation suggests that the sharp narrative U-turn and undermining of genre-based expectations in the final twenty minutes of the film are not simply part of an aesthetic experiment but a deliberate political move to address both straight and queer audiences.

As the first Korean queer film directed and produced by openly gay activists (respectively, Leesong Hee-il and Kimjo Gwangsu, another gay filmmaker who puts members of South Korea's LGBTQ communities in the spotlight through his independently produced motion pictures), *No Regret* passes the final litmus test of the third category of Deleuze and Guattari's minor literature: "everything has a collective value. . . . It is a literature which produces an active solidarity. . . . If the writer lives on the margin, is set apart from his fragile community, this situation makes him all the more be able to express another, potential community, to force the means of another consciousness and another sensibility."[24] Here, we are not discounting the appeal of *No Regret* to heterosexual women (who accounted for approximately 80 percent of all theater patrons) or a more flexible definition of queerness—such as the one put forth by Alexander Doty: "a range of nonstraight expression in, or in response to, mass culture," inclusive of but not limited to "gay, lesbian, and bisexual expressions."[25] Unsang Kim is right in arguing that there is "a need for the conceptual expression of the term, 'Korean queer cinema,' beyond those films that deal explicitly with 'coming out' stories or that focus on social acceptance of sexual minorities" when a variety of big-budget genre films made by and for heterosexuals over the past decade and a half (from Yi Chun-ik's *The King and the Clown* [*Wangŭi namja*, 2005] to Park

Chan-wook's *The Handmaiden* [*Agassi,* 2016])—can be counted as relevant to the discussion.[26] However, the "collective value" of *No Regret* as a "minor" text written and directed by a gay activist who publicly came out on national television seven years before the film's release resonates powerfully and is distilled to its emotional core in an anecdote reported in the Korean edition of *Newsweek.* According to the magazine, Leesong shed tears when a twenty-year-old approached him in a meeting with fans and told the filmmaker that his parents had accepted his coming out after watching *No Regret* together.[27] It is difficult to imagine a more uplifting example to illustrate Deleuze and Guattari's idea of "collective utterance" and "an active solidarity" facilitated by minor literature.[28]

In various media interviews, Leesong has refused to be pigeonholed as a gay director and has repeatedly declared that he would stop making films about LGBTQ individuals—a promise that he has not kept, as he has continued to churn out queer romance tales such as the feature-length motion pictures *White Night* (*Paekya*, 2012) and *Night Flight* (*Yagan pihaeng*, 2014) and the short films *Suddenly, Last Summer* (*Chinan yŏrŭm kapjagi*, 2012) and *Going South* (*Namjjokŭro kanda*, 2012). In his recent article on Leesong's films, Kyungtae Kim argues that the characters who populate the indie auteur's works are "queer anarchists" prone to expressing dissent through their "pursuit of personal freedom" and their resistance to being absorbed into mainstream civil society.[29] This is evident in scenes in which the main characters opt not to belong to any community—gay or otherwise—that "obeys heteronormative demands."[30] For example, *White Night* features Leesong's signature lone queer protagonist. In this case, it is Wŏn-gyu (Wŏn T'ae-hŭi), a flight attendant for a German airline who left Korea two years earlier, after being victimized by a homophobic street assault (an event loosely based on a real-life incident in 2011 involving a gay couple who were attacked by three strangers in the gay bar district of Chongno). When Wŏn-gyu visits Seoul overnight between flights, he arranges a blind date for a one-night stand with T'ae-jun (Yi I-kyŏng), a working-class delivery man whom he meets in an online chat room. The two men's attempts to initiate a sexual encounter fail (once in a public restroom and later in Wŏn-gyu's hotel room). They almost part company multiple times before developing an unexpected bond over Wŏn-gyu's impulsive plan to exact revenge on a group of homophobic thugs (who had attacked him and his ex-boyfriend, leaving the latter's leg severely injured). When the flight attendant dashes out of the bar (where the couple had been having nightcaps) to chase one of his assailants into the street and his underclass companion joins the pursuit without knowing what is going on, the mode abruptly shifts from melodrama to crime, as in *No Regret.* Having become an inadvertent accomplice in revenge against homophobes, T'ae-jun beats one of the gang members to a pulp to protect Wŏn-gyu, and finally the two men—once strangers but now closely aligned—consummate their passion in the main storyline's cathartic aftermath.

As Kyungtae Kim points out, Leesong expresses his distrust of the gay community through his fictional mouthpiece, Wŏn-gyu, whose anger is directed not just at "the perpetrators [but also at] gay onlookers who do not respond and help [when] a member of the community faces a crisis."[31] Describing himself as a "refugee," the character who vows not to return to his homeland is a lost soul, belonging neither to Korea nor to Germany, and he is unable to find a comfortable embrace outside of fleeting encounters such as the one he forms with his online date. Kim's observation rings true to an extent, if we limit our focus to the diegetic worlds of the filmmaker's work. But Leesong's activism and his published writings in popular magazines attest to his desire to build bridges between different identities and maintain a dialogue with mainstream society. His prolific cultural commentary and social activism make him, in the words of Deleuze and Guattari, "all the more able to express another, potential community"—in particular, that of independent filmmakers, regardless of their sexual orientation.

Leesong's recent writings have become more concretely policy oriented. In a 2015 essay titled "Film, the Return of Politics," he harshly criticizes vertically integrated major film companies' monopolistic control of multiplex screens and the South Korean government's shift of exhibition support from low-budget independent films to "diversity films" that include medium-budget commercial releases and art-house exports from abroad.[32] Toward the end of his essay, he expresses concern about the depressing future of Korean cinema in the face of oligopolistic practices among conglomerates and calls for the "return of politics" (which he defines as critical reflections on the entire cinematic ecosystem and the restoration of nonmonetary values). Leesong sees an urgent need for collective action, not in the form of militant resistance to the past's authoritarian dictatorships, but through "trickster" subterfuge and subversions, inspired by the gay American artist Keith Haring.[33] Leesong's evocation of Haring (famous for his AIDS activism pieces such as "Ignorance = Fear, Silence = Death") in his writing on the crisis of Korean independent cinema is illustrative of his converging identities and interests. In his contribution to the winter 2001 issue of the *Independent Film Magazine*, Leesong declares, "My dream is simply to become a trickster. . . . I want to cope with my fear of the world with this fantasy of tricksters flooding and reconstituting the moral order of society."[34] More recently, Leesong's inner trickster seems to be pursuing the dual goal of resisting both heteronormative patriarchy and conglomerates' control of the Korean film industry. According to Kyungtae Kim, Leesong's LGBTQ protagonists dream of "the possibility of a *queer utopia*."[35] Their creator dreams bigger and longs for a new role played by South Korean cinema in spreading "a garden variety of germs" without the tyranny of a handful of majors sterilizing the earth so it can grow only formulaic blockbusters.

New Queer Cinema and LGBTQ Rights in South Korea

Phil Ho Kim and C. Collin Singer divide the history of South Korean queer cinema into three periods, "according to the manner in which queer content is displayed and the reception of the films by both the government authorities and the public: the Invisible Age (1976–1998), the Camouflage Age (1998–2005), [and] the Blockbuster Age (2005–present)."[36] The first period is somewhat equivalent to the Motion Picture Production Code–governed era of classical Hollywood, when so-called sex perversion was explicitly banned by the industry's self-regulatory cleansing—although certain characters were either covertly coded or subjectively interpreted by audiences as being queer. The only Korean film during the invisible age to feature gay-identified characters was Pak Chae-ho's *Broken Branches* (*Naeillo hŭrŭnŭn kang*, 1995), a three-part family saga that spans four decades of narrative time. While the film's first two parts ("Father" and "Hope") thematize an extended family's tragedies against grand historical backdrops (such as the Korean War and the assassination of Park Chung-hee [Pak Chŏng-hŭi]), the final part ("Family") is in a different tone, adopting a comic mode and exploring the closeted sexuality of the family's heir—an advertisement producer who dates an older, married man. Homosexuality in the narrative functions as a shorthand for the younger generation's new values, which are diametrically opposed to the traditional Confucian patriarchy represented by the gay producer's two departed fathers (his biological father who was killed during the Korean War and his stepfather, who died the same year that President Park—the nation's patriarch—was assassinated).

Such displacement of LGBTQ content onto a related yet different theme (old versus new, traditional versus modern, and so on) is evident in the narrative strategy of the second era, the camouflage age. Commercial genre-based productions such as the all-girls' high school horror film *Memento Mori* (*Yŏgo koedam tubŏntchaeiyagi*, 1999) and the reincarnation-themed romance *Bungee Jumping of Their Own* (*Pŏnji chŏmp'ŭrŭl hada*, 2001) similarly dilute or compromise queer themes in an effort to, as Kim and Singer put it, "avoid costly run-ins with either the viewer, rating authorities or the homophobic conservatives."[37] The third era, the blockbuster age, opened with the sleeper hit *The King and the Clown*, a revisionist historical drama that portrays as queer King Yŏngsan, a real-life tyrant of the Chosŏn Dynasty who has been the subject of numerous biopics and historical TV dramas since the Golden Age of Korean cinema in the 1960s. Kim and Singer give credit to this film for starting "the 'gay man = gorgeous beauty' formula now prevalent in Korean mass media, known as the 'flower boy' (*kkonminam*) phenomenon."[38] Found in subsequent queer blockbusters such as *Antique* (*Sŏyang koldong kwajajŏm aent'ik'ŭ*, 2008) and *A Frozen Flower* (*Sanghwajŏm*, 2008), this trendy formula has been both celebrated (particularly by straight female audiences) and criticized for alienating some LGBTQ communities with superficial images of pretty young gay men.

What distinguishes *No Regret* from the abovementioned films is not simply the fact that it was independently produced and directed by openly gay individuals (the producer, Kimjo, publicly came out during the press conference at the film's premiere) but also its indirect call for marriage equality and social recognition of minorities, whose members frequently struggle to come out in a country that has long suppressed civil liberties and frank discussions of sexual identity. Despite romantic clichés associated with their all-too-familiar genre situation, the two lovers are ordinary individuals, and audiences can relate to their character flaws and weaknesses regardless of their sexual orientation. As Kim and Singer point out, "The film starts encroaching on heteronormativity when it lays the second layer of queerness on top of the 'men love other men' storyline, by borrowing the narrative structure of the so-called 'hostess film' and giving it a twist."[39] According to Unsang Kim, *No Regret* belongs to one category of South Korean queer cinema, focused on LGBTQ-identified characters and their same-sex romantic relationships. Kim argues that more recent queer films, such as Chŏng Chu-ri's *A Girl at My Door* (*To-hŭi-ya*, 2014), Yi Kyŏng-mi's *The Truth Beneath* (*Pimilŭn ŏpta*, 2016), and E. J-yong (Yi Chae-yong)'s *The Bacchus Lady* (*Chukyŏjunŭn yŏja*, 2016), helped bring about a "critical social turn" and are "more concerned with intimate relations that bind various social others together."[40] Instead of celebrating dating or marriage equality, self-identification (coming out), and social acceptance, this new group of films fundamentally challenges "the value of the normative family structure and [envisions] a more radical type of kinship."[41]

While a diversification of what Unsang Kim calls the "queer cinemascapes in South Korea"[42] is undoubtedly an encouraging trend from the perspective of genre studies scholars, the receding of openly LGBTQ characters from the center of the new queer cinema can also be read as a troubling phenomenon within the current political zeitgeist. This concern has been on our minds lately, especially after we gained insights from our conversations with human rights activists and practitioners such as Kim Min-a, a film production manager at the National Human Rights Commission of Korea (NHRCK; Kukka ingwŏn wiwŏnhoe), whose interview we cited in chapter 1. In that interview, conducted on December 22, 2015, we asked Kim about the public backlash against the NHRCK's films, and she referred to conservative Christian organizations' complaints about the "Lie" episode in *If You Were Me: Anima Vision 2* (*Pyŏlpyŏl iyagi*, 2008)—a short segment about contract marriages between gay men and lesbian women. Detractors were in an uproar over that episode, taking issue with a public institution that was, in Kim's paraphrase, "promoting homosexuality." We followed up by asking Kim where LGBTQ rights fell in the ranking of the most challenging issues being championed by human rights advocates (compared to the subject of migrants' rights, for example). She responded that while hate speech against migrants continues to flare up in the public sphere (and has been reported by the press), explicit racism and xenophobia are, for the most part, stigmatized and self-censored among the general population.[43] However, homophobic hatred continues to be freely and openly expressed, as shown by highly visible street demonstrations that bring together members of "morally upright" religious and civic groups, united in their stand against same-sex relations. Kim pessimistically added, "coming out is not an option for most LGBTQ individuals" in South Korea, given how conservative the social climate there currently is.

The subaltern status of LGBTQ rights within the larger corpus of human rights discourse is likewise evident in legislative battles and homophobic lobbying surrounding a comprehensive antidiscrimination bill (*ch'abyŏl kŭmjibŏp*), which the NHRCK recommended in 2006 to the liberal administration of President Roh Moo-hyun (No Mu-hyŏn) and which the Ministry of Justice (Pŏmmubu) announced in 2007. The bill was originally conceived of as including twenty protection categories (including military service status, national origin, ethnicity, race, skin color, language, family status, sexual orientation, educational background, and criminal background), but due to opposition from the religious right, the ministry dropped seven categories—the most controversial of which is sexual orientation—before submitting the bill to the National Assembly (Kukhoe). The legislature failed to pass the bill in 2007. Between 2008 and 2013 it was reintroduced five times (with the sexual orientation protection reinserted) and again failed to pass. In 2013, legislators from the Democratic Party of Korea who had reintroduced the bill were forced to withdraw it as a result of organized lobbying from Protestant church members and pastors (who criticized the bill for advocating homosexuality and suppressing the constitutional rights to free speech and religious freedom). Currently, both the administration of President Moon Jae-in and the NHRCK are maintaining a kind of detached silence, effectively avoiding having to spell out their official position on suspended legislation for fear of the political repercussions likely to arise from mentioning such controversial subjects. As Hong Sŏng-su, a law professor at Sookmyung Women's University, aptly states, "People think that it will hurt their support ratings if they so much as mention the word 'discrimination.'"[44]

Even if the comprehensive antidiscrimination bill were to pass by some legislative miracle, it would be difficult to change public opinion or the mass consciousness of South Korea overnight without persistent educational and cultural efforts. If one were to turn to the United States (another Protestant-majority nation), where same-sex marriage was legalized in 2015, as a source for inspiration, the "normalization" of LGBTQ characters on prime-time TV programs such as *Will & Grace* (NBC, 1998–2006 and 2017) has played a crucial role in influencing public attitudes toward homosexuality. In 2012, on NBC's *Meet the Press*, then–vice president Joe Biden (who as a senator in 1996 had voted for the discriminatory Defense of Marriage Act) publicly supported same-sex marriage and credited *Will & Grace*, a popular sitcom about the friendship of two characters (a gay corporate lawyer and his best friend, a straight female interior designer), "as having done more to shift public perception on the issue than anything else."[45] Although much shorter-lived than *Will & Grace*, SBS's *Life Is Beautiful* (*Insaeng ŭn arŭmdawŏ*, 2010) was just as groundbreaking in terms of its sustained focus on a romantic gay couple: T'ae-sŏp (Song Ch'ang-ŭi), a doctor, and Kyŏng-su (Yi Sang-u), a divorced photographer. T'ae-sŏp is the oldest son of the Yang family, which runs a resort motel on Jeju Island. His father is a retired civil servant who remarried after the death of T'ae-sŏp's mother. His stepmother had also married before and has a daughter from a previous marriage. T'ae-sŏp's grandparents, parents, uncles, and four siblings (as well as his stepsister's husband and daughter) all live together. T'ae-sŏp's sexual difference is introduced as one of the many conflictual factors in this otherwise traditional Korean family drama, an obstacle that tests and ultimately reaffirms the characters' strong familial bond. As one might have anticipated at the time of its broadcast, the TV drama's prominent LGBTQ content drew criticism from religious groups, whose members ran homophobic newspaper ads (including one with the headline "SBS Should Be Responsible If My Son Turns Gay and Dies from AIDS after Watching *Life Is Beautiful*") that blamed the broadcaster for beautifying homosexuality and leading "impressionable" young people astray.[46] The cast and crew members were asked to leave a Catholic cathedral while shooting a private engagement ceremony between two gay lovers, and the broadcaster decided not to air the partial footage they had shot.[47] Despite such setbacks, the writer for *Life Is Beautiful*, Kim Su-hyŏn, was honored with the Rainbow Human Rights Award from Ch'ingusai, a gay human rights organization, in recognition of her commitment to "correcting prejudice about sexual minorities among viewers."[48]

A decade has elapsed since this hot-button television drama aired (with an average rating of 20 percent). A decade and a half has gone by since Leesong's *No Regret* broke Korean independent cinema's box-office record. However, the rekindled political debate over the antidiscrimination bill attests to the fact that the path to equality is fraught with obstacles, though eventual passage of the bill is not impossible. The recent "critical social turn" in South Korean queer cinemascapes might lead to increased acceptance on the part of mainstream audiences, who are more sympathetic toward the general understanding of social marginality and unconventional family formation than they are to the specific human rights claims and commitments of LGBTQ communities. In a recent interview with *Hankyoreh 21*, Kimjo, who participated in the first same-sex public wedding ceremony (in 2013) and filed unsuccessful lawsuits demanding official recognition of his marriage to Kim Sŭng-hwan, states, "Coming out is the best solution to eradicate homophobia. There is a huge difference between those who have close gay friends and those who do not. . . . The moment you come out, you gain self-recognition and you can also change people around you. In this respect, coming out is the most difficult yet the easiest way to change society."[49] If the goal of new queer cinema is to change society and help foster a tolerant environment in which antidiscrimination legislation and equal rights can be accepted without resistance, then perhaps including a greater number of LGBTQ characters on screen as people who are extraordinary in their ordinariness—and whom mass audiences can identify with or simply envision as their friends or family members—might well be its most pressing agenda.

Part 3

Disability Rights in Mainstream and Minoritarian Filmmaking

5

Always, *Blind*, and *Silenced*

Disability Discourses in Contemporary South Korean Cinema

In recent years, several South Korean films documenting or dramatizing the lives of people with disabilities have garnered local and global attention. They include the art-house feature *Oasis* (*Oasisŭ*, 2002) from director Lee Chang-dong (Yi Chang-dong), which earned the actor Moon So-ri (Mun So-ri) critical accolades and festival awards for her portrayal of a woman with cerebral palsy (*noesŏng mabi*); and the mainstream production *Marathon* (*Malat'on*, 2005) from Chŏng Yun-ch'ŏl. The latter film, a box-office hit with over five million admissions in South Korea, tells the story of Ch'o-wŏn, a young man with autism (*chap'yejŭng*) who is a diegetic stand-in for the real-life long-distance runner Pae Hyŏng-jin. *Marathon*'s commercial success, mimicking the protagonist's triumphant display of athletic prowess by narrative's end, made it possible for other previously risky subjects and marginalized figures to take center stage in subsequent features, as demonstrated by the theatrical release of *Silenced* (*Dogani*, 2011), a disturbing motion picture from the director Hwang Tong-hyŏk that brought to light an actual case of sexual abuse that dates back to 2000 and involved children and administrators at a school for hearing-impaired students in Kwangju, South Korea.

FIGURE 5.1 Hwang Tong-hyŏk's *Silenced* (*Dogani*, 2011) is one of the few recent South Korean productions to feature a human rights activist as a main character. Here, a young woman named Yu-jin (Chŏng Yu-mi) assists the male protagonist—a recently hired schoolteacher named In-ho—in bringing a case of sexual abuse to light, acting as a literal spokesperson for a trio of deaf kids who are largely silent in the presence of adults.

In the first half of this chapter, we seek to explain how *Silenced* and other Korean-language films (including Song Il-gon's 2011 romantic drama, *Always* [*Ojik kŭdaeman*], and An Sang-hun's 2011 crime thriller, *Blind* [*Pŭllaindŭ*]) highlight a problematic tendency in contemporary disability rights cinema, which can be considered a subset of human rights cinema. While certainly well-intentioned in terms of their paternalistic privileging of individuals and groups that challenge normative (able-bodied) understandings of character-based drama or documentary filmmaking, such productions reflect an infantilizing tendency in popular culture more generally. That is, in the words of Kenneth L. Robey, Linda Beckley, and Matthew Kirschner, they reproduce "implicit (unconscious) attitudes" that "associate disability with child-like features."[1] In bringing to the fore a trio of deaf kids (Min-su [Paek Sŭng-hwan], Yŏn-du [Kim Hyŏn-su], and Yu-ri [Chŏng In-sŏ]) only to have them recede into the background once two able-bodied adults (Kang In-ho [Kong Yu], the main character, and a human rights activist named Sŏ Yu-jin [Chŏng Yu-mi]) take up their fight as the basis for a lawsuit, *Silenced* unfortunately silences individuals who are doubly marginalized, owing to their young age as well as their perceived lack (of hearing or of full mental capabilities) (see figure 5.1). Simply stated, the children in this film become objects rather than subjects of disability rights discourse.

This representational schema would seem to align with what Janet Lord, May Sabatello, Duane Stroman, and other disability scholars refer to as the standard medical approach to the topic, which sees disability as a sickness, a childlike helplessness (regardless of the person's age) that results from an inability to do something, a marked deficit in one's physical or mental performance. As Lord states, such an approach "leaves out of the equation a more holistic understanding . . . beyond medical intervention that situates the disadvantages associated with disability as a social phenomenon."[2] After all, as one of the teachers (who has been at the school for ten years) tells In-ho, "There's something *strange* about these kids"—reductively concluding that he and his colleagues should not think of them as "normal." "A disability in the body leads to an impairment in mentality," he states flatly, articulating in the process the simplistic and pervasive notion that corporeal and psychological problems are not only linked but also the root of societal problems (rather than vice versa). This notion accords with Jane Erin's argument concerning the stereotypes that inform many people's misunderstanding of disability. She states: "When a disability affects competence in one area, the individual may be assumed to be incompetent in all ways. The common tendency to treat those with disabilities as childlike or to assume that they cannot make their own decisions is one example."[3]

Moreover, in *Silenced* Min-su, Yŏn-du, and Yu-ri open up to In-ho and Yu-jin, sharing their traumatic experiences of sexual abuse, only to have those stories taken away, appropriated, and absorbed into the legalese that emerges once criminal prosecution begins and the children become doubly victimized objects of pity rather than subjects of agency and self-determination. However, *Silenced* at least gestures toward what the abovementioned scholars call the "social model" of disability, in which silence itself—whether of impaired individuals or of the wider community that permits prejudicial policies and discriminatory practices to continue—is part of the oppressive landscape in which people with disabilities are forced to live.

Before textually unpacking the themes and representational strategies of *Silenced*, we situate the film in two contexts: that of disability rights cinema and that of disability rights discourse, which has largely been split into medical and social paradigms. In doing so, we refer to other motion pictures that conform to some of the tropes typically found in human rights cinema. These two contextual zones are part of a third epistemological frame, an overarching legal structure that has been pieced together over the years at both global and local levels—starting in the 1970s, when the U.N. General Assembly issued its first nonbinding declarations and resolutions concerning the rights of people with disabilities and including more recent efforts in South Korea and elsewhere to formalize rights-protection policies through welfare laws and international conventions. Venturing into this textual and contextual analysis necessitates a look at the manner in which *Silenced* has been received by Korean audiences since its September 22, 2011, theatrical release. As we elaborate below, the film has had a significant impact not only on the general public but also on government officials, including legislators in the National Assembly (Kukhoe) who passed a revised law (named the Dogani Law after the motion picture) a mere two months after the film's release (as we discussed in chapter 1). That important piece of legislation, which calls for heavier punishments (including longer prison terms, up to life sentences) for offenders convicted of abusing children and people with disabilities, will doubtless ensure the legacy of a widely celebrated cultural production that nevertheless demands scrutiny as a troubling example of disability cinema's infantilizing impulse.

Disability Discourses in South Korea: From Welfare Support to Human Rights Protection

Before delving into our main case studies, it will be helpful to first consider the status of people with disabilities in South Korea. Data from the 2011 National Survey on Persons with Disabilities indicate that an estimated 2,683,400 people are reported to be living with disabilities in South Korea.[4] In a country with a population of roughly fifty million, that national share (5 percent) falls considerably short of the global share (10 percent), which suggests that official records underestimate the actual number of people living with disabilities.[5] Indeed, as the Korean film scholar Chung Wan Woo points out, "a higher numeric figure, ranging from five to seven million," is more accurate and should be used by scholars in the fields of both disability studies and media studies.[6] Why is there such a disparity between official records and unofficial accounts? In his study of *Oasis* and *Marathon*, Woo acknowledges several factors, including Korean parents' "unwillingness to register their children as disabled at an early age" and a general "lack of awareness about the registration process," despite the government's recent, much-publicized efforts to raise public consciousness and introduce legislation that addresses various needs in South Korea's disparate disability communities.

The South Korean government's first effort to provide legislative support to disabled citizens dates back to the 1961 Livelihood Protection Act (Saenghwal pohobŏp), which purported to safeguard the general well-being of people who might otherwise sink into poverty due to disability. It would take another twenty years before a major shift in Korean policies took place—a change that occurred in 1981, proclaimed by the United Nations as the International Year of Disabled Persons. South Korea joined other nations in responding to the United Nations's call for "equalization of opportunities, rehabilitation and prevention of disabilities"[7] and promulgated the Welfare for Persons with Physical and Mental Disabilities Act (Simsinchangaeja pokchibŏp). As Dong Chul You and Se Kwang Hwang point out, because of the act's focus on medical and vocational rehabilitation, it benefited individuals "living in institutions"[8] more than people with disabilities who were not institutionalized and had different needs. Moreover, its binding power as law is questionable since it recommends rather than mandates the use of antidiscriminatory measures in employment. In 1984, after the International Coordinating Committee of the International Paralympic Games had selected Seoul as the host city of the 1988 Games, the Ministry of Health and Welfare (Pogŏnbokchibu) announced a plan to implement corporate quotas for disability employment. According to official statistics provided by the Ministry of Labor (Nodongbu) in 1985, 35 percent of South Korea's disabled population was unemployed, but the actual unemployment rate was estimated to be as high as 50 percent in the mid-1980s.[9] After a bill to promote disability employment was discarded by the National Assembly in 1984, the issue was not followed up legislatively despite presidential campaign promises made to disability groups after the 1987 June Uprising (a mass democratic protest movement that ended South Korea's military dictatorship and enabled a return to direct presidential elections). In April 1988, six months before the Paralympics (whose budget was four times larger than that of the total welfare budget for disabled people in South Korea), disability advocates voiced their frustrations and demands publicly, organizing street protests and hunger strikes in rehabilitation facilities.

With the formation of the National Association for People with Disabilities (Changaein ch'ongyŏnmaeng) in 1988, activists of various disability organizations consolidated their efforts and resources to focus on two legislative demands: the revision of the 1981 welfare act to increase benefits and protection and the enactment of a disability employment law. Grassroots activism was partly responsible for the 1989 comprehensive amendment of the Welfare for Persons with Disabilities Act (Changaein pokchibŏp), which expanded financial support for disabled people to include "social security pensions, medical cost allowance, children's education tuition fee allowance, mortgage and tax exemption."[10] Another major legislative victory was the 1990 Disability Employment Promotion Act (Changaein koyong ch'okchin tŭngae kwanhan pŏmnyul), which required employers with more than a hundred employees to hire disabled persons at a rate of 1–5 percent of the total workforce (flexibly accommodating activists' demand for a 2 percent employment quota). As You and Hwang note, *dangsajajuwei* (*tangsajajuŭi*, roughly translated as the principle of "self-determination" or "self-representation") emerged as a philosophical touchstone that has defined the Korean disability movement since the early 1990s. This principle was a latent element of the self-initiated movement (supported by sixty disability groups) launched in 2003 to enact a new antidiscrimination act that would adequately reflect "disabled people's experiences and opinions."[11] In 2007, the same year that a comprehensive antidiscrimination bill was abandoned in the National Assembly (as discussed in chapter 4), the Anti-Discrimination against and Remedies for Persons with Disabilities Act was passed; it was enacted in the following year. This groundbreaking piece of legislation signaled a marked progression of Korean disability policies from welfare support to human rights protection.

As Katharina Heyer points out, several human rights instruments have helped remedy the problem of the invisibility and exclusion of people with disabilities in recent years, most notably the Convention on the Rights of Persons with Disabilities, "which was adopted by the UN General Assembly with speed, enthusiasm, and consensus" on December 13, 2006. Before that landmark treaty, the 1993 Standard Rules on the Equalization of Opportunities for Persons with

Disabilities was the first far-reaching effort to progressively recognize people with disabilities as entitled "to enjoy all human rights in the same way as other members of the community."[12] Significantly, between 1998 and 2012, the South Korean government introduced three five-year plans that attempted to operationalize, at the local level, the laudable if still abstract ideals at the heart of the 1993 Standard Rules.[13] The first of these initiatives, effective in the period 1998–2002, expanded the range of welfare services provided to people with disabilities, allowing individuals in need of assistive devices (such as orthotics or prosthetics and wheelchairs) to have the costs of them and other rehabilitation-associated expenses covered through public funds. Not long after the introduction of this plan, cochlear implants (to assist people with hearing impairment) were included in the National Health Insurance benefits.[14] The second five-year plan (in effect in 2003–2007), building on the first, sought to make Korean society more inclusive and more amenable to the idea of active participation in the body politic by those who for so many years had been denied equal rights as citizens. Furthermore, that plan was designed to increase educational and professional opportunities for people with disabilities. The third five-year plan, effective in 2008–2012, built on the previous two plans by promoting job creation and proactive investments in disability communities. This plan also set out to restructure South Korea's welfare delivery system, bringing it into compliance with international standards and increasing the National Health Insurance's budget for physiotherapy and occupational therapy.[15] Since the introduction of these five-year plans, tremendous strides have been made to ensure that people with physical, sensory, and intellectual or developmental impairments are afforded the same opportunities given to nondisabled individuals.

Yet according to cumulative data provided in the 2016 annual report of the National Human Rights Commission of Korea (NHRCK; Kukka ingwŏn wiwŏnhoe), of the 23,410 complaints of discrimination received between November 2001 (when the NHRCK opened) and December 2016, 10,970 (46.9 percent) were related to disability. No other categories among twenty preselected reasons received 10,000 complaints. Coming a distant second in that list of reasons was sexual harassment (2,184, or 9.3 percent), followed by social status discrimination (1,904, or 8.1 percent).[16] This alarming fact appears to validate You and Hwang's comment that "while the Korean Disabled People's Movement has raised public awareness of disability, the traditional Korean culture, which praises physical perfection, has still largely failed to fully grasp the challenges of disability.... Definitions of disability and their effects on disabled people are still based on medical and cultural perspectives. Disability is traditionally conceived [of] as a tragic medical problem in Korea and it has been taken for granted that solving the issues relating to disability is the responsibility of the families of those affected."[17] In South Korea's "highly homogenized culture" (to borrow Woo's words), disability is still seen as "something undesirable."[18] Because it disrupts "the idea of harmonious interdependence (cooperation, solidarity, and oneness)" that Woo and other scholars see as part of a neo-Confucian Korean culture of conformity, disability presents a social problem that reflects long-held prejudices about those who do not "fit in."[19]

To what can we attribute this overwhelmingly negative public perception of disability in South Korea? In their 2003 article about Korean adolescents living with physical disability, Shin Jeong Kim and Kyung Ah Kang allude to "deep-rooted" superstitious beliefs that are a testament to the pervasiveness of "shamanistic thinking" in the country.[20] This line of reasoning corresponds with Weol Soon Kim-Rupnow's statement that "some Koreans believe disability can be caused by supernatural agents, such as punishment from God or the curse of the devil for their sins, or those of their parents, or even their ancestors"—in other words, disability can be an "imbalance of metaphysical forces" (*ŭmyang*).[21] But metaphysics or superstition alone do not adequately explain the long-standing prejudices that people with disability face in an economically developed, heavily industrialized country where the per capita gross domestic product and life expectancy rates have dramatically increased over the past half-century. The idea that individuals with disabilities "are less valued" in Korean society and "bring shame to their families" is likewise mentioned by Hyun-Kyung You and Lori McGraw in their study of motherhood and disability.[22] As You and McGraw acknowledge, for years the derogatory term *pyŏngsin* has frequently been used to denote disability. Depending on context, this colloquialism can mean anything from "dumbass" or "retard" to "crippled body" or "deformed person." A more sensitive, less dehumanizing expression (*changaein*) is preferred by Korean disability rights activists, even though this newer term carries various connotations (of individuals faced with "obstacles" and marked by "abnormality" or beset by "dysfunction") that can be construed as negative. A *changaeu*, or "friend with disabilities," might very well be recognized and respected as a person, but disability itself remains the locus of a "shameful experience" for both the individual and his or her family.[23]

Always: Infantilizing Feminine or Disabled Others

In the introduction to their edited volume *The Body and Physical Difference*, David Mitchell and Sharon Snyder provide a working definition of the term "disability," stating that it designates "cognitive and physical conditions that deviate from normative ideas of mental ability and physiological function."[24] In contrast to words like "crippled" and "handicapped"—which, as Mitchell and Snyder remind us, "suggest inherent biological limitations and individual abnormalities"—"disability" and its associated meanings hint at the "social, historical, political, and mythological coordinates that define disabled people as excessive to traditional social circuits of interaction and as the *objects* of institutionalized discourses."[25] Although it "defies precise definition and measurement,"[26] we have opted to use the word "disability" throughout this chapter when referring to a broad range of physical, sensory, and intellectual or developmental impairments that generally lack "the biological luxury of recovery,"[27] stretching it to accommodate representations of individuals with mental health problems, disorders on the autism spectrum, emotional disorders, speech disorders, hearing impairments, vision impairments, and other health and learning challenges that are visible or invisible facets of those individuals' identities. As a catchall signifier,[28] the term brings together the functional limitations or obstacles faced by people with disabilities and the reduction of opportunities that results from the attitudinal and societal barriers placed before them as they journey toward inclusion and equality—journeys that, when cinematically depicted, are frequently sensationalized or sentimentalized.

As stated above, the subject of disability has gained increased prominence in a variety of Korean cultural productions over the past two decades, with independent artists and mainstream filmmakers alike contributing to this contemporary phenomenon. Besides *Silenced*, other contemporary Korean-language films dealing with potentially debilitating forms of sensory impairment include *Sopyonje* (*Sŏp'yŏnje*, 1993), *Sympathy for Mr. Vengeance* (*Poksunŭn naŭi kŏt*, 2002), *Au Revoir, UFO* (*Annyŏng! Yuep'ŭo*, 2004), *The King and the Clown* (*Wangŭi namja*, 2005), *Love Me Not* (*Sarang ttawin p'ilyo ŏpsŏ*, 2006), *No Mercy for the Rude* (*Yeŭiŏmnŭn kŏtdŭl*, 2006), *Blades of Blood* (*Kurŭmŭl pŏsŏnan talch'ŏrŏm*, 2010), *The Recipe* (*Toenjang*, 2010), *Glove* (*Kŭlrŏbŭ*, 2011), *Themselves* (*Pada*, 2011), *Planet of Snail* (*Talp'aengiŭi pyŏl*, 2011), *Wind on the Moon* (*Talae punŭn param*, 2015), and *Miracles on the Piano* (*Kijŏkŭi p'iano*, 2015). Regardless of whether deaf or blind characters in these generically diverse motion pictures are protagonists or merely secondary characters who play minor supporting roles in the diegesis, for the most part the social dimension of disability is not the point on which narrative content pivots. With few exceptions, even in those rare cases in which characters with sensory impairments are given more than a modicum of screen time, disability is largely treated as an "isolated phenomenon" that is "a matter of individual fortitude, will-power, and perseverance," in the words of Mitchell and Snyder.[29] Summarizing the earlier arguments of Paul Longmore, the authors state that most films dealing with the subject of disability fail to delve into "questions of social accommodation," opting instead to use disability "as a sop to our beleaguered cultural consciences by assuring the viewer that the problem is a largely isolated affair that needs to be treated one disorder at a time."[30]

This representational tendency is particularly salient in the 2011 film *Always*, a generically titled romantic drama about a generically attractive twentysomething couple—a brooding boxer and a blind woman—who first meet inside a tiny pay booth at a parking garage (a claustrophobic space that is itself indicative of the isolating tendency in South Korea's disability cinema). Chang Ch'ŏl-min (So Chi-sŏp), the struggling pugilist, has recently taken over the night shift as a parking attendant. We initially see him whiling away his working hours by watching boxing matches on the small TV inside the booth. The accomplishments of the onscreen fighters stand in stark contrast to his own history of failures, and his deadened stare at the screen suggests that he has given up all hope of attaining professional success inside the ring.

At this point—a mere three minutes into the film—a young woman bursts onto the scene, interrupting his viewing and thrusting sweet jellies and tangerines into his hands. "I even brought soju," she whispers into his face, before giggling, "I can see that you're really impressed." As soon as the young man, who is clearly confused, opens his mouth to speak (asking about the stranger's identity), the woman, whom we later learn is a telemarketer named Ha Chŏng-hwa (Han Hyŏ-ju), changes her demeanor from childlike enthusiasm to startled apprehension. She has mistaken Ch'ŏl-min for the previous parking attendant, a much older man who has recently retired. In fact, Chŏng-hwa has not seen Ch'ŏl-min at all, and her blindness in this and subsequent scenes indicates a rather indelicate use of sensory impairment on the part of the director, Song Il-gon. That is, Chŏng-hwa's inability to visually discern the individual who, because of their forced proximity inside the pay booth, is literally inches away from her, is introduced in the opening minutes of *Always* as a way to generate romantic tension and laughter (before audiences have developed a connection to her and an understanding of her tragic backstory). Humor thus results from the sight of someone whose lack of sight puts spectators on the side of the male protagonist, who gazes curiously and voyeuristically at Chŏng-hwa. After this scene, Ch'ŏl-min adopts a paternalistic, protective role vis-à-vis an excessively infantilized woman whom he will grow to love over the course of this cliché-ridden, saccharine narrative.

Indeed, subsequent scenes show Ch'ŏl-min habitually rushing to Chŏng-hwa's aid or defense (fending off a violent male attacker at one point), and these acts of demonstrable heroism are a convenient way for him to reclaim his masculine prowess as a boxer and lover. Further conforming to gender stereotypes, Chŏng-hwa is "sweetness personified," to borrow the words of one critic, who writes that this indomitable female character "won't allow a handicap [to] dampen her vivaciousness."[31] Throughout *Always*, femininity and childlike naiveté veer dangerously close to one another—a rhetorical maneuver undertaken not only by the filmmaker but also by the film's many critics, who might point derisively toward its melodramatic conventions and sappy sentimentality while still referring to Chŏng-hwa as a "blind girl" rather than a blind woman.[32]

In this and many other examples of disability cinema, "heroes" and "victims" proliferate, becoming implausible narrative linchpins that correspond to long-entrenched cultural clichés about individuals who are paradoxically "better than" yet also "less than" the normative model of able-bodied agency. By narrativizing and stabilizing impairment in this way, accentuating the childlike cuteness of the female protagonist, and locating the romantic couple in a cordoned-off space relatively free from other sociopolitical entanglements (aside from debt collectors and bounty hunters), *Always* sentimentalizes and trivializes the subject, linking it, in the words of Lennard Davis, "to the bourgeois sensibility of individualism and the drama of an individual story."[33] Thus, "we do not perceive experiences of disability as . . . generated by the social environment,"[34] but instead come to understand disability abstractly, as something that must be personally overcome or dealt with before heterosexual love can reach its cinematic apotheosis (which, in *Always*, culminates with an act of self-sacrifice, as Ch'ŏl-min helps Chŏng-hwa to pay for an expensive eye operation that restores her sight). As we explain below, Hwang Tong-hyŏk (the director of the more noble but no less problematic *Silenced*) adopted some of the same generic tropes and representational strategies used in *Always*. But Hwang did so in ways that actually inspired human rights advocacy and social change in the public sphere, a result that few cultural productions can claim. Besides pointing toward *Silenced*, the above discussion lends contextualizing depth to another film that was theatrically released in 2011: a taut, ostensibly apolitical crime thriller that seems to offer little of substance beyond satisfying the criteria of the genre. However, as a motion picture that is partially concerned with the academic and occupational opportunities afforded to differently abled individuals, director An Sang-hun's *Blind* deserves at least passing consideration for its contribution to disability discourses.

Blind: Double Victimhood and Mastery as Maturation

The main character in *Blind* is Min Su-a (Kim Ha-nŭl), a young police cadet whose promising career in law enforcement is cut short when she loses her eyesight. That event, the tragic outcome of a highway accident that also took her brother's life, is depicted in the film's opening sequence. Significantly, those first few minutes of *Blind* establish the double victimhood of the female protagonist, as she not only experiences sensory loss but is forced to cope with the traumatizing death of a loved one. Her trauma is laced with guilt, for she had handcuffed her brother's arm to one of the roof handles inside the car, making it impossible for him to escape when the vehicle fell from a city bridge. Following that expository opening, another extended sequence, which takes place three years later, begins with her waking from sleep, suiting up her guide dog, Sŭl-gi, and setting out to be readmitted to the police academy. Having been released from her post during her convalescence, Su-a is eager to return to the life she once knew, but she acknowledges to the director of the program that she does not expect to be put back on the "front lines." Interrupting her speech, Su-a's former superior—staring at the blind woman in shocked disbelief—explains that she had not been expelled because of her disability. "It *wasn't* because you are *blind*," he insists, but rather because "you no longer qualify to be an officer." "You left without permission during training," he grumbles, before reminding her that she bears responsibility for her brother's accidental death. Overlaying an exterior shot of Su-a walking sadly away from the building, the director's patronizing voice-over concludes that there is nothing he can do (that is, he cannot help her). His condescending statement positions the protagonist as a person in need (despite her apparent self-sufficiency), someone for whom special accommodations would have to be made if she is to reclaim her former position.

With the academy director's words still stuck in her mind, the distracted woman begins to cross the street. At this point (the first of many such occasions in the film), the screen goes black, as if plunging the spectator into the sensory-deprived psyche of a depressed character who relies on assistive technologies to navigate the world. Oddly, the soundtrack also becomes murky, with the environmental noises surrounding Su-a now muffled. The darkness and near silence are suddenly interrupted by the sound of a blaring horn and the image of screeching car nearly colliding with her. Honking madly at the woman, the male driver is so irate that he calls her a *pyŏngsin* ("retard"). "If you can't see anything, stay home," the man yells at her from inside his vehicle, before speeding off. Confused, Su-a pivots on her feet, rushes back to the sidewalk, and falls to the ground, scraping her leg in the process. This scene, similar to a moment in *Always* when Chŏng-hwa is nearly hit by a car at the parking garage, thus culminates with the image of a vision-impaired woman taking a spill and experiencing pain in the social sphere (that is, falling in full view of others), far removed from the comfort and relative safety of her apartment.

Tellingly, the next scene shows Su-a at home, receiving a phone call from her doting "mother" (actually, the director of the orphanage where Su-a grew up). The older woman, who is planning a visit, tells Su-a not to cook anything, as doing so might risk yet another injury. Not heeding the older woman's advice, Su-a burns her hand while heating milk on the stove. Even the domestic sphere, it seems, is fraught with danger. The purpose of this and many other moments in *Blind* is to showcase the protagonist's tenacity while also reminding audiences that she has a long way to go before gaining the confidence and skills required to be a police officer. But this scene, capped with a shot of Su-a, now-bandaged, giggling while wrestling playfully with her dog, also demonstrates the need for this childish character to grow up—a maturation process, enacted over the course of the narrative, that problematically reproduces the infantilizing tendencies in so much of South Korea's disability cinema.

That maturation process begins once Su-a becomes embroiled in a crime case, a series of murders involving a psychopathic gynecologist (masquerading as a taxi driver) and his female victims (see figure 5.2). From the moment she is picked up by the homicidal cabbie until the film's concluding scenes, which show her miraculously graduating from the police academy one year after the mystery has been solved (thanks in large part to her independent investigation), the plot of *Blind* focuses on the victim-hero dyad that is such an entrenched facet of the disability genre. In fact, at times the female protagonist's heroism can be read as superheroism, as when Su-a informs an incredulous policeman, Detective Cho (Cho Hŭi-bong), that she can discern a person's height and physique simply from the sound and reverberation of his or her voice. During that scene (which occurs thirty minutes into the film), Su-a explains that she can tell what Cho ate for

FIGURE 5.2 In director An Sang-hun's 2011 thriller *Blind* (*Pŭllaindŭ*), the social dimensions of disability are sidelined in favor of showing the female protagonist, Su-a (Kim Ha-nŭl), getting embroiled in a suspense-filled crime plot. Throughout the second half of the film, she is stalked by a mysterious man who has been masquerading as a taxi driver.

lunch (black bean noodles) from the smell of his breath, even though she is seated at a distance from him. Her mastery of these other senses (hearing, smell, and touch) is what eventually leads to the arrest of Myŏng-jin (Yang Yŏng-jo), the serial killer whom she first met (that is, heard and smelled) when he picked her up in a luxury taxi—one with fine leather seats that, to her fingers, felt distinctly different from those in a normal taxi.

This kind of "impairment vitalism" (to borrow the words of Jan Grue) is not specific to Korean disability cinema: there is a long history of films that visually and verbally encode the "disabled" as the "super-abled," culminating most recently with a wave of Hollywood action films based on Marvel and DC comic book franchises that include *X-Men* (2000) and *Daredevil* (2003).[35] What may set Su-a apart from the superheroes in those U.S. productions is the correlation between mastery and maturation, as if the woman is able to overcome her girliness (or her infantilizing cuteness) only by learning to harness the hypersensitized abilities (such as superhearing and supersmelling) that will serve her well as a police officer in the years to come. Tellingly, once she has received her degree and had her photograph taken by her "mother" (the director of the orphanage) outside the police academy, the signifying elements of the film conspire to return her to figurative childhood in its closing seconds. She is a girl once more, posing for a celebratory photo next to Ki-sŏp (Yu Sŭng-ho), a young man who was an eyewitness to the crimes and who stands in for her missing brother in the film's final shot: a freeze frame accompanied by a mawkishly sentimental melody swelling up on the soundtrack. In this and other contemporary motion pictures, the infantilizing impulse operates on a metaphorical level as adults with disabilities are made into childlike emblems of vulnerability and victimhood. However, another important cultural production from 2011—the controversial *Silenced*—foregrounds the plights of actual young people. As we show below, the hearing-impaired kids in this film are the literal embodiments of rights violations as well as allegorical reminders that such abuses often fall on deaf ears in a society that, ironically, has grown accustomed to cultural representations of disability.

Silenced: Seeing through the Fog

As indicated above, the origins of *Silenced*, a film produced by Samgŏri Pictures and distributed by CJ Entertainment, are to be found in South Korea's recent history of human rights violations. According to police reports, beginning in 2000 a group of deaf-mute children at Inhwa School in the city of Kwangju were habitually subjected to sexual abuse by teachers and administrators. At least nine students were brutally raped by staff members over a four-year period, and many other children experienced various forms of mistreatment (if not outright molestation) before a formal investigation was launched by local authorities in 2005. Representatives of the Kwangju Sexual Violence Counseling Center initiated that inquiry, responding to a single plea for help from a newly hired teacher who was especially shocked to discover such abuses occurring at an educational center that was designed to assist children with disabilities. A subsequent trial resulted in the indictment of two school officials (including an executive administrator, the school founder's son, who had sexually molested six students ages 7–20), who were found guilty of assaulting minors. However, despite gaining national notoriety thanks to a November 1, 2005, investigative network news program broadcast on MBC (Munhwa Broadcasting Corporation), and despite the fact that several residents of Kwangju staged a sit-in for eight months outside municipal offices, the case quickly evaporated from public consciousness outside of the city. Equally speedy were the prison terms of the two accused (a rehabilitation teacher and the abovementioned administrator), who received jail sentences of only two years and one year, respectively. As discussed in the introduction, in 2006, the NHRCK's investigation revealed that four additional individuals, including the school headmaster, were responsible for abusing children, and two of them faced trials in the following year. But as Evan Ramstad and Sooah Shin explain in their coverage of the events, "the two received suspended sentences on the grounds they had reached 'an agreement' with the parents of the victims."[36] Not until the 2011 theatrical release of *Silenced* did Koreans across the country become truly involved in this case, which was reopened by the

Kwangju Metropolitan Police Agency that November, leading to additional charges of sexual harassment, assault, negligence, or misuse of public funds being made against fourteen educators.[37]

Tied to those historical events but also based on a 2009 online novel of the same title by Gong Ji-young (Kong Chi-yŏng), *Silenced* is set in the fictional, mist-shrouded town of Mujin rather than Kwangju. Like Gong's story, the film begins with the main character, Kang In-ho, driving from Seoul to that small town, where he will begin work as an art teacher at the ironically named Benevolence Academy (Chaae hakwŏn), a school for hearing-impaired students. As his car travels through the thick fog, which the author describes as clinging to the vehicle like "a witch's white hair,"[38] this opening scene crosscuts to the image of a young boy walking along train tracks. His nose is bloodied, and he appears to have been harmed. He is alone and looks despondent. Meanwhile, In-ho seems distracted, chatting with his mother on his cell phone and swerving to avoid an oncoming truck with blinding lights as his vehicle enters a tunnel. The boy, too, makes his way into a tunnel, standing squarely on the icy tracks as a high-speed train barrels toward him. His suicide, timed to correspond with a shot of In-ho accidentally hitting and killing a deer (significantly, a young doe), is sudden and shocking. But the correspondence of those two deaths suggests that the child, who is later revealed to be a student who had been abused at Benevolence Academy, is as vulnerable and voiceless as the animal—a rhetorical equivalency that foregrounds this film's general approach to disabled youth.

As a point of contrast, the main character in Gong's novel is not so much distracted by a phone call from his mother as lost in thought about his own earlier experiences as an adolescent:

> Kang couldn't have said why, but for some reason he recalled the time many summers ago that he had almost drowned. He had been fishing, and he could still remember the sticky, slimy feel of the vegetation on his bare legs when he had jumped into the reservoir to retrieve the fishing rod that had been pulled from his grasp. The way the water weeds clung to him he felt as though they would swallow up everything, and instead of swimming back to shore he had called to his friend for help. The energy had drained out of him, and even though he knew how to swim, he felt paralyzed. That this memory had suddenly surfaced just now gave him a bad feeling. He stiffened, overcome with a brief surge of terror: if he wasn't careful, this journey might be the end of him.[39]

Tellingly, this passage introduces the themes of trauma and foreboding, collapsing past and future. But rather than channel that traumatic experience through the cognitive lens of one of the many children being exploited and sexually molested at Benevolence Academy, the novel presents it through the psyche of an adult reflecting back on his life, recalling a moment from his past when he felt helpless.

It is worth pointing out that the geographic relocation of the narrative is one of the many creative liberties that both the novelist and the filmmaker took when cinematically translating true events for online and cinematic consumption. By setting the story of deaf children's rights violations in Mujin, Gong and Hwang draw upon the accumulated lore surrounding that culturally mythologized place, which is best known to Koreans as the eponymous locale in Kim Sŭng-ok's 1964 novella *Record of a Journey to Mujin* (*Mujin kihaeng*). Kim purportedly modeled that locale on his hometown, Sunch'ŏn, a remote fishing village in South Chŏlla Province that is accessible mainly by train or boat. Once that literary text was adapted into a film three years later—director Kim Su-yong's *Mist* (*Angae*, 1967)—audiences began to associate Mujin with the avoidance of shame and regret, the painful traumas or ugly realities that must remain hidden beneath a blanket of gray melancholy.

This explains the allegorical implications of the fog in *Silenced*, which can be said to represent a collective unwillingness on the part of the townspeople to acknowledge the depths of human despair at Benevolence Academy. It is at the deaf school that children have been molested by the headmaster, a respected member of the community named Kang-bok (Chang Kwang), who has police officers on his payroll. Indeed, by the time the narrative concludes, the vaporous clouds that were introduced in the first scenes (showing In-ho driving to his destination and careening into a deer) have become a distinguishing feature of the town and the film. Tellingly, in the penultimate scene of *Silenced*, after having successfully fought for the rights of children whose voices would not otherwise be heard, In-ho leaves Mujin and returns to Seoul, only to encounter a subway poster promoting the touristic appeals of that now-tainted place. The poster reads: "Come to Mujin. City of white fog." Mujin is tainted because it serves as the backdrop for a series of tragic events that robbed students of their innocence and set off a firestorm of controversy once the participants—the pedophilic headmaster, his twin brother, and the school superintendent—were brought before a jury of their peers, only to be given light sentences.

The film's narrative centerpiece is the lengthy courtroom sequence that begins at its midpoint, after In-ho has witnessed firsthand the abuses occurring at the school and gathered evidence from the children's tearful pretrial testimonies (videotaped at the Mujin Human Rights Center). Working with a human rights activist named Sŏ Yu-jin, who assists him in bringing the abuses to light, the protagonist has spent much of the first half of the film acting as a literal spokesperson for the kids, vocalizing their traumatic experiences and initiating legal proceedings on their behalf. In court, however, he becomes a passive audience member (see figure 5.3), forced to silently look on as the demonstrative defense attorney makes one of the children, Yu-ri, wet herself while seated on the witness stand. Another young girl, Yŏn-du, has her testimony challenged when she indicates, through sign language, that she could actually hear music playing when she stumbled upon the headmaster raping Yu-ri, her friend. To determine if

FIGURE 5.3 In a legal setting that is central to the genre of the human rights film, *Silenced* shows the male protagonist, In-ho (Kong Yu), sitting alongside children in a courtroom.

Yŏn-du is lying, the judge has the young girl take a hearing test in court (which she passes), with the soundtrack's lowered volume conveying her perceptual limitations. These occurrences, in addition to an earlier courtroom scene in which Yu-jin is forced to remind the apparently oblivious judge that a sign-language interpreter is needed for audience members in the courtroom who cannot hear, illustrate the institutional failures of a society and legal system that have not yet determined how to fairly treat persons with disabilities. Or, rather, the South Korean government's implementation of rights-protection policies and adherence to international conventions leave much to be desired, if *Silenced* is an accurate representation of what transpired in Kwangju a decade ago.

Significantly, the film's social field opens up and introduces additional voices once the court proceedings end and public outrage begins to fuel street demonstrations outside the courthouse. That outrage is a result of the reduced jail time given to the headmaster and his brother, but is also a response to the revenge suicide of Min-su (the elder brother of the boy who was seen killing himself in the film's opening). Near the end of the film and like his younger brother, Min-su throws himself (along with his rapist teacher, charges against whom have been unjustly dropped) in the path of an oncoming train. In the protest scene that follows, amid the cacophony of voices yelling on behalf of the deaf children, In-ho, dazed and doused with a violent spray of water, holds the dead student's portrait and repeats the words, "This boy cannot hear or speak. His name is Min-su. He cannot hear or speak. This boy's name is Min-su. He cannot hear or speak. Please. His name is Min-su. He cannot hear or speak. . . ." In the seconds leading up to this moment, before the police have turned their hoses on the unruly crowd, protesters rush the vehicle carrying the corrupt prosecutor and defense lawyer. They throw eggs at the car, and Yu-jin beats her fists against the window, as if trying to break the glass.

This is the third occasion in which spectatorial attention is directed toward a car window, a barrier between interior and exterior that, with enough effort, can be breached. The first occasion occurs much earlier in the film, when Yu-jin gives In-ho a ride from a repair shop (where he has dropped off his car after a collision with a deer) to Benevolence Academy. He shivers in the passenger's seat of her ramshackle van, property of the Mujin Human Rights Center, and asks her why one of the windows has been broken. Yu-jin explains that a stranger attempted to break into the van one night but ran away before she could catch him. The second occasion takes place after the midpoint of the film, when In-ho expresses his mounting anger by breaking the driver's side window of his former professor's sedan only minutes after the old man—the mentor who had recommended In-ho for the teaching job at the deaf school—has tried unsuccessfully to bribe him with money in the hope of keeping him silent. This visual motif of car windows being shattered, when positioned alongside the abovementioned moment when Yu-jin tries desperately to break through the glass of the lawyer's automobile, lends imagistic support to the idea that barriers separating the privileged and the underprivileged, or the entitled and the enslaved, need to be removed for social and political change to occur. Not coincidentally, during its theatrical run in Seoul and other cities, *Silenced* was one of the first Korean films to receive the "Barrier-Free" treatment, the use of a newly created platform for the screening of motion pictures accompanied by descriptive audio and subtitles to assist audience members with hearing or visual impairments.[40]

As Cho Hŭp and O Sŭng-hyŏn point out, *Silenced* is a politically engaged text that goes beyond "representing society from the perspective of the disempowered and the weak" and positioning itself as "a private protector."[41] By this the authors indicate that, instead of objectively conveying narrative information, the film is suffused with the filmmakers' subjective sentiments about a negligent society and therefore adopts an affective mode of communication. The film's Korean-language poster, which features a first-person pronoun, prominently foregrounds the able-bodied protagonist's declaration that he is a "private protector" of the both literal and figurative voiceless: "*I* decided to reveal the incident to the world." *Dogani*, the title of the novel and its film adaptation, has dual meanings: a crucible, or a container for heating metal or ceramic substances to high temperatures, and an emotional state of intense excitement, anger, or catharsis. In Hwang's film, when Yu-jin is informed about unimaginable abuses against institutionalized children, he is shocked and says incredulously: "What is this crazy thing? A crucible of insanity (*kwangran ae dogani*)?" "A crucible of insanity" in the narrative successfully prompted a *dogani* of rage (*punno ŭi dogani*) and collective action on the part of audiences because, as the film director and critic Kim Hong-jun point out, an ordinary Korean might feel imperiled by realizing that, like the children, "I could be that marginalized and could suffer their pain" if the system continues to protect only the wealthy and powerful.[42] Ultimately, despite its contribution to increasing public awareness of the actual abuses that occurred at the Inhwa School during the 2000s and bringing positive legislative changes to prevent future offenses, *Silenced* uses emotionally wrought, deeply traumatized hearing- or vision-impaired characters as vehicles for their advocates—the "heroes" of this and other South Korean films—to demonstrate society's capacity for charity, compassion, and understanding. Unlike *Always* and *Blind*, however, this film locates people with disabilities almost exclusively within institutional contexts (the oppressive school, the human rights center, the police station, the court of law, and so on), where they are largely reliant on intermediaries to speak and fight on their behalf. This is a double-edged knife of sorts, slicing through the empty rhetoric that is so prevalent in rights-protection policies but further wounding the very individuals—in this case, sexually abused deaf children—who are posited as the most vulnerable among us.

Conclusion

Throughout the history of South Korean cinema, disability has been a recurring theme, frequently mobilized as an allegory for the various social ills faced by a formerly colonized nation. Burdened with an authoritarian past, the Korean people have witnessed multiple forms of oppression related to gender, class, region, and political orientation, as evidenced in dozens of films produced since the 1920s. For example, in Na Un-gyu's silent-era classic *Arirang* (1926), the protagonist's mental illness and murder of a villainous steward of a greedy landlord have been widely interpreted as embedded textual references to the Korean people's rebellion against Japanese colonial exploitation and discrimination. Similarly, in Yu Hyŏn-mok's Golden Age classic *Stray Bullet* (*Obalt'an*, 1961), a Korean War veteran dealing with physical disability experiences humiliation and sorrow when he accidentally discovers that his former fiancée has become a prostitute for American soldiers. Directed by the legendary auteur Im Kwon-taek (Im Kwŏn-t'aek) and partly set during the colonial period, *Sopyonje* is credited with reviving Korean national cinema, and in that film the female protagonist—a *p'ansori* (traditional folk opera) singer—is poisoned by her adopted father (who is also her mentor) and loses her eyesight. This unforgivable act is narratively justified, at least from a nationalist or patriarchal perspective, as an artistic form of self-sacrifice that results in the daughter's vocal maturation and mastery of a disappearing folk art.

Unlike *Arirang*, *Stray Bullet*, and *Sopyonje*, the three motion pictures examined in this chapter signal a cultural shift toward individualization and diversity in South Korean cinema—which, to paraphrase the historian Michael Robinson, is liberated from the "master narratives" of the past in which disability has long served as an allegorical stand-in for the nation, disempowered by foreign occupiers and their masculine, military, and cultural dominance.[43] Yet *Always* is a conventional melodrama in which disability is one of the many obstacles that the central couple has to overcome to attain a romantic union. The vision-impaired female protagonist, while beautiful and desirable, is doubly infantilized because of her gender and disability and becomes an object of protection for the physically fit male protagonist. In *Blind*, the female protagonist is an independent and capable investigator whose compensatory reliance on senses other than sight helps her solve a serial murder case that baffles her able-bodied colleagues. However, this story of "impairment vitalism" is escapist at best, constructing an illusory meritocracy and shifting spectatorial attention from social failures to personal triumphs and individual accountability. *Silenced*, in contrast, is a more politically committed example of disability-themed human rights cinema that not only successfully raised national awareness of rights violations for individuals in corrupt institutions but also provoked legislative changes that strengthened the protection of minors. Its impact has been referred to as the "Dogani effect" or the "Dogani phenomenon" in South Korea. Despite its positive role in bringing justice and greater equality to children with disabilities, the film's narrative ironically silences the affected people, who must be represented by two able-bodied adults: a sympathetic teacher and a human rights activist. Tellingly, the film eliminates important characters in Gong's original novel—a disabled teacher at Benevolence Academy and Yŏn-du's parents, who help file the report of child abuse with the police and bring charges against the school. Deprived of that support network in the film version, Yŏn-du as an orphan is depicted as more passive, vulnerable, and dependent on the kindness of righteous outsiders: In-ho and Yu-jin.

The emergence of disability cinema beyond the scope of South Korea's traditional metanarratives of an ailing nation is both noteworthy and welcome. However, as genre films (a melodrama, a thriller, and a social problem film, respectively) aimed at mainstream audiences, these three productions resort to familiar tropes of the disabled figure as an object of paternalist protection or affection, a superhero, or a silenced child victim. Additional work must be done before people with disabilities achieve equal rights and fair cinematic representations, not just in South Korea but in other countries around the world. Despite their failure to grant full subjecthood and agency to characters with physical and sensory impairments, these films invite their audiences to reflect on societal prejudices and to become more engaged citizens for whom human rights is a matter of pressing national concern.

6

Barrier-Free Cinema

Caring for People with Disabilities and Touching the Other in *Planet of Snail*

In the introduction to her 2017 book, *Curative Violence: Rehabilitating Disability, Gender, and Sexuality in Modern Korea*, Eunjung Kim cites a recent example of "nationalist spectacle" involving a metaphorical "folding" of time and the virtual erasure of disabled embodiment.[1] The incident in question revolves around Kang Won-rae—who, with another dancer and singer, Koo Jun-yup (Ku Chun-yŏp), made up the 1990s dance duo Clon. Kang's career was cut short by a motorcycle accident in November 2000 that injured his spinal cord and left him paralyzed from the waist down. The incident captured the attention of many Koreans, especially after Kang began making appearances on public television programs that promoted scientific efforts to cure his condition a few years later. One such program was the KBS (Korean Broadcasting System)'s music-variety show *Open Concert* (*Yŏllin ŭmakhoe*, 1993–), which brought Kang back to the stage in 2005—albeit this time in a wheelchair alongside other (able-bodied) dancers.[2] The TV episode featured a message of hope recorded by President Roh Moo-hyun (No Mu-hyŏn), who touted the centrality of science and technology to his country's ongoing efforts find solutions to incurable diseases. It also included a distinguished medical scientist, Hwang U-sŏk, whose pioneering work in stem-cell research and therapeutic cloning was held up as a promise of something positive to come, such as a way to restore Kang to his former life as an entertainer unburdened by physical disability. Kim describes the scene's sentimental underpinnings in detail, noting how this compulsive "desire for cure" on the part of the nation's top researchers and highest elected government officials was "captured emotionally" by the show's producers. Switching to slow-motion close-up shots of the wheelchair-bound man dancing to concert music, the camera effectively turned Kang into an object of the audience's sympathy and pity. Similarly, Hwang's spoken words (relaying the "agonizing sadness" that he experienced while watching the disabled man's performance) rhetorically transformed the young entertainer into a "magician's assistant to prop up the illusion of cure." "In these folded temporalities," Kim concludes, only Kang's "nondisabled past and his cured future become meaningful."[3]

Like many examples of nationalist spectacle that Kim cites in her study, the producers of the KBS program exploitatively framed this onstage footage of Kang in his wheelchair as a "powerful drama of imagined bodily transformation," one that furthermore might reveal "the power of the nation" if only Hwang and other government-funded stem-cell researchers were able to follow through on their promise to make disability "disappear" once and for all.[4] Such disappearing acts, however, are just that: illusory attempts to bring stability to the body politic through appeals to healing an individual's bodily handicap. Such appeals are practically magical in the sense that scientific breakthroughs in biotechnology and related fields resemble a kind of divine intervention, though in the case of Kang (and thousands of other paralyzed Koreans) the so-called cure has yet to materialize. It is as if the line between medical practitioner and soothsayer or shaman had begun to blur with the airing of that episode of *Open Concert* and would eventually evaporate altogether once it was reported that Hwang's findings were, in fact, fraudulent. Having attained questionable results through improper and illegal methods, the once-respected scientist was arrested on various charges, creating a scandal in the scientific community and lending credence to South Korean disability activists' long-standing claim that "the emphasis on curing and normalizing disabled people," even in its most benign form, "generally reinforces prejudice against [them]."[5] That is, curative processes ironically tend to destroy human subjects by pointing toward their perceived deficiencies or lacks rather than societal failings or systems of oppression as the problem in need of fixing. Hence the reference to "violence" in the title of Kim's book, which argues for a culturally specific interpretation of such seemingly benevolent but ultimately destructive acts (including preventive eugenics), contextualized within colonial and postcolonial epistemes that have treated the nation as a body in desperate need of healing.

Notably, the concept of *ch'iyu* (a Sino-Korean expression referring to healing that consists of "two individual words: ch'i, 'to govern,' and yu, 'to cure'")[6] snakes its way through a host of South Korean cultural productions revolving around disability, from classic folktales to modern literature. Motion pictures in particular display a knack for maximizing the melodramatic appeals of cure-themed stories, affectively tapping into the audience's presumed need to witness nonconforming bodies—those that are marked by a specific loss (such as of seeing, hearing, movement, or mental capacity)—be made whole by the narrative's end through the restoration of that absent ability. Melodrama, a mode of storytelling that has long permeated Korean cinema, is especially conducive to such allegorical readings, given its binaristic tendency to paint the world in black and white as a series of structured oppositions (including that between good and evil) and thereby supplying stories with a requisite amount of agonistic tension that must itself be "cured" if catharsis is to be experienced. As Kim notes, the term "cure," which "typically means to restore 'health' by removing illness and disability through medical treatment," is also figuratively used as an expression of "moral judgment." Drawing upon a definition supplied by the *Oxford English Dictionary*, she reminds us that "it also means 'to remedy, rectify, or remove (an evil of any kind),'"[7] a plot point in several South Korean films.

In chapter 5, we alluded to the narrative trajectory of director Song Il-gon's 2011 romantic drama *Always* (*Ojik kŭdaeman*), which builds toward the moment in which the blind woman Chŏng-hwa (Han Hyŏ-ju) has her sight restored following an expensive eye operation (paid for by the self-sacrificing Ch'ŏl-min [So Chi-sŏp], who raises the money by subjecting his own body as a boxer to pain and potential disability in a Bangkok fight club). Forty years prior to that motion picture's release, another blindness-themed action film—director Pak No-sik's *Quit Your Life* (*Ingansap'yorŭl ssŏra*, 1971)—put a unique spin on the idea that a failing masculinity might be restored through a similarly sacrificial act on the part of a male character who literally and figuratively *sees* his unseeing female companion as an object of pity. Specifically, this latter cultural production hinges on the exploits of Ch'ŏl-ho (played by the director), a conscripted soldier who works in a Manchurian gold mine during the Japanese occupation. Early in this film's narrative, the protagonist, along with his one friend (a fellow miner named Chŏng-su [Kim Hŭi-ra]), is falsely accused of stealing precious metal from the mine. Though Chŏng-su is executed by the tyrannical overseer of the mine, Tal-gyu (Hŏ Chang-kang), Ch'ŏl-ho manages to escape the hangman's noose and twelve years later makes his way to Chŏng-su's wife, Yŏng-suk (Kim Chi-mi). Realizing that she is blind (a condition that was "caused indirectly by the shock of her husband being drafted"), he pretends to be his fallen friend (whose death, unbeknown to her, he will seek vengeance for). While some audiences might question the too-convenient way that Yŏng-suk readily accepts this stranger into her arms (if not her bed, though the still-virginal thirty-one-year-old woman does make overtures in that direction), *Quit Your Life* successfully demonstrates the functional value of disability as a source of melodramatic pathos, turning her literal and figurative blindness into a decidedly feminized plight that only he, the newly masculinized hero, can remedy. Indeed, like *Always* forty years later, this film builds toward a denouement in which the woman (whom he describes as a "poor maiden") is to receive a cornea transplant made possible by the male lead, someone so smitten by this object of "pure love" that he is willing to given up his own eyes as part of the story's ophthalmological intervention.[8] However, the catharsis that such cures promise is deflected in this film's closing scene, which shows a mortally wounded Ch'ŏl-ho (the victim of Tal-gyu's gunfire) stumbling to the ground before he is able to hand Yŏng-suk the cornea transplant consent forms. As she passes by within a few inches of Ch'ŏl-ho's slumped body, oblivious to his presence, the blind woman mutters the film's final lines, telling the man whom she has mistaken as her missing husband that she is content despite her disability. "Being the person I am now suits me better," Yŏng-suk says, concluding that the tears that pour down her face are for both "happy moments" and "sad moments" and suggesting that perhaps she was never really in need of a cure in the first place.

Regardless of its unique twist on the frequently reductive trope of disability (as an engrained feature of several melodramas), *Quit Your Life* is aligned with the long-standing view that a "cure" for an otherwise permanent ailment "was something more likely to be bestowed than earned, something that came from outside rather than from within."[9] In that sense, it is like many other cinematic treatments of physical, emotional, and/or cognitive "affliction," which tend to celebrate "the power and skill of the healer" (that is, the savior figure who, through medical or religious intervention, is able to make "the lame walk and the blind see") rather than the less spectacular, more quotidian activities entailed in actually caring for people with disabilities. As Catherine Kudlick points out, such generic formulas, as "prevailing orthodoxies" (be they of a scientific or a spiritual bent), have shaped the public's understanding of disability as a form of imperfect embodiment and contributed to the valorization of curing over caring.[10] Narratives like these also have consequential effects on the material circumstances that make barrier-free accessibility (or the lack thereof) a contested terrain for disability rights activists. As Eunjung Kim argues, "the compulsion of cure, regardless of whether any cure is available, preempts social and practical solutions to many of the problems and struggles that disabled people experience."[11]

Thankfully, the ableist fantasies about disabled "others" that we encounter in several mainstream South Korean films have been partially offset by alternative modes of representation in which caring, rather than curing, becomes the operative means of tending to their day-to-day needs. A few independently produced documentaries, including Kye Un-gyŏng's film *Pansy and Ivy* (*P'enji wa tamjaengi*, 2000) and Sŏ Tong-il's *Pink Palace* (*P'ink'ŭ p'aellisŭ*, 2005), have moved away from the infantilizing impulse that we alluded to in chapter 5 and that can be detected in recently released big-budget productions such as Cho Yŏng-jun's *The Preparation* (*Ch'aebi*, 2017), Ch'oe Sŭng-hyŏn's *Keys to the Heart* (*Kŭgŏtmani naesesang*, 2018), and Yuk Sang-hyo's *Inseparable Bros.* (*Naŭi t'ŭkpyŏrhan hyŏngje*, 2019). According to Eunjung Kim, to varying degrees the female-focalized *Pansy and Ivy* and the male-focalized *Pink Palace* allow a "shared sensibility of the experiences of disability" to emerge organically, giving audiences the opportunity to spend time in the virtual company of onscreen subjects, but on their terms, "in everyday relationships in which individuals invest in each other's lives."[12] The former film communicates the desires and dreams of two small-stature sisters who lean on one another in times of personal setbacks and romantic interest in potential mates. The latter film shows the sexual yearnings of men with various disabilities (for example, spinal-cord damage, cerebral palsy, polio, deafness, and blindness). The title refers to a barrier-free brothel in Melbourne, Australia, which generated international media attention for its efforts to serve customers with disabilities by installing wheelchair-accessible doors and sit-in showers. Without access to such a care-based establishment, most interviewees in *Pink Palace* struggle to find a sex partner, let alone a wife or girlfriend, and are forced to lead a life bereft of sexual intercourse. These two documentaries treat their disabled subjects with dignity and respect by focusing on the most basic needs, with which any adult audience member can identify. In the following pages, we turn our attention to another Korean documentary that likewise showcases the mundane yet meaningful everyday activities and conversations of a disabled couple—two people who are deeply devoted to each other and who demonstrate a level of care and support that is rarely seen in more cure-focused mainstream productions.

The toast of festivals around the world and the winner of the Best Feature-Length Documentary award at the twenty-fourth International Documentary Film Festival Amsterdam (IDFA), South Korean director Yi Sŭng-jun's *Planet of Snail* (*Talp'aengiŭi pyŏl*, 2011) makes a significant break from traditional cinematic representations of people living with disabilities. From Bucharest to Melbourne, this intimate, noncondescending look at individuals who might otherwise serve as objects of pity (in other examples of human rights cinema) has garnered international attention for its sensitive approach to a largely underrepresented or misrepresented community: that of deafblind individuals who experience the world primarily through touch and smell (see figure 6.1). Yi had met one such individual—Cho Yŏng-ch'an—in 2008 while making a science documentary about human fingers for the EBS (Educational Broadcasting System), a South Korean television network, and had asked him and his wife Sun-ho (a woman who possesses all five senses but is burdened with a spinal disorder that has stunted her growth) if they would like to be the subjects of a feature-length film. Initially reluctant, the couple agreed to participate in the project in hope that it would be a corrective counterbalance to the many formulaic depictions of differently abled bodies in the mainstream media. In our interview with Yi Sŭng-jun on December 16, 2015, the documentarian discussed fondly the close relationship that he developed with the film's subjects over the two-year course of production: "I tried to become their friend, their brother, and not just because I was making a film. . . . I was invited to their home once or twice a week, and I didn't plan much initially. If something interesting caught my

FIGURE 6.1 Yŏng-ch'an and Sun-ho, the two main subjects of director Yi Sŭng-jun's disability-themed documentary *Planet of Snail* (*Talp'aengiŭi pyŏl*, 2011), share a tender moment in a natural setting.

attention, I filmed it. When nothing was happening or they were not in a good mood, I chatted with them over coffee or played chess with them. Respect was key to how I gained their trust."[13]

Despite its narrow focus on the quotidian lives of sightless and hearing-impaired people living in the Korean city of Taejŏn, *Planet of Snail* is a truly transnational production, bearing the traces of foreign input at the level of creative and financial participation if not conception. With participants ranging from Japan's NHK (Nippon Hōsō Kyōkai)[14] to Finland's Vaski Filmi, and with production supported through the U.S. Cinereach Grant and Sundance Documentary Fund, *Planet of Snail* announces a new stage in nonfiction filmmaking in South Korea. The fact that a Lebanese editor (Simon El Habre) and a Finnish sound designer (Sami Kiiski) also lent their talents to the project only further accentuates this film's distinctiveness as a small-scale, yet globally oriented, portrayal of the day-to-day lives of physically challenged people.

In this chapter, we use *Planet of Snail* as a case study through which to gauge the relationship between human rights and the human sensorium, the latter concept referring to a person's perception of his or her environment as it is felt through the mind and body—that is, through psychological and physiological interfacing. Human rights, both as a legislative ideal (if not actuality) and as a discourse (spread through cultural productions, including motion pictures), calls upon compassionate subjects to feel the pain or suffering of others (objects of the humanitarian gaze), despite the presence of literal or figurative obstacles that make such intersubjectivity a difficult, or even impossible, undertaking. By rejecting some of the common tropes of human rights cinema (including the framing of physically "handicapped" individuals as victims of an indifferent social system), Yi's unusual documentary encourages an alternative type of phenomenological engagement with subjects who communicate chiefly through touch. Scenes showing Sun-ho tapping on her husband's fingers—a coded approach to language adapted from Braille—demonstrate the need to pursue nonaural and/or nonvisual approaches to human rights discourse. This, admittedly, is an unusual proposition for audiences who are, indeed, interfacing with the film through their eyes and ears. And indeed most critics who have called *Planet of Snail* "touching" (that is, emotionally moving) speak or write from embodied positions far removed from those of the film's protagonists, whose own touching (of one another, trees, pinecones, sand, raindrops, and so on) hints at the limits of spectatorial feeling for and toward the other.

After discussing *Planet of Snail*'s themes and representational strategies (as well as the possible meanings of its polysemic title), we explain how this and other examples of Barrier-Free cinema are being used to enable different viewing opportunities for diverse audiences (including those who are hearing-impaired and/or vision-impaired). Recently, in Seoul and other cities, the newly created Korean Barrier Free Film Committee (founded by Yi Ŭn-kyŏng, a film producer turned rights activist) has created platforms for the screening of motion pictures accompanied by descriptive audio and subtitles to assist audience members with hearing or visual impairments. As one of the first films to be shown in this barrier-free format, *Planet of Snail* points toward a future in which textual features and themes associated with human rights cinema might infuse the spaces in which such motion pictures are seen, heard, and felt.

The Poetics of Touch and Sensorial Identification

Besides the Nuremberg International Human Rights Film Festival, which is where we first encountered *Planet of Snail*, other festivals around the world have showcased Yi Sŭng-jun's production as an exemplary, award-worthy work of nonfictional filmmaking. In May 2012, the film began attracting international attention after playing in Melbourne's Human Rights Arts and Film Festival. Six months later, it kicked off the ninth Verzio International Human Rights Documentary Film Festival, an event held in Budapest during the second week of November 2012. And in March 2013, *Planet of Snail* was included as part of the One World Romania festival, an event modeled on the One World International Human Rights Documentary Film Festival, which, for nearly twenty years, has been held in over forty towns and cities in the Czech Republic. These and other venues have given audiences around the world an opportunity to feel as if they have temporarily gained entrance into the private lives of real rather than fictional characters whose stories are told in a refreshingly original way.

The "characters" in question are Yŏng-ch'an and Sun-ho, the man and woman who appear in nearly every one of *Planet of Snail*'s deliberately paced scenes. The audience is first introduced to this couple in a pretitle sequence that shows them flying a kite on a lonely country road outside Taejŏn, a burgeoning city that is sometimes referred to as the Silicon Valley of South Korea, owing to the large number of technology centers and research institutes located there. The couple participates in a simple, somewhat childish activity that is far removed from the hustle and bustle of the urban environment situated just beyond the hills in the background. Apart from the occasional car that speeds across the frame in the distance, as well as the offscreen presence of a dog that can be heard barking, they are alone. Or, rather, they *seem* to be alone—a fiction that this documentary film sometimes undermines through handheld camera movement that should remind attentive audiences of the presence of another person: Yi, the filmmaker. Although throughout *Planet of Snail* Yi adopts an observational mode of nonfiction filmmaking that rarely calls attention to itself (at least, he does not do so in an intentionally reflexive way), the director's physical proximity to his filmed subjects is what allows spectators to feel that they too are close to individuals who might otherwise be kept at a distance in real life and who are not able to return the cinematic-spectatorial gaze. However, such positioning of Yŏng-ch'an and Sun-ho does not mean that they are reduced to simply being objects of the camera's or audience's potentially invasive gaze—at least, not in the way that characters are in many of the disability narratives alluded to above.

It is telling that, in the English-language version distributed internationally (the one shown at film festivals and released on DVD in the United States and throughout Europe), both Yi Sŭng-jun's name and the title of the film appear as text against a backdrop of clouds—an image that directly follows a shot of Yŏng-ch'an "looking" up. Presented this way, the credits seem to be part of the sky toward which Yŏng-ch'an gazes. Yet a few seconds are all that most audiences need to see that he in fact cannot see. Sun-ho, his diminutive partner in this scene (and in life, as we come to learn), functions as his "eyes," instructing him on how to fly a kite that initially darts to and fro against a cloudy firmament only to be replaced by the textual inscription of the director's name and the film's title moments later. As those words disappear, sunlight pierces the gray clouds before the shot fades to black. That subtle solar burst, a sign of the film's expressive, poetic tendencies, may suggest the hopefulness that infuses much of *Planet of Snail*, despite the day-to-day challenges that this couple will face in ensuing scenes.

Additionally, that fleeting image of the sky—a moment that appears to be an impossible point-of-view shot (from a blind man's perspective)—introduces a theme that will develop over the course of this ninety-minute documentary. As further indicated by its title (which can more accurately be translated as "Star of Snail"), the film is paradoxically organized around images and ideas of earthbound activity as well as a kind of heavenly or astronomical distance from the earth. Therefore, a tension between the terrestrial and the extraterrestrial, the earthly and the otherworldly, thematically structures this motion picture and distinguishes it from many other examples of disability rights cinema. Audiences are cued in on *Planet of Snail*'s phenomenological commitment to both extremes, to each of those two experiential aspects of living abstractly and materially in the body or presence of a person with disabilities.

Following the first scene, an establishing shot takes us to the apartment complex in the city where Yŏng-ch'an and Sun-ho live. Inside, we watch as they partake of a hot meal that Sun-ho has prepared. Cutting from medium shots to extreme close-ups and back again, the camera observes the couple as they eat. The bottom branches of a Christmas tree can be seen on the left side of the frame, and this—not to mention the snow that blows visibly outside the window—provides information about the seasonal setting (a wall calendar flipped to the page for January will also appear a few minutes later). Even though this holiday dinner scene lacks voices, it is not wordless, for Sun-ho can be seen sharing a prayer with Yŏng-ch'an, who receives her words through his fingers. Tapping on her husband's fingers, the woman communicates a private message, one that is not subtitled for the film's audience. Their sense of touch is accentuated here and in the ensuing scene, which shows Yŏng-ch'an still in his apartment, now sculpting a small animal from white putty while Sun-ho washes the dishes.

Hands are at the heart of these people's lives, whether they are pursuing artistic endeavors or attending to mundane domestic chores. Pacing back and forth with a braille-style reading device strapped across his shoulder, the young man can be seen feeling his way through a tactile fairy tale, using his fingers to read the story of a father and son who are looking for their lost cow, which was last seen in the mountains. Reciting what at first seems to be a passage from that tale, Yŏng-ch'an actually shares an extract from his own poem: "The earth / a smooth train / I'm traveling by the earth from morning to noon / noon to night / lying still in bed." In a way, he can be said to take temporary command of the film, something that rarely ever happens in other disability narratives. In a later scene, Yŏng-ch'an enjoys riding an inflatable tube with his wife and a friend down a snowy slope. As the image transitions to an out-of-focus shot of the radiating sun with black dust particles speckling the screen, the poet's voice steals onto the soundtrack, musing, "One's sight and hearing are not something that is lost. They are just wandering around far in space and shall come back to their master all in good time." In yet another scene (set on a train), Yŏng-ch'an recites an impromptu poem to his wife, who sits next to him: "Still am I / an astronaut dreaming / under my fingertips? Being isolated / without talking to anyone, / I am left in space alone. / All deaf-blind people / have the heart of an astronaut."

According to Kye Un-gyŏng, Yŏng-ch'an's narration enables audiences to take momentary leave of *Planet of Snail*'s narrative and enter a "space of darkness, stillness, loneliness . . . silence," the desolate yet beautiful inner terrain of the deaf-blind poet.[15] Poetic speech is accompanied by dissonant sound effects, which can be said to express the narrator's existential crisis. Although Yŏng-ch'an's poems are not explicitly related to human rights issues, as Kye observes, his confession-like recitals open a ruminative space that can be imaginatively inhabited by the spectator and filled with personally held feelings about disabilities. "Audiences participate socially," argues the Korean film scholar, "not by actively doing something for disability rights but through self-reflection on issues related to disabilities"[16] while listening to Yŏng-ch'an's space travel-themed poems (full of longing for freedom, mobility, and connection to the outside world).

Although many commentators have described Yi's film as being observational, he explained to us that he did not consciously approach his subjects as an observer. Instead, he insisted, he "tried to reveal something, certain moments that [he] discussed or debated" with them in advance. Many of the film's poetic interludes, including the intimate shots of Yŏng-ch'an touching trees, raindrops, and other natural forms were based on sensorial experiences that he had relayed to the filmmaker in advance of shooting. "Even though Yŏng-ch'an explained how he felt," Yi told us, "I could not convey his sensations completely, 100 percent. So I tried to interpret and translate with my own visual images."[17] The subject's embodied experiences and the filmmaker's artistic vision fuse together in the film's most lyrical scene, which shows Yŏng-ch'an putting his fingers onto raindrops dangling from his apartment's steel balcony. The director's use of an extreme close-up of the man's digit pressed against water lends a sense of haptic visuality, a tactile experience that likely triggers associative memories in the minds of many spectators who have also touched raindrops in this manner (and who are thus prompted to identify with the deafblind man's most basic human feelings). Here, the poet's inner voice (spoken narration) returns against an abstracted close-up shot of a raindrop in which a view of the street outside Yŏng-ch'an's apartment is reflected upside down: "The eyes, ears, and heart of a man are often deeply hypnotized or caught in obsession or are in the deep swamp of ego. And one is getting old, unaware of the world. If you wish to be free from eyes and ears, be an astronaut like me." These words suggest the feeling of being differently abled and invite audiences to reflect on their own disability of not being able to experience life fully, beyond the shallow façades of commercial entertainment and capitalistic achievement in a fast-paced world.

As the author of his own story, Yŏng-ch'an exudes agency and self-determination, which Katharina Heyer and other scholars believe is an essential part of the disability rights movement.[18] Although frequently associated with civil rights–era attempts to secure equal opportunities for members of ethnic minority groups and women in the United States (culminating with the passing in 1990 of the Americans with Disabilities Act), this more globally expansive political movement was launched on multiple national fronts throughout the second half of the twentieth century, and it has been linked to developments in adaptive technologies, new accessibility standards, and independent living opportunities that would contribute to the gradual dismantling of institutional barriers. But for all of those advancements, self-determination has remained the conceptual crux of the disability rights movement. In the South Korean context, as alluded to in chapter 5, *dangsajajuwei* (*tangsajajuŭi*), a principle that emphasizes "disabled people's rights to self-determination and self-representation," was introduced as a core tenet of the disability movement in 1991.[19] As noted by Dong Chul You and Se Kwang Hwang, disability activists saw the need to "make their own decisions" and forge their own path, as "non-disabled activists and professionals are not able to create suitable content and establish systems or facilities for disabled people."[20] Although Yŏng-ch'an is not seen participating in organized political movements or social justice campaigns, this same principle is the means by which individuals like him are able to project their autonomy or their ability to function independently and thus have a hand in how their identity will be defined.

Significantly, the main character's spoken words in this early scene accompany yet another shot of the sun partially obscured by gray clouds, an image that might recall our description in chapter 5 of Mujin (the setting of the film *Silenced* [*Dogani*, 2011]) as a city engulfed in white mist. In both textual instances, clouds or fog denote what spokespeople for the medical model of disability might call a perceptual limitation or biological inability inscribed in the body of the so-called handicapped individual—specifically, vision-impaired people restricted to blurry images of the world (or even to seeing less than that). Yŏng-ch'an himself puts it in such metaphorical terms, when—speaking to a classroom full of actors—he explains that his inability to see is "like being surrounded by a thick fog." But such recurring shots more accurately serve as a sign of what advocates of the social model of disability would say is a failure on the part of society, or at least a general unwillingness to engage differently abled people on their own terms. Stated in another way, individuals such as Yŏng-ch'an are rarely ever seen, in the sense of acknowledging not only their existence but also their goals, motivations, and abilities. Like the sun that remains a veiled presence in *Planet of Snail*, people with disabilities are often obscured or abstracted in even the most well-intentioned motion pictures, including those (like *Silenced*) that use hearing- or vision-impaired characters as vehicles for their advocates—the true heroes of those films—to demonstrate their charity, compassion, and understanding.

Unlike *Silenced*, which locates deaf characters almost exclusively within institutional contexts (the oppressive school, the court of law, and so on) where they rely on intermediaries to speak and fight on their behalf, *Planet of Snail* lavishes attention on individuals who are not helpless victims of violence. Nor are Yŏng-ch'an and Sun-ho voiceless recipients of charity. Instead, they are self-determined social actors who participate in the public sphere, communing with other people who have physical and/or sensory impairments. They also pursue educational opportunities at learning centers where technological accommodations have been made to assist in the process of social inclusion. With Sun-ho's editing help, Yŏng-ch'an even submits his memoir to a literary contest (his submission is rejected later, but he plans to try again in the next contest).[21] Yes, these characters are shown living normal, uneventful lives at home, where they sometimes entertain deaf and/or blind friends to break up the day-to-day monotony; but they can just as often be seen venturing into the wild and reveling in their natural surroundings alongside other Koreans.

Several scenes, for example, show the couple enjoying outdoor activities, from sledding down hills on snow tubes to walking along sandy beaches once winter gives way to spring and they go on vacation. Despite the warmer temperatures, when Sun-ho and a friend playfully nudge Yŏng-ch'an toward the water and push his hand down to the sand to meet an incoming wave, he jokes that it is as cold as a refrigerator. Laughing even though he cannot shake the shock of touching that frigid water, he retreats a few steps on the beach and muses that "the sea is dancing." Here it is revealed that certain sounds, like the crashing of waves, can be heard by the young man, if only faintly. That dim, barely discernible noise becomes the soundtrack of his ocean's "dance" in this scene, just as the faint rustling sound of leaves accompanies the shaking of a tree—something we see Yŏng-ch'an do much later in the film, as part of his full-bodied exploration of the natural world. When Sun-ho translates the sound and image of the moving leaves to her partner, she once again taps on his fingers. In this case, she says, "They touch each other and make crunchy sounds." She also forms a bird-like shape with her hands to mimic the rotating movement of the tree's limbs—a back-and-forth motion that lends visual texture to the film's themes, including its oscillation between earthly and heavenly pursuits. Her hands, positioned in this way, furthermore visually echo the kite that was witnessed at the beginning of *Planet of Snail*, one that featured the image of a bird taking flight even as it remained tethered by a string to the ground.

Bringing visual symmetry to Yŏng-ch'an's story, *Planet of Snail*'s final scene recalls the first scene by showcasing yet another tethered object. This time, however, it is the protagonist himself who is being prevented from flying away or, rather, drowning in the ocean, thanks to the rope that connects him to a small boat (see figure 6.2). The two images—one of a kite being flown and the other of a man swimming alone—reflect one another. Both hint at the idea of limited movement as well as the prospect of freedom, kept in check though the latter is by institutional forces and medical discourses that define disability as an inability. Not insignificantly, in a recent essay concerning international humanitarian law, Janet Lord draws upon a similar connective metaphor when arguing that the standard approach to disability privileges diagnosis and treatment at the expense of "a more holistic understanding and approach beyond medical intervention that situates the disadvantages associated with disability as a social phenomenon." As she states, such an approach "relegates persons with disabilities to the role of the 'sick' and inexorably tethered to illness (read helplessness)."[22] Yŏng-ch'an is not "tethered" to illness or helplessness, yet the barriers to full inclusion are subtly registered in the form of a rope tied around his waist—the

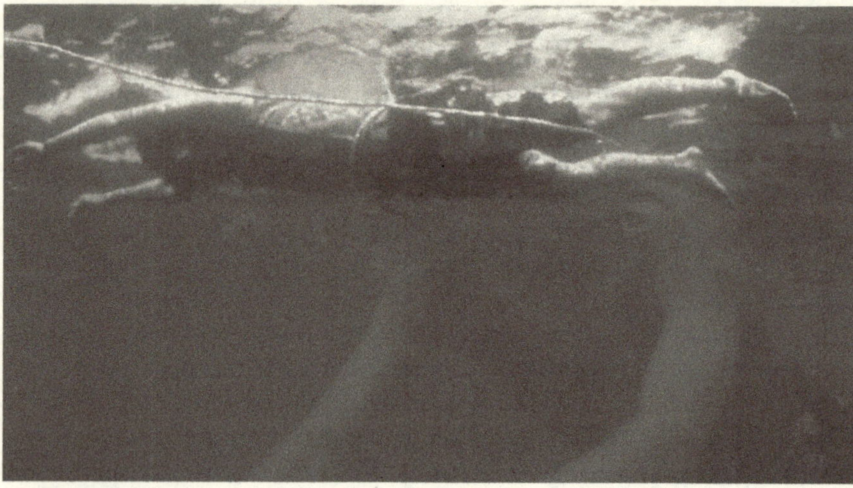

FIGURE 6.2 Toward the end of *Planet of Snail*, Yŏng-ch'an, a deafblind man, is shown entering the ocean—an expansive space of possibilities—while tethered by a rope to a nearby boat.

thing that ensures his safety but that hampers forward movement. Significantly, the first time we witness Yŏng-ch'an moving in a similarly vigorous yet stunted manner is just after the abovementioned dinner scene. Not long after eating his meal, he begins exercising inside the small apartment, running in place for several seconds. Ironically, his momentum sends him backward, not forward, a subtle counterimage at odds with the notion of historical progress and societal advancement embedded in the disability rights movement.

In a study of disability in postsocialist Ukraine, Sarah Phillips uses the expression "mobile citizenship" to denote the "creative strategies being used by people on the margins to assert claims to full citizenship."[23] As she states, "the concept of mobile citizenship is particularly rich for exploring intersections and intertwinings of disability and mobility in a variety of contexts."[24] Although the first and final scenes of *Planet of Snail* stage the barriers to full inclusion as a form of limited movement or tethered activity (a potentially emancipated object or person is prevented from breaking free), there are many more moments when Yŏng-ch'an enters the lives of others as a self-motivated and enterprising subject, demonstrating in the process his capacity for mobility and, indeed, citizenship.

One such scene involves Yŏng-ch'an's participation in a theater company's rehearsals for a play titled "Three Days." Before he arrives at the acting troupe's rehearsal space, he and Sun-ho meet a young actress named Ch'oe Chŏng-a, who—along with her cohort of other actors—greets the couple with great enthusiasm. The performers are excited because the deafblind man will be able to provide pointers and tips as they practice their parts, granting them access to the experience of living without the faculties of hearing and sight. To "hear" and "see"

Chŏng-a's performance as a deafblind woman, Yŏng-ch'an follows close behind her, offering polite criticisms while putting his fingers on hers. He instructs her on the right way to walk and explains that she is using her hands "in the wrong way." Compared to the struggling actress, who strives to imitate the behaviors of a deafblind person, our protagonist is the embodiment of authenticity and authority, using his body in a confident way and, in doing so, dispelling some of the cultural myths associated with "handicapped" individuals (including the notions that they are noble warriors triumphing over diversity, tragic figures consumed by anger or resentment, or childlike beings incapable of taking care of themselves).[25]

This is an important, revealing scene for many reasons, not least for its suggestion that these performers—the actors who are copying Yŏng-ch'an's physical characteristics but are unable to evoke the reality of disability in quite the same way that he can—will come to represent that reality in the minds of audiences who eventually attend their play. A reminder of the dramatic power and inherent artifice of both theatrical and cinematic fictions, this seemingly trivial moment points toward the ways in which able-bodied performers are typically privileged over people with disabilities in the casting process. Thankfully, that scene is counterbalanced by a later one, which shows Yŏng-ch'an, Sun-ho, and their friends staging their own religiously themed play for a church congregation—an audience whose audible laughter and palpable respect for the performers may coincide with the feelings of the film spectator.

Speed, Slowness, and Snails

Don't let the title fool you. It's not a nature documentary about snails.

—Peter Knegt, "Seung-Jun Yi on His IDFA Award-Winning *Planet of Snail*"[26]

Following *Planet of Snail*'s 2011 theatrical release, numerous online movie critics reflected on the film's unusual and evocative title. Mark Feeney, writing for Boston.com, muses that its title reflects Yŏng-ch'an's reliance on touch when experiencing the world.[27] Similarly, albeit in a more poetic vein, Christopher McQuain alludes to the slow, tactile way in which the deafblind protagonist relates to his physical surroundings, stating, "Like a snail emerging from its shell to engage with the world, not so much with the aid of its eyes (which barely sense shifts in light) as through its halting and hypersensitive physical orientation to the world around it," Yŏng-ch'an feels "the rich extremes of inward and tactile experience with less effort than the rest of us normally sighted and hearing people find readily possible."[28] Snails evoke not only the tactile but also the terrestrial, as decidedly earthbound creatures that have a sluggish commitment to the soil. Although no mollusks actually appear in *Planet of Snail*, the distinctiveness of the film's English-language title demands that we acknowledge its metaphorical suggestiveness—its capacity to synthesize and foreground otherwise unstated themes by drawing upon culturally specific associations. During our interview with the filmmaker, he explained that the title was partly inspired by Yŏng-ch'an's own analogy in which deafblind people are compared to snails due to the "slow speed" of their communication with others. Moreover, a snail's antennae are shaped like braille, a tactile form of communication for individuals who have experienced the loss of sight or were born without it. Furthermore, the "planet of snail" concept was suggested to the filmmaker by Antoine de Saint-Exupéry's 1943 French novel *The Little Prince* (*Le petit prince*), about a little boy from a tiny volcanic planet uninhabited by other humans. Yi imagined that his main character was like this solitary fairy-tale prince who lives in his own world, disconnected from the rest of humanity.[29]

Judging from the consensus that emerges from the literature in sociology, anthropology, and political science and drawing upon anecdotal discourse, twentieth- and twenty-first-century Seoul (specifically) and South Korea (more broadly) can be described as spaces of ceaseless transformation and frenetic speed. In "From Insularity to *Segyehwa*," Nahzeem Oluwafemi Mimiko remarks that "the rapidity with which Korea moved from its rural and poor origins to an industrial nation is unprecedented in economic history." The speed of that achievement is such "that a parallel cannot be found in human history," according to the author.[30] Dal Yong Jin puts it more succinctly, stating, "Korea is nothing if not dynamic."[31] Taking these comments into consideration, it is clear that the expression "moving at a snail's pace" does not accord with the rhetoric surrounding contemporary South Korean identity and society. Indeed, the animal least likely to evoke the nation's character is the snail (*talp'aengi*), given that creature's negative associations (synonyms for the word include "dawdler," "idler," "plodder," "procrastinator," "sluggard," and "straggler").

Quoting the theorist Paul Virilio, the Korean film scholar Kyung Hyun Kim draws attention to the historical crises that resulted from South Korea's stress on "amazing speed and mechanical overload," a government-mandated emphasis that also led to industrial growth but at the expense of internal dislocations and social ruptures that remain unmended today.[32] From the International Monetary Fund (IMF) Crisis of 1997–1998 to the recession and credit market crash that began in 2008 and affected South Korea as much as any other developed nation, potentially traumatic events tied to the country's rapid growth have served as both offscreen (contextual) and onscreen (textual) facets of films focusing on citizens for whom success is often defined by material acquisition, upward mobility, higher education, and competitive one-upmanship in a free-market economy. Writing in 2003 about the largely negative perception of people with disabilities in their home country, Shin Jeong Kim and Kyung Ah Kang similarly argue that, during the IMF Crisis, such individuals were the first to be subjected to personnel cuts in businesses and other organizations. "People with disabilities are considered useless as they cannot contribute to their families' financial gains," the authors state, and indeed this "last-to-be-employed," "first-to-be-dismissed" mentality so endemic in the South Korean labor market (with its emphasis on speed and efficiency) needs to be undone by more thoroughgoing attempts to rehabilitate society rather than "handicapped" or "crippled" individuals.[33]

One consequence of the rapid industrialization that began in Seoul and other metropolitan areas in South Korea during the 1960 and 1970s is that people with disabilities "have formed the poorest group in the lower social stratum" of the country, making it nearly impossible for many of them to "escape poverty."[34] Writing more generally about global perceptions, Ellen Ryan and Karen Bannister state: "Disability is seen as a constraint that may require more time off and greater accommodation within the work place. . . . This stereotype can place individuals with disability in a perpetual underdog position in the hiring processes. Indeed, global studies show that most people with disabilities are unemployed or underemployed, and consequently many live near or below the poverty line."[35] Conspicuously absent from *Planet of Snail* is any mention of the economic hardships faced by Yŏng-ch'an and Sun-ho, although spectators can likely guess that the couple is not wealthy, based on material signifiers within their small apartment. In an interview for the Korean-language website *No Cut News*, Yi Sŭng-jun acknowledges the absence of such references, saying that it was an intentional decision on his part. In fact, Yi shot an interview in which Yŏng-ch'an confesses to finding it difficult to earn a living, but (after consulting with the film's editor, Simon El Habre), Yi opted to leave that footage out of the film for fear that it would engender a feeling of sympathetic pity in the audience—something he strived to avoid throughout the filmmaking process. "I intentionally avoided money issues in order to concentrate on themes," stated the director, who in multiple interviews has said that his goal was to showcase the quotidian lives of individuals who, unlike "busy modern people," stop long enough to touch raindrops, hug trees, and have themselves buried in sand. These small actions, which we see the main characters of *Planet of Snail* doing in several extended scenes, "are what truly matter," according to Yi.[36]

According to a 2007 report from the International Labour Organization (published after the Convention on the Rights of Persons with Disabilities was adopted by the United Nations, on December 13, 2006), there are approximately 650 million individuals in the world (or 10 percent of the global population) living with some form of physical, sensory, or cognitive impairment[37]—which makes them part of the largest minority in the world, a "planet" unto themselves. Roughly 70 million of those people use sign language as their primary means of communication. In recent years, cochlear implants and other listening devices have made it possible for people to counteract hearing loss. Notably, the cochlea, a part of the inner ear that translates sound vibrations into nerve impulses,[38] is "a snail-shell-shaped bony tube that is flexible on the inside." In fact, the word cochlea "actually means 'snail shell' in Latin."[39]

For the philosopher Slavoj Žižek, the snail is an uncanny creature, similar to tortoises insofar as both are simultaneously squishy and hard, spongy and firm—a bundle of contradictions dialectically contained in the image of an outer shell that protects the animal's otherwise vulnerable, largely hidden interior.[40] The slimy body inside, lacking a skeleton, evokes a figure of the Real, one that is actualized only when it disappears—that is, when the shell around it (a kind of symbolic representation of the animal's thingness) delineates the contours of a void or absence. Yet the body is always there, a "something rather than nothing" that is, in Žižek's words, "defective, vulnerable, ridiculously inadequate." He thus sees in the snail a sign of "the fundamental vulnerability, the need for a safe haven of a home specific to humans," which is "projected back into nature, into the animal kingdom." In other words, snails can be thought of as "humans who carry their houses around with them."[41] Although this latter metaphor does not necessarily lend itself to a deeper understanding of *Planet of Snail*'s themes, the tension between softness and hardness, as well as Žižek's emphasis on vulnerability as a latent characteristic or demonstration of human defectiveness, point toward some of the representational dilemmas attending cinematic portrayals of persons with disabilities. Fittingly, at various points throughout the film, Yŏng-ch'an can be heard imagining himself as an astronaut, someone with his own shell-like protective gear that serves to preserve life in the vacuum of space. Perhaps his poetic inner self is an inverse shell that protects him not only from an inhospitable or barrier-filled environment but also from an uncaring, speed-driven society that continues to marginalize disabled people despite efforts to raise public consciousness about such matters.

Becoming "Barrier Free"

The term "barrier free" was first used in a 1974 meeting in New York City of a U.N. expert group that discussed design accommodations. The term was adopted in the field of architecture and urban planning to increase accessibility in the construction of building, road, and cross signals. As Carolyn Stevens points out, although "the international 'barrier free' movement began in 1974 . . . it was not until 2001 that the term was adopted by the United Nations as part of the work in preparation for the 2006 Convention on the Rights of Persons with Disabilities."[42] In South Korea, the term entered the lexicon in 2010 to refer to a broader cultural movement to bring down actual and metaphorical obstacles that audiences with disabilities might encounter as consumers of broadcasting, motion pictures, and live performances. The recent rise of the Korean barrier-free movement is a direct response to the 2007 Anti-Discrimination against and Remedies for Persons with Disabilities Act (discussed in chapter 5). Under Article 24 of this act, state and local governments as well as cultural and artistic entrepreneurs are mandated to "provide legitimate convenience" to people with disabilities to enable their participation in "cultural and artistic activities."[43] As one particular application of this law, movie theaters with more than three hundred seats for a given screen are legally required to provide accessible facilities and accommodation. Despite these general legislative principles, several impediments still stand in the way of people with disabilities who might wish to attend movie screenings. According to a 2013 study by the Ministry of Culture, Sports, and Tourism (Munhwa ch'eyuk kwankwangbu), out of 119 surveyed film theaters across the nation, only 50 (42 percent) were equipped with wheelchair-accessible seats. Of those seats, 80 percent were placed in the front corner of the auditorium, at a close angle to the screen and next to the exits (a location that is not conducive to comfortable film viewing, despite its safety benefits).[44] It is not surprising that a 2011 study on the status of disabled people showed that only 6.0 percent of respondents were able to attend movies or plays within the past week, while 65.5 percent felt dissatisfied with their cultural and recreational opportunities.[45]

Visually impaired and hearing-impaired audiences face other obstacles besides seating accessibility. While network broadcasters are now legally required to air all programs with subtitles for the deaf and hard of hearing, audio descriptions and subtitles for theatrical film screenings have been limited to nonprofit exhibition sponsored by the Korean Film Council (Yŏnghwa chinhŭngwiwŏnhoe)'s public funds since 2005. As a film producer and distributor, Yi Ŭn-gyŏng had an idea that departed from the model of state-subsidized, noncommercial film exhibition for largely segregated audiences with content accessibility needs. Based on the Japanese model of barrier-free cinema, she wanted to introduce an integrated approach that brings disability experts and industry practitioners together in the professional production of alternative versions of original prints (which would be created by the same people who produced the original prints in the case of domestic motion pictures)[46] intended for all audiences, both in film festivals and commercial venues. To achieve that goal, Yi hosted the first Barrier Free Film Symposium in November 2011 (before it was renamed as the Barrier Free Film Festival in 2013) and launched the Barrier Free Film Committee in 2012. Giving exhibition sites a barrier-free treatment is an expensive endeavor, costing 15–20 million won (approximately $13,000–18,000) for visual description script development, sound remixing or re-recording, voice acting, and directing. By 2013, the Barrier Free Film Committee had produced eighteen barrier-free versions of films (ten Korean and eight foreign), and the committee's website now lists sixty-seven available films, including animations and shorts.[47] The first Korean film that received barrier-free treatment was An Sang-hun's *Blind* (*Pŭllaindŭ*, 2011) and the first Korean film to have a barrier-free version released simultaneously along with a regular print in commercial theaters (as opposed to only in film festivals or community screenings) was *Planet of Snail*.

In her 2012 interview printed in the Korean Film Council's monthly magazine, Yi Ŭn-gyŏng explains the significance and uniqueness of *Planet of Snail*'s barrier-free theatrical release, which was presented on commercial screens "with the same level of frequency as the regular version." She states: "Because barrier-free is still an unfamiliar format, it is very rare that audiences come without being invited and normally, disability organizations arrange group screenings in theaters in advance. However, even without such organizing efforts, *Planet of Snail* [the barrier-free version] was watched by 7,000–8,000 paying audiences. Out of the 20,000 total audiences for the film, approximately a one-third of them saw the barrier-free version. . . . GCV [the largest multiplex chain in South Korea] allowed us to screen it on regular screens . . . and able-bodied audiences saw the barrier-free version comfortably."[48]

Although the barrier-free format is not exclusively for visually impaired and hearing-impaired audiences (it has been used to entertain audiences of an advanced age as well as to educate children and minors through public screenings), the simultaneous release of original and barrier-free prints of *Planet of Snail* was unprecedented. Particularly noteworthy was the fact that some able-bodied audiences chose to watch the barrier-free version despite not needing subtitles or audio description narration, thus experiencing a vicarious sort of disability-adjacent spectatorship. In both content and form, an integrated, barrier-free experience of *Planet of Snail* in the presence of both able-bodied and differently abled viewers represents an ideal that is rarely achieved by other examples of disability rights cinema. It thus shows the merits of South Korea's antidiscrimination disability law, which promises to fully integrate people with disabilities into the larger society and to "establish their right to equality which will ensure their human dignity and sense of value."[49]

Part 4

Representing Prisoners of the North and South

7

Beyond Torture Epistephilia

The Ethics of Encounter and Separation in Kim Dong-won's *Repatriation*

After CBS News published photos documenting prisoner abuses and torture by U.S. military personnel in the Abu Ghraib prison in Iraq in April 2004, a few American independent documentaries—including Alex Gibney's investigative exposé *Taxi to the Dark Side* (2007) and Errol Morris's meditative film *Standard Operating Procedure* (2008)—tackled those controversial issues. Despite the liberal intent of criticizing the U.S. government's policy of detention and interrogation of Middle Eastern prisoners and invoking sympathy for innocent victims of cruelty and inhumanity, these films have been seen as failing the litmus test of ethical representations of torture on screen, as put forth by Marnia Lazreg. According to her, "Representations of torture in films need to be clear about the arbitrariness of torture, its routinization, as well as the hollowness of its political justifications. They can do so only by being clear about the illegality of torture and by depicting its consequences for the victims, who must be allowed to present their experiences of psychological and physical pain and degradation."[1]

The abovementioned documentaries about torture either reduce victims to informers who support the indictment of U.S. policy on the War on Terror or treat them as anonymous (often naked) subjects in enlarged still photographs (such as the images from Abu Ghraib) whose documented degradation engenders pity on the part of compassionate spectators. In contrast, the veteran Korean documentarian Kim Dong-won (Kim Tong-wŏn) approached his subject from an entirely different perspective in *Repatriation* (*Songhwan*, 2003), the winner of the 2004 Sundance Film Festival's Freedom of Expression Award. What radically distinguishes Kim's film from its American counterparts is his long-term commitment to, and intimate relationship with, his subjects. It took Kim twelve years—a full decade of shooting footage plus another two years of editing that material into the finished film—to complete *Repatriation*. Alongside his staff in PURN Production (P'urŭn yŏngsang, a progressive documentary collective that he founded in 1991), he shot eight hundred hours of footage on five hundred tapes that showcased the daily lives and struggles of released long-term prisoners who had spent as much as 30–40 years in the prisons of authoritarian South Korean regimes, where torture and abuses were routine. In the spring of 1992, Kim was asked by a Catholic priest to give a ride to two recently released North Korean spies—Cho Ch'ang-son and Kim Sŏk-hyŏng—who had been staying in a nursing home in Asan, a city in South Ch'ungch'ŏng Province. After their move to Pongch'ŏn-dong, a mountainside shantytown in Seoul, where they became Kim's neighbors, the director started to develop a surrogate father-son relationship with Cho, the gentler of the two men. The director became a driver, cameraman, and advocate for a group of long-term prisoners, recording various events such as reunions, picnics, support group meetings, rallies, funerals, and visits to gravesites. Mundane everyday activities are interspersed with talking-head testimonies about prison experiences, tense moments of conflict with South Korean relatives (who disowned or avoided released prisoners), and ideological confrontations with anticommunist groups or bystanders. In his documentary, Kim intermittently historicizes their stories with archival footage and explanatory voice-overs.

After another prisoner of war, Yi In-mo, was sent back to North Korea in 1993, the repatriation campaign to return other unconverted prisoners (those who refused to denounce their communist beliefs and allegiance to North Korea in exchange for a reduced sentence or parole) to their homes began. Kim Dong-won wanted to contribute to the campaign by raising public awareness about the issue through his documentary. Before he could complete his project, the repatriation of long-term political prisoners on humanitarian principles was agreed upon in the June 15 North-South Joint Declaration of the inter-Korean summit between Kim Jong-il (Kim Chŏng-il) and Kim Dae-jung (Kim Tae-jung) in 2000. On September 2, 2001, Cho and sixty-two others were voluntarily repatriated to Pyongyang, where they received a hero's welcome. Kim Dong-won wanted to complete his film after meeting Cho and his family in Pyongyang. In August 2002, he was elated to be invited to participate in a reunification festival in North Korea's capital. However, the day before departure, his permission to visit North Korea was canceled after a security background check brought up his arrest record from 1996. As shown in the documentary, he was arrested and investigated for a violation of the National Security Law (Kukka poanpŏp) because of his association with long-term prisoners. Kim sent a video greeting to Cho through a friend, who was able to shoot the footage of Cho and other repatriated prisoners in place of the director. In the tape brought back to Seoul, Cho sends his regards to Kim and says that he thinks of him as if he were his own son. Kim's final voice-over states, "Mr. Cho said that I was like a son to him. I was ashamed for not being much of a son. That shame spurred me on to complete this film. I miss Grandpa Cho."

Nicknamed the "godfather of Korean independent documentaries," Kim is touted for a series of "committed documentaries" that focus on the urban poor and social activism.[2] After completing a fifteen-minute short on a teenager's baptism, *James's May* (*Yagobo-ŭi owŏl*) in 1986, Kim was called upon by a Catholic priest to document the demolition of housing in the Sanggye-dong ghetto and the forced eviction of its two hundred residents as evidence for a legal case. The underclass inhabitants of the slum lost their homes due to the government-led gentrification project, designed to eliminate an eyesore from the sight of foreign visitors to the Seoul Olympics games in September 1988. What was intended as a single day's job for Kim turned out to be a long-term participatory commitment and "an ethical manual for independent documentary filmmakers."[3] The day after the shooting, Kim went back to Sanggye-dong to re-record sound due to technical errors and inadvertently bore witness to brutal violence against evictees by a group of gangsters hired by the development company. This incident awakened a spirit of activism in the fledging documentarian, and Kim decided to move to Sanggye-dong to become one of his subjects. He joined the evicted residents' year-long fight against the developers and assisted their resettlement in makeshift housing in Puch'ŏn, a satellite city of Seoul, running a day care facility for embattled parents.

The director-turned-subject explained this life-altering decision by reflecting on his own fluctuating status between assistant and filmmaker: "I always agonize over the relationship between those who are filming and those who are filmed. . . . At first, I wanted to help with things I could do to my best ability but there still remained a problem. Even if I declared my intention to help the urban poor, there was ambiguity about my qualification. Ultimately, the method I chose [to solve this] was to become an urban poor [person] myself. To this day, I feel that it was the best decision of my life. . . . I was afraid of nothing when I considered myself a resident. I felt proud to be together with them and I thought I could do anything."[4] Initially developed as short newsreel-style videos documenting the demolition and forced evacuation of tenants, the three-part Sanggye-dong series culminated with *The Sanggye-dong Olympics* (1988), a twenty-seven-minute film that is now considered a foundational text in the history of Korean independent documentaries. It is a prime example of collective filmmaking in which the distinction between documentarian and subject is not just blurred but eradicated.

Narrated by a female resident who consistently uses the collective pronoun "we" and other pluralistic rhetoric in her voice-overs, *The Sanggye-dong Olympics* closes with the credit "produced by the residents of Sanggye-dong fighting against evacuation" rather than naming individual creative personnel. As creators of the documentary, the evictees embraced filmmaking as an integral part of their community activism. As Kim observed, "When the gangsters and police turned up to force them out, the residents' morale slipped. But when the camera started rolling, they would pick up the courage to move forward. It seemed that filming and being filmed gave them a sense of pride."[5] After completing the Sanggye-dong project, Kim demonstrated his sustained commitment to urban poverty by making two documentaries about another redevelopment area and its residents' opposition to forced eviction: *Haengdang-dong People* (*Haengdangdong saramdŭl*, 1994) and its sequel, *Another World We Are Making: Haengdang-dong People 2* (*Haengdangdong saramdŭl 2*, 2000).

Twelve Years of Dedication: The Ethics and Politics of Participatory Documentary

According to Bill Nichols, a "participatory mode" of documentary filmmaking emerged in the 1960s as a result of earlier technological developments that made it possible to record synchronized sound on location.[6] This allowed documentarians to step out of the invisible, at-the-keyhole position of the observational mode and interact with their subjects more directly. As Nichols elaborates, "When we view participatory documentaries, we expect to witness the historical world as represented by someone who actively engages with others rather than unobstructively observing, poetically reconfiguring, or argumentatively assembling what others say and do. The filmmaker . . . becomes a social actor (almost) like any other."[7] Using examples such as *Chronicle of a Summer* (1961), *Portrait of Jason* (1967), *Tabloid* (2000), and *Citizenfour* (2014), Nichols argues that participatory documentaries "involve the ethics and politics of encounter."[8] This is the very thing that obsesses Kim Dong-won. In *Repatriation*, unlike in *The Sanggye-dong Olympics*, Kim would not be able to become one of his subjects. He confides: "I agonized over the fundamentals of documentary. Although this applies to every subject, it is particularly difficult to film long-term prisoners without trust. And trust requires time." Explaining that he is "a timid person" who often feels "uncomfortable" when meeting people for his work, Kim states: "I constantly ask myself, 'Am I using this person?' To overcome such skepticism, a great deal was required beyond building trust. I had to think about my own life as a whole. For any documentary filmmaker, it is natural to ask one's own qualification for filming."[9]

Repatriation's participatory mode is apparent from the opening black-and-white sequence, shot inside a van traveling on the highway. The director's voice-over opens the narrative, recollecting the day when a neighborhood priest requested the use of his car to transport two unconverted long-term prisoners. The priest cautiously added, according to Kim, that the passengers had been North Korean spies. The narrator confesses, "I hesitated momentarily. Words like 'unconverted' and 'spies' terrified me." As if contextualizing the deep-rooted fear of communism of Kim and, by extension, the South Korean populace, the camera lingers on a series of anticommunist police billboards on the roadside: "Achieve democratic security by destroying communist violence. Call 113 for anticommunist reporting," "Achieve a secure society through the spirt of reporting," "One word of reporting can protect yourself and your neighbors. Call 113 to report spies," "Look around and report communist forces disguised as democrats," and so forth. This slow-motion, monochromic travel sequence exudes an oneiric mood that is reminiscent of psychological film noirs of the 1940s and 1950s. While shooting this scene toward the end of postproduction in 2003 (eleven years after the diegetic timeline of 1992), Kim was amused to spot the same antispy signage that had existed a decade earlier.[10] The diegetic journey from Seoul to Asan via Highway 1 symbolizes not only Kim's personal flashback to the day when he first met his documentary subjects but also societal introspection within the collective unconscious of South Koreans, who had been indoctrinated by mandatory anticommunist education since the Korean War (1950–1953).

The next scene of the film, set in the nursing home where Kim Dong-won and his crew go to pick up two patients, contrasts sharply with the opening scene in its realistic home video aesthetic. The caption on the upper right shows the date March 7, 1992. Two elderly gentlemen flash bright smiles in an institutional bedroom after they are told by an unidentified speaker to pack their things. Kim's voice-over chimes in to share his first impression: "They look unexpectedly ordinary. But I glimpsed obstinacy in their words and expressions." The camera cuts to a close-up of Kim Sŏk-hyŏng (introduced by a caption indicating that he had served thirty years in prison), who gently indicts the societal preconception about unconverted prisoners with a wry smile on his face: "They think we are a bit more obstinate." The next shot shows a profile-angle talking-head image of Cho Ch'ang-son, who had also served thirty years, as he speaks in a matter-of-fact way of his experience of discrimination. A cut to a medium-long shot of the bed on which Kim Dong-won holds a microphone shows him seated between the two older men. The voice-over informs the viewer: "Somehow I found myself seated between the two. It made the shooting harder but I had no choice. I didn't want them to be conscious of the camera" (see figure 7.1).

In this two-and-half-minute exposition, Kim unveils himself as both a narrator and a participant in the drama, departing markedly from observational modes of subject-object engagement in which the documentarian is expected to be as invisible as the proverbial "fly on the wall." In contrast, Kim makes his presence (both acoustic and visual) and the cinematic apparatus as conspicuous as a fly in the soup. Although Kim had several hours of footage to choose from during postproduction, he selected the shot of himself awkwardly sandwiched

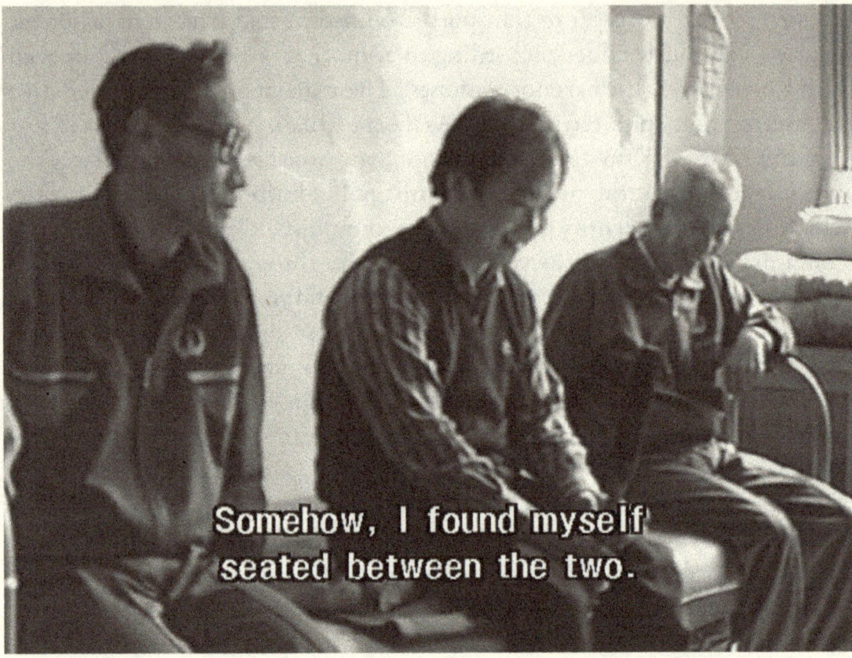

FIGURE 7.1 Kim Dong-won tends to form close personal connections with his subjects, and this shot of the documentarian sitting between two of those subjects in *Repatriation* (*Songhwan*, 2004) is one of many instances in his work in which physical proximity denotes spiritual kinship.

between the two former spies to appear early in the film with a reflexive commentary on the filmmaking process. The director's positioning between Kim Sŏk-hyŏng and Cho Ch'ang-son is politically symbolic. As a voice-over explains a few minutes later, the former subject had been a top North Korean official before being sent as a political agent in 1961 to win South Korean intellectuals to the communist cause. Although he was highly educated and an accomplished public speaker, as the documentarian's narration informs the viewer, Kim Sŏk-hyŏng's "inclination to 'enlighten' us sometimes put us off." This disposition is showcased in the following talking-head scene in which the former spy attempts to convince his off-screen neighbors that South Korea is a subordinate nation to the United States and that Korean reunification is not possible under such circumstances. The camera pulls back to show Cho silently sitting next to his more loquacious comrade at a dinner table. Kim Dong-won's voice-over introduces the self-effacing man: "Cho Ch'ang-son was from a poor farming village. He worked on the boat that transported agents." With narration forming a sound bridge, the scene transitions to another neighborhood gathering, this time with a roomful of worshippers singing a hymn led by the church choir. Cho is seen sheepishly sitting in a back corner, observing others rather than singing. The director continues: "He was quiet, kind, and hardworking. He never missed community meetings, and willingly worked for others. People felt more comfortable with him than with Kim."

During the early stage of filming, Kim Dong-won had no intention of foregrounding Cho as the protagonist of his film. Because of Kim Sŏk-hyŏng's eloquent speeches, the early footage favored him as the camera followed the talking subject. The director explains the shift of his film's focus: "As time went by, Cho Ch'ang-son proved to be much more humane so my protagonist changed. I didn't want to film too much ideological stuff. . . . Also, Mr. Kim did not go out much in the neighborhood but Grandpa Cho came over to our house often and we became friendly. So the camera naturally gravitated toward my friend. . . . He was affectionate and warm. He was friendly with all neighbors and treated my children as if [they were] his own grandchildren."[11] The film includes a brief montage of four still photos of Cho being chummy with Kim's two young sons. The director's narration explains that "Grandpa Cho" came over early in the morning to babysit the children and doted on the youngest, who reminded the old man of the toddler daughter he had left behind in North Korea. Kim Dong-won's decision to spotlight Cho rather than Kim Sŏk-hyŏng humanizes the political subject matter and makes it relatable to a wide demographic group of viewers across the ideological spectrum (notably, *Repatriation* became the highest-grossing Korean documentary at the time of its release, with 24,000 viewers). As Nam Lee points out, the widely distributed film deals with "sensitive ideological questions in a new and different way from the previous era," one that is "more accessible and approachable for the audience"—which she attributes partly to "recent changes in [the] political climate."[12] In particular, the 1998 inauguration of the long-time political dissident and opposition leader Kim Dae-jung as president and the progressive rhetoric of his Sunshine Policy (a policy of engagement with North Korea) were instrumental in creating an environment in which the film could be completed and released. Kim Dong-won gives due credit to the Korean leader (who won the Nobel Peace Prize): "*Repatriation* owes its existence to late President Kim Dae-jung. Without him, there would have been no *Repatriation*. . . . All my tapes would have been rotting."[13]

Kim's documentary is a deprogramming text of sorts, one that counters the kind of sinister images of North Korean spies that had become firmly engrained in the minds of the postwar generation through theatrical propaganda newsreels screened before movies and televisual anticommunist police dramas. This is exemplified by way of archival footage, which Kim introduces with a voice-over about his childhood memory of being exposed to scary images of spies and listening to his father's anticommunist lectures afterward. As a middle-age female neighbor in Pongch'ŏn-dong puts it during her interview in *Repatriation*, "They are no different from our own [South Korean] grandpas"—an attitude that would be widely accepted once people overcame prejudice and got to know North Koreans personally. As Young-a Park points out, though, "the transition of

[Kim Sŏk-hyŏng and Cho Ch'ang-son] into civilian life" was made easier by the "strong sense of community and acceptance" in a shantytown like Pongch'ŏn-dong. Park quotes the director's interview, in which he speculated that "in an urban middle-class high-rise apartment building with double and triple rings of security guards and high-tech security gates, this could hardly have happened."[14]

Repatriation encourages audience members' empathy for and identification with political prisoners through the use of close-ups. A particularly memorable photogenic face belongs to Kim Yŏng-sik, Cho's shipmate and a wireless operator who was captured in 1962, tortured in prison, and forcefully converted in 1972. Now a farmworker in Chŏnju, Kim—who is shown sitting on the front porch of his humble home—has scars on his knees caused by repeatedly being kicked in prison, and he pleads to shoemakers, "Please make soft-toed shoes. It was shoes with hard-toes that ruined my legs." The camera tilts up from a close-up of Kim's wounded legs to a close-up of his face bursting into a childlike, radiant smile. He adds lightly, "But you have to go through it to understand. Others haven't experienced it." The director's voice-over offers a commentary on a slow-motion close-up of Kim's smiling face (an image that is featured prominently in the film's Korean poster): "I've never seen a more honest face than his. Looking at his face makes you believe in the inherent goodness of all humans" (see figure 7.2). Referring to the slow motion in this shot, the director explained, "I deliberately slowed the shot and made it look like a still picture in order to stress my subjective perspective."[15] This shot might explain why Kim received comments from several American audiences at the 2004 Sundance Film Festival that they found North Koreans (whom they had encountered as cinematic subjects for the first time) looking warmhearted and good-natured.[16] In an interview, the filmmaker stated that when he gets old he would like to look like these long-term prisoners, whose innocent faces appealed to him from the first encounter.[17] With such stylistic choices as close-ups, slow motion, and still photos, Kim allows his audiences to observe those faces patiently, intimately, and form an emotional bond that would otherwise be difficult to achieve.

In *Repatriation*, Kim Dong-won held the "ethics of encounter" of participatory documentary to the highest standard by supporting his subjects beyond the call of his project and at the risk of his own safety. As Park explains, "Kim's ostensibly simple act of chauffeuring these released prisoners [in 1992] was in fact a very risky task," as attested by his police arrest and detention in 1996 (referred to in the documentary). These latter events rallied independent filmmakers in Kim's defense and galvanized their efforts to found the Association for Korean Independent Film and Video (Han'guk tongnipyŏnghwa hyŏphoe), which was launched two years later with Kim as its first president.[18] He also displayed the utmost respect for what we call the "ethics of separation," a rarely discussed subject in documentary studies. A few days before he was due to be repatriated to North Korea, Cho contracted pneumonia and was hospitalized. This unexpected

FIGURE 7.2 Kim Yŏng-sik, one of the subjects in *Repatriation*, breaks into a wide smile while being interviewed—a moment that underscores his good nature despite a lifetime of personal tragedies as a former political prisoner and victim of abuse.

illness prevented Kim from conducting a long interview with Cho as planned. The director gave up on the interview and presented several copied tapes to him as a memento of his life in South Korea. On the day of departure, Cho was transported to the Demilitarized Zone in an ambulance. In the film, the parting of Kim and Cho is fleetingly inserted into a montage of both celebratory and tearful interactions of farewell between former prisoners and their friends and supporters who came to see them off. The filmmaker's offscreen voice intones, "Take care of yourself. Let's meet again within a year." The camera zooms in on the crying face of Cho in the ambulance. This is the last time that the two saw one another. Kim finally managed to visit Pyongyang in 2005 (two years after the film's release) and was reunited with ten of the repatriated prisoners, but he was unable to see Cho because of the latter's illness. Recalling the day of repatriation, Kim stated: "I hated my profession that day. It distressed me that I had to shoot while saying goodbye to them. I was in agony and wanted to throw away my camera. . . . That's when I thought that documentary filmmaking is a cruel business."[19] This statement attests to the fact the ethics of participatory documentary pertains as much to separation as to encounter.

As described above in this chapter, Kim's film closes with the ostensibly apolitical statement, "I miss Grandpa Cho," although its subject matter touches on controversial topics such as North Korea, anticommunism, torture, and the unconditional repatriation of political prisoners without reciprocity (that is, not in exchange for the return of South Korean abductees and prisoners of war). In his interview with the film scholar Nam In-yŏng, Kim said: "My radical classmates from the Korean National University of Arts complained about that statement. They wanted me to clarify my political position. . . . But my position has never been radical. . . . My standards are humanistic and universal but that could be political in and of itself."[20] He elaborated: "I wanted to express two things in the statement. . . . First, even if we are not yet ready for reunification, I would like us to visit freely between North and South Korea. Second, like grandfathers themselves put it, it is important to keep one's own conscience. But if I have to choose one, the first meaning is more important."[21] Despite his ethical engagement and deep camaraderie with his subjects, Kim tiptoed around the ideological divide between him and the unconverted prisoners. In an early picnic scene, while admiring the childlike innocence of the people who had spent most of their lives in prison, the narrator also expresses his discomfort at hearing them sing a song that explicitly praised North Korea. Fifty minutes into the film, Kim's narration expresses a neutral position: he does not side with the political prisoners, who place the sole blame for the mass famine in North Korea in the mid-1990s on U.S. sanctions, and he expresses his doubt about the sensationalist reports in the South Korean press of millions of starved victims and hunger-driven cannibalism in North Korea. The director's voice-over further elaborates his political thoughts: "I'm critical of the human rights condition in the North. I'm also well-aware that North Korea has as many inequalities as the South. Above all, I know a liberalist like me couldn't survive where I can't make films freely."

As Jung Han-seok describes, Kim cautioned against portraying political prisoners as "ideological victors" or apologists for North Korea and "accept[ed] them as humans," as that was "the only way that [he] could respect and relate to them."[22] The film's opening dedication caption reads, "To my late father and all long-term prisoners who were jailed for their faith in reunification. My anticommunist father would have been furious at my work. The long-term prisoners might not be happy with it either."[23] *Repatriation* deliberately circumvents questions of political commitment and opts not to take a side in an ideological debate personified by his two fathers (the biological one in South Korea and the surrogate one from North Korea). As Nichols explains, "Ethics need not mean taking a stand for or against the values and beliefs of others so much as acting in ways that do not withhold respect from subjects or undermine trust from audiences."[24] Kim's understated final voice-over ("I miss Grandpa Cho") balances the "ethics and politics of encounter" by implicitly supporting reunification, a common goal of the divided nation as well as a lifetime political mission of long-term prisoners, without politicizing the North Korean issue.

Beyond Victimhood and Epistephilia: An Ethical Witnessing of Torture

Segregated from general prison populations, unconverted prisoners had been invisible in South Korean society, and their presence had been denied by the authoritarian government until the mid-1980s. In the 1950s and 1960s, all political prisoners were either prisoners of war or spies and agents from North Korea. In the 1970s and 1980s, homegrown dissidents and communist sympathizers became the majority of political prisoners. In the immediate aftermath of the Korean War, unconverted prisoners accounted for 60–70 percent of all prisoners. Their numbers dwindled in the latter part of the 1950s and the early 1960s due to executions of inmates on death row and the ideological conversion system (*sasang chŏnhyangjedo*), which became official state policy in 1956. In May 1961, when Park Chung Hee seized power through a military coup, there were an estimated eight hundred unconverted prisoners, most of whom were in Taejŏn Prison. Park's military regime strengthened the government's political prisoner policy and subjected all unconverted prisoners to solitary confinement along with absolute silence. In the early 1970s, the number of the unconverted prisoners (scattered across four prisons) was reduced to an estimated 450–500. After surviving an enhanced conversion program during the harshest period of Korean military dictatorship (the Yushin, or revitalizing reform, system of the Fifth Republic under Presidents Park Chung-hee [Park Chŏng-hŭi; 1972–1979] and Chun Doo-hwan [Chŏn Tu-hwan; 1980–1987]), 102 unconverted prisoners were released from those prisoners between 1988 and 1999.[25] *Repatriation* includes in captions the names of those prisoners who did not survive: 19 who were killed by torture and abuses and another 117 who died of illness in prison.

Kim's soft-spoken voice-over occasionally injects historical context that informs the viewer of these prisoners' plights under Park Chung-hee's staunch anticommunist policy, which classified North Korean spies and communist sympathizers into two categories: "converts" (*chŏnhyang*) and "converts to be" (*michŏnhyang*). Park's military dictatorship and capitalist regime was determined to convert all communist prisoners to demonstrate the South's "superiority" over the North. In the early 1970s, a special conversion task force was formed in each prison to carry out a brutal and inhumane conversion scheme that included various dirty tactics (for example, beating, waterboarding, stimulating the sexual urges of prisoners with pornographic materials and aphrodisiacs, and enlisting family members to emotionally manipulate prisoners). One of the film's interviewees, Grandpa Cho's former captain (Chin T'ae-yun), was forcefully converted while he was unconscious following excessive beatings. The aging captain testifies in talking-head shots in his shabby room in a provincial dog farm: "Five men took turns beating me. I counted up to 600 times, then I fainted, so I don't know how many [times I was beaten]. They almost killed me. They hung me upside down. My legs were broken. Then, they taped a pen to my hand. They moved my hand to sign, and there I was, converted." In the interior scene preceding the slow-motion shot described above, Kim Yŏng-sik testifies about the waterboarding practice in prison during the Park Chung-hee era: "There was a water tank. They laid me out like this. Fixing my hands and feet with bolts. They stretched me out so I couldn't move at all. They put a thin towel over my face and poured water on me. I couldn't breathe. They kept on pouring and after a while it was so awful and I wanted to die. Others might have stood it but I couldn't. I just couldn't take it." The director's narration in an earlier scene, when he first meets Kim Yŏng-sik (who is being reunited with Cho and Chin after thirty years), describes the deep psychological scar that this forced conversion left on such a soft-hearted, vulnerable individual: "Kim's [lowered] face showed well enough the pain, hidden but indelible, of one who renounced his faith."

Not only does the documentary expose the meaninglessness of paper-thin conversions such as those of Chin and Kim Yŏng-sik, but it also pays tribute to the collective humanity of unconverted prisoners who persevered in the face of unspeakable state violence. Sonically superimposed atop a montage of still-frame close-ups of these former prisoners' faces, Kim Dong-won's solemn voice-over intones,

> In the total isolation of imprisonment, fighting against loneliness and fear for decades, what made them go on? How could they withstand the cruel torture that ordinary people would succumb to in a few days, or even minutes? What were they trying to uphold with their life? These were questions asked by many people, including myself. . . . When asked, they usually answered, "I couldn't abandon my political belief," or "It was for the people and the nation." Even while they were in prison, they'd exchange encoded messages, study ideology, and encourage one another. They didn't sit idle and whine, but were always active, as far as their ideology was concerned. But what they were trying to uphold wasn't just nationalism. Nor did their strength come only from socialism. Ideology is just part of the reason, which in turn is just one of many human attributes. The most convincing answer I received was that the reason they held out or the reason why they couldn't give in, lies in the very atrocity of the conversion scheme. The pain inflicted on them justified their resistance and gave them strength. Inhuman violence trampled their human dignity and pride. To protect their human dignity, they had no choice but to fight.

This approximately two-minute montage showing fifty expressive, soulful faces is compelling evidence that "the documentary film is best suited for exposing viewers to the unjustifiable character of torture, arguing for its accountability, and unambiguously calling for its eradication."[26]

This montage does not privilege Kim's protagonist, Cho. In fact, Cho's close-up is buried in the middle of the montage (his is the twenty-seventh image) without receiving special attention. Unlike the names of their dead comrades inscribed in the caption against the black screen preceding the montage, these fifty faces are not identified by name. The montage presents unconverted prisoners as a dignified collective linked by common humanity rather than ideology, as Kim's narration emphasizes. The montage is followed by a talking-head statement from one of the unconverted prisoners, Sŏ Chun-sik, who served seventeen years in prison: "Let's say that there is a hill. Reason won't help you get over it. It's not reason. It's your outrage at unfair treatment, at being beaten, that makes you grit your teeth. This gives you strength to climb the hill." Another talking-head comment from Sin Hyŏn-ch'il, who served twenty-five years, follows: "Even if no one else acknowledges what I do, even still, I have to believe in myself. If even I don't have faith in myself, what's sadder than that?" These two sequences are followed by a long shot of a public panel of long-term prisoners, at which Yi Kong-sun (who served thirty-three years) is heard speaking. The camera cuts to Yi's close-up as he passionately testifies: "Those who try to change my mind by beating me with clubs are lower beings than me. Why should I submit to such despicable people?" Next is a cut to a long shot of the audience, whose members applaud Yi's statement.

In the Korean Film Directors series on Kim Dong-won published by the Korean Film Council (Yŏnghwa chinhŭngwiwŏnhoe), Jung observes, "In *Repatriation*, it is difficult to spot the prisoners' testimonies on torture or resistance inside the prison." Noting the tremendous amount of time that Kim devoted to this project, Jung acknowledges that there must have been plenty of footage of testimonies concerning the subjects' life in prison, yet the director chose not to portray that in his film. "Instead," Jung states, "he focuses more on the time after he had met the prisoners and their present life. It is because the torture and struggle inside the prison only reflect the prisoners' learned insights . . . as ideologists, the value of their resistant spirits, and not their state as natural men."[27] Kim explained that he edited out many prison stories because other films, such as Hong Ki-sŏn's *The Road Taken* (*Sŏnt'aek*, 2003) (a biopic about Kim Sŏn-myŏng, the world's longest-serving political prisoner, who was released in 1995 after spending forty-four years in prison), had already covered the topic well.[28] Although the subject of imprisonment is not the main focus of *Repatriation* (compared to the everyday lives of released prisoners and their struggle for repatriation), the abovementioned testimonies and montage in the first thirty minutes of the film provide powerful indictments of torture and ideological conversion, the likes of which had not been committed to the screen prior to its release.

Kim does not portray his subjects as passive victims, a trope that consistently pops up in well-meaning liberal documentaries produced in the United States and Europe. According to Elizabeth Cowie, to qualify as victims, documentary subjects "must be properly helpless, as well as voiceless, or at least voicing only their plight, their suffering, and must not make any overt demands for help."[29] Errol Morris's Abu Ghraib documentary *Standard Operating Procedure* depicts such victims—specifically, tortured Iraqi inmates who appear only in enlargements of archival still photos of abuse or as fragmented abstract bodies in expressive reenactment sequences (one of the aesthetic hallmarks of Morris's visually distinctive documentaries). Most interviewees are torturers (low-ranking military policemen and women) who provide context for these notorious photos and express remorse for their wrongdoing or justify their actions. Thomas Austin sharply criticizes this approach: "*Standard Operating Procedure* never grants interiority to the Iraqi victims and has little room for their perspectives. To this extent, something of their objectification and loss of agency in Abu Ghraib persists in the film's use of archival photos, reenactments, and interviews with US personnel only." He goes on to argue that this film's "use of reenactments (and at other times still photographs) . . . invites audiences to sympathize with prisoners via an insistence on their humanity."[30] Yet *Standard Operating Procedure* does not grant its subjects a sufficient degree of "voice" or "subjectivity," opting instead for what Patricia Zimmermann has called "stagnant empathy."[31]

Empathy in *Repatriation* is not stagnant, but active and dynamic. Instead of pity and sympathy, Kim provokes audiences' respect and admiration for these prisoners' courage, humanity, and resilience. In a manner that recalls Pyŏn Yŏng-ju's equally committed intergenerational solidarity with the subjects of her seven-year trilogy about so-called comfort women—*The Murmuring* (*Najŭn moksori*, 1995), *Habitual Sadness* (*Najŭn moksori* 2), and *My Own Breathing* (*Sumgyŏl*, 2000)—Kim's empathy did not end with the completion of his documentary. Not only did he maintain his personal friendships with the remaining former prisoners in South Korea, but he also worked on a sequel focusing on Kim Yŏng-sik and thirty-two other converted prisoners' efforts to nullify their forced conversion and campaign for another round of repatriation. The sequel remains incomplete, due in part to the rise of ultrarightist political groups and the resurgence of nationalist sentiments during the administrations of Presidents Lee Myung-bak (Yi Myŏng-bak; 2008–2013) and Park Geun-hye (Pak Kŭn-hye; 2013–2017), which deflated any hope for a second repatriation, and the inability to obtain North Korea's permission for these prisoners to visit their hometowns. Kim Dong-won still plans to complete the film with the footage set in South Korea alone.[32] As for the people who were repatriated in 2000, audiences see them rewarded handsomely for their loyalty in a clip of the North Korean propaganda film *Children of the Sun*. After showing a massive welcome parade and a tour of luxurious housing for repatriated prisoners, the socialist realist–style propaganda film culminates with a long shot of prisoners in workers' outfits marching forward with the superimposed image of the oversize sun in the background. The impassioned female narrator pays tribute with the following words: "These unconverted prisoners are children of the sun, loyal warriors of our Great Leader and General. . . . Eternal soldiers of the Great General, children of the sun." Kim talks over the North Korean narration, stating: "The North used them to beef up its propaganda. The dear men must have been embarrassed to pose for this photo. But they'd have obliged willingly."

Nam Kyu-sŏn, Kim's friend who filmed Cho and other repatriated prisoners in Pyongyang on his behalf in 2002, describes her impression in a talking-head shot: "In Seoul, they didn't even have their own rooms. They had to do menial labor and endure poverty. Naturally, they live a better life there. But perhaps more than anything, they looked so happy because they were back home, reunited with their families, and reacquainted with old friends. After all, coming home is like the ultimate completion in a person's life." Kim's final voice-over accompanies Nam's footage from Pyongyang, which shows former prisoners singing an old war song together, shoulder to shoulder. The director offers an introspective commentary:

> They had overcome total failure and prolonged suffering, and were now singing with strength and dignity. Their lives have yet to reach a happy ending. Still the endless road of revolution and struggle lies before them. The road they must travel on might be even rougher. They no longer have visible enemies. And it's time for their soul-searching to begin. I was still curious about how they lived. Yet I gave up my trip to Pyongyang and started editing. It was so hard to get there, and I heard that even if I made it to Pyongyang, I might not be allowed to film them. "I already know them well enough," I told myself.

Kim artificially pans and zooms in on the image of Cho, closing his film with the deeply personal statement discussed above.

Although a voice of opposition within Korean critical opinion has maintained that Kim's approach in *Repatriation* is old-fashioned and fails to shed new light on unresolved political issues,[33] the filmmaker remained faithful to the "ethics of encounter" by refusing to use his subjects to satisfy "torture epistephilia." Julia Lesage defines the latter concept in the U.S. context as a "historically unique aspect of the torture documentaries as well as of the larger public discourse in the United States about torture since the publication of the Abu Ghraib photos in 2004." She elaborates: "By torture epistephilia, I refer to the thirst for knowledge about official U.S. support of torture."[34] South Korea's ideological conversion system under Cold War authoritarian regimes (1956–1988) is still a taboo subject that is largely dependent on oral histories and memoirs of released prisoners. Although a famous case like that of Kim Sŏn-myŏng, labeled by the *New York Times* as "the world's longest-serving known political prisoner,"[35] attracted a great deal of public attention and became the basis for a narrative fiction film (*The Road Taken*), the stories of other unconverted prisoners did not attract much attention.

Given Kim Dong-won's access to a large amount of footage with interviews about prison experiences (which were his subjects' favorite topic to talk about),[36] the film could easily have been a detailed recounting of the conversion system and its torture practices, one that would satisfy the thirst for historical knowledge or "torture epistephilia" on the part of many viewers. Instead of using his subjects to indict South Korea's authoritarian past and its inhumane political prisoner policy, however, Kim evokes their past with restraint, in the form of character background, to define who they are today and who they will continue to be as they carry on the struggle in their twilight years. In doing so, the director remains true to his documentary philosophy, which can be summed up in the following words: "It is my belief that when a documentary alienates its subjects, the ethics and truth become casualties. I have always thought that subjects and their lives should take precedence over my work. I edited *Repatriation*, which took 12 years to complete, with this philosophy in mind."[37] Alienation occurs in a film like *Standard Operating Procedure* which, in Austin's view, is "illustrative of some of the ethical and political problems that attend mediations of distant suffering" by "leaving [the] victims in continued silence."[38] In contrast, Kim's film succeeds not only in breaking the silence of his subjects and empowering them as speakers, participants, and collaborators, but also in setting new standards of ethical conduct for socially engaged documentary filmmakers in South Korea and beyond.

8

Story as Freedom or Prison?

Narrative Invention and Human Rights Interventions in *Camp 14: Total Control Zone*

> Shin's life . . . is not fiction. It is journalism and history built around one young man's memory, as refracted through a collapsed scheme to hide from trauma, torture, and shame.
>
> —Blaine Harden, *Escape from Camp 14: One Man's Remarkable Odyssey from North Korea to Freedom in the West*

Currently, in North Korea an estimated 80,000–120,000 political prisoners are detained in five penal colonies (*kwalliso*, literally "control centers") or labor camps that are operated outside the trials, sentencing, and other activities of the regular judicial system and frequently violate the prisoners' human rights.[1] The harshest of these colonies are Camp 14 (Kaech'ŏn), Camp 15 (Yodŏk), and Camp 16 (Myŏnggan), which are known as "total control zones" that deny prisoners the ability to return to society.[2] The other two colonies are Camp 25 (Myŏngjin) and Camp 18 (formerly Pukch'ang, now Kaech'ŏn), where abusive conditions (forced labor, beatings, malnourishment, lack of medical care, and so on) are still prevalent, but from which prisoners can be released upon rehabilitation. The purpose of these penal labor colonies, whose existence is denied by the North Korean government, is to punish so-called enemies of the state for their political misdemeanors. The term "political misdemeanors" refers to an amorphous set of crimes or ideological infractions for which there is no judicial oversight or due process and which includes engaging in antistate propaganda, importing or possessing so-called decadent cultural artifacts (that is, foreign audiovisual and written materials), attempting to leave the country without permission, and displaying insufficient loyalty to current or past administrations (those of Kim Il-sung [Kim Il-sŏng], Kim Jong-il [Kim Chŏng-il], and Kim Jong-un [Kim Chŏng-ŭn]).[3]

In the foreword to the second edition of his 2012 profile of a former North Korean prisoner named Shin Dong-hyuk (Sin Tong-hyŏk), whose harrowing escape from the notorious Camp 14 at the age of twenty-two drew the attention of human rights organizations around the world, the American journalist Blaine Harden addresses revelations that were made public three years after the publication of his book's first edition. During those intervening years, it had come to light that his subject had stretched the truth and misrepresented his experiences as the only known person to have been born in—and to have escaped from—such a place. Shin now claims that, at the age of six, he was relocated to a different forced labor site (Camp 18, located on the opposite side of the Taedong River, where a majority of the population from the early 1980s to the mid-2000s consisted of freed prisoners and guest laborers)[4] before fleeing to China and defecting to South Korea. He revised his original claim that at the age of thirteen, he had been tortured for seven months after informing on his fugitive brother and complicit mother and being forced to witness their public executions. According to his new account, his family's executions took place in Camp 18 (not 14), and he was tortured when he returned to Camp 14 after a failed escape attempt at the age of twenty.[5]

Shin was forced to change his testimony after the North Korean regime released several video interviews (on the state-controlled website Uriminjokkiri in October and December of 2014) with his father, stepmother, and former classmates as well as neighbors collectively contesting his original story. According to North Korean witnesses, Shin (known as In-gŭn to his family and friends) worked as a laborer in Camp 18's mine, but neither he nor his family were political prisoners. He allegedly received eleven years of public schooling and was a troubled child with a history of minor offenses, such as theft. Following his father's instructions, he reported his mother and older brother to the authorities because they were responsible for murdering a village woman after stealing her money (according to the witnesses, the mother and son were executed for their crime). Shin's father testified that the burns on his younger son's body were caused by a childhood accident and were not the result of torture (as described in the book). Pyongyang further insisted that Shin had sexually assaulted a thirteen-year-old girl before escaping from North Korea and defecting to the South. Nearly all points of these North Korean allegations (with the exception of the rape charge) were corroborated by other defectors in South Korea, who claim to have known Shin and his family in his childhood.[6]

To the skeptics in South Korea (for whom his incoherent correction of factual details seemed only to expose more fundamental fabrications in *Escape from Camp 14*, an international best seller translated into twenty-seven languages), Shin replied, "Torture scars on my body are my evidence. I have been a sincere activist for North Korean human rights. I do not know those people who claim to know me. They are spreading false rumors."[7] However, Chu Sŏng-ha, a defector turned journalist, shares the feeling of distrust within the North Korean defector community: "In the past, prisoners of Camp 18 were harshly treated as if they were less than animals. Shin's book feels like a collection of prisoner anecdotes he heard while growing up [as the son of a former prisoner who is presumed to have been freed by the early 1980s] but disguised as his own experiences. False testimonies about North Korean human rights are crimes that bring suspicion to true testimonies. One cannot defeat evil with lies."[8] Reliable supporters of Shin's testimony include An Myŏl-ch'ŏl—an escaped former guard from the now-inoperative Camp 22 who is president of NK Watch and who vouched for Shin's familiarity with the language and rules of the total control zone, which would be unknown to outsiders—and British medical examiners who verified that the scars on Shin's body are consistent with the marks of torture.[9] As Harden admits in his 2015 foreword, Shin is an ultimately "unreliable narrator" whose memory has been distorted by trauma or whose story has primarily been invented, depending on whose version of the story one chooses to believe.[10]

The appropriate question to ask is not whether Shin has lied but rather why someone in his position might do so. Approximately thirty-three thousand North Korean defectors currently live in South Korea, most of them having fled their homeland in search of food, freedom, and a better life. However, many defectors whose families remain north of the Demilitarized Zone have experienced not only separation anxiety (being far from parents, spouses, children, and so on) but also culture shock, discrimination, and unemployment after relocating to a fiercely competitive capitalistic society. According to estimates from South Korea's Ministry of Unification, because of their failure to fully assimilate, twenty-eight defectors have returned to North Korea via an unofficial route (by way of China). Moreover, in a recent survey, 20 percent of interviewed defectors expressed a desire to go back to their country of birth.[11] The average wage of defectors is approximately half to two-thirds of that of native-born South Koreans, and the defector unemployment rate is 9.7 percent, three times higher than the national average. Moreover, one in five defectors is a temporary worker, a situation that further jeopardizes their economic stability. The most lucrative (and therefore most coveted) employment prospect for defectors is to become a paid witness to North Korean atrocities and human rights violations on network talk shows, on the national security lecture circuit (hosted by the Ministry of Unification), and in various civil or church group meetings. As Jiyoung Song points out, cash payments vary depending on defectors' ability to meet "the demand for 'saleable stories': the more exclusive, shocking or emotional, the higher the fee."[12] The capitalist market system inevitably encourages certain defectors to embellish their stories with fabrications, exaggerations, and distortions to satiate South Korean and Western cravings for sensationalistic tales about the most isolated country on earth.

This hidden side of North Korean human rights violations in South Korea is explored in *Shadow Flowers* (*Kŭrimja kkot*, 2019), a feature-length documentary by Yi Sŭng-jun, whose earlier work *Planet of Snail* (*Talp'aengiŭi pyŏl*, 2011) is examined in chapter 6. *Shadow Flowers* follows the everyday travails of a middle-age North Korean woman, Kim Ryŏn-hŭi, who defected to South Korea but whose intent was to go back home once she had saved up enough money for medical treatment in China. Little did she know that her open acknowledgment of that plan during her defection interview would put her on the South Korean government's watch list, making such clandestine repatriation efforts impossible. Toiling as a factory worker, the determined woman relentlessly pursues her dream with the help of local human rights activists. She maintains regular contacts with her relatively well-do-do family in Pyongyang—her husband is a doctor and her daughter an apprentice chef—via cell phone and Skype. Intercut with scenes of Kim's demoralized life in South Korea is rare footage shot in North Korea showing the everyday routines of those she left behind. By contrasting Kim's mounting despair with her family's small moments of happiness in the socialist North, Yi's remarkably complex and nuanced film forces audiences to broaden their understanding of human rights in a part of the world that remains at least partially hidden in the proverbial shadows. The filmmaker's observational camera stays neutral in more tense scenes, such as when Kim takes her frustration out on South Korean authorities over the phone or retreats to a defensive position when confronted with an anticommunist protester's denunciation of Kim Jong-un's dictatorship. We are left to judge whether Kim's longing for North Korea derives from her privilege (as a member of the elite class in the capital city who is reduced to performing menial labor in the South) and attachment to her family or genuine allegiance to the political and economic system in the North.

Turning our attention to the transnational spread of rights advocacy, this chapter focuses on another nuanced portrayal of a more celebrated yet equally controversial North Korean defector (Shin Dong-hyuk), a German–South Korean coproduced documentary based on Harden's *Escape from Camp 14*. That film, *Camp 14: Total Control Zone* (2012), is less skeptical of Shin's testimony than Harden's revised text, which foregrounds the ethical dilemmas that he and other journalists face when trying to report facts that cannot be checked. However, in combining seemingly straightforward talking-head interviews and poetically rendered animated sequences showing the life Shin endured under a repressive totalitarian regime, the film adopts a hybridized form in which the line between history and fiction is blurred. As such, *Camp 14* is a useful case study through which to examine the relationship between "the art and freedom of animation" and "the realism and social purposes of the documentary"—a relationship that, in the words of Jonathan Dawson, might be thought of as being "diametrically opposed," but which we see as being complementary, or at the very least not as contradictory as theorists have maintained.[13]

Indeed, making a distinction between what Hayden White calls "historical story-telling" and "historical reality"[14] is not as straightforward as some theorists claim, and the emergence of fully animated or partially animated documentaries such as *Chicago 10* (2007), *Waltz with Bashir* (2008), *The Wanted 18* (2014), *Nowhere Line: Voices from Manus Island* (2015), *Chris the Swiss* (2018), *Samouni Road* (2018), *The State against Mandela and the Others* (2018), and *Camp 14* suggests not only the zeal with which cultural producers are embracing aesthetically freeing forms of narrative invention in their reconstruction of past events, but also a growing willingness on the part of audiences to question ostensibly oppositional modes of discourse. Moreover, *Camp 14*, directed by the German documentarian Marc Wiese, adopts the perspective of an outsider—that of the European filmmaker as well as that of his North Korean subject—in highlighting how Shin remains a prisoner of sorts, even after finding refuge in democratic South Korea: he is spiritually drained and isolated from the millions of middle-class consumers flooding the streets and supermarkets of Seoul. Ultimately, we hope to reveal how *Camp 14* distinguishes itself from other animated documentaries by dramatizing the life of a prisoner for whom escape was not only a survival tactic but also a potentially captivating plot point, part of a partially fabricated story that has both galvanized and undermined the efforts of Amnesty International, NK Watch, and other nongovernmental organizations to end human rights abuses in North Korea. In fact, as Harden writes in his revised book's foreword, Shin's story, which the young Korean was obliged to repeat when interviewed by other journalists, "had become a kind of prison" by the time he finally owned up to its partial fictiveness a few years ago.[15] Telling the truth and opening up about discrepancies in his eyewitness reports thus became his release—a reversal of the manner in which narrative invention, poetic license, and fabulation have long been conceived of as a kind of "prison break" from the confines of history and the dictates of facticity.

Hidden No More: Exposing North Korea's Total Control Zones

Before we venture into an analysis of *Camp 14*'s representational modes, it will be useful to contextualize this unconventional text by placing it alongside other contemporary accounts of North Korean prisoner abuse. Doing so might suggest correlative tendencies among a host of cultural productions, across different media forms (from feature-length films to literary memoirs and working papers aimed at policy makers and government officials). But the distinctiveness of Wiese's documentary—its incorporation of animated sequences as well as lengthy live-action scenes of its traumatized subject sitting silently before the camera, sometimes resisting the tell-all imperative of talking-head interviews in favor of the director's less invasive approach to truth telling—will likely stand out when juxtaposed against more traditional forms of reportage. As we will elaborate near the end of this chapter, the unorthodox style of visual witnessing that Wiese uses in *Camp 14*, with its emphasis on artistically rendered evocations of a personal tragedy that cannot be fully accessed by the spectator, is not unlike the kind of comics journalism discussed by Hillary Chute in her recent study *Disaster Drawn*. Although that study is concerned with printed rather than cinematic texts, it highlights the cultural significance of alternative modes of documentary representation.[16]

Since the 2003 publication of David Hawk's *The Hidden Gulag*, which was one of the first English-language efforts to expose "crimes against humanity in North Korea's vast prison system" (to quote from the book's subtitle), several books on that subject have brought attention to the problems faced by arbitrarily incarcerated individuals in a part of the world that is still largely misunderstood by outsiders.[17] Examples of those recent publications include first-person testimonies of the inhumane conditions endured by North Korean prison camp inmates, such as Kim Yong's *Long Road Home*; autobiographical tales of survival by defectors who fled into neighboring China, such as Hyok Kang's *This is Paradise!*; and former high-ranking party members' indictments of a corrupt political system that, because of economic mismanagement, is responsible for mass starvation and other hunger-related illnesses, including Jang Jin-sung (Chang Chin-sŏng)'s *Dear Leader*.[18] As the subtitle of *Dear Leader* (*Poet, Spy, Escapee—A Look inside North Korea*) suggests, such texts promise readers an insider's view of an otherwise hidden society that has come under increased scrutiny following reports of prisoner abuse and other human rights violations. Regardless of how clearly and emotionally those experiences are presented to non-Korean audiences, a feeling of literal and figurative distance makes the prospect of imaginatively crossing over to the other side a difficult, if not impossible, endeavor.

Notably, even among North Koreans who have spent their entire lives eking out a meager existence under the repressive regimes of Kim Il-sung, Kim Jong-il, and Kim Jong-un (authoritarian leaders from three successive generations of one family whose collective cult of personality has become something of a running joke in U.S. popular culture), a sense of distance separates those who have been subjected to both physical and mental bondage from those who have never set foot inside a prison camp. Kang Chol-hwan makes this clear in his 2001 memoir *The Aquariums of Pyongyang: Ten Years in a North Korean Gulag*. Translated into French by coauthor Pierre Rigoulot and then into English by Yair Reiner, this book paints a vivid yet depressing picture of Kang's decade-long internment at the notorious Yodŏk concentration camp in South Hamgyŏng Province.[19] In chapter 16 of his book, after detailing the horrifying deprivations experienced by the author and his father, grandmother, uncle, and younger sister (who were all rounded up by the authorities in 1977, once his grandfather had been imprisoned for suspected anticommunist activity), Kang discusses what happened to them following their inexplicable release ten years later.[20] That was when they were set "free" to work the land, as members of a farm commune alongside peasants who "had little sympathy for [their] plight."[21] Because North Koreans are taught from an early age that "former counter-revolutionary prisoners were, by definition, bad, shady people," and because most of their countrymen have little or no idea about what happens to people when they are hauled off to labor camps, Kang felt simultaneously close to and remote from the men and women with whom he was forced to work following his "liberation." However, that "distance between [the two groups] lessened" over time because the author and his family "were able to share parts of [their] story" with their new neighbors, being sure to leave the details of their former lives as political prisoners vague "for the sake of everyone's safety."[22] As we shall see, a similar sense of vagueness hangs over other first-person accounts of North Korean prisoner abuse—including that of Shin in the documentary film *Camp 14*—even as they help to fill in a "missing picture" of past and present rights violations that would remain inaccessible to most audiences were it not for the incorporation of animation, photographs, reenactments, and other visually expressive storytelling devices.[23]

It is telling that before musing about the gulf separating himself from other individuals who lack his firsthand knowledge of concentration camp life, Kang indirectly refers to the all-encompassing, spiritually debilitating nature of the North Korean prison system as a "total institution." In the chapter referred to above, Kang explains that, even after being released from Camp 15, he and his family "were constantly being watched" in their neighborhood and while at work, "both by security agents and ubiquitous snitches, who were just as plentiful on the outside as they had been in the camp."[24] Although "everyone in North Korea . . . is under surveillance," according to this former prisoner, the scrutiny of his activities and movements was more intense than what his neighbors had to deal with, primarily because he was forced to wear clothing and carry identification cards that betrayed his tainted background. So pervasive was that surveillant gaze that it ceased to be necessary, for Kang unwittingly began to monitor his own actions, as if he "had a policeman inside [his] head."[25] His words recall Michel Foucault's description of a circular prison block in which inmates are controlled day and night by a watchman who—presumed to be hidden inside a central control tower that looks out at their open cells—is not visible and need not even literally be present to exert power over them.[26] Based on the panopticon design of the English philosopher Jeremy Bentham, this hypothetical layout of eighteenth-century correctional facilities metaphorically registers the way that society can impose a disciplinary sway over its subjects from a distance, forcing them to self-regulate even without the presence of an all-seeing eye.[27] Moreover, in abiding by the social norms and ideological dictates of a state security apparatus that has seeped into every nook and cranny of public and private life, such subjects become ensnared in a different kind of "prison," a truly total institution that is not confined to actual carceral settings.

The sociologist Erving Goffman first developed his concept of total institutions sixty years ago, narrowing the focus on differently enclosed environments of top-down social control that whittle away at individuals' dignity and leave them feeling isolated even in the company of others.[28] Although Goffman's definition, articulated most famously in his 1961 book *Asylums*, encompasses a range of sequestered spaces of enforced austerity that are administratively organized around a disciplinary gaze (for example, boarding schools, convents, nursing homes, orphanages, poor houses, and sanitariums), prisons and other structures designed for carceral punishment best represent the pernicious way that external regulations can become internalized—so much so that people who have been involuntarily locked up inside such structures can be made to feel still imprisoned after their release.[29] Moreover, the metaphorical unfolding of those enclosures, their opening out onto a society that looks apprehensively and suspiciously at former inmates (who, like the convicted character Charles Darnay in Charles Dickens's *A Tale of Two Cities* [1859], are subjected to a kind of universal watchfulness even outside of prison), makes them total in terms of promoting conformity among the greater populace.[30] Perhaps more than any other form of confinement and punishment, though, the total control zones of Camps 14, 15, and 16 pile on the "abasements, degradations, humiliations, and profanations of the self" that Goffman first detected in U.S. mental hospitals over a half-century ago,[31] leaving prisoners—including those who (through a mixture of daring, determination, and luck) have managed to leave the camps behind—in a state of perpetual mortification.

As detailed in *The Aquariums of Pyongyang*, *Escape from Camp 14*, and other published memoirs about the experiences of North Korean prison camp survivors, life behind the proverbial barbed-wire fence is bleak, consisting of a series of dehumanizing experiences that, in the words of Kim Yong, leaves inmates wishing "they were dead" at the end of each workday.[32] Many inmates, like Kim (who was a lieutenant colonel in the North Korea National Security Agency before being sent to the labor camp), had thoughts of suicide from time to time but persevered against what he and other survivors have called "indescribable torment."[33] Indeed, the existential dilemmas and rigors of an indefinite incarceration are difficult to fathom, even for those readers who have found their way into any of the more benign types of total institutions listed above. Besides coping with unhygienic facilities and (barely) subsisting on a rationed diet of corn gruel, watery soup, and cabbage leaves for years on end, prisoners at Yodŏk (Camp 15) and Kaech'ŏn (Camp 14) must perform hard labor, day and night.[34] Forced to carry out manual tasks such as bricklaying, coal mining, farming, and logging under the close supervision of guards, these prisoners are worn down physically and mentally so that they are unable to put up any resistance, individually or collectively.[35] Underfed, overworked, and frequently subjected to the guards' beatings, the bodies of the inmates bear the marks of a cruel and humiliating system of oppression that some North Koreans—including those like Kang Chol-hwan and Shin Dong-hyuk, who eventually escaped their respective camps—are never able to fully leave behind. Tellingly, in a few of his video recorded testimonies featured in *Camp 14*, Shin offers up his physical self—his slightly deformed limbs and occasionally visible skin abrasions—to the camera as a kind of corporeal testament or living proof of the harsh realities visited upon him and his family members throughout the 1980s and 1990s (even if the North Korean rebuttal is true and the Shin family's living arrangements in Camp 18 were freer than what is described in the first edition of Harden's book). The experiences are unimaginable, and ironically, no photographic equipment was able to document during their actual unfolding. It is to his body, and to the similarly ruptured form of the film itself, that we now turn.

The Body in the Mirror and the Voice inside My Head: Locating Shin Dong-hyuk

From its opening seconds until its final scene, *Camp 14* draws attention to Shin's body and, paradoxically, his disembodied or displaced voice as vessels through which past traumas are indirectly communicated to the spectator. Consider, for instance, the film's first scene, a seemingly innocuous moment in which the surface details of cinematic signification are imbued with deeper meanings, at least on subsequent viewings (and through contextualizing readings of the abovementioned books). In a single shot from a handheld camera that lasts one minute, the viewer has a quotidian vantage on the protagonist, who brushes his teeth in front a bathroom mirror. The brightly lit lavatory, which is later revealed to be part of his fairly spacious yet sparsely furnished apartment in Seoul, is lacking in decorations or accouterments, suggesting a pared-down, ascetic existence that is at odds with the apartment's larger surroundings—a city of commerce and consumption that, in subsequent scenes (and in stark contrast to what we see here), appears to be driven by materialistic desires. The former prisoner moves his toothbrush vigorously, even as he seems to be in a partially somnambulant state, as if caught between sleep and wakefulness. Shin's eyes remain closed for much of this opening shot's duration, and his refusal to cast his gaze toward the mirror might initially be chalked up to early morning sluggishness. But the young man's action, or rather inaction, can also be read allegorically, as a rebuke to the visualizing impetus of documentary films that promise to lay bare a person's painful memories for all to see. Rejecting the opportunity for literal self-reflection, Shin nevertheless opens up about his feelings via offscreen narration, an aural component that—crowding out the sound of water pouring from the bathroom faucet—will be familiar to anyone who has seen (or rather heard) a traditional documentary film.

The voice-over, as several scholars of nonfiction cinema have pointed out, has acquired a "miserable reputation" over the years, primarily because it is perceived as "inherently didactic," a heavy-handed means of guiding the audience toward a particular interpretation of onscreen events and visual images that would—and perhaps should—exude their own autonomy as signifying elements.[36] The voice-over was an engrained facet of the earliest documentary talkies as well as classic newsreels of the 1930s (for instance, the March of Time series of short films produced in the United States and narrated with booming "authority" by Westbrook Van Voorhis),[37] and the term brings to mind certain stereotypical features of nonfiction cinema, which are detectable in a diverse cross section of contemporary productions (from the Morgan Freeman–narrated *March of the Penguins* [2005] to the Tom Hanks–narrated *Defying the Nazis: The Sharps' War* [2016]). Even these later films can be said to adopt (though less obviously) an "aggressive" stance toward each member of their audiences, who—like a "prisoner" to the presumed "truth" of the text—is held captive by an invisible or offscreen source of historical facts or pertinent information concerning the lives of distant others.[38]

Sometimes referred to as "voice-of-God" narration, such commentary—often delivered by a stentorian male speaker—carries "insinuations of patriarchy, dominance, [and] omniscience," as Stella Bruzzi notes in her recent study of documentary filmmaking.[39] Similarly, Bill Nichols has drawn attention to nonfiction cinema's "tacit proposal" to its audience, whose "desire to know" something about the world and its subjects is invoked and gratified by a medium that is most "instructive" or "didactic" when it adopts expositional devices like the voice-over.[40] But *Camp 14*'s incorporation of narrational commentary is complicated by the fact that two voices, rather than one, vie for the audience's attention simultaneously in this and several subsequent scenes. The voices are those of Shin (who naturally speaks Korean) and of Steven Charles (who, remaining offscreen, provides English-language translations in lieu of subtitles). Notably, the native Korean speaker's voice is all but drowned out by the dulcet tones of Charles's British-accented speech as the invisible narrator explains (on Shin's behalf) that the former prisoner still suffers from nightmares. "It's not as bad as it used to be," Charles continues, before concluding that those nightmares, which Shin has tried to ignore, are nevertheless "part of my everyday life." The narrator's adoption of the personal pronoun "my," which claims ownership of—or dominion over—a life that is revealed and hidden in equal measure during this opening scene will recur throughout the film, just as its aurally displaced subject, Shin, will eventually let his body speak for him in several wordless passages.

Intentionally or not, by combining those two narrational elements, Wiese erases or at least smudges the boundaries between fictional and nonfictional modes. As Bruzzi explains, the voice-over of fiction film is often "that of a character in the narrative" (and thus is tethered to a physical body), whereas the same device in a documentary generally indicates "a disembodied and omniscient narrator."[41] Furthermore, by beginning *Camp 14* in this way, the filmmaker perhaps unwittingly brings together the ordinary and the extraordinary, highlighting in this most banal of everyday activities (brushing one's teeth) one of the essential aspects of life that most audiences take for granted and that was denied to penal colony inmates in North Korea. In *Long Road Home*, Kim Yong mentions the lack of mirrors in that penal labor colony, which meant that "there was no way of seeing one's own physical decline." Only by "looking at the ghastly faces of other prisoners" could he "picture what kind of half-beast half-ghost [he] had turned into."[42] Significantly, the first page of Harden's book introduces the reader to Shin by drawing attention to his teeth, "which he could not brush in the camp."[43] Although Shin has since received cosmetic dental work in Los Angeles, his body (including his once-blackened gums) is marked by that traumatic past and, in the words of Harden, remains "a road map of the hardships of growing up in a labor camp that the North Korean government insists does not exist."[44]

A similar "there but not there" atmosphere hangs over the documentary *Camp 14*, both during the expressionistic sequences in which monochromatic animation is used to fill in the missing picture of that past and whenever Shin gives in to his own silent reckoning with it as part of the film's many nontalking talking-head interviews. Those personal testimonies are spread out over the course of film's nearly two-hour running time and are distinctive for the way that Wiese holds on the practically static image of Shin even when his subject cannot verbally articulate his feelings—for instance, when he is asked by the director what "water torture" is (see figure 8.1). Long stretches of time are thus spent in the virtual company of someone so weighed down by his past experiences and so visibly haunted by what he is asked to relive for the sake of other peoples' enlightenment that his silences speak as loudly as the English narrator's frequent intrusions. As the director indicates in the film's press-kit notes, Shin was "profoundly traumatized" by what he had been forced to endure ever since his birth in the penal labor colony on November 19, 1983. "He could barely speak for more than half an hour . . . could barely answer my questions," Wiese explains, and his decision to include footage of the former prisoner sitting in his sparsely furnished apartment in dazed silence renders the "unspeakable" and "unrepresentable" in a genuinely discomforting way.[45]

Nevertheless, Shin does gradually open up and let his interviewer in, cautiously providing details about his incarceration at various points in *Camp 14*, through halting onscreen interviews and offscreen ruminations translated into English by Charles. The audience learns much of the same information that readers might have gleaned from Harden's book (albeit with a few notable discrepancies), including specifics about Shin's backbreaking labor in the coal mines

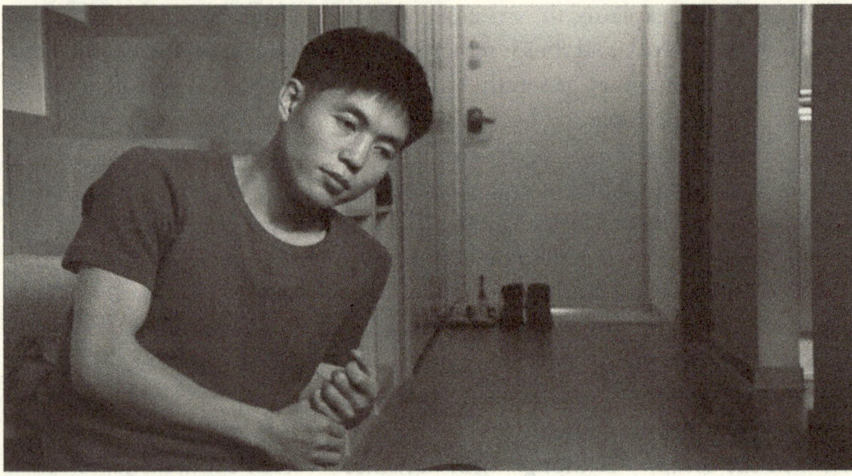

FIGURE 8.1 In *Camp 14: Total Control Zone* (2012), a multinational coproduction directed by the German documentarian Marc Wiese about the life of the former North Korean prisoner Shin Dong-hyuk, the subject frequently struggles to articulate his feelings during the film's talking-head interviews.

below the mountains surrounding the camp, where he was sent to work starting at the age of six (or the age of ten, according to the second edition of Harden's book).[46] Those mountains are literally sketched in by an artist, Park Kŭn-un, who appears with Shin during an early scene set inside an upscale café in Seoul. Sitting side by side and working together, the former prisoner and the cartoonist provide our first glimpse of what the camp might have looked like. Shin supplies the verbal descriptions on which Park bases his charcoal drawings of the barbed-wire fence running along the mountain, the guards' living quarters, the entrance to the coal mine, the unfurnished one-room domicile where Shin lived with his mother, and so on. Close-ups of the artist's hand moving freely across a large sheet of white paper suggest the gestural aspects of the comics medium as an expressive language even though the cartoonist's purpose—the reason for his presence in this scene—is simply to illustrate the main character's experiences. That is, the velvety drawings that fill the screen, like the sometimes smudgy animated sequences that pepper this documentary, serve the dual function of diagramming the physical layout of the Kaech'ŏn internment camp (which can only otherwise be seen via satellite imagery) and aesthetically rendering a prisoner's perhaps hazy memory of that actual space. In much the same way that a "true picture" of prisoner abuse can be said to emerge in director Leon Lee's *Letter from Masanjia*, a 2018 documentary about a former Falun Gong member whose recollections of a Chinese labor camp are visualized through animation, the black-and-white cartoons of *Camp 14* serve as a form of visual witness. This is something to which the comics medium—as much as the cinematic medium—is particularly disposed, according to Hillary Chute.

In *Disaster Drawn*, Chute alludes to the functional usefulness of hand-drawn images in bringing human rights violations in secluded or shadowy corners of the world to light, an act of aestheticized witnessing that even photojournalism cannot achieve when access to such places is limited or prohibited. The celebrated work of comics journalist Joe Sacco (the creator of such graphic novels as *Palestine* [1996], *Safe Area Goražde* [2000], and *Footnotes in Gaza* [2009]) is most clearly in line with Chute's claim that artists literally and figuratively "draw out" past atrocities from their respective historical frameworks (the Suez Crisis of 1956, the siege of Sarajevo during the early 1990s, and so on) and, through the use of comic-book panels and gutters, reframe them as material objects for present-day contemplation.[47] Sacco and other cartoonists "picture the other . . . by inhabiting his point of view," Chute emphasizes, in an act that is physical rather than metaphysical, with the experience of pain or trauma communicated through the artist's hand. The drawer of lines on a page thus leaves a trace of his or her own body in the material form of a memory object, the visual rendering of other marked bodies' forced flirtation with death or physical anguish.

Not coincidentally, Chute ends *Disaster Drawn* with a paragraph partly devoted to Kim Kwang-il, a forty-eight-year-old defector from the North who had spent more than two years in a prison camp before escaping to the South and whose own simple yet evocative line drawings were included in a widely disseminated U.N. report on human rights abuses in February 2014.[48] Those images, which depict abusive interrogation techniques and painful torture positions as well as mass graves in which rotting corpses have been deposited, came from the hands of someone who directly witnessed what the U.N. Human Rights Council has called (in that nearly 400-page document) "crimes of extermination, murder, enslavement, torture, rape and persecution."[49] As Chute summarizes, hand-drawn images play an increasingly important role "in the public sphere as a form of witness that takes shape as marks and lines because no other technology could record what it depicts."[50] By illustrating Shin Dong-hyuk's memories of prison life through the incorporation of both hand-drawn images (by the South Korean artist Park Kŭn-un) and computer-generated animation (by the Iranian-born German artist Ali Soozandeh), *Camp 14* thus acknowledges the importance of cartooning as a form of visual witnessing. And like the above-mentioned *Letter from Masanjia* (which similarly shows an artist—brush and pen in hand—bringing the past to life on the page), the film contributes to expanding the boundaries of nonfiction cinema.

Breaking and Obeying the Rules of Genre

In combining various elements associated with both fictional and nonfictional discourses, including what could be perceived as dramatic pauses on the part of someone who might be suffering from post-traumatic stress disorder and whose story of incarceration and death-defying escape is thrilling in a way that conforms to genre-based entertainment, *Camp 14* also expands the parameters of what a prison film looks like. In recent years, a number of important studies of prison films have been published, and the work of Nicole Hahn Rafter, David Wilson and Sean O'Sullivan, Paul Mason, Michelle Brown, Frances Pheasant-Kelly, Alison Griffiths, Kevin Kehrwald, and other media scholars has been instrumental in setting out the boundaries or limits, as well as the textual affordances or possibilities, of the genre.[51] Ironically, in providing critical lenses through which to better see the prison film's inner workings and sociocultural significance, academically trained theorists have constructed a hermeneutic apparatus that could be said to resemble a panopticon-like correctional facility or any other institutional site in which objects of a disciplinary gaze are subjected to the power of authorities. Of course, one could make the same argument about other categories of cultural production, or rather about the epistemological frameworks that enclose particular genres (for example, the Western, the romantic comedy, and the horror film) within a kind of prison of familiar tropes, stock characters, iconography, and so on. One could also respond that such contrarian claims work to maintain asymmetrical power relations by criticizing the critical act itself—that is, by deflecting attention from the ways that media texts frequently perpetuate stereotypes and cultural misunderstandings (and therefore need to be "dissected" or "interrogated" until alternatives to the status quo become commercially viable).

In a way, though, the relative narrowness of the critical frame surrounding the prison film emulates the physical limitations placed on inmates in the penal system. As Michelle Brown states in *The Culture of Punishment*, since the earliest years of the motion picture medium many examples of carceral cinema have "operated as primers in prison sociology, introducing their viewers to the mechanical daily routines and bureaucratic processes of imprisonment typically through the entry of a central character into the overwhelming subculture of the institution."[52] But equally routinized are the hermeneutic moves of critics and historians who have sought to unpack what Brown calls "penal representation," turning again and again to the same set of iconographic features (including bars, cells, fences, gates, guard towers, razor wire, and stone walls), thematic motifs (such as control, oppression, and transgression), and "punitive conditions" from which the spectator's questionable "pleasure" in the text is dependably derived. Stock characters (for example, "convict buddies, a paternalistic warden, a cruel guard, a craven snitch, a bloodthirsty convict, and the young hero, who is either absolutely innocent or at most guilty of a minor offense that does not warrant prison") and stock plot points or narrative events (such as beatings, riots, and escapes) are "staples of the genre," according to Nicole Rafter, and the repetitiveness with which they occur in representative Hollywood productions (including *I am a Fugitive from a Chain Gang* [1932], *Brute Force* [1947], and *Riot in Cell Block 11* [1954]) makes those films cohere as a generic corpus.[53]

To be sure, "media representations of incarceration contribute, at some level and in some way, to public knowledge and comprehension of penal culture." This, Paul Mason reminds us, is one reason why prison movies matter.[54] But the "spectacle of punishment" that the genre offers, like the voyeuristic fantasy or vicarious thrill of being able to enter a carceral setting with the guarantee of "release" once the story ends, complicates the prison film's edifying and socially productive function.[55] Indeed, conventional examples of the genre "are essentially fantasies," Rafter argues, insofar as they "purport to reveal the brutal realities of incarceration while actually offering viewers escape from the miseries of daily life through adventure and heroism."[56] The "carceral fantasies" of the genre (to borrow the words of Griffiths) are such that the lure of identification—our alignment with protagonists who respond heroically to belligerent guards, malevolent wardens, and other oppressors—often "runs up against a specific voyeuristic spectacle" that is morally repulsive, for it hinges upon "manipulative acts of personal and collective violence." Such acts of "obligatory" brutalization include torture (*Cool Hand Luke* [1967] and *Hunger* [2008]), rape (*American Me* [1992] and *American History X* [1998]), and execution (*I Want to Live!* [1955] and *The Green Mile* [1999]).[57]

Torture, rape, and execution are all referred to in *Camp 14*, as is the one "major incident"—that of the protagonist's escape—which, according to Rafter, most clearly announces a motion picture's membership in the prison film genre.[58] But the film does so in ways that depart somewhat from traditional representations. For instance, and perhaps fittingly, the last of the three violent acts—execution—is typically the final major event to befall the tragically doomed hero (at least in a certain subgenre of the prison film), or else it is witnessed near the end of the narrative as a reminder of the life-and-death stakes involved in that character's heroic escape. However, execution is presented early in Wiese's documentary, as the source of Shin's first traumatic experience as someone born in a North Korean labor colony where public executions were common occurrences.

When Wiese asks him to recall his earliest memory of the camp, Shin hesitates and then says, "There's no particular event that I remember." However, he quickly contradicts himself, adding that his earliest memory is "when I went to a public execution with my mother." The flat matter-of-factness of his statement emphasizes how habituated Shin had become to extraordinary events, which for him had become ordinary circumstances starting around the age of four. This talking-head scene, occurring at the seven-minute mark of the film, comes immediately after a shot of Park Kŭn-un's hand-drawn image of stick-figure prison guards aiming their rifles at camp inmates who are tied to wooden posts.[59] And it immediately precedes Soozandeh's animated rendering of Shin's memory, which includes point-of-view shots from his younger self's position in the crowd of gathered onlookers, looking at the firing squad killing two blindfolded prisoners. Following the sound of gunfire, a reverse-angle shot zooms in on the young

FIGURE 8.2 In one of the many animated sequences in *Camp 14*, Shin is depicted as a young boy witnessing a public execution—a traumatic experience rendered as a highly stylized dramatic reenactment (in lieu of nonexistent photographic evidence).

boy's face (see figure 8.2). His shocked stare, fixed on what he calls "a perfectly ordinary field," sharply contrasts the blank gaze of the older Shin as he sits silently before the camera, clearly affected by that painful recollection. Shifting between newly recorded footage of the protagonist in Seoul and imaginative reenactments of what he claims to have happened when he was in Camp 14 (including images and sounds that no camera was present to record), this early passage of the film crystallizes their complementarity as a form of "documentary dramatics," demonstrating in the process how nonfictional and fictional modes can be harnessed for the sake of both educational enlightenment and emotional connectivity.

Besides this scene of execution, this originary moment of deeply engrained trauma in the life of the inmate, references to rape and torture are sprinkled throughout the documentary, but once again in ways that depart from traditional prison films. Notably, it is from a former secret service officer in North Korea's Ministry of State Security, a middle-age man named O Yŏng-nam, that we hear about the sexual victimization of female prisoners, whose voices are conspicuously absent in a section of the film devoted to a gendered power differential that resulted in many women's losing their lives—or the lives of their babies—after being forcibly impregnated. Although no former female inmate was interviewed by the filmmaker,[60] O's comments, like those of Kwŏn Hyŏk (a former commander of the guards at Camp 22, who also appears onscreen as a talking-head interviewee), are self-incriminating, thus breaking from the genre's normal method of depicting male antagonists (prison guards, wardens, and so on) as either irredeemably bad or utterly unable to hold themselves accountable for their past offenses. Along with the brief, unsettling footage, shot on low-resolution video and "smuggled out of North Korea by a human rights organization," of prison guards brutally interrogating inmates, the two former officers' comments (which are subtitled in English rather than spoken over by Steven Charles) help substantiate or authenticate victims' claims of abusive treatment. As Kwŏn remarks in the film, prisoners in his camp were not "treated as human beings" and were of less use to the officials than animals would have been. "In the camp," he states at one point, "the life of an inmate is worth less than the life of a worm"—a statement that occurs in between blurry video images of an unidentified female prisoner crying in agony as she is beaten on the head with a stick and kicked in the stomach by a guard.

The most emotionally riveting or dramatic scene in *Camp 14* arrives at the film's halfway point, as Shin describes (after a series of lengthy hesitations) how he was involved in his mother's and brother's deaths. After his older sibling escaped from the camp's cement factory and made his way into his mother's cement-floored hovel, the protagonist witnessed him receiving the maternal affection that she had long denied Shin, and this enflamed the fourteen-year-old's jealousy. When the authorities in the camp caught wind of what had happened, they arrested Shin while he was in the camp's meagerly furnished school (where he had been receiving ideological proselytizing rather than any actual education). They then transported him to another type of total institution: a prison *inside the prison*. Like many other internment or labor camps around the world, Kaech'ŏn has a maximum-security detention area inside it to house prisoners deemed most dangerous to the state, and the seven months that Shin spent inside that area were the most mentally and physically challenging.

This jaggedly animated sequence, in which sketchy cross-hatched lines convey the regulated chaos of the situation, shows the blindfolded boy being taken to an interrogation room that recalls the location—witnessed earlier in the film—where guards had been secretly videotaped while beating and berating an unnamed woman. There, guards tie Shin up in ropes and hoist him to the ceiling, leaving him to hang there for hours on end and occasionally lighting a fire under his back to burn away his flesh. Beside this painful flame torture, he experiences water torture, although Shin—in recounting that episode—lets Soozandeh's animation do the work of visually explaining what that entailed. "Many years have passed," he says, clearly ill at ease while seated before the camera. "I don't want to remember these experiences anymore." Yet in present-day Seoul, he raises his arms, which bow unnaturally upward, in front of the lens, and testily turns the line of questioning toward his interviewer, asking why he is cursed with such "deformed" appendages. Once again, the subject's body fleshes out what even the animation is unable to fully reveal, metaphorically putting the viewer in the skin of a man who is "filled with anger" whenever he stands "in front of the mirror." But such corporeal interfacing—between the subject and object of this film's humanitarian gaze—can go only so far in transporting the audience into the space of the other, someone who was tortured regularly while

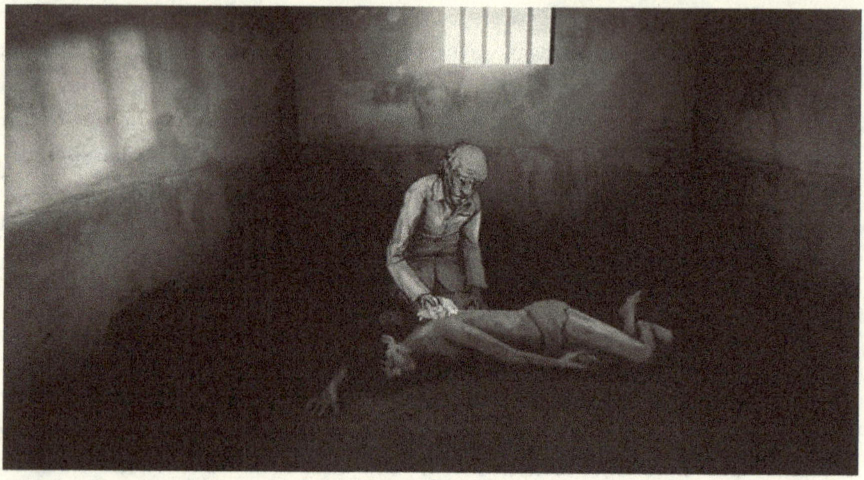

FIGURE 8.3 Shin's friendship with a much older prisoner provided him with the emotional support that he claims was lacking in his family (particularly after the deaths of his mother and brother). This moment of male camaraderie in *Camp 14* suggests that Wiese's unusual documentary includes some of the tropes found in other examples of the prison film genre.

the authorities investigated his mother's and brother's suspicious activities beginning in April 1996.

It is in this section of the film where Shin mentions his friendship with an older prisoner, who kindly tended to his wounds and was the closest thing he had to a caring parent. Meeting the feeble old man in the underground prison was, according to Shin, "a stroke of fortune," and he attributes his survival throughout that seven-month period to his cell mate. For the first time in his life, Shin was the recipient of human affection, and, in a manner that suggests the strong bonds that develop between cell mates in more traditional prison dramas, the man's show of "emotional support"—so needed after Shin's mother was hung and his brother was shot by a firing squad—was enough to sustain him for years after returning to the camp's general population (see figure 8.3). As Rafter notes in *Shots in the Mirror*, one source for prison movies' "enduring popularity" can be found in these onscreen representations of "perfect," unsullied friendships between men (or, in some cases, women). Despite their outward differences, the paradigmatic pair of buddies who together form the heart of many prison films, from *Papillon* (1973) to *The Shawshank Redemption* (1994), are "ideal companions" in that they are "more loyal and true" to one another than they can be, spiritually or emotionally, with anyone else (including family members) outside the carceral setting.[61] Bringing in Shin's feelings about the old man with whom he shared a cramped prison cell, *Camp 14* thus puts itself in league with more traditional examples of carceral cinema, though its failure or refusal to abide by the "rules" of the genre mark it as different.

Tellingly, a list of the "rules and regulations of the labor camp" is read aloud by the offscreen narrator, as if reinforcing the film's status as a plot-driven prison drama for which literal and figurative enforcements are tied to the inmates' closely monitored behavior and to the filmmaker's willingness to abide by the dictates of the genre. Over grainy footage of guards and prisoners secretly recorded at a distance by the former commander Kwŏn in another penal compound (the Hoeryŏng labor colony, or Camp 22), the voice of the English-speaking narrator returns, only this time it is not tethered to that of the Korean-speaking subject. Instead, it operates in much the same way that expositional voice-overs do in more traditional documentaries, didactically informing the audience of something that they would presumably not comprehend without such a device. The narrator intones, with a booming command of the facts:

> Firstly, inmates aren't allowed to escape. Anyone trying to escape *will be shot immediately*. Anybody who sees an inmate trying to escape and doesn't report it *will be shot immediately*. Secondly, stealing is forbidden. Anyone who steals or hides any food *will be shot immediately*. Thirdly, inmates must obey the officer of the state security department completely. Those who display improper or disobedient behavior towards the teacher of the state security department *will be shot immediately*. Fourthly, outside of work, men and women are not allowed to be in contact privately. If physical contact exists between men and women without permission, they *will be shot immediately*. Lastly, inmates must have the deepest remorse for their own mistakes. Those who cannot take responsibility for their own guilt, or who have an opinion about their guilt, *will be shot immediately*.

These are a condensed set of "laws" that Shin and other inmates were forced to memorize and abide by lest they "be shot immediately." A lengthier list, containing ten items, is attached as an appendix to Harden's *Escape from Camp 14*:

1. Do not try to escape.
2. No more than two prisoners can meet together.
3. Do not steal.
4. Guards must be obeyed unconditionally.
5. Anyone who sees a fugitive or suspicious figure must promptly report him.
6. Prisoners must watch one another and report any suspicious behavior immediately.
7. Prisoners must more than fulfill the work assigned them each day.
8. Beyond the workplace, there must be no intermingling between the sexes for personal reasons.
9. Prisoners must genuinely repent of their errors.

The tenth and final rule—"Prisoners who violate the laws and regulations of the camp will be shot immediately"—is simply a reminder of the force and speed of punishment that prisoners will face should they be held in violation of the previous nine rules.[62]

Although no humor can be derived from the dire situation faced by Shin and others, the enumeration of the above items, each carrying the threat of death by gunfire should an infraction occur, might bring a smirk or chuckle of recognition among those viewers who have seen the Hollywood chain-gang picture *Cool Hand Luke*. Indeed, an early scene from that 1967 film, depicting the title character (the Korean War veteran Lucas Jackson, played by Paul Newman) arriving at a Florida prison camp, features dialogue that anticipates the voice-over in *Camp 14*. Specifically, a grizzled floorwalker named Carr informs Luke that a "night in the box" awaits anyone who breaks the following rules:

> Any man forgets his number *spends a night in the box*. . . . Any man loses his spoon *spends a night in the box*. . . . Any man playing grab-ass or fighting in the building *spends a night in the box*. . . . Any man not in his bunk at eight *spends the night in the box*. . . . Any man caught smoking in the prone position in bed *spends a night in the box*. . . . Any man turns in the wrong sheet *spends a night in the box*. . . . Any man with dirty pants on sitting on the bunks *spends a night in the box*. . . . Any man loud talking *spends a night in the box*.

Just as "nearly all prison films" are said to "dwell on the theme of rebellion against injustice,"[63] which *Cool Hand Luke* certainly communicated to its audience in the late 1960s (when people were primed to question the legitimacy of those in command), so do more than a few examples of the genre exhibit this seemingly contradictory predilection for laying down the law. The fact that *Camp 14* does so through the spoken narration of Charles (who, for the first time in the film, is not translating something that Shin is saying but is instead acting as the voice of state authority) suggests that the above rules have seeped so deeply into the psyche of its subject, whose scarred and bent body mirrors the fractured form of the film itself, that such utterances are indeed redundant.

Conclusion

Camp 14 is one of several recently produced cultural artifacts that foreground social injustices and rights violations in North Korea. It thus contributes to shedding light on a subject and a region of the world that previously had been couched in a language of "shadows." But it is also part of a new trend in documentary filmmaking, whereby hand-drawn and computer-generated animation is seen as an instrumental means of expressing the seemingly inexpressible or simply assisting in the full disclosure of private moments that cannot be accessed otherwise. Given the increased output of animated documentaries, it is not surprising to see this recent development—which in fact has roots in much earlier productions (going back to the cartoonist Winsor McCay's 1918 silent twelve-minute short *The Sinking of the Lusitania*)—receive so much scholarly attention. Indeed, some of the most important recent studies of nonfiction cinema have devoted space to animation as an accepted addition to filmmakers' tool kits, alongside more traditional means of getting at the truth or facts of a given topic (including interviews and archival footage).[64]

Foremost among those studies is the work of Annabelle Honess Roe, who has delineated the primary ways in which animation is used in documentary films.[65] As she and other scholars, including Lucia Ricciardelli, have noted, animation can be harnessed as "mimetic substitution," lending visual expression to "events that could not be captured with the camera but that have been documented either auditorially or in written form."[66] This last point anticipates Hillary Chute's argument concerning comics journalism, which frequently "materializes histories from places where photography cannot travel."[67] In a slightly different vein, animation as "non-mimetic substitution" can be used to "showcase the documentarian's imaginative rendering of historical events that have only been recorded verbally."[68] Additionally, animation opens a space for the portrayal of what Ricciardelli describes as "subjective, phenomenological experiences of the real, giving spectators the opportunity to 'imagine the world from someone else's perspective.'"[69] Most famously exemplified by director Ari Folman's *Waltz with Bashir*, a 2008 Israeli production in which the filmmaker excavates his memories of being a soldier in the 1982 Lebanon War, the "expressive function" of documentary (or what Roe refers to simply as "evocation") "responds to a . . . representational limitation" faced by makers of live-action documentaries, who sometimes struggle to bring forth the "emotions, feelings and states of mind" of their filmed subjects[70]—especially those individuals whose lived realities and subjectively felt experiences are so far removed from the day-to-day experiences of most moviegoers.

Bringing together the mimetic, nonmimetic, and evocative functions of documentary animation, *Camp 14* further distinguishes itself from other examples of the prison film genre by demonstrating how the total institution that once confined its protagonist to a life of forced labor north of the 38th Parallel has been internalized and is mentally extended into his new life in the South. On the surface, this aligns with sociologists' claim that "once confined in a total institution, it can be extremely difficult to make the transition back out into the community."[71] Indeed, the totalizing experience from which Shin escaped (but which he carried with him to his new home in Seoul) is evident whenever he is shown walking by himself down the aisles of a sprawling South Korean supermarket or dining alone at a restaurant, while multigenerational families sit at nearby tables. But it also manifests itself on distant shores, as when Shin travels to Geneva (where he speaks at the 2013 Summit for Human Rights, Tolerance and Democracy and receives UN Watch's Moral Courage Award) and Los Angeles (where he meets the young members of Liberty in North Korea, an activist group that sends goods to Shin's former countrymen). In each of these scenes, the former prisoner, quiet and reserved in the company of others, seems emotionally detached from those around him. "My home is over there," he says during a touching scene shot near the Demilitarized Zone, and he points toward North Korea, which he can see only at a distance. This sentiment echoes another of Shin's most revealing comments: "When it comes to my body, I live in South Korea, but in my mind I still live in the camp." Thus, the film disturbs the typical character arc and narrative trajectory at the heart of carceral cinema, giving us an unconventional hero who in some ways longs to return to the place that robbed him of his dignity.

There is much that is contradictory about Shin, who seems resigned to a life of quiescence yet travels the globe to share his experiences with others. The apparent inconsistencies in his character have become magnified recently, as his testimonies have come under scrutiny. As mentioned at the beginning of this chapter, Shin admitted to Harden and others in January 2015 that his initial accounts of prison life were not entirely accurate, following the North Korean regime's rebuttal with his own father as their star witness. Since those highly publicized "revelations," human rights advocates with a vested interest in North Korea have "seriously questioned" Shin's moral standing and credibility, if not the legitimacy of his and other camp survivors' claims about rights violations. Although the harsh conditions of Camp 14 have been revealed "to some extent" by this film, in the words of one group of researchers, the fact that "some of his testimonies were not true" might sit uneasily with those viewers who want and expect documentaries to be fictionless transcriptions of "real life."[72]

However, it is worth remembering, as Jonathan Dawson prompts his readers to do in his study of animated documentaries, that most debates concerning the apparent opposition "between the 'actual' and the 'constructed'" lead to a philosophical "dead end" when it comes to this hybridized mixing of communicative forms.[73] In fact, a great deal of emotional and artistic authenticity—and perhaps even truth—is to be found in the dramatic use of hand-drawn and computer-generated imagery. Although it is impossible to distinguish between facts and fiction in *Escape from Camp 14* and the film *Camp 14*, as the North Korean specialist Andrei Lankov puts it, "even if [Shin] indeed spent a significant part of his life in the 'mild' Camp 18, the Camp 14 did once exist and the abuses of the North Korea's 'absolute control zones' are documented through other independent sources."[74] What is depicted in the book and the documentary are thus true in a fundamental sense as the creative testimony of collective, if not strictly personal, experiences of many voiceless, unknown inmates in the world's harshest penal colonies. If freedom is indeed one of the operative themes in the prison film, then our willingness to grant it to cultural producers who are drawn to stories of incarceration—or, in Marc Wiese's case, drawn to subjects who find themselves somehow trapped by their newfound freedom—might unlock new ways to expand the genre beyond its own barbed-wire confines.

Part 5

Migrant Worker Rights in Hybrid Documentaries

9

Between *Scenery* and Scenario

Landscape, Narrative, and Structured Absence in a Korean Migrant Workers Documentary

> If I am in a car and I look at the scenery through the window, I can at will focus on the scenery or on the windowpane. At one moment I grasp the presence of the glass and the distance of the landscape; at another, on the contrary, the transparence of the glass and the depth of the landscape; but the result of this alternation is constant: the glass is at once present and empty to me, and the landscape unreal and full.
>
> —Roland Barthes, *Mythologies*

The first images that appear in *Scenery* (*P'unggyŏng*, 2013), a feature-length documentary from the Korean-Chinese director Zhang Lu (Chang Ryul), are of cars slicing through a nighttime veil of fog on their way to Incheon International Airport, as seen through the windshield of a moving vehicle. After a few seconds, against the droning whoosh of expressway traffic, an offscreen male voice emerges on the soundtrack. The speaker announces, in a language that is not Korean (thus necessitating subtitles), "I came to South Korea in 2010. I've been working in this country for two and a half years. I'm on my way back to East Timor." Suddenly, we find ourselves inside the brightly lit airport, on an escalator taking the man a few steps closer to his destination. Carrying two pieces of luggage and wearing a San Francisco Giants cap, he is shown from behind as he cryptically explains, in another voice-over, that this is not what he wanted. He is returning to his place of birth out of necessity (for "health reasons"), not for pleasure, although he does plan to reconnect with his family in person for the first time since his mother's recent death. "Every night in my dream I could see her face," states the young man, who—now standing in line before an airline's check-in counter—turns his head to finally reveal his own face. The camera remains at a distance, but the telephoto lens endows this brief airport scene with a degree of intimacy, even as it shifts position to show, behind him, another group of travelers who might likewise be preparing to return to their homeland. Then, racking focus from that trio of men in the background to this lonely figure in the foreground, the camera allows our vision to momentarily settle on someone who, only a few seconds later, will once again disappear in a crowd, never to be seen again in this most transnational of rights-advocacy films.

For all intents and purposes, Augustino, the East Timorese man whose name eventually appears onscreen, might be the main character in a more straightforward and crowd-pleasing motion picture about South Korea's increasingly multicultural society. In that hypothetical film, audiences might discover details about his health problems and witness the family's reunion in his mother country. After receiving medical care, the protagonist would eventually return to Seoul, where he would resume his life as a low-skilled laborer whose trials, tribulations, and ultimate triumph over adversity would serve as reassuring proof that, while foreigners sometimes face obstacles in South Korea, the country's civil society ensures fair and equal treatment in the end. However, Augustino, the downhearted individual whose face goes from being an obscured blur to an in-focus object of our spectatorial gaze (before getting lost in the crowd), is just one of the many migrant workers (*oegukin ijunodongja*) who populate Zhang's *Scenery*, an episodic film that is as torn between cultural spaces and experiential states as Augustino is.

As the writer-director of several critically lauded films concerning Sino-Korean relations, diasporic communities, and the rights of ethnic minorities as well as other marginalized members of Chinese society, Zhang has earned a reputation as one of the most socially conscious filmmakers in his home country. Born in Yanbian, China, as a third-generation ethnic Korean, this former novelist and short-story writer made a midcareer leap into the world of cinema in the early 2000s, leading to the production of such feature-length works as *Tang Poetry* (*Tang si*, 2003) and *Grain in Ear* (*Mangzhong*, 2005).[1] After his

2012 relocation to South Korea, Zhang has continued to grapple with the above themes—albeit with a newly transplanted focus on Korean society's often discriminatory attitudes toward its own cultural outsiders, many of whom live in the ethnic enclaves of Seoul and other cities. Among his most recent independent productions, which include the languidly paced narrative features *Kyŏngju* (2014), *Love and . . .* (*P'ilrŭmsidae sarang*, 2015), *A Quiet Dream* (*Ch'unmong*, 2016), and *Ode to the Goose* (*Kunsan: Kŏwirŭl nolaehada*, 2018), *Scenery* stands out as an exemplar of what Marcia Landy, Sean Redmond, Daniela Berghahn, Claudia Sternberg, and other scholars call "minoritarian cinema."[2] "Minoritarian cinema" can be defined as a form of cultural expression that begins on the margins but crosses or unsettles boundaries between inside and outside, or the personal and the collective, while emphasizing processes of *becoming* (rather than being) through such migratory maneuvers. It is often oppositional toward official histories and traditional storytelling techniques that present a straightforward account of heroic feats on the part of a select few celebrated figures, and it uses alternative devices instead (for example, narrative gaps, nonchronological structures, and large ensemble casts featuring a mix of ethnic and/or sexual identities).

Distinguished from Zhang's other films by its nonfictional form, *Scenery* is also unique as a structurally fragmented and aesthetically hybrid text comprised of separate episodes in which fourteen migrant workers share their dreams with the unseen filmmaker, speaking directly to the camera through talking-head interviews. That episodic structure is significant insofar as multiple perspectives on the plights of foreigners (hailing from such places as Bangladesh, Cambodia, the Philippines, Thailand, and Uzbekistan) are presented alongside a series of experimental interludes and exterior shots (of factories, building sites, and agricultural zones) in which this long-marginalized part of South Korea's labor force is either visually peripheralized or simply not to be found. Thus, the "scenery" in this fittingly titled film is marked by an uncanny absence as well as presence: that of a growing population of laborers who, until recently, were part of the backdrop of the nation's economic growth but who have increasingly come to the fore both in official governmental campaigns and in cultural productions that highlight their predicament as an exploitable resource forced to perform often physically demanding and sometimes demeaning work.[3]

In this chapter, we provide a lens through which to witness the rise of such cultural productions as a response to neoliberal policies and multicultural initiatives on the part of the South Korean government (during the administration of President Lee Myung-bak [Yi Myŏng-bak; 2008–2013] as well as earlier administrations). Theoretical concepts that are native to film studies as well as those traditionally located in other scholarly fields (including sociology, urban geography, and political science) will be joined together to offer a broad framework for the textual analysis that follows. Then, turning to our main case study, we explore the dialectical tensions in *Scenery*, including that between the seen and the unseen, or the visible and the invisible. Notably, it is through the diasporic subjects' own verbalized (rather than visualized) recountings of their dreams—as well as of their feelings of loneliness, longing, and loss—that a semblance of "story" begins to compete with nonnarrative forms in this experimental yet scenario-driven documentary. Fixated on the physical landscapes in which migrant workers have toiled invisibly for so many years, yet also drawn to the private day-to-day lives of individuals who are tasked with telling their own stories, Zhang's *Scenery* ultimately resists easy categorization just as the interviewees—visually framed by the ever-sensitive filmmaker (who, as an outsider himself, is sympathetic to their struggles)—cannot be reduced to mere statistics. It is therefore telling and indeed ironic that this film begins with a scene involving a migrant worker's departure from rather than entrance into a space (Incheon International Airport) that signifies South Korea's global connectedness to other regions as well as the hopes and dreams that often spur foreigners like Augustino to leave their pasts and home countries behind in pursuit of a better future.

Setting the Scene(ry): Contextualizing Migrant Workers' Rights

Discussions of the topic of transnational migration in South Korea have exploded in recent years, owing to internal and external pressures that have been placed on government organizations and civil society as a whole to uphold the rule of law while protecting the rights of an ever-growing number of documented and undocumented workers. Today, approximately 25 percent of the 2.3 million foreigners living in the country are migrant workers (including both those with and those without papers), hailing from such disparate places as China, Sri Lanka, Uzbekistan, and Vietnam. As the objects rather than subjects of neoliberal discourse and policy making, these men and women continue to be exploited and mobilized as evidence of South Korea's hospitality as a host country even as they are gaining a voice in the public sphere and becoming a more visible presence in television programs like the JTBC (Joonang Tongyang Broadcasting Company) talk show *Non-Summit* (*Pijŏngsanghoedam*, 2014–) and motion pictures like Sim Sang-guk's *Where Is Ronny . . .* (*Roni-rŭl ch'ajasŏ*, 2008) and Sin Tong-il's *Bandhobi* (*Pandubi*, 2009).[4] That is, migrant workers are leaving a significant cultural and demographic imprint on a nation that now prides itself, perhaps prematurely, on the great strides that it has made in transitioning from a "hermit kingdom" with a long history of "cultural homogeneity" to a cosmopolitan space of multiethnic inclusiveness (if not quite heterogeneity).[5] Of course, xenophobic attitudes still percolate below that optimistic surface, and foreigners continue to be exposed to discrimination, surveillance, passport confiscation, and outright abuse at the hands of their employers. Moreover, most migrant laborers lack access to health care, social security, welfare support, and workers' compensation, as Hakjae Kim and other scholars remind us.[6] But it would be shortsighted not to admit that, in this age of human rights advocacy and labor movements supported by nongovernmental organizations (NGOs), progressive steps have been taken to extend democratic liberties to all people living in South Korea, including immigrants.

As summarized in a 2006 Amnesty International report, South Korea began to transition to an economy based on product exportation and labor importation around 1987, when approximately 6,500 undocumented migrant workers sought employment in agriculture, construction, manufacturing, and other blue-collar fields requiring little or no formal education.[7] Not coincidentally, a self-organized prodemocracy movement swept through the country in the summer of 1987. That movement called for political reform and an end to the corruption that during the authoritarian administration of President Chun Doo-hwan (Chŏn Tu-hwan; 1980–1988) had been seeping into every sector of society, from the highest echelons of large firms like Daewoo, Samsung, and Lucky-Goldstar to the mining and fishing industries in the mountains and along the coasts. A series of sometimes violent mass protests, collectively known as the Great Workers' Struggle, was initiated in the three-week period from June 10 to June 29. It came to a head in August, when millions of strikers (from shipyard workers to taxi drivers) took to the streets of Seoul, Ulsan, and other cities to demand wage increases, overtime bonuses, and better working conditions. By the time the dust finally settled at the end of the year, Roh Tae-woo (No T'ae-u) had won the presidency. Not long after that national election, which officially terminated South Korea's long history of dictatorships, over 3,400 new trade unions were founded, a sign that the mass insurrection had been successful despite the enormous price that had been paid by a populace willing to give their lives to a cause greater than their own self-interest.

In 1991, the same year that the Roh administration greenlighted a controversial program called the Industrial Trainee System (Sanŏp yŏsujae; overseen by the Korean Federation of Small Businesses, this system treated temporary, unskilled foreign workers "as trainees rather than as legal laborers"),[8] the number of migrant workers in the country jumped to approximately 40,000.[9] That sharp increase, coming a mere four years after the 1987 uprising, can be attributed to a number of factors, including the emergence of volunteer activists and nonprofit advocacy groups; the lobbying efforts of the federation; and the rapid growth of the South Korean economy, which attracted the attention of people in developing nations throughout East and Southeast Asia.[10] As one of the four so-called Asian Tigers (along with Hong Kong, Singapore, and Taiwan), South Korea had witnessed its per capita gross domestic product soar in a relatively short span of time, and—at least until the International Monetary Fund (IMF) Crisis a few years later (foretold by the accumulation of foreign debts and the devaluation of the Korean won)—the country was flush enough to provide aid to other nations after the establishment of the Korean International Cooperation Agency in 1991. And while many of the country's manufacturing giants and financial sectors began to turn their attention to high-tech industries in which most jobs were held by college-educated, white-collar business professionals, cheap labor was still needed to sustain that level of economic development. Thus, it is easy to see why entrepreneurial business owners, in the midst of labor shortages and plummeting birthrates, saw foreign workers as an attractive resource, and why farmers, bricklayers, fishermen, and other people from countries like Bangladesh, Cambodia, and Myanmar might have looked to South Korea as a beacon. Indeed, it was an opportunity for them to step into the so-called 3-D jobs (that is, jobs considered to be dirty, dangerous, and difficult) that fewer and fewer Koreans were willing to do cheaply.

Despite the abovementioned events, it would take another four years before the issue of migrant workers' rights first gained national prominence, which occurred thanks to a widely reported sit-in protest staged by thirteen Nepali workers outside Myŏngdong Cathedral between New Year's Day and January 9, 1995. Located in the heart of Seoul, this place of Catholic worship has long been a "site of labor and democracy movement demonstrations,"[11] and it is shown in documentarian Kim Dong-won's *The 6-Day Struggle at the Myŏngdong Cathedral* (*Myŏngsŏng, kŭ 6-ilŭi kirok*, 1997). Hence its significance as a staging ground for social justice and human rights advocacy in the eyes of those "industrial trainees" who, despite having grown accustomed to economic hardship in their home countries, chose to leave their factory jobs in Seoul after being forced to work fifteen hours a day while putting up with "physical and verbal assaults" from their employers and coworkers.[12] As EuyRyung Jun notes, before the protesters had grabbed their placards and chained themselves together for nine chilly winter days (a half-dozen of which are the focus of the documentary), they had sought help from several civic groups, including the Chun Center for Migrant Workers and the Citizens' Coalition for Economic Justice (the headquarters of which had been the location of a less-publicized sit-in one year earlier).[13] Silently making their demands known through large handwritten placards (which carried messages like "Please don't beat us," "We are not slaves," "Pay us our wages," and "Return our confiscated passports"), the protesters not only forced native-born South Koreans to confront the dehumanizing conditions in which they had been forced to work but also served as a source of inspiration for other immigrants, making it possible for the voices of the latter to eventually be heard as well. Because the Nepali workers' request for fair and equal treatment was witnessed and documented by news reporters for *Chosun Ilbo* and other media outlets, the demonstration's impact on South Korea's governmental and religious institutions was "immediate," according to Keiko Yamanaka, who notes Cardinal Stephen Kim's public apology to the people of Nepal as well as the increased number of prosecutors' investigations that followed the protest.[14] The eventual arrest of "law-breaking brokers and employers," as well as the "establishment of a special court" that became part of a larger public policy apparatus (one designed to safeguard the basic human rights of immigrants in the country) provided further evidence that South Korea was finally willing to undertake significant institutional changes for the sake of improving the lives of foreign workers.[15]

Several scholars have claimed that the Nepali workers' protest of 1995 was a pivotal moment in the recent history of South Korean labor politics. For example, EuyRyung Jun maintains that the sit-in "opened up an emergent field of migrant advocacy comprising various individuals (church ministers, human rights activists, labor activists, lawyers, lay volunteers, and college students, as well as migrants themselves) and various groups (churches, migrant centers, labor unions, lawyers' groups, and college students' support groups, as well as migrants' own communities)."[16] In an effort to combine resources and unite around a common cause, several immigrant organizations, religious groups, charities, and local NGOs launched the Joint Committee for Migrants in Korea, a multiethnic collective that, according to Hakjae Kim, eventually partnered with labor unions to push for structural changes in the Employment Permit System (Koyong hŏgaje; EPS).[17] Ostensibly, the EPS was enacted in 2003 to protect the rights of foreign workers, and the system has certainly made it possible for migrant laborers to enjoy the benefits of labor laws such as the Industrial Safety and Health Act, the Labor Standards Act, and the Minimum Wage Act. Thus, it was initially seen as a considerable improvement over the Industrial Trainee System, which it replaced in 2004. However, as Timothy Lim and other political scientists have argued, the EPS, which actually gives employment priority to ethnic Korean workers rather than transnational workers, ultimately diminished the already limited power of the latter group and put more power in the hands of management (who "have the right to dismiss migrants without justification").[18] Yes, migrant workers' rights to organize and engage in collective bargaining remained intact, but, as Jun reminds us, "in reality . . . [workers'] rights can be easily overridden by the employers' right to hire and fire, and, above all, by the clause that puts limitations on the length of stay for migrants."[19]

It is significant that 2003, when the liberal administration of President Roh Moo-hyun (No Mu-hyŏn; 2003–2008) enacted the EPS, also witnessed another sit-in protest at Myŏngdong Cathedral, one that was led by the Joint Committee for Migrants in Korea and the Equality Trade Union's Migrant's Branch.[20] This time, a mixed group of foreigners—not only from Nepal but from other countries as well—were reacting to an ultimatum that had been issued by the government in November of that year and that threatened to deport 120,000 illegal workers as well as people who had overstayed their visas. Facing the prospect of compulsory expulsion, several dozen men and women spent 380 days at the protest site, where they solidified their pan-ethnic solidarity in the presence of numerous cameras and reporters. Intermittently, they were joined by South Korean media activists from MediAct (a public institution partially funded by the Korean Film Council) and other local groups. As Hyun Mee Kim and other scholars have described it, besides giving the strikers an opportunity to gain a broad media-based education during those days, MediAct played a part in the

December 2004 creation of Migrant Workers' Television, an alternative to South Korea's mainstream media, which had largely silenced foreigners' voices and denied them the ability to tell their own stories.[21] In contrast, Migrant Workers' Television—along with the annual Migrant Workers' Film Festival that was initiated by social activists in 2006 (and that would thereafter receive support from the Ministry of Public Administration and Security, the South Korean Film Council, and the National Human Rights Commission of Korea), gave these men and women a public forum in which to speak truth to power.[22] As extensions of the 2003 Myŏngdong Cathedral sit-in, these developments were among the first inklings that South Korea's cultural producers, including filmmakers and television writers, had begun to direct their attention to a topic that previously had largely been confined to newspaper pages and websites.

These contextualizing comments about the recent history of migrant workers' advocacy efforts might seem tangential or unrelated to the thematic concerns and stylistic distinctiveness of Zhang Lu's *Scenery*. Certainly, nothing as dramatic or harrowing as a hunger strike, kidnapping, or forced deportation takes place in the film, though these did occur during the Myŏngdong Cathedral sit-in of 2003–2004. However, because of *Scenery*'s apparent lack of such historical details and its focus on the uneventful quotidian lives of over a dozen individuals, an informed understanding of the stakes involved in migrant workers' ongoing fight for human rights helps flesh out the otherwise cryptic dreams and incomplete stories spoken by its fourteen subjects. Additionally, the documentary's unique status as a text situated between reality and representation, observation and narration, and outsider and insider views of migrant workers, as well as the spaces they occupy, is thrown into relief when we consider the two main strains of cinematic activism that were showcased at the Migrant Workers' Film Festival (as well as its contemporary incarnation, the Migrant World Film Festival)—namely, large-scale feature-length motion pictures *about* foreigners living in South Korea and small-scale short films and videos *by* foreigners living in South Korea. *Scenery* brings these strains together, although it tilts in favor of the latter—which, as Hyun Mee Kim notes, serves as "a platform for migrants to express themselves as autonomous or culturally cosmopolitan beings in resistance to the restrictive and discriminating conditions imposed upon them."[23]

Before we transition to a textual analysis of this film, it is helpful to reflect on the words of one of the Nepali protesters at the 1995 Myŏngdong Cathedral sit-in, who explained to a reporter that he and his cohort had decided to come to South Korea "because there was no work in our country and because we wanted to get out of our poverty." "We all had good dreams when we left for Korea," he continued, but "we can hardly describe the situation we are facing here." The protester's statement, which concluded with an appeal to Koreans "to treat us not as animals but as equal brethren and human beings" (a sentiment also expressed by a Chinese Korean protest leader in Zhang's 2018 *Ode to the Goose*), will likely resonate with anyone who has seen *Scenery*, a film that dwells on both the "good dreams" and the "bad dreams" that a mixed group of migrant workers individually share with viewers during its ninety-six-minute running time. However, that protester's statement—which appears to have been a genuine, truth-filled speech act on the part of a disenfranchised group when it first began to circulate via South Korea's mainstream media–was "carefully structured through the gaze of the host and of its neoliberal developmentalism," according to Jun.[24] Therefore, we should be circumspect about this or any other film's ability to truthfully lay bare the migrant worker experience without the least hint of complicity in neoliberal policies and national agendas.

Episodic Cinema and Ethnic Enclaves: "Permanent Temporariness"

> Home is wherever you settle down.
>
> —Noodle shop owner Lily (Moon Suk), speaking to main characters Yun-yŏng (Park Hae-il) and Song-hyŏn (Moon So-ri) in writer-director Zhang Lu's *Ode to the Goose* (2018)

As alluded to above, Zhang's *Scenery*—a project requested by officials for the Jeonju International Film Festival (who in 2013 asked the director to make a film about "strangers")[25]—distinguishes itself from earlier motion pictures about foreigners living in South Korea through its refusal to abide by some of the conventions of commercial filmmaking and traditional storytelling. One of the film's most unusual characteristics is its episodic structure, its digressive approach to the subject of the migrant worker experience. Rather than focus on the travails of one person, who is elevated to the status of a universal heroic symbol of the determination required to combat prejudice and to survive (or even thrive) in a labor regime that is inherently discriminatory, *Scenery* opts to spread its observational gaze across a panoramic array of differently situated individuals (see figure 9.1). Structured around a series of entrances and exits interrupted by poetic shots of natural and man-made environments, the film provides a continuous change of scenery for viewers who might wish to delve more deeply into a given person's backstory or current situation as a migrant worker but who ultimately witness a broadly evocative cross section of testimonies rooted in the quotidian. In a way, this discursive documentary is both smaller and larger than other cinematic incursions into the ethnic enclaves of Seoul. In chaining together short interviews with fourteen immigrants from nearly as many countries, all residing in various parts of the capital city and its surrounding environs, Zhang presents the viewer with a panoply of discrete life experiences. This is indicative of the film's tactical, bottom-up approach, with its attentiveness to small, unremarkable moments in the lives of its subjects. Any thematic overlap between the otherwise autonomous episodes that the spectator might notice contributes to

FIGURE 9.1 Korean-Chinese filmmaker Zhang Lu's 2013 film *Scenery* (*P'unggyŏng*) consists of separate episodes in which fourteen migrant workers share their dreams with the unseen filmmaker, speaking directly to the camera through talking-head interviews. *Scenery*'s title alludes to the spaces and places in which the subjects live and work—agricultural, industrial, and residential vistas that are shown in extreme long shots.

the film's countervailing universalism and structural coherence, its strategic top-down view of those subjects' cross-ethnic connectedness.

The idea of the ethnic enclave—an ethnically concentrated geographic area in which a group's cultural identity is retained as an alternative to the host society's dominant culture—is one way to begin unpacking this film's structure. Each of the film's short segments opens a window onto a world that is contained within the larger setting of South Korea, a landscape of assimilative belonging that has become increasingly peppered with sites of social and cultural difference. Thus, it is useful to consider the work of sociologists and geographers who have researched the recent growth of ethnic enclaves in Seoul and other cities. For instance, Seonyoung Seo and Tracey Skelton have discussed the ways in which the capital city's Nepali diaspora—specifically, the men, women, and children living and working in the neighborhood of Ch'angsin-dong, colloquially known as Nepal Town—have created a space of "connection, leisure time, and resistive possibilities."[26] Like the areas of Daerim-dong and Yŏnnam-dong (where concentrated pockets of Chinese people can be found), Ch'angsin-dong is a burgeoning "home away from home" for many immigrants who have managed to find "mobility, freedom and safety" in a sometimes inhospitable environment.[27] Other neighborhoods and towns, including Kwanghŭi-dong (for Mongolians), Hyehwa-dong (for Filipinos), and Wangsimni (for Vietnamese), likewise demonstrate foreigners' ability to create "a sense of security for themselves in precarious working and living conditions and in the face of processes of exclusion in the host countries."

Despite the positive aspects of community building described by Seo and Skelton, who acknowledge some of the various ways in which migrants "challenge labour politics" in the company of others with whom they share cultural traditions, Ch'angsin-dong—like other ethnic enclaves or "villages" in and around Seoul—is becoming "a space of *permanent temporariness*."[28] Borrowing the latter concept from social geographers such as Francis Leo Collins, the authors' use of that term conjures up the in-between status of migrant workers "on temporary visas or permits as a long-term or permanent part" of Korean cities' "economic, social, cultural and political landscapes."[29] But the authors also provide a clue as to how episodic films like *Scenery* evoke that liminal status through a conjoining of seemingly contradictory narrative and nonnarrative modes. Indeed, the fleeting encounters with cultural outsiders provided by the film, in addition to the regularity with which Zhang applies certain formal and rhetorical devices, suggest a perpetual state of being on the move, despite each episode's incorporation of static talking-head shots in which there is little or no movement on the part of the speakers.

Consider, for instance, the fifth interviewee to appear in the film, a lettuce picker from Bangladesh named Oaliullah Bhuiyan. He is framed by Zhang's immobile camera inside his small apartment, praying while facing in the direction of Mecca and sharing a meager meal with two other workers. Although he has been living apart from his wife since he came to South Korea, she has begun to appear in his dreams. One recent dream has been especially memorable, according to Bhuiyan: In it, he and his wife take a trip to Jeju Island, a tourist destination off the coast of the Korean Peninsula. Humorously, the Bangladeshi admits that he has never been to the island and does not even know where it is located, but he found it to be "beautiful" in his dream. "We went there and we saw mountains," he says to the camera, continuing with a description of the tangerine trees and grapevines that he and other "tourists from various countries" encountered when they set foot on that imaginatively constructed but wholly artificial version of the actual vacation spot. Here, the film's emphasis on the constructedness of a cultural ideal—in this case, a tourist destination that presumably welcomes vacationing couples from around the world—maps onto the general misperception of South Korea as a country that is hospitable to foreigners. The speaker's description of the island in this segment is thus the verbal equivalent of *Scenery*'s visual privileging of natural and man-made landscapes that are at once transporting and stultifying, liberating and incapacitating.

Bhuiyan's fantasy of Jeju as a beautiful paradise reminds us of the similar dream that drew over 550 Yemeni asylum seekers and refugees to the island in 2018 (taking advantage of the tourist island's policy of allowing foreigners to spend up to thirty days there without a visa). One of those Yemenis is Jamal Nasiri, a former agricultural officer who brought his wife and five daughters to Jeju, a faraway place that the family saw as an attractive alternative to their war-torn home country. In his interview with the *New York Times*, Nasiri explained,

"We think about our future, how to keep our children safe and send them to school for a better life, because we are humans."[30] However, such hopes were effectively squashed, and Jeju turned out to be a mirage akin to what is expressed by Bhuiyan in Zhang's film. The temporary presence of a few hundred refugees on a remote island (barred from entering the mainland while their asylum applications were reviewed) sparked widespread xenophobia throughout South Korea, with more than 714,000 petitioners directly pressuring President Moon Jae-in to deport the Yemenis. From Jeju to Seoul, thousands of protesters took to the streets with prorefugee picket signs marching opposite anti-immigrant demonstrators whose slogans read "Korean Nationals Should Come First," "Abolish Asylum Law," "Islam Fake Refugees Get Out," and "We Want Safety, Not Hatred." In the midst of controversy, the South Korean government granted asylum status to only 2 applicants. It permitted 412 others to stay for one year on humanitarian visas that restrict employment and exclude many benefits provided to people who are given asylum, such as health care and the right to invite family members to join them. Those people were left with broken hearts and shattered dreams, like so many migrants before them.

Instead of politicizing his subjects (that is, turning his interviewees into witnesses who criticized South Korea's immigration policies and labor relations), Zhang and his cinematographer, Cho Yŏng-jik, maintained an empathetic yet ethical distance from their subjects, whom the diasporic filmmaker has called "people who have different lifestyles from me but are in a similar position [as foreigners]."[31] As the Korean critic Chŏng Han-sŏk states, "*Scenery* is not a film of or about dreams," as they are merely a means of revealing the "collective unconsciousness" and "emotional episteme of underclass migrant workers."[32] Such tension between the singular (the individual dreamers and their stories) and the collective (the larger environment or context in which social alienation is experienced) becomes evident around the film's midpoint, at the forty-seven-minute mark.

In the span of just two minutes, we are introduced to a young woman named Ganga Basnet. Images of a cramped yet empty apartment lead to a static long shot of Ganga in profile as she sits alone on her bed. Her voice-over informs us that she moved from Nepal to South Korea two years earlier in search of a job. After becoming a housekeeper, she met a Cambodian woman who may have eased Ganga into the assimilation or integration process (the audience cannot be sure about this, however, and must intuit many of the details that are left unspoken). However, because she and her friend had to sleep in different bedrooms, Ganga (who now speaks directly to the camera) often felt alone and suffered from recurring nightmares. Her testimony echoes the sentiments of another interviewee (from the film's third episode): a young woman from Vietnam named Hoang Thanh who, while repetitively inserting metal rings into plastic packages at work, describes a nightmarish vision of her drunk and abusive father chasing her. Returning to Ganga's voice-over, the film provides a new view of the woman (now shown in a medium close-up), who slowly slips out of the frame as the camera pans to the left. We learn that she eventually went to work in Kyŏnggi-do, a province surrounding Seoul that has seen its number of Nepal-born workers rise in recent years. Indeed, because there were already four Nepali employees at her new job, the hiring process was relatively easy for her, Ganga states. Although she began to have back pains after relocating, "the city hall helped [her] to get proper treatment," apparently paying some of the medical fees so that she could receive surgery at Seoul's St. Mary's Hospital. Nevertheless, despite this unusually strong show of support for a migrant worker on the part of the local government, Ganga's nightmares returned—dreams in which dead people from her village back in Nepal tried to take her away from her new (yet temporary) home. By the time she wraps up her commentary and says that she can no longer "sleep properly" as a result of her accumulated stress, the camera has panned fully to the left, leaving her out of frame and focusing instead on an empty bedroom seen through an open doorway.

The open doorway, which provides a view of nothing of particular importance, marks the end of this segment and the beginning of the next one (another short interview, this time featuring Prayoon Puekhunthod, a man from Thailand who likewise suffers from nightmares involving ghosts from his past). Similarly unconventional compositions—framings of interior or exterior spaces lacking human figures—are threaded throughout the entire film, as if Zhang has been inspired by earlier art film directors like Michelangelo Antonioni and would rather leave the mystery of certain characters' musings intact than fill in details about their backstories or have them explain their potentially heated encounters with Korean authorities. Indeed, *Scenery*'s empty yet full mise-en-scène, denoted as well by the landscape shot that begins Ganga's episode (that of ocean waves lapping onto an unspecified beach), encourages audiences to fill in the gaps of this enigmatic text and to detect similarities among the fourteen subjects who are shown (and frequently not shown) in compositionally consistent ways. Thus, vacancy of image correlates to narrational incompleteness, indicating the way in which scenery and scenario are linked together by a filmmaker who rejects traditional forms of storytelling in favor of techniques that Angela Ndalianis associates with art cinema. According to her, "Art cinema adopts a looser narrative form that breaks up linearity and causality through . . . ellipsis (which creates narrative gaps); 'dead time' (action that has little or no effect on narrative progression); episodic sequences paralleled by drifting, aimless protagonists; and an open-ended structure."[33] Although typically the "cinematic image" is prioritized over "narrative exposition" by art film directors, Zhang's documentary reveals how scenery, as the "visual esthetic experience of nature,"[34] is no less artificial or dubious than narrative as a representation of reality.

One of the most consistently employed visual markers in *Scenery* is that of fog or some other atmospheric or material screen coming between the viewer and the landscape or figures who are the film's ostensible subjects. The first time this

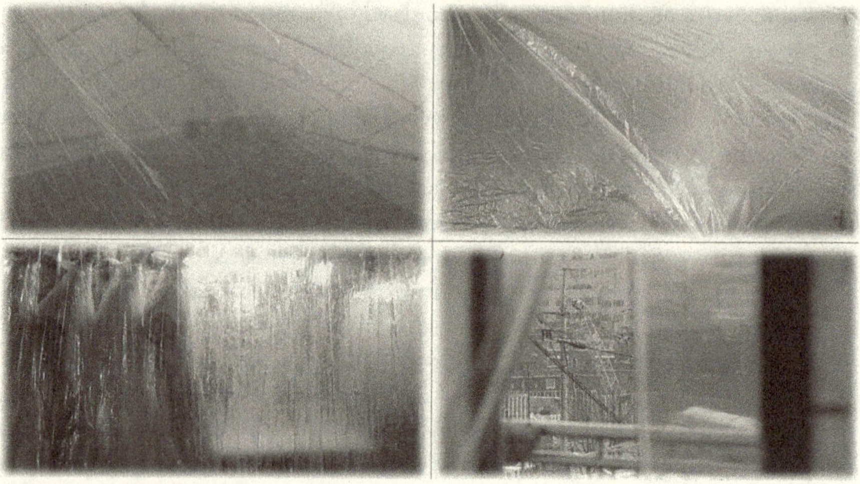

FIGURE 9.2 Throughout *Scenery*, Zhang obscures the spectator's view of the environment by filming through semitransparent curtains and plastic sheets—an approach that hints at his unusual approach to the subject of migrant workers (a largely "invisible" labor force in cultural productions until recently).

obscuring device occurs is immediately after the opening episode of the film (Augustino's segment) ends. Mimicking the film's first scene, shot through the windshield of a moving car, the camera once again travels down the expressway, only this time the wintry view is obscured by a dense layer of white fog that blots out the background. A palimpsest-like assemblage of tall, ghostly buildings in the distance is faintly suggested, but there are no details. Against this empty yet full scenery, the film's title (*P'unggyŏng*) appears. This shot, eerily similar to the landscape paintings by the Chinese artist Qiu Shihua,[35] is the first of many such occasions when Zhang restricts our vision, veiling what would otherwise be a source of spectatorial contemplation. For example, subsequent sequences feature exterior and interior shots in which the framed image is blurred by semitransparent curtains, plastic sheets, and protective shells that direct our gaze away from the objects and toward the medium itself (see figure 9.2).

The filmmaker's approach to the subject of migrant workers in South Korea, then, is both unorthodox and entirely in keeping with their long history of nonrepresentation in popular culture. That is, Zhang delivers two contrasting ways of seeing foreigners' invisible but paradoxically hypervisible presence in a country where their many contributions to society have largely gone unrecognized or been obscured by a legalistic discourse that reduces migrants to the dehumanizing level of statistics or other data. But the director, in beginning *Scenery* in this way, also brings to mind a passage from Roland Barthes's "Myth Today," quoted as an epigraph at the beginning of this chapter. The French philosopher discusses the idea of scenery as something that is either accessed by or denied to the viewer through the intervening window of a vehicle in motion. For

Barthes, attention alternates between the presence of the glass and the distance of the landscape, between emptiness and fullness—contradictory modes of experience that are collapsed in this film.[36]

Landscape, Nature, and Scenery: Locating and Pictorializing Otherness

It is worth pointing out that there is a subtle difference between "landscape" and "scenery," although the Korean term *p'unggyŏng*, which can be translated as either of those English words, obscures such distinctions. In *Man in the Landscape*, the environmental theorist Paul Shepard reminds readers that the word "scenery" is derived from the Greek term for "stage," and indeed the concept evokes a theatrical organization of the visual field as an "immobile display," in the words of Larry W. Riggs—one that is "viewed by a detached observer."[37] Besides theater, other pictorial forms of expression such as painting and photography have solidified the idea of scenery as a "beautiful" abstraction of nature. Unlike landscape, which captures a sense of the natural geography and physical layout of a given space, scenery is more concerned with picturesque appearances and "the world of illusion." The Chinese American geographer Yi-Fun Tuan perhaps puts it best: although "often used interchangeably" as signifiers of nature, such commutability blinds us to the fact that the word "landscape," in its original sense, "referred to the *real* world, not the world of *art* and *make-believe*" that is bound up in the word "scenery."[38] Yet for all of the latter term's suggestion of the kind of static, consumable images that are found in a theatrical or photographic frame, "the itinerant eye" of the traveler or tourist must first encounter an environment before it can be translated or pictorialized into scenery.[39] Therefore, movement as well as stasis contributes to the latter's dialectical blending of elements.

Notably, discussions of scenery can be found in several writings about South Korean cinema. A representative use of the term pops up in Eunsun Cho's study of *Adada* (1987), director Im Kwon-taek (Im Kwŏn-t'aek)'s exploration of colonial-era patriarchy and female suffering in which "women's bodies are exploited to fabricate 'the scene of han' . . . by being inserted or transfigured into the scenery of premodern Korea."[40] And what, exactly, is that film's scenery comprised of? In Cho's words, it is "mountains veiled in mist, the green rice fields of spring where people have just scattered seeds, or the golden rice fields of autumn waving in the wind." The diffused light and colors of these tranquil natural settings, she concludes, evoke "the textures of oriental watercolor painting" and "produce a feeling of natural harmony, nostalgia, and pictorialized sadness."[41] However, Cho goes beyond the standard meaning of scenery to suggest how the title character in *Adada*, a deaf-mute woman who—in the words of Adam Hartzell—has been "married off to a noble but poor family for her desirable dowry of rice fields,"[42] is subjugated as a kind of natural resource of the nation.

As she states, the female protagonist is "not allowed to articulate her suffering but [instead] becomes the mythic scenery of Korea," as silent yet pictorially enticing as the valuable agricultural land that she gives her cruel husband.[43] Similarly, Cho Hae Joang, in her discussion of *Sopyonje* (1993), another period piece directed by Im that concerns the plight of a woman with disabilities, refers to Korea's rural scenery and the musical storytelling tradition known as *pansori* as "props" that "put 'Korean' clothes on modern subjects."[44]

Going beyond questions of pictorial beauty and outward appearances, other film scholars have drawn upon the suggestiveness of the word "scenery" to evoke the social milieu in which Koreans find themselves as a result of decades of Westernization and foreign intrusion. For instance, Hyangjin Lee, author of *Contemporary Korean Cinema*, paints a vivid picture of the "frantic social scenery of post-war Korea" when discussing, ironically, the sounds rather than images one encounters while watching Yu Hyŏn-mok's *A Stray Bullet* (*Obalt'an*, 1961)—including those of church bells, English phrases, and an aging woman's repetitive statement "Kaja! Kaja!" ("Let's go!"). In this reading of Yu's postwar classic, "scenery" has less to do with any imagistic evocations of natural beauty than it does with the harsh urban landscape that has witnessed "local" or national culture being replaced or threatened by international signifiers and U.S. American hegemony.[45] Lee's use of the word "scenery," then, corresponds to the manner in which Cho Jun-hyoung discusses another Golden Age film of the 1960s, director Yi Man-hŭi's *A Day Off* (Hyuil, 1968). In his notes accompanying the DVD of this film (released by the Korean Film Archive), Cho explains that the "lead character . . . is the scenery." Implied in his use of the word is not only the physical locations through which an unemployed young man named Hŏ-uk listlessly drifts (including "the windy and desolated Mt. Nam, the back alleys around Myŏngdong and Ch'ungmuro filled with coffee shops and bars, the deserted spaces filled with construction debris," and so on), but also the time of modernization and military dictatorship ("when traditional values were collapsing rapidly and intellectuals and youngsters seemed insecure and lacking in either guidelines or role models"). Concluding that the scenery in *A Day Off* is used "as a medium to strengthen the coexistence" of the inside and the outside, Cho points us in the direction that Zhang's more recent film takes in plotting a course of social transformation after the fall of military dictatorships, once South Korea's international agenda of neoliberal globalization had begun to replace its national agenda of industrial modernization.[46]

On numerous occasions throughout *Scenery*, the filmmaker lingers on natural and manufactured environments that appear to be devoid of people. This visual motif begins immediately after the film's title appears against a fog-veiled backdrop and the director's name appears against a black screen. A wide-angle establishing shot shows snowcapped mountains rising above the roofs of several gray apartment buildings and factory spaces. A second shot, positioned closer to one of the structures, reveals the dinginess of the run-down setting, which is crisscrossed by cables and wires. Still closer is the third shot in this sequence, taken from a standing position just outside the entrance of a construction site. Seemingly insignificant details, like a black plastic bag, a cardboard box, and a green wheelbarrow parked partly in the sunlight, attract our attention, as does a dog that scans his surroundings while sitting outside another entrance in the fourth shot. Finally, following this protracted series of scene-setting images, whose function is still unclear, the fifth and sixth shots show small groups of migrant laborers walking down the street, presumably on their way to work. The ensuing shot, set inside a cramped and cluttered woodworking and furniture shop, seems to confirm this. Suddenly, the restless camera lurches forward and begins to explore the space, as if searching for a human subject to settle on. This is the first of several moments in *Scenery* when factory floors and other work spaces are initially presented as bereft of human labor, as if they were haunted sites of an immaterial and invisible labor force that has ceased to be seen by most Koreans. Panning to reveal an eerily empty, unusually quiet workplace, the handheld camera eventually locates the same group of men shown earlier, who are now performing physical labor in silence save for the muted sound of electric drills and saws.

Soon, one of the men is introduced with onscreen text that informs us of his name, Thasila, and his country of origin, Sri Lanka. This introduction is staged inside a small food shop, where Thasila stands before the camera in medium-long shot and, like Augustino before him, tells the audience about his dream. Spoken in Korean, the man's unhurried monologue, like so many of the other migrant workers' recountings of their dreams in this documentary, concerns an imagined homecoming. In Thasila's case, national landmarks like Lankatilaka Vihara (an ancient Buddhist temple in Udunuwara) and Sigiriya (a rock fortress outside the town of Dambulla) are referred to as places he visited in his dream, highlighting his desire to return to Sri Lanka despite his need to earn a living while working in South Korea. Other examples of this kind of longing for one's place of birth can be seen in the film's penultimate and final interviews, which respectively show an agricultural worker named Ourn Ramou discussing his dream of going home to Cambodia and administering medicine to his sick grandmother and a machinist named Nguyen Van Nguyen, who likewise pines for a reunion with his family in Vietnam, where his mother's home-cooked meals await him. In the film's eleventh episode, a young man named Xu Chun Ming is shown working inside a meat-processing plant and complaining about his hard life in South Korea, where he spends several hours each day scraping intestines out of pigs' carcasses. He is paradoxically torn between his constant fear of immigration officers, who represent the threat of deportation, and his desire to return to China. In the film's most overt statement of annoyance (if not anger) on the part of a migrant worker who is constantly reminded of his otherness in South Korea, the Chinese man states, "I don't want to live like this anymore. I hope I can go back home soon." Following this talking-head moment, in which the speaker stands outside his place of work against another drab backdrop of industrial buildings, is a series of shots in which the heads of livestock that have been severed from the animals' bodies are piled up inside a butcher's shop. It is a grisly image, to be sure, but just part of the everyday "scenery" encountered by migrant workers like Xu Chung Ming.

A few segments besides this one (including interviews featuring Choup Chanphearun from Cambodia and Prayoon Puekhunthod from Thailand) provide firsthand views of foreigners' negative or gloomy experiences in South Korea. Shekhal Mamun, a Bangladesh-born employee at the Free Port Migrant Art and Culture Center, appears in the film's tenth episode and shares his memories of working at a factory seven or eight years ago. Speaking flawless Korean (evidence of the length of time he has lived in the country), Mamun talks directly to the camera, opening up about the discrimination that he faced at his previous job, where Korean coworkers questioned his weekly wages (implying that he was not worth the money he was being paid) and threatened him with physical violence. Now he teaches carpentry to Korean students at the center, a further testament to his tenacity as a foreigner who may have integrated himself more fully into the host country's social structures than some of the other individuals in this documentary.[47] Thus, the problems of South Korea's labor regime are consigned to the past, whereas the present situation appears to be more hopeful for people like Mamun. Besides him, several other interviewees gesture toward the more lighthearted aspects of living abroad. Two separate talking-head scenes, each focusing on workers from the Philippines (the machinist Philip Gonzales and the office assistant Katherine Ann Corteza), highlight the quotidian aspirations of people who yearn to take part in the material spoils of an affluent, middle-class society. In the case of Philip (who speaks English in the film), that means buying and owning a luxury car and taking his friends to tourist destinations like Seoul Tower; in the case of Katherine (who speaks Korean), it translates into marriage with her boyfriend, for whom she dreams of performing a "sexy" dance at their forthcoming wedding reception. Like the dream recounted by Sherzod Akbarov, a man from Uzbekistan who lives apart from his wife while working at a fabric design and textile company in South Korea, Katherine's monologue reminds us that romantic connections are sometimes put on hold for the sake of gaining financial footing and accessing opportunities that, ironically, were initially sought so as to raise families and nurture relationships with loved ones.

Scenery's Final Scene: The Undecided Fate of Migrants on the Run

Zhang Lu's experimental yet realistically grounded documentary *Scenery* is built around dialectical tensions, including that between absence and presence. This paradoxical dynamic is evident, for instance, when the unseen and silent director puts his soliloquizing subjects front and center during interviews in which only they can be heard. Cinematographically framed in this way, migrant workers have thus moved from the periphery to the center of agential discourse, even though the film's episodic structure works against such centeredness through a discursive, distributive trajectory that leaves each person behind only minutes after his or her introduction, in search of someone else. But the fourteen individuals who are sensitively showcased (if only momentarily) in this film's segments are also present in their absence during scenes in which natural and man-made landscapes appear eerily unpopulated. It is as if the director has figured out a way to suggest the idea of an invisible labor force through scenery that is both conventionally beautiful and horribly abject. The film's titular foregrounding of the ostensible backdrops of social life in South Korea is, in fact, uncanny: the spaces and places on view in the film—be they crowded city streets where vendors make a meager living or empty factory floors and rice fields where the absence of workers is conspicuous—are at once familiar and strange. One is tempted to say that any sense of estrangement that the spectator feels while watching *Scenery*, achieved by means of distantiation devices not uncommon in other examples of international art cinema (such as dead time, direct address, and open-endedness), is an experience that is perhaps all too familiar to foreigners living in a strange land, separated physically from loved ones back home and culturally distanced from the native populations that surround them. Liminally situated between the known and the unknown, migrant workers living in the ethnic enclaves of cities like Seoul are often forced to navigate gaps both social and spatial—something that audiences likewise face when watching representatives of such a broad cross section of humanity express their hopes, fears, and dreams across an episodic series of personal encounters.

As invisible as the Chinese Korean director is throughout much of *Scenery*, in the final minutes Zhang abandons his distant, observational mode of documentary filmmaking in favor of something entirely different. The last sequence of the film begins after the final interview has ended, once Nguyen (the Vietnamese machinist) is shown eating a humble meal by himself, in lieu of tasting his mother's food back home. The lengthy, wordless passage that follows that quotidian scene consists of several exterior shots, showing everything from a helicopter flying menacingly overhead to a violinist of European descent playing his instrument outside an Italian restaurant. Dozens of pedestrians enter and exit a subway terminal, and—in one of the most suggestive shots in the entire film—a train in the background zooms past heavy equipment vehicles operated by men who are barely visible within the garbage-filled mise-en-scène (which appears to be a dump site or a recycling plant). In this latter image, the industrial progress and speed historically associated with railway transit seem to clash with the comparatively glacial movement of the dump truck and excavator, which continues digging through steel scraps well after the train has left the frame. South Korea's post-IMF recovery and growth, much of which would have been impossible without blue-collar workers, are neatly symbolized in this ugly but evocative piece of scenery. A slow fade to black further underlines the significance of this image, which initially appears to be the final shot of the film.

However, it is followed by one more scene, a sudden burst of movement in which the handheld camera frantically darts from place to place before making its way to a dark alley. First, it crosses a busy intersection in a heavily commodified shopping area, thronged with middle-class Koreans enjoying their leisure time. Then, a jump cut takes the viewer inside a tunnel, where the camera continues rushing forward, toward the light at the end. Before it reaches the end of the tunnel, another shot—this time of a factory looming above a barren field on the outskirts of the city—thrusts itself into the chaotically bobbing frame. Finally, another jump cut transports the viewer into a back alley, as if to suggest the panicky feeling of someone who is on the run, desperate to escape from his or her pursuers.

The frenetic pace of this final scene, accentuated through the jarring juxtaposition of shots and the jittery manner of the camera operator's movement, is completely at odds with everything that preceded it. That is, the director's rigorous commitment to a particular aesthetic that might seem detached or cold, on view throughout most of the film, is replaced here by a gestural form of expressive cinematography, in which the body and presence of the filmmaker is almost palpable in the image. If this is interpreted as a point-of-view shot, it seems as though Zhang has put himself in the shoes of the film's final, fifteenth character, an unseen migrant worker perhaps trying to evade capture by the police or immigration officials. Audibly panting from shortness of breath, the figure who is there but not there sits down on the ground, designated by the camera's lowered position relative to its surroundings. The place itself is highly symbolic: the alley, home to small, traditional eateries and mom-and-pop shops, hints at an older Korean society at odds with the commercial district of high-end shoppers seen earlier (and suggested by the modern high-rise buildings and city traffic still visible in the background). Appearing unable to escape from this labyrinth of passages, the camera casts its gaze upward, toward the blue sky, as if searching for an alternative to the scenery that it has captured so far. This final image, held for a few seconds, is accompanied by the distant sound of an airplane. Although it too is unseen, the audible plane soaring somewhere overhead might remind audiences of the film's first scene, in which Augustino, a man from East Timor, was shown awaiting his return flight to his country of origin. Closing with this indeterminate moment, *Scenery* leaves the fate of this and other migrant workers undecided, rhetorically countering the false happy endings of most mainstream narratives.

10

"Powers of the False" and "Real Fiction"

Migrant Workers in *The City of Cranes* and Other Mockumentaries

In *Representing Reality*, Bill Nichols defines documentary film as an example of the "discourses of sobriety [that] have instrumental power [to] alter the world itself."[1] Discourses of sobriety, exemplified by those of science, economics, politics, foreign policy, and education as well as documentary film, according to Nichols, have "direct, immediate, transparent" relationships with reality.[2] This view of documentary film as an objective art of reality and authenticity has been challenged by several scholars, including Michael Renov, who points out that "nonfiction contains any number of 'fictive' elements, moments at which a presumably objective representation of the world encounters the necessity of creative intervention." "Among these fictive ingredients," Renov explains, "we may include the construction of character . . . the use of poetic language, narration, or musical accompaniment . . . or the creation of suspense via the agency of embedded narratives . . . or various dramatic arcs."[3] Three years after the publication of *Representing Reality*, Nichols updated his position, arguing: "More recently . . . documentary has come to suggest incompleteness and uncertainty, recollection and impression, images of personal worlds and their subjective construction. . . .

Documentary and fiction, social actor and social other, knowledge and doubt, concept and experience share boundaries that inescapably blur."[4]

No other subgenre of documentary is more representative of this shift from a discourse of sobriety to a postmodern mixture of fact and fiction than mockumentary, which is defined by Jane Roscoe and Craig Hight as "a 'fact-fictional' form having a close relationship with both drama and documentary."[5] Expanding Nichols's original premise, Roscoe and Hight encourage us to "think about documentary as existing along a fact-fictional continuum, each text constructing relationships with both factual and fictional discourses."[6] Mockumentary, as described by Ohad Landesman, is "a formal conundrum placed at the meeting point of fiction and documentary, blurring fact and fabrication with a twist of irony and parody."[7] Although the origins of mockumentary can be traced back at least to the 1960s, when *A Hard Day's Night* (1964) and *David Holzman's Diary* (1967) were produced and released, this mode of documentary gained mainstream popularity in the United States following the box-office success of the low-budget, independently produced "found footage" horror film *The Blair Witch Project* (1999), which presents its realistic yet fictional scenes as recently discovered video recordings and which grossed nearly $250 million thanks to the power of viral marketing.

Sometimes referred to as fake documentary, mockumentary is a relatively rare mixed mode of discourse in the context of South Korean cinema. Some notable examples include *Modugi Video* (2005), *Actresses* (*Yŏbaeudŭl*, 2009), *Invisible 2: Chasing the Ghost Sound* (*Kwisinsori chatgi*, 2010), *Arirang* (2011), *577 Project* (2012), *Navigation* (*Naebigeisyŏn*, 2014), *No Tomorrow* (*Sŏm sarajin saramdŭl*, 2016), and *Gonjiam: Haunted Asylum* (2018). While these motion pictures are either self-reflexive portraits of stars or directors (*Actresses*, *Arirang*, and *577 Project*) or horror films and thrillers using purportedly found footage (*Modugi Video*, *Invisible 2*, *Navigation*, *No Tomorrow*, and *Gonjiam*), two additional examples stand out for their use of the mockumentary mode to explore the socially relevant subject of immigration and migrant labor. Those films—director Mun Sŭng-uk's *The City of Cranes* (*Sit'i obŭ k'ŭrein*, 2010) and director Pak Che-uk's *Love in Korea* (2010)—foreground the experiences of Mahbub Alam (or Mustaque Ahmed Mahbub), a Bangladeshi immigrant who became a naturalized Korean citizen and who plays a fictionalized version of himself. Although he dreamed of pursuing an advanced degree in accounting in Finland, Mahbub Alam ended up coming to South Korea as a migrant worker in 1999 to raise money for surgery that his mother needed. His travel visa expired in three months, his mother passed away a few months after that, and what had been intended as a temporary work stay became indefinite. Then an undocumented Bangladeshi worker, Mahbub Alam became involved in the labor movement after injuring his hand in a textile factory and receiving no compensation from his employer. In 2001, he took a leadership position in the Equality Trade Union's Migrant Branch. From November 2003 to December 2004, the Bangladeshi migrant participated in the 380-day sit-in of 120 migrant workers of various ethnic origins at Myŏngdong Cathedral (mentioned in chapter 9), calling for an end to immigration crackdowns and the legalization of undocumented workers. After becoming disappointed by the Korean mainstream media's coverage of the migrant labor movement, Mahbub Alam turned his attention to creating alternative media for and by migrants. In 2005, he became a founding member of Migrant Workers' Television (also mentioned in chapter 9), which produced biweekly news in eleven languages and a monthly current affairs and discussion program titled "The World of Migrant Workers," in partnership with the Korean community cable channel RTV. As a television producer, filmmaker, and actor, Mahbub Alam also directed the annual Migrant Workers' Film Festival, made documentaries about deported Bangladeshi and Nepali migrant workers (including *The Deported* [2007] and *The Returnee* [2009]), and appeared in multicultural-themed films such as *Where Is Ronny . . .* (*Roni-rŭl ch'ajasŏ*, 2008) and *Bandhobi* (*Pandubi*, 2009). Additionally, he has served as director of the Asia Media Culture Factory, a cultural organization for diversity, and Free Port, a migrant art center. More recently, he founded an import and distribution company for European and Southeast Asian art films. In 2012, he was the recipient of the thirty-first Sejong Cultural Award.

Financed by the Ministry of Sports, Culture, and Tourism (Munhwach'eyuk kwangwangbu) and Arirang TV (an international English-language network based in Seoul), *The City of Cranes* is a part of a tourism-enhancing film project called Korea through Movies (*Yŏnghwa, Han'gukŭl mannada*). Each of the first five entries in this series focuses on a different city or region, from Seoul to Jeju Island.[8] As an entry for the industrial city of Incheon, *The City of Cranes* tells the story of Yu Ye-jin, a local cable television station reporter playing a version of herself,[9] who is partnered with Mahbub Alam to make a documentary about the elusive Mongolian migrant Baatar Ad Moru (Nyamsambuu Gombosuren). The migrant has disappeared without a trace after becoming a local celebrity due to his eccentric antics (for example, dancing and communicating with an orphaned crane in the zoo) as well as his heroic achievements (such as saving the lives of four Korean colleagues from a construction site). Independently produced by Mahbub Alam, who also stars in the film, and directed by Pak Che-uk, *Love in Korea* is based on a real incident in which six Bangladeshi film crew members disappeared after arriving in Seoul for location shooting of a Bollywood-style romantic musical. As it turns out, the film shooting is a ruse for the crew members to enter South Korea with the intention of staying as undocumented workers. Mahbub Alam begins a futile search for his missing compatriots and visits his homeland to solve the mystery. In both *The City of Cranes* and *Love in Korea*, documentary and road-movie modes of cinematic discourse are used as narrative tools to pose open-ended questions about immigration, migrant labor, and national or transnational identity. To borrow Gilles Deleuze's terms, these films harness the "powers of the false" by freeing themselves from "*a system of judgment*" of truthful narration.[10]

In his analysis of Wayne Wang's *Chan Is Missing* (1981), the Asian American critic Peter Feng proposes a "doughnut" theory for cultural identity: "Each character in *Chan Is Missing* holds a doughnut that contains the possibilities of Chinese American identity in the center. . . . The big doughnut made up of all of the little doughnuts—a doughnut akin to the construction of Chinese American identity that the spectator viewing *Chan Is Missing* is left with—is almost meaningless, almost wholly 'hole.' . . . *Chan Is Missing*, by showing us why it is impossible to know who we are as Chinese Americans, shows us how we might discover how we can become Asian Americans."[11] In terms of both aesthetics (as low-budget, cinema verité–style, open-ended quest narratives) and content (as compilations of multiple interviews about missing immigrants), *The City of Cranes* and *Love in Korea* take an approach to the issue of identity that is strikingly similar to that in the Asian American independent film *Chan Is Missing*. The injection of fictional discourses into the documentary frame can be interpreted as the filmmakers' admission of their own inability to tell a single truth about heterogeneous immigrant experiences or present an authentic account of what happened to undocumented workers who went missing. The use of mockumentary conventions in these texts is not simply a demonstration of tongue-in-cheek parody: rather, it is a manifestation of the "subversive potential of those texts . . . which play with [the constructed nature of documentary representations of reality],"[12] as well as a thought-provoking challenge to essentialist notions of national identity, belonging, and alterity.

"Powers of the False" and Mockumentary Aesthetics in *The City of Cranes*

Deleuze borrows the concept of the "powers of the false" from Friedrich Nietzsche's philosophical writings. In *Nietzsche and Philosophy*, Deleuze paraphrases Nietzsche: "Being, the true and the real are aviators of nihilism. Ways of mutilating life, of denying it, of making it reactive by submitting it to the labor of the negative, *by loading it with the heaviest burdens*. Nietzsche has no more belief in the self-sufficiency of the real than he has in that of the true: he thinks of them as the manifestations of a will, a will to depreciate life, to oppose life to life. . . . The world is neither true nor real but living. And the living world is will to power, *will to falsehood*."[13] As Daniel Smith summarizes, for Nietzsche and Deleuze "the power of the false is a power of metamorphosis: that is, a power of *creation* . . . the power of the false is creative of truth—but that is, precisely, *a new concept of truth*: truth is no longer a timeless universal to be discovered, but a singularity to be created (in time)."[14] In *Cinema 2*, Deleuze applies this concept to film studies, naming Orson Welles as a Nietzschean director who "has constantly battled against the system of judgment" with such documentary fictions as *It's All True* (1941–1942, unfinished) and *F for Fake* (1975).[15]

The City of Cranes (the fourth feature from the Lodz Film School graduate Mun Sŭng-uk) is likewise conducive to a Deleuzian reading.[16] Mun's film skillfully interweaves fact and fiction, underscoring the "power of the false" to break free from the system of truth. Mun authenticates his documentary by introducing its main actor-characters—Yu Ye-jin and Mahbub Alam—with Ye-jin's talking-head interview footage intercut with still photos from her previous career as a stewardess with Singapore Airlines. Additionally, *The City of Cranes* includes a film clip from *Bandhobi*, which depicts an interethnic romance and friendship between a Bangladeshi migrant worker and a Korean high-school girl, followed by video footage of Mahbub Alam's question-and-answer sessions with audiences after the screening of his independent documentary *The Returnee*. A compilation of archival images segues to a dramatic scene in which Ye-jin is instructed by her producer to collaborate with Mahbub on the new documentary project about Mr. Baatar, a Mongolian immigrant, as "Mr. Mahbub is also a foreigner and knows the subject well." However, this scene is presented in a four-panel split screen with a frame of Ye-jin's conversation with her producer (a staged scene) on the upper right-hand side and three other frames showing various archival footage of Mahbub (from actual film festivals and public events). This experimental composite of the real and the false is emblematic of the "power of creation" underscored in Nietzsche's and Deleuze's philosophy and inherent in the process of making a mockumentary.

Following this scene, Mahbub's talking head is featured, and the subject of the documentary within the documentary speaks: "Mr. Baatar is a famous person in Korean society, so I got interested in this documentary project about him. There are still a lot of problems about Korean perspectives on migrant workers, so I would like to participate in a project that can help Korean society become a bit more open." While the premise of making a documentary about the mysterious Mongolian man who is famed for his bizarre crane dance is pure fiction, Mahbub's comment about Korean prejudices toward migrants and the need for more inclusive media programming could not be more truthful and echoes the media activist's own commitment to increasing progressive multicultural productions. Not surprisingly, in his autobiography, *I Am an Earthian* (*Nanŭn chiguinida*), Mahbub describes his character in *The City of Cranes* as a "70 or 80 percent identical portrait of [his] ordinary self."[17] To amplify the film's cinema-verité realism, Mun shot it without a screenplay and instructed his actors to improvise dialogue after he described the overall setup of each scene. In other words, while staging dramatic or fictional scenes, actors could freely use their own verbal and behavioral antics, drawing upon personal experiences.

The dramatic tension builds after a Mongolian interpreter who has promised to deliver their documentary subject to the production team unexpectedly bows out, claiming that he does not really know Baatar. Mun's handheld camera records an emergency meeting of the production team in which the Korean crew's

FIGURE 10.1 Mahbub Alam remains silent while Korean production staff members speak ill of Mongolian and Southeast Asian immigrants in Mun Sŭng-uk's *The City of Cranes* (*Sit'i obŭ k'ŭrein*, 2010).

xenophobic attitudes toward Mongolians and other migrants are revealed. After the frustrated manager explains that advertisers have already booked the programming spot and they cannot cancel the project, a staff member says, "This occasionally happens when you try to book Mongolians or other foreigners because of language barriers." Another producer chimes in: "It is so common that they do not keep appointments after making them. Not just Mongolians but Southeast Asians too. Thailand, India, Ski Lanka, and so on. They are very poor at keeping appointments." A third staffer adds, "We had similar experiences when dealing with foreigners in the past." The manager gently intervenes, correcting them in this way: "We are in front of Mr. Mahbub and cannot say that all foreigners are like this. But we are in trouble. What can we do?" The fly-on-the-wall camera is positioned at a distance. Its telephoto lens is used to flatten the spatial gap between the foreground (which is partly blocked by blurry images of oversize books) and the background (where half a dozen people, including Ye-jin and Mahbub, are sitting on a sofa). The camera pans and zooms in to a close-up of each speaker while cutting to several reaction shots of Mahbub, who remains stoically silent as the Koreans speak bluntly about the people of his region (see figure 10.1). This uncomfortably realistic scene is staged in an observational mode that, according to Nichols, "hinges on the ability of the filmmaker to be unobstructive" and "conveys the sense of unmediated and unfettered access to the world."[18]

In the ensuing two talking-head interviews with Mahbub and Ye-jin, however, Mun shifts his aesthetic mode and breaks the 180-degree rule of continuity editing, disorienting the spectator and calling attention to the constructedness

FIGURE 10.2 During Yu Ye-jin's talking-head interview, writer-director Mun crosses the 180-degree axis of action and intentionally calls attention to the constructedness of his documentary images.

of his documentary images.[19] Mahbub is initially positioned on the right side of the frame when he starts to discuss the difficulty of finding Baatar and explains that he proposed to make a documentary about the search process itself. In the following shot, Mahbub is on the left side of the frame and continues to elucidate his intention of presenting the bigger picture of immigrant lives and the status of migrant workers while working on this documentary. After cutting to a long shot showing both Mun (the offscreen interviewer and the film's director) and Mahbub, the camera transitions to another close up of Mahbub, now back on the right side of the frame. He confides that he could have made a more serious project by himself, but the broadcasting station would not have appreciated such an approach, which is probably why Ye-jin has been assigned as his production partner.

The next talking-head interview is set in the broadcaster's editing room, where Ye-jin is asked by the offscreen interviewer (Mun) who has the final say over the documentary. The female reporter confidently replies, "Of course, it is me," directing her gaze toward the right side of the frame (see figure 10.2). In the following shot, she is repositioned and now addresses the offscreen interviewer on her left side. She continues to explain that she initiated this project and Mahbub is simply offering assistance because of his expertise. The camera cuts back and forth again, crossing the 180-degree axis of action, while Ye-jin compares herself to a plastic surgery patient and Mahbub to a doctor—making the point that it is her decision how to reconstruct her own face. Mun's violation of the 180-degree rule of screen direction in these talking-head interviews is consistent with the general characteristics of mockumentaries, which "self-reflexively manifest their artifice, exposing the production process and cinematic apparatus to deconstruct their effect on the viewer."[20] More than just a self-reflexive aesthetic experiment, however, the repeated shot patterns in these two scenes have a mirroring effect, underscoring the commonality of the two characters who are equally mistrustful of—and combative with—one another. Imitating the shot–reverse-shot format of a narrative fiction film's dialogue scene, these talking heads accentuate the theme of failed communication as each character looks like both the speaker of and the listener to their own speech. Minute stylistic details, such as reversing the left-right rotating order of Mahbub's and Ye-jin's close-ups, further convey a subtle message that these two individuals, who are supposed to be engaging in a shot–reverse-shot dialogue, end up delivering monologues, talking past one other in a way that undermines cross-cultural empathy.

As foreshadowed in these talking-head interviews, the relationship between Ye-jin and Mahbub throughout the shooting process is marked by conflict. Reflecting the status of *The City of Cranes* as a tourism promotion film, Ye-jin suggests that they include beautiful landscape shots of Incheon, while Mahbub opposes the use of such "unnecessary shots" and advocates interviewing diverse people. These comments are ironic, as Mun's film is filled with picturesque landscape shots of Incheon, accentuating the beauty of its ports, bridges, high-rise buildings, beaches, and islands. As the Korean critic Yi Yŏng-jin states, "Director Mun Sŭng-uk wanted to ask if Incheon or Korea is an open space for enabling communication [between natives and migrants], but his social consciousness fails to be fully reflected in the film. A few shots inserted to promote Korea's tourism [industry] appear to be excessively naive and fake."[21]

After a few futile attempts to track down their documentary subject, the bickering production duo is connected with a local Mongolian school teacher named Chimddorj Otgontuya, who informs them that Baatar was a famous wrestler in Mongolia.[22] This revelation underscores Mun's hybrid documentary aesthetic. First there is a talking-head interview with the teacher in the courtyard, which segues to ethnographic shots of Mongolian traditional costumes, dolls, and paintings in the school's interiors—combined with a soundtrack of traditional Mongolian music. Then there is a montage of exterior shots of Baatar in traditional wrestling costume performing an eagle dance (which resembles a crane dance) before participating in a wrestling match on a soccer field. Dynamic wrestling footage from multiple camera angles dissolves into a close-up of a painting depicting two horses in a tussling embrace. When the camera pulls back, it turns out that the painting is on the wall behind the three characters—Ye-jin, Mahbub, and Chimddorj—who are in front of a computer screen on which Baatar's wrestling video is playing. What appeared to be parallel editing (cutting back and forth between school interiors and the outdoor playground where wrestling is taking place) turns out to be cutting between close-ups of interior objects and an enlargement of the screen within a screen.

This scene is reminiscent of the first scene in director Michael Haneke's *Caché* (2005), in which an exterior static long shot of a Parisian house turns out to be the screen enlargement of an enigmatic surveillance video that the bewildered homeowners have received and are watching inside the same house. As Ipek Celik explains, "because both the film itself and the surveillance video are shot with a high-definition digital camera, the transition between the two kinds of images is seamless, distorting the spectator's sense of space."[23] This description can be applied verbatim to the corresponding scene in *The City of Cranes*. Like his use of jump cuts in the abovementioned talking-head interview scenes, the mise-en-abîme screen within a screen calls attention to the process of image manipulation and the artifice of Mun's documentary realism. Like Haneke, Mun "situates images as suspect" and invokes, however indirectly, the Deleuzian power of the false.[24]

The Death of a Mongolian Migrant and the Story of Incheon Bridge

During their interview with the Mongolian teacher, the conflict between Ye-jin and Mahbub intensifies as the latter becomes impatient with the former's constant interruptions while he is talking. Later on the road, Mahbub confronts Ye-jin and demands that she wait until he finishes asking all the questions and then take her turn. In the midst of growing tension, the two go to meet Baatar's girlfriend (who was referred to them by the teacher), but they face communication problems. Mahbub asks the girlfriend if she speaks English and starts interviewing her in that language. He inquires about what kind of a man Baatar is. The girlfriend answers in halting English that he is "good" and "really Mongolian." Mahbub goes on to probe into their relationship, but the woman is reluctant to answer, telling him that this is her private life. Now Ye-jin grows anxious and intervenes in Korean, asking the Mongolian woman if they can meet Baatar today. This interruption prompts Mahbub to bolt out of the door, telling Ye-jin to conduct the interview by herself.

However, the two are soon reconciled and join Baatar's close friends at a restaurant where a traditional Mongolian dinner party is taking place. Ye-jin and Mahbub ask when Baatar is expected to arrive and receive a surprising reply: "He is already here with us in spirit." It turns out that Baatar has passed away in a traffic accident while working at a horse-riding track as an undocumented migrant (after losing his legal status due to a scam). While touring the horse-riding establishment where Baatar had resided before the accident, Ye-jin and Mahbub learn that the Mongolian had to live in a cramped container but never lost his smile due to his love for horses. Against a long shot of a Korean girl riding a horse around the track, Ye-jin intones in an elegaic voice-over: "Baatar means 'hero' in Mongolian. His friends would prefer to remember him as a real Mongolian riding through the plains instead of acknowledging his empty death." During his interview with Baatar's girlfriend, Mahbub had asked what she meant by "really Mongolian," a question that she was unable to answer. While openly challenging the fixed notion of national identity in this and other scenes, the film also reaffirms ethnic stereotypes through ethnographic shots of Mongolian school interiors as well as Ye-jin's voice-over, which defines "real" Mongolianness in narrow terms.

As of May 2016, according to statistics released by the Ministry of Justice (Pŏmmubu), 31,253 Mongolians were living in South Korea.[25] Most of them are low-skilled migrant laborers who are allowed to work in South Korea for up to four years and ten months in the manufacturing, agriculture, fishery, construction, or services industries under the Employment Permit System (Koyong hŏgaje; discussed in chapter 9).[26] The sixteen developing nations in the Asia-Pacific region that signed memoranda of understanding to send their workers to South Korea under this system are Bangladesh, Cambodia, China, Indonesia, Kyrgyzstan, Laos, Mongolia, Myanmar, Nepal, Pakistan, the Philippines, Sri Lanka, Thailand, Timor Leste, Vietnam, and Uzbekistan. Between the system's introduction in 2004 (replacing the more controversial Industrial Trainee System [Sanŏp yŏsujae])[27] and 2015, 540,000 migrant workers had come to Korea (as of 2020, approximately 200,000 migrant workers are employed under the system by 63,000 small or medium-size companies). The limited-term government-run labor program resulted in a sizable share of permit laborers being converted to illegal immigrants after their legal status expired. Of all migrant workers in South Korea, the share who stayed in South Korea after their permits expired amounted to 16.9 percent in 2013, 15.6 percent in 2014, and 15.3 percent in 2015.[28] In March 2016, the Ministry of Employment and Labor (Koyong nodongbu) announced that it would reduce the quota of work visas for countries with high numbers of overstaying laborers in South Korea, thus applying further pressure on undocumented workers living in the constant fear of immigration crackdowns and deportation.[29]

According to official government statistics, as of 2019, 390,281 foreigners are residing in South Korea without legal documentation. Thailand, China, and Vietnam account for the most undocumented foreigners, and Mongolia accounts for the fourth highest number: 17,510 of its nationals reside illegally in South Korea.[30] According to a survey by the Kyŏnggi Institute of Research and Policy Development for Migrants' Human Rights of 560 foreign residents in 2015, 43.7 percent said that they felt discriminated against at their workplaces.[31] In a 2007 interview with the *Korea Times*, a Mongolian journalist named Batmonkh shared his nightmare tale of working in South Korea as a manual laborer for the minimum wage (three dollars an hour): "Recently, whilst working in a wood yard which supplies fuel to *jimjilbangs* [saunas], I filled a chainsaw with the wrong mixture of oil and petrol, I was beaten by the supervisor with a metal tool until I bled."[32] It is not uncommon for a well-educated person with a professional career back home to fall victim to abusive, inhumane conditions as a migrant worker in South Korea. According to Batmonkh, "It is unfortunate that 95 percent of the Mongolian workers here are educated people. Mongolians are only allowed [to hold] very basic jobs and have no chance to assert themselves. Koreans make it clear who is boss." The Ministry of Gender Equality and Family (Yŏsŏnggajokpu)'s 2015 survey is a telling indicator of the inhospitable environment that migrants face in South Korea. According to this survey, 60 percent of Koreans said that Korean nationals should be given priority over foreigners for jobs, and more than 31 percent of Korean adults stated that they did not want immigrants as neighbors.[33]

As a tourism promotion project, *The City of Cranes* shies away from confronting such harsh realities faced by migrant workers. Although Ye-jin's voice-over notes in passing that Baatar was a victim of a scam by a Korean who "borrowed" his name for unspecified illegal activities, causing the Mongolian to lose his legal status, the owner of the horse-riding track is depicted as a benevolent friend who offered shelter to a migrant in trouble. The Mongolian's death was caused by bad luck (a traffic accident), not by exploitation or depression. He had a community of support and a close circle of friends who remember him fondly, unlike Batmonkh—who said, before leaving South Korea, "I am glad to leave as it is lonely and boring, here each man is for himself working hard, there is no time for life."[34]

Despite such shortcomings, *The City of Cranes* contains powerful scenes in which Korean discrimination against migrant workers and immigrants is evoked if not indicted. After a drunken quarrel with Ye-jin, and in a style that recalls the use of slow motion by the Hong Kong filmmaker Wong Kar-wai, Mahbub is seen walking along a street brightly lit by neon signs, passing a succession of vendors, shops, and pedestrians. His voice-over is intimate and morose: "I speak Korean well and eat Korean food well. No matter how much I try to be a Korean, Koreans do not recognize me. I am still an outsider in Korea." This confession is strikingly autobiographical, a pouring out of emotion on the part of Mahbub Alam, whose Korean father-in-law has not accepted him and refuses to even meet him officially, although the Bangladeshi immigrant married his youngest daughter in 2004 and has become a Korean citizen since.[35]

Toward the end of the film, Ye-jin and Mahbub visit the bridge construction site where Baatar worked as a welder. Against a series of long shots of the newly opened Incheon Bridge, a six-lane structure that connects Yŏngjong Island (where Incheon International Airport is located) and the mainland of Incheon, Mahbub muses in a voice-over: "The construction work is hard, dirty, and dangerous. Countless people will drive on this bridge. But how many people who built it will drive on it?" Then the camera cuts to a talking-head interview (against an image of the bridge) with Sin Sŭng-hwan, a publicist for Korea Expressway Corporation. Sin cites statistics not well known to the Korean public: "The total number of workers for Incheon Bridge was 260,000 per year. Among them, 100,000, or 40 percent, were migrant laborers. They took care of the hardest, most physically demanding, labor. Throughout the entire bridge, their touch can be felt. But most of them have gone back to their homelands by now, and the rest are working in other construction sites." Sin goes to compliment the fictional worker Baatar for his work ethic and gregarious personality. This short segment is representative of the film's seamless blending of documentary and fiction as well as touristic shots and social messages. Under the pretext of visiting Baatar's former workplace, Mun's film acknowledges (however briefly) the enormous contribution that 100,000 migrant workers made each year during the four-year construction of the bridge, the magnificent view from which is captured from multiple angles. By providing the context for the use of migrant labor in the bridge's construction and underscoring the exclusion of those limited-term guest workers from the benefits of the bridge (which, as the banner shown in the background of the scene reads, functions as a "gateway to the world"), Mun's film quietly invites the viewer to question the fairness of immigration policy and labor practices without explicit political commentary.

Ultimately, *The City of Cranes* is a flawed multicultural film whose touristic raison d'être betrays its underlying subtext of exposing Koreans' discriminatory attitudes toward immigrants and the hardships of migrant workers. Ye-jin's and Mahbub's struggle brings attention to communication problems and the feelings of neglect that even the most assimilated naturalized citizens might experience in South Korea. Their symbolic reconciliation on a sunny, mud-caked beach where they harmoniously practice the crane dance and wrestle in honor of the late Baatar (a medium-range two-shot that visually represents the film's Korean DVD cover tagline, "We became friends who share hearts by being together") transforms a narrative of alterity, alienation, and dissent into a picture-perfect multicultural spectacle, further enhancing the agenda of the film's state sponsor: the Ministry of Sports, Culture, and Tourism. However, the film might also be a step in the right direction in terms of its audacious stylistic experimentation, which not only blurs the boundaries between documentary and fiction but also rejects truth claims related to the authenticity of images or the constructed notion of national identity. According to Sissy Helff, mockumentary creates "an open space for speaking out unpleasant truths" paradoxically because "all claims of truth might be light-heartedly thrown overboard," and "as a kind of countermove . . . a buffer zone for the narration" is created.[36] As Helff suggests, mockumentary is much more than a gimmick or hoax and can "provide great artistic freedom to invent refugees' and asylum seekers' stories outside political schemes and particular national motivations"—as demonstrated by her case study *In This World* (2002), Michael Winterbottom's mockumentary about an Afghan orphan's life-risking journey from a Pakistani refugee camp to London. Mun's mockumentary similarly harnesses the creative potential of the genre to highlight another border-crossing story of a symbolic fictional subject that reflects the shared experiences of migrant workers in South Korea. The film's accommodation of the "powers of the false" is compelling as it makes it possible to create a new type of cinematic praxis, a new identity, and a new Korea, but only when one is willing to accept that there is no such a thing as a fixed reality or unshakable truth in this world.

Part 6

Nonhuman Rights in a Posthuman World

11

Animal Rights Advocacy, Holocaustal Imagery, and Interspecies Empathy in *An Omnivorous Family's Dilemma* and *Okja*

Over the past several years, animal rights advocacy has become an increasingly conspicuous element in international cultural productions. Literary texts such as Karen Joy Fowler's *We Are All Completely beside Ourselves*, nonfiction publications such as Melanie Joy's *Why We Love Dogs, Eat Pigs, and Wear Cows*, and documentary films such as D. A. Pennebaker and Chris Hegedus's *Unlocking the Cage* (2016) confront readers and audiences with a subject that, until recently, had been thought of only as a peripheral concern or trivial matter running a distant second to the more pressing call for human rights reforms and protection policies around the world.[1] Throughout recorded history (and still today, despite legislative successes in safeguarding the welfare of animals), nonhuman beings have been denied the rights and freedoms afforded to humans. This kind of speciesism—the prejudicial privileging of humans over nonhumans (akin, some rights advocates claim, to racism, sexism, and homophobia)—continues to color mainstream works despite the efforts of the above writers, researchers, and filmmakers to shine a light on the suffering experienced by animals who are either subjected to inhumane factory farming techniques or simply prevented from living a life of comfort rather than one of cruelty. In South Korea, legal debates over the relative value of animal life and human life—a false binary that privileges species over sentience and too often treats cows, pigs, and other creatures as "food" rather than "people"—have likewise crept into public consciousness, as evidenced by the production and distribution of contemporary motion pictures tackling the theme of nonhuman rights.

In this chapter, we examine a representative cross section of those films, including the low-budget documentary *An Omnivorous Family's Dilemma* (*Chapsik kajokŭi tilema*, 2014) from the director Hwang Yun and the transnational coproduction *Okja* (2017) from Bong Joon-ho (Pong Chun-ho), which to varying degrees pose porcine-focused alternatives to the speciesism that underlies most narratives about animal-human relationships. The latter film, a high-profile action-adventure comedy-fantasy funded by Netflix (the online streaming media service that released *Okja* on its website in June 2017, after debuting it at the Cannes Film Festival a month earlier), is especially significant as a site of contested meanings and contradictory impulses. These include the Korean filmmaker's desire to cater to an international audience while delving into a subject that has particular resonance in his home country, which Bong calls "a BBQ paradise" (where "every street on every corner is burning meat").[2] Indeed, meat consumption is part of daily life for most middle- and upper-class citizens (many of whom, ironically, identify themselves as pet owners, putting the lives of cats and dogs above those of fish and fowl). A rise in vegetarianism and veganism, undertaken for ethical rather than strictly dietary reasons, can be partially attributed to growing public awareness of the South Korean government's failure to adequately address long-standing concerns about slaughterhouse conditions as well as the environmental impact of raising animals (including domestic creatures such as cats and dogs) for food. However, such consumption practices continue to be stereotyped as merely fashionable or trendy lifestyle choices. Worse, vegetarianism and veganism are sometimes represented in Korean popular culture as pathological signs of an individual's past traumas or enduring familial problems, a topic broached in Han Kang's award-winning novel *The Vegetarian* (*Ch'aesikjuŭija*, 2007).[3]

Limited space prevents us from discussing this important literary intervention into questions of changing forms of dietary intake in South Korea, where today's annual meat consumption statistics (over 50 kilograms [110 pounds] per person) represent a quadrupling of the national average just thirty years ago.[4] However, we would like to dwell briefly on the frequency with which vegetarianism has been mentioned in both the print and online reviews of *Okja*. For instance, the critic Tom Philip wrote in *GQ* that if one wants to "convert carnivores to vegetarians," an audience-friendly action film like this is a good alternative to taking them to a "real-life pig farm" or subjecting them to a potentially "boring" documentary about slaughterhouses.[5] In his January 2018 article, Philip includes anecdotal evidence that Bong's film has prompted people to rethink their consumption habits, thus serving as "a jumping-off-point for their own study of the ethics of meat-eating." Jacob Oller likewise believes that this "Netflix hit is a great movie and even better activism," telling his readers at the website *Film School Rejects* that *Okja*'s "philosophical punch"—its power to change people's hearts and minds—comes not only from its rejection of preachy proselytizing (the thing that most gnaws at viewers of vegan documentaries) but also from the distributive reach of the online streaming media provider, which currently serves more than a hundred million subscribers in 190 countries.[6]

If only a small percentage of Netflix subscribers watch the film, it will have reached the eyes and touched the hearts of more people than the American Society for the Prevention of Cruelty to Animals (ASPCA) and People for the Ethical Treatment of Animals (PETA) have members.[7] Chris Fuhrmeister, the pop culture assistant editor for the website *Eater*, goes so far as to compare the Korean director's film to Upton Sinclair's 1906 novel *The Jungle*, a muckraking classic that sought "to expose the ugly side of America's mass-market meat industry." As Fuhrmeister states, *Okja* might prompt "a harder look [at] Big Meat" and "change the system" in a way that Sinclair hoped to do, converting "a generation of omnivores into bleeding-heart vegans who worship at the altar of PETA."[8] Notably, a few weeks after *Okja*'s release, PETA's official bloggers compiled a representative list of viewers' tweets, indicating eleven ways that the film had "changed lives."[9] Whether or not one agrees with Simon Ward, author of the recently published coffee-table book *Okja*, who claims that this might be "the most vegetarian film ever,"[10] it is clear that this much-discussed cultural production has engendered dialogue about issues that animal rights activists have sought to bring to public awareness for decades.

We will circle back to *Okja* in the second half of this chapter, further exploring the film's international reception as well as the connection between acting and activism, or performance and politics, that is central to its discombobulating mix of silliness and seriousness. But before returning to Bong's film, which furthermore combines childlike whimsy and the kind of mature themes one would expect to encounter in the case studies from our previous chapters (for example, global capitalism, corporate greed, exploitation, and political protest), we dwell momentarily on a few examples of Korean fiction in which nonhuman animals are mobilized either as main characters or as allegorical metaphors. These include stories for children that treat their nonhuman subjects in both sympathetic and symptomatic ways. Specifically, two novels by Hwang Sun-mi (Hwang Sŏn-mi)—her 2000 *Madangŭl naon amt'ak* (translated as *The Hen Who Dreamed She Could Fly*) and her 2012 *Purŭngae jangbal* (translated as *The Dog Who Dared to Dream*)—deserve special consideration, given their transnational popularity and transmedia proliferations (the former text was adapted for the big screen as *Leafie, A Hen into the Wild*, a commercially successful animated family film distributed to theaters by Lotte Entertainment in 2011 before receiving a limited international release under the title *Daisy, A Hen into the Wild*). Moreover, both of Hwang's most famous works, ostensibly aimed at young readers who are perhaps more accustomed to, or accepting of, anthropomorphized animals as protagonists than older readers might be, adopt a paradoxically fantastic yet realistic mode of representation in which far-fetched or fanciful elements are grounded in the banal, quotidian realities of casual cruelty and abuse—the very subjects taken up in the abovementioned narrative fiction films and documentaries (which notably hinge on the presence of children to make their points).

Animal Rights as Flights of Fancy in South Korean Literature and Film

Long before Hwang Sun-mi gained fame as one of South Korea's premier authors of children's literature, numerous other writers and storytellers had incorporated nonhuman creatures into their works. The word "vast" leaps to mind when one thinks of the amount of premodern (classical) poetry and prose in which animals figure prominently, often functioning as pedagogical tools through which disseminators of the relevant culture's dominant ideology might communicate moral lessons to their listeners or readers. For example, cows, dogs, and horses were frequently presented as "exemplary defenders of virtue, in particular of loyalty toward one's master," during the reigns of King T'aejong and King Sejong, as Elmer Veldkamp has noted.[11] This idea is echoed by the literary scholar James Grayson, who suggests that there was a reciprocal relationship between traditional folktales and traditional society, which reinforced one another as well as "the values of Confucianism" while being influenced by those same values.[12] However, a strain of contrarian antiauthoritarianism courses through that same cultural history, with animal fables and *p'ansori* such as *Sugungka* (*Song of the Water Palace*) satirizing the royal court's unchecked corruption and abuses of power. Kichung Kim discusses *Sugungka* in his overview of classical Korean literature, stressing that the behavior and relationships of that story's small menagerie (consisting of a tortoise, fish, rabbit, and fox) "are unmistakably human, and we have no difficulty recognizing in their actions those of people in contemporary Chosŏn society."[13] While the tale's surface details might suggest light comedy or frivolity, its darkness and depth are borne out in scenes depicting "the constant bickering between . . . civil and military officials, their shirking of difficult or risky tasks, official appointments based on family connections rather than merit or ability, and worst of all, the readiness of the king and his court to sacrifice the lives of the common people for their own interests."[14] As we shall see, the dueling tendencies of animal-themed literature to either support the sociopolitical status quo or shine a satirical light on those in power remain a fixture of contemporary Korean fiction (and film), especially in examples that are also torn between fantastic and realistic modes of representation.

Certainly, supernatural beings and fantastical creatures such as dragons and ogres can be found in the earliest Chosŏn-era cultural productions. But more mundane, if still magically endowed, animals (including those found in the real world, such as bears, tigers, rabbits, and magpies) would become discernible elements of the myths, legends, fables, satires, short fiction, novels, and other genres that collectively constitute Korean literature over its 1,500-year span. As Kim Hŭng-gyu reminds us, perennial animal folktales, handed down from generation to generation, eventually inspired several novels of the late Chosŏn period, including *Tale of the Tortoise and the Hare* (*T'okkijŏn*), *Tale of Sŏ Taeju, the Rat* (*Sŏ Taejujŏn*), and *Tale of a Male Pheasant* (*Changgijŏn*). These stories, Kim argues, use their eponymous creatures to allegorically "express the conflicts of human society."[15] Similarly, heroic tales like "A Fight between a Centipede and a Toad" (which was first transcribed by Son Chin-t'ae in November 1921, when he was collecting his country's oral traditions in a North Chŏlla village) have been cited by Grayson as illustrations of the ways in which animals are endowed with "human-like feelings and a sense of responsibility, thus reinforcing in the minds of listeners the importance of the Confucian code of social propriety." In his words, "the assumed disparity between the world of man and the animal world is used to illustrate the idea that if even animals can be virtuous *so too should men*."[16] Thus, the "transmutability of animal and human life," a facet of classical Korean literature that endures in contemporary fiction, has aesthetic and ethical dimensions, enriching the semantic repertoire of anthropomorphized characters from which twentieth- and twenty-first–century authors draw while reminding us that a creature's seemingly far-fetched ability to speak for herself or himself (and be understood by humans) is itself a political act in the current context of animal rights discourses.

To be clear, the title characters in Hwang's *The Hen Who Dreamed She Could Fly* and *The Dog Who Dared to Dream* cannot verbally communicate their hopes and desires to their human "masters."[17] Sprout, the feathered hero of the former novel, is unable to express her desire to leave her cramped battery cage to the farmer whose livelihood depends on her productivity. She is also unable to convey her displeasure with being "culled," a word that she does not understand until she is dumped by the farmer into an open grave along with several other unproductive hens. Clucking in panic as she treads on poultry corpses, her utterances are nevertheless understood by others in the animal kingdom, including a one-eyed weasel that will prey on the bird from this early scene until the story's concluding moments. Similarly, Scraggly—so named because of her long black hair—engages in interspecies dialogue throughout *The Dog Who Dared to Dream*, verbally sparring with an antagonistic cat whose companionship she begins to appreciate by narrative's end. But her words fall on deaf ears among the human cast of characters, which includes the old man who owns Scraggly and her canine family. Nevertheless, these animal protagonists' psychological states as well as their ambitions in life are rendered in such a way that the reader may experience a degree of kinship or connection. This is foundational to the interspecies empathy that is needed to unlock the literal and figurative cages that too often define and delimit nonhuman existence.

Notably, both of the author's two animal narratives begin with a carceral image, that of a cage constraining the movement of livestock or pets. The opening sentence of *The Hen Who Dreamed She Could Fly* reads, "The egg rolled to a stop upon reaching the wire mesh of the coop," and it is followed by a description of the underfed and exhausted protagonist, Sprout, who is worrying about her inability to lay eggs over the previous two days.[18] These first few words highlight the relative value that farmers place on hens as egg producers but also remind the reader of the prison-like environment in which such production takes place, an environment that is made all the more depressing due to the tantalizing proximity of Sprout's cage to the entrance of the building—an open doorway through which a fragrant, blooming acacia tree is visible. The barnyard outside the henhouse beckons to her, just as the leaves of that tree, which "lived on until late fall before turning yellow and then dropping quietly" only to be "reborn in green light the following spring,"[19] give the hen—her neck now featherless and raw because she had shoved her head through the wires of the cage so many times—hope for a life beyond the henhouse's four walls. Similarly, *The Dog Who Dared to Dream* opens with a scene in which a thin and starving canine (not the main character, Scraggly, but her mother with swollen teats) nurses her newborn pups inside a large metal cage while growling at the apparent lack of concern shown by the old man who freely comes and goes through a wire mesh gate.[20] Although these two novels plot different narrative trajectories for their nonhuman protagonists, they both foreground the existential predicament faced by many animals who are forced to live alongside—or, rather, under the disciplining gaze of—their human masters. And these books do so by front-loading their stories with the semiotically charged imagery of metal cages.

Across different cultural and national contexts, children's stories concerning animals have long relied upon a kind of carceral semiotics. Indeed, the cage, which fences in and cordons off nonhuman beings, has been used by authors and filmmakers to denote the figurative and literal obstacles to be surmounted by animals on their journeys toward an ever-elusive freedom. Consider, for instance, the manner in which such animated films as Walt Disney's *Lady and the Tramp* (1955), Don Bluth's *The Secret of NIMH* (1982) and *All Dogs Go to Heaven* (1989), and DreamWorks' *Spirit: Stallion of the Cimarron* (2002) treat zoos, bird cages, dog pounds, and horse stables as prison-like environments that, in the words of Kathryn Gillespie and Rosemary-Claire Collard, partially constitute a uniquely "animal geography" of suffering and servitude. As Gillespie and Collard point out, cages, pens, chutes, and other spaces of species-based subordination enable humans to exert "control over animal bodies."[21] Letting an animal out of its place of confinement, as the title character does to a lark in P. L. Travers's *Mary Poppins Comes Back* (1935), is evidence of a person's capacity for intersubjective understanding and compassion (in this case, the English nanny expresses indignation at the sight of a wild songbird, who has spent two years in captivity, being reduced to a household ornament for the amusement of humans).[22]

The old man who finally brings Scraggly, her siblings, and her mother a pot of food in the third paragraph of *The Dog Who Dared to Dream* eventually lets these dogs out of their cage. But his motives, as someone who will profit from their sale to a local buyer, are less noble than those of Mary Poppins. Tellingly, the first chapter of Hwang's novel is titled "The Old Man," giving pride of place to the human character who will be referred to as "master" and "owner" in subsequent chapters, and whose actions will have disruptive (at times, devastating) effects on the dogs' lives at various points throughout this quietly tragic story. The dogs give the aging, nerve-frayed junk-shop owner the name "Grandpa Screecher," owing to his tendency to shout whenever they act out (for example, pooping on his vegetables, chewing up his shoes, and sending his wife's freshly washed laundry to the ground). Naturally precocious, the dogs demonstrate a willful nature and a desire for unadulterated pleasure; the seeking of which, Jonathan Balcombe reminds us, is as central to the call for animal equality as is the avoidance of physical pain and psychological suffering (a desire that is likewise shared by most humans).[23] Pain and suffering surely await the initially carefree canine hero at the heart of Hwang's story, and its place in the emerging canon of animal rights fiction should be secured by the author's subtle handling of difficult subjects (such as death, familial separation, and loss of innocence) as well as her capacity to make the reader empathetically experience a dog's life and longings. This facet of *The Dog Who Dared to Dream*—its ability to engender what Clive Phillips calls "interspecial empathy" and what Julien Dugnoille calls "transspecies empathy"—puts it in the company of classic animal-themed children's literature (for example, E. B. White's *Stuart Little* [1945], Robert Lawson's *Rabbit Hill* [1945], Eleanor Estes's *Ginger Pye* [1951], and William H. Armstrong's *Sounder* [1970]) while setting it apart from the typical triumphalist narrative that sees nonhuman creatures ultimately overcoming hardships and succeeding.[24]

Indeed, by the end of Hwang's novel, readers are made to feel the accumulated weight of Scraggly's suffering, a significant portion of which comes at the hands of Grandpa Screecher, who is ironically the person with whom she develops the closest bond. Notably, the opening chapter of *The Dog Who Dared to Dream* tells us that his hands "smelled of metal," a scent that suggests that this man is more machine than human. Indeed, his actions over the course of the novel (selling off Scraggly's siblings and eventually her offspring to a shady neighbor until she is left emotionally drained and virtually alone by narrative's end) appear to be utterly lacking in compassion. One reason why the mangy mutt takes an initial liking to Grandpa Screecher, despite his tendency to take a broom to the dogs when disciplining them, is that Scraggly is the only one of her mother's offspring that the old man names. Her specialness is further denoted by the bluish tint of her black hair, which appears to glow in the moonlight (according to her nemesis, the cat). Significantly, a more accurate English translation of the title of Hwang's novel would be "Long-haired Blue Dog," which would emphasize the main character's distinguishing physical feature (her "outer" form) rather than

FIGURE 11.1 A disturbing "culling" scene in the children's animated film *Leafie, A Hen into the Wild* (2011), the big-screen adaptation of Hwang Sun-mi's 2000 novel *The Hen Who Dreamed She Could Fly* (*Madangŭl naon amt'ak*).

her thoughts and dreams (her "inner" life). From both a transnational and translational standpoint, this shifting of hermeneutic energy from the "outside" to the "inside" of the dog mimics the ethical movement needed to dismantle the binaries of self versus other and human versus animal and encourages divergent interpretations across cultural contexts in which the expression "animal rights" (*tongmulkwŏn*) has different meanings.

It is worth pointing out that the abovementioned culling scene in *The Hen Who Dreamed She Could Fly*, when translated to the big screen in this story's transmedia flight from one storytelling medium to another, is lent an additional affective charge. After visually evoking the prison-like setting of the henhouse, which the shadowy figure of the farmer enters with wheelbarrow in tow, the opening sequence of the film *Leafie, A Hen into the Wild* culminates with shots of the open grave—a haunting and indeed haunted image that, like a palimpsest, registers the residual markings of past traumas (see figure 11.1). Such images, which might be described by cultural commentators as "holocaustal," serve as rhetorical invitations to perceive in this otherwise light animated kids' film darker subtexts that give the lie to the notion of fantasy-based entertainment's relative emptiness as a diverting escape from the "real." Such representational strategies have long been adopted by both mainstream cultural producers and animal rights activists who seek to appeal to the hearts, if not always the minds, of their easily swayed audiences. Moreover, images such as these, which might be perceived as being tasteless or unsavory (given their conflation of animal suffering with human misery), in fact accurately depict the manner in which dead, dying, or simply unwanted creatures have been disposed of by humans. This idea is likewise broached in the 2014 independent documentary *An Omnivorous*

Family's Dilemma, a film that ratchets up the affective charge through its inclusion of live-action, rather than hand-drawn and computer-animated, images of real animals being slaughtered or buried alive in mass graves.

Courting Controversy and Killing Pigs: From PETA to *An Omnivorous Family's Dilemma*

Before addressing the direct and indirect references to the Holocaust in *An Omnivorous Family's Dilemma*, it will be useful to place such rhetorical maneuvers in the context of previous efforts to raise consciousness about the topic of animal welfare through images and language that—even to the most ardent champions of nonhuman rights—are not only objectionable but offensive. Unquestionably, the most notorious instance of an animal rights campaign that harnessed this kind of analogous discourse is the one that was launched by PETA in early 2003, when a traveling exhibit consisting of eight large panels made its way across the United States and was eventually uploaded as a looping slideshow on the nonprofit organization's website. That antimeat, provegetarian campaign, titled "Holocaust on Your Plate," was controversial to say the least, but it was consistent with PETA's previous publicity-grabbing attempts to shock audiences into greater sympathetic alignment with nonhuman creatures through the use of advertising and public-relations campaigns noted for their "strong visual impact."[25] For instance, ten years earlier, Dan Matthews, PETA's senior vice president, introduced the "I'd Rather Go Naked than Wear Fur" campaign, first in Tokyo (where he and a small group of fellow protesters—unafraid of appearing nude in public—demonstrated outside an international fur fair) and then, once news of that event began to spread, all over the world. But little about that long-running antifur campaign (which garnered widespread celebrity support until it ended in 2020) could have prepared people for the morbidly unsettling exhibit that would draw the ire of many cultural commentators (including human rights and animal rights advocates) almost immediately after it debuted in 2003.

What, precisely, was so provocative and upsetting about that campaign? As suggested by its title, a comparison was made between the twentieth century's most conclusive evidence of humans' capacity to act inhumanely (the Holocaust) and the history-spanning suffering of nonhumans (who have long been deemed "disposable" in the eyes of humans). Juxtaposing genocidal images from World War II with photos from factory farms and slaughterhouses, the brochures, posters, and online material that made up "Holocaust on Your Plate" have been roundly criticized by anti–animal rights spokespeople as proof that PETA and other, more militant organizations (such as the Animal Liberation Front) are not only misguided in their exploitative use of potentially "triggering" imagery but also morally bankrupt as provocateurs willing to "compare children behind barbed wire [to] pigs looking out from behind bars."[26] One of the most outspoken critics is Wesley Smith, who wrote *A Rat Is a Pig Is a Dog Is a Boy* and who has referred to such public-relations stunts as "odious" and "despicable," a subversive form of moral equivalence that merely underscores the "twisted reasoning at the heart of the animals rights/liberation movement."[27] Brusquely condemning the decision of Ingrid Newkirk, PETA's cofounder and president, to show "emaciated concentration camp inmates in their tight-packed wooden bunks alongside chickens in cages," Smith states plainly what others have attempted to say in their more measured responses to the problem of drawing moral equivalencies between animals and humans.[28] Those others include renowned thinkers such as Raymond Gaita, who—in his 2002 book *The Philosopher's Dog*—argues that "one need not be susceptible to such extravagant comparisons in order to fully acknowledge that our cruelty to animals is abominable and to hope that future generations will find it so."[29]

Nevertheless, "Holocaust on Your Plate" and other PETA campaigns (including "Meet Your Meat," a twelve-minute video montage narrated by Alec Baldwin that shows animal mistreatment in industrial agriculture) have succeeded in attracting media attention and influencing the public-facing business practices of fast-food chains, clothing manufacturers, drug companies, and multinational corporations (which, in some cases, have adopted more humane policies). This is covered in the director Matthew Galkin's feature-length documentary *I Am an Animal* (2007), which provides biographical details about Newkirk's upbringing as a dog lover and her early commitment to animal rights, as well as her unapologetic response to those who have decried PETA's description of the mass killing of sentient creatures within the meat industry as a "Modern-Day Holocaust." Galkin also includes talking-head interviews with representatives of the Anti-Defamation League (such as its national director, Abraham H. Foxman, a Holocaust survivor) and other nonprofit advocacy groups, including Friends of Animals and the Humane Society of the United States, who have distanced themselves from such sensationalism—which, in the words of one interviewee, has "trivialized animal rights." Newkirk stands her ground in this documentary, defiantly telling her many critics that the only way to get this important discussion on the table is to do something "jarring," and that ultimately "we must *get over ourselves*" if we are not only to free nonhuman creatures from their enslavement to humans but also to emancipate ourselves from the hubris of believing that one species is superior to all others. Notably, director Mark Devries's *Speciesism: The Movie* (2013), another in a long list of documentaries to explore this subject, directly interrogates the flawed premise of humans' ontological superiority, building toward a conclusion in which such pernicious thinking is linked to the rise of Nazism in the 1930s and the propping up of eugenic principles as a justification for human rights abuses since the 1940s.

Importantly, PETA and its media-savvy president (who would eventually become implicated in the illegal activities undertaken by black-hooded members of the Animal Liberation Front) were not the first to suggest that "killing pigs and caging chickens is Auschwitz all over again" (to borrow Smith's unsubtle phrase).[30] In fact, Isaac Bashevis Singer, a Polish American writer who was awarded the Nobel Prize in Literature in 1978, argued that "in relation to [animals], *all people are Nazis*; for the animals, it is an eternal Treblinka"—a phrase that inspired Charles Patterson's 2002 book *Eternal Treblinka: Our Treatment of Animals and the Holocaust* (published one year before PETA began its notorious campaign).[31] But in equating "the experience of Jews in torture camps like Buchenwald and Dachau with the meat and leather industries," Newkirk played up the outrageousness of her organization's headline-grabbing deeds, thus distinguishing PETA from other advocacy groups through its "sustained, all-encompassing media presence."[32] As Brett Lunceford explains, "PETA seems to recognize," perhaps better than any other animal rights group, "that protest can function as entertainment and spectacle."[33] Not only has PETA—the largest animal rights organization on the planet (based in Norfolk, Virginia, and boasting approximately 6.5 million members and supporters worldwide)—been adept at inserting itself into popular culture ("including music, fashion, and their own print outlets aimed at the true believers"), but it has also inspired smaller activist groups in other countries to follow its lead, adopting equally outrageous tactics or theatrical "performances" in the spirit (if not the letter) of "I'd Rather Go Naked than Wear Fur" and "Holocaust on Your Plate."

Julien Dugnoille, one of the foremost scholars of interspecies relations in South Korea, has commented on the influence of PETA on local groups like Coexistence of Animal Rights on Earth (CARE, established in 2002) and Korea Animal Rights Advocates (KARA, established in 2005), two of the many organizations whose leaders tend to "think outside the box" in their highly publicized efforts to promote the welfare of nonhuman creatures.[34] Although we say more about these groups and their often creative forms of social activism near the end of this chapter, it is bears mentioning here that they each have sought to raise public consciousness about animal rights through a variety of media-based educational campaigns that include citizen journalism, celebrity-endorsed "*sajimalgo, ibyanghaseyo* (don't buy, adopt)" print ads, and the creation of videos celebrating heroic acts of animal rescue. They have also associated themselves with filmmakers such as Im Sun-rye (who was appointed KARA's president in July 2009) and Hwang Yun, director of *An Omnivorous Family's Dilemma* (whose networking through the film festival circuit might extend those organizations' reach even further).

Although *An Omnivorous Family's Dilemma* is something of an outlier, distinct from many of the nonfiction motion pictures made in South Korea over the past decade, it is part of a larger—indeed, global—cultural phenomenon in which documentarians have played a vital role in catalyzing a truly transnational animal rights movement. In the first decade of the twenty-first century, the animal rights question had already begun moving "from the periphery and toward the center of political and legal debate," according to Cass Sunstein, who notes that in 2002, Germany voted "to guarantee animals rights in its constitution, adding the word's 'and animals' to a clause that obliges the state to respect and protect the dignity of human beings."[35] Luxembourg and Austria have followed suit, going so far as to equate the importance of animal life to that of human life in legislative acts and anticruelty laws that were passed in the early 2000s. Not coincidentally, when those constitutional changes were introduced, an initial wave of animal-themed documentaries arrived on the scene, including *The Witness* (2000), *Shelter Dogs* (2003), *Peaceable Kingdom* (2004), *Earthlings* (2005), *Sharkwater* (2006), and *Dealing Dogs* (2006). The second wave can be said to have occurred during the next decade, around the same time that the abovementioned U.S. production *Speciesism: The Movie* was distributed. In 2013 and 2014, a host of similarly themed films (all released within months of one another) brought the topic of animal exploitation to millions of viewers. Examples from that period include Gabriela Cowperthwaite's *Blackfish* (2013), Liz Marshall's *The Ghosts in Our Machine* (2013), Amy Schatz's *An Apology to Elephants* (2013), Marc Pierschel's *Live and Let Live* (2013), Chris Delforce's *Lucent* (2014), and Kip Andersen and Keegan Kuhn's *Cowspiracy: The Sustainability Secret* (2014). Although their specific concerns vary considerably (including scientific testing, dietary and environmental ethics, industrial farming and agribusiness, and so on), these films share a common understanding that nonhumans deserve respect and that moral rights are not reserved exclusively for humans (a line of reasoning put forth by Peter Singer, Richard Dawkins, Gary Francione, Steven Best, and other interviewees who appear with regularity in these productions). The films also occasionally show atrocity photos depicting the pain and suffering of animals, a rhetorical tactic that Hwang Yun takes in her 2014 documentary *An Omnivorous Family's Dilemma*—which was one of several internationally distributed works of transnational animal rights advocacy that year.

Images of pigs being buried alive in mass graves, taken from television broadcast news footage recorded during the 2010–2011 foot-and-mouth disease outbreak in South Korea (which led to mass disposals of 3.5 million cows and pigs), appear early in Hwang Yun's film, immediately following an opening sequence that establishes her backstory and personal investment in the plight of animals. Over still photographs highlighting how central her pet dogs were to her childhood and early motherhood, Hwang's voice-over narration explains that, when she visited the zoo one day, she realized that the animals asked her "to tell people their story." "So," she continues, "I made a film about them." What follows from that point is a series of personal investigations into the spread of factory farming in South Korea, the dwindling number of alternative farms where pigs and other animals enjoy a relatively healthier and happier life, and the lengths to which her own family members are willing to go (or not go) to support her cause and adopt her new lifestyle as a vegetarian. The aptly titled *An Omnivorous Family's Dilemma* (a nod to the American author Michael Pollan's 2006 best seller, *The Omnivore's Dilemma*) is both an autobiographical essay about Hwang's conversion to animal rights activism and a metatextual meditation on the limitations faced by filmmakers who feel the need to speak for voiceless others. Tellingly, this documentary—which consists in part of video diary footage of her family's domestic life as they negotiate some of the challenges involved in weaning themselves from a diet of meat to vegetable-based meals, as well as talking-head interviews with farmers, other animal rights activists, and governmental representatives—brings together voices of assent and dissent. This dialogic element of the film, similar to the approach that Galkin takes in *I Am an Animal*, is most apparent whenever Hwang's husband, a veterinarian who provides medical care to wild animals, appears onscreen to grudgingly announce his opposition to her project, occasionally shooing her camera away when her persistent questioning grows tiresome or too invasive. Her pesky camera is even present when he receives news that he will need to take temporary leave of his family and join a group of other animal specialists and scientists at poultry farms to deal with the outbreaks of a highly pathogenic avian influenza that have affected millions of birds across East Asia (in particular in South Korea and Taiwan, where thousands of ducks, chickens, geese, and doves were culled in 2013 and 2014 to arrest the spread of the virus). It is during this penultimate section of the film when the questionable moral equivalencies referred to above are most nakedly apparent.

At the ninety-minute mark of the film, we encounter Kim Chŏng-su, a visibly shaken civil servant at the Chinchŏn District office who had been ordered to take part in the culling of livestock after an earlier outbreak of avian influenza. Accompanied by documentary TV news footage of squawking hens being stuffed into bags and hogs being scuttled into open pits, Kim describes the trauma he continues to experience as a result of that process. The four hundred ducks that he pushed into a one-ton sack "were warm . . . like babies." "You could hear their heartbeat," he says, and at this point Hwang inserts close-ups of children's drawings—crude yet expressionistic renderings of the horrors being described by the government employee. Explaining that his memories of that event still haunt him years after its occurrence, Kim states that it "reminds [him] of the massacre of Jewish people by German soldiers." This rhetorical maneuver of the text, echoing those earlier scenes showing the killing of pigs during the swine flu epidemic, is likely to draw as many looks of disbelief as nods of agreement, effectively splitting the choir to whom *An Omnivorous Family's Dilemma* preaches. Although the civil servant directs his questions toward himself (asking, "If I were ordered to kill a human, would I be able to carry out the order?"), his gaze remains fixed on the camera, an invisible apparatus that stands in for the film's director as well as its audience—both of whom are implicated in the ethical dilemmas that such government-mandated policies, ostensibly designed to safeguard humans from deadly disease, inevitably create.

Juxtaposed against this somber archival footage of Kim's television interview is the filmmaker's more lighthearted autobiographical journey toward creaturely awareness. It is a literal and figurative journey that she takes with her son,

To-yŏng, as the two develop a bond with a mother and baby pig after numerous trips to a traditional country farm (owned by a good-natured old man named Wŏn Chung-yŏn and located in Kangwŏn Province), one of only a few such alternatives to the cramped industrial farming spaces that operate outside the public's view in South Korea. In contrast to the many animals that are shown being scuttled into a dirt pit in the film's harrowing TV news footage, the pigs with whom Hwang develops a strong emotional bond are given names by Wŏn, who genuinely cares for his animals. One pig in particular, Sip-sun, attracts the attention of the filmmaker, who initially travels to the remote mountain village where the farmer lives because she is searching for a viable alternative to the many factory farms that have left her shaken and feeling sick. When she arrives, she is introduced to Sip-sun, a sow who is lying on a warm, luxurious bed of hay and being fed cabbage and root vegetables by Wŏn. Described as being "mild-tempered," Sip-sun is nevertheless visibly wracked with pain, having endured a six- or seven-hour labor that finally ends the following day with the birth of eight piglets, who immediately begin suckling milk from their mother's teats and burrowing under the hay for warmth, while hens cluck away inside their spacious pen.

These moments, which are recorded by Hwang with quiet and respectful tenderness, are intercut with scenes from factory farms that show a very different and more industrialized approach to porcine birth, illustrating how successful Wŏn has been in creating an atmosphere of compassion for the animals that are central to his livelihood. Part of that compassion comes from his decision to name the piglets not long after their birth, a move that not only helps him identify individual pigs but also endows them with an individuality that contributes to interspecies bonding. As Stephen Clark states, "once named and attended to," an animal is revealed to be "more than 'just an animal,' more than a replaceable part" (something that the abovementioned children's stories by Hwang Sun-mi reveal through their foregrounding of a hen named Sprout and a dog named Scraggly).[36] The black sows who receive multiple close-ups in *An Omnivorous Family's Dilemma* and who are shown breast-feeding their babies in unison, including Yong-sun (who has "stiff hair" and is "finicky") and Chi-sun (who has "pretty eyes"), are thus brought into the moral orbit of the activist-filmmaker and revealed to be just as much a part of South Korea's animal rights debates as any named human is.

Besides expressing an empathetic understanding of the pain that Sip-sun must have felt during labor, Hwang Yun—a lullaby-singing mother who has recently given birth to a son—forms an attachment to a small piglet that she names Ton-su. Because Ton-su was the last of the eight pigs that Sip-sun gave birth to, the filmmaker sees something of her own child in the small animal. That interspecies parallelism is underlined by her frequent cross-cutting between scenes at Wŏn's farm and quotidian moments at her own home, where To-yŏng grows from a baby in a crib to a toddler who plays with a collection of stuffed animals and then to a precocious young boy who, against his will, is being groomed to be a vegetarian. During these domestic scenes, *An Omnivorous Family's Dilemma* seems less like an animal rights film than a home movie, but the child's foregrounding is central to the film's message that a "humane education" of the Korean populace is needed if legislative steps are to be taken to enhance the welfare of nonhuman creatures. In the words of Frank Ascione (a researcher who has advocated parents' use of fiction as a way to guide young people toward an empathetic relationship with animals, an entryway into animal understanding), one of the most fruitful ways to instill a philosophy of respect and kindness toward nonhuman creatures is to "focus on teaching children these humane principles,"[37] and in accordance with that approach Hwang Yun takes time to explain to To-yŏng why she has to pack daily meals for him (to replace the meat-heavy school lunch menu). She also takes him to the farm to see Ton-su and the other piglets, encouraging an interspecies bond between them that might further promote prosocial behavior once the boy has grown into a man and (his mother hopes) has learned to empathize with others beyond his kin. At the very least, he, like his filmmaker-mother (who initially struggles to tell the pigs apart), comes to see each animal as an individual capable of feeling pleasure and pain just as humans do.

The interrelated issues of animals' naming and individuality emerge later in the film, during an interview with a veterinarian friend of Hwang's husband named Yi Yun-kwŏn. As someone who works with factory farms to treat their sick pigs, he has frequently been forced to put "corporate profit" before his "personal feelings," and he matter-of-factly explains to Hwang why it is sometimes advantageous to kill pigs as an alternative to curing them with costly medication. When he is asked if he and other vets perform the culling, Lee says yes, through the use of drugs or electrocution. "Those animals were born simply to be eaten," he flatly states. Though they are "living things," according to Yi, "we don't name them," since doing so would interfere in the professional obligation to see them as "food" and not "friends." Here, the interviewee makes a distinction between a pig and a dog, the latter being a domestic creature that he regards as an "individual" who in times of need (for example, in case of an injury or infection) would be given traditional veterinary care.

Yi's words, echoed in the filmmaker's subsequent voice-over narration when she notes that sows in factory farms are "locked in stalls all their lives" and eventually "butchered when their performance fails," remind us that the mass manufacturing of pigs on corporate farms is tantamount to an indefensible form of carceral abuse. But the animals are also shown suffering on Wŏn's traditional farm, once the time comes for them to be castrated (a bloody ritual that the clearly unnerved farmer must perform so that the meat will be free of boar taint). Because he does not use anesthetics, the sows become violently angry and attempt to shield their babies from his blade, putting up a maternal defense that any parent would appreciate.[38] The filmmaker watches this grisly scene with a mixture of sadness and confusion, acknowledging that even so-called alternative farms are ultimately more concerned with making life better for humans than for animals—a point made salient in the film's open-ended final scene in which Hwang, standing in her kitchen, receives a package of organic pork meat, a gift from Wŏn, and wonders what to do with it.

Although Hwang's earlier work—*Farewell* (*Chakbyŏl*, 2001), *Silent Forrest* (*Ch'imukŭi sup*, 2004), and *One Day on the Road* (*Ŭnŭnal kŭ kilaesŏ*, 2006)—also deals with animal-related issues (such as the treatment of zoo inhabitants and the traffic kills of wild creatures), *An Omnivorous Family's Dilemma* can be thought of as her magnum opus, one that took four years to shoot and complete. And it highlights the weakest of the weak: farm animals that, though numerous, generally attract little interest from people, including self-described animal lovers.[39] What is especially ironic is that the pig, a largely misunderstood creature (once commonly linked to maternal fertility and earthly abundance, but now negatively associated with dirtiness, filth, and greed), has long been thought of as a sacred animal in Korean culture, representing the good fortune that awaits the most morally upstanding or virtuous members of society (a theme found in classical Korean literature and shamanist rituals as well as cinematic productions of the 1950s and 1960s, the so-called golden age).[40] Although several different creatures, from snakes to swallows, can be interpreted as good omens if encountered in a dream, the pig occupies a special place in the minds of many Koreans, the most superstitious of whom will sometimes buy lottery tickets after waking up from such a dream. But writers and filmmakers have also deconstructed the pig's symbolic and literal currency. For instance, director Han Hyŏng-mo's *A Pig's Dream* (*Twaejikkum*, 1961) begins with a cartoon rendering of the eponymous animal as it kicks a man in the neck. Those opening credits hint at this film's broadly comical tone as well the cruel misfortune that eventually befalls the main character, a cash-strapped man named Son Hak-su (Kim Sŭng-ho), who—after having a dream about a pig and then receiving one as a potentially profit-making gift—ends up losing his young son to a fatal traffic accident.[41]

In the years following the theatrical release of *A Pig's Dream*, a number of other Korean cultural productions have likewise conveyed contradictory feelings toward this creature, which appears as a violent threat to humanity in one film (the mutant killer pig in *Chaw* [*Ch'au*, 2009]) and a medium through which to expel evil from the world in another (the container of an exorcised demon in *The Priests* [*Kŭmŭn sajedŭl*, 2015]). In the director Chang Mun-il's *My Sister, the Pig Lady* (*Twaeji kat'ŭn yŏja*, 2015), the animals are merely a means to an end: a way for the titular female protagonist, Chae-hwa (Hwang Chŏng-ŭm), to earn a living as a restaurant owner in a small fishing village. Throughout this film, pigs are treated horrendously by humans, who beat them with sticks whenever they attempt to escape from their cramped quarters and who cut off their tails as snack food. The animals are nearly killed when two other women, Yu-ja (Ch'oe Yŏ-jin) and Mi-ja (Pak Chin-ju), crash their moped into the pig house, and are taunted with the words, "Bacon? Sirloin? Tenderloin? Ribs?" by Chae-hwa, who inconsiderately asks the pigs what they think about her idea of opening a barbeque restaurant near the ocean. In the film's most troubling scene, after Chae-hwa forces one squealing pig onto a cart, she plunges a knife into its head—a shot (framed with the animal just offscreen) that is soon followed with images of her skinning it and then of grilling meat on a restaurant table as the patrons sing the words "Awesome pork!" But perhaps no Korean cultural production better illustrates Laura McMahon's argument that "the place of the pig in cinema has so often been one of deathly subjugation"[42] than Pak Ch'ŏl-su *Farewell, My Darling* (*Haksaengpugunsinwi*, 1996), a film about a rural family's funeral preparations in which one mourner, a wealthy villager named P'al-bong (Kim Il-u), guns down a pig (shown fleeing for its life) as part of the Confucian service. This moment, in which an actual animal's death appears to take place within a fictional drama, and that culminates with an image of the pig hemorrhaging in the dirt, is perhaps more disturbing than the culling scene in *An Omnivorous Family's Dilemma* insofar as it is presented as a comical grotesque—a mixing of tonal elements that is similar to what Bong Joon-ho's *Okja* would do (with greater sensitivity and skill) two decades later.

Hamming It Up with *Okja*: Activist Actions and Performative Distractions in a Transnational Animal Rights Film

Since the passing of the Animal Protection Act of 1991, which went largely unenforced until it was overhauled in 2007, South Korea has come under increased international scrutiny in terms of its questionable commitment to universal norms in the age of globalization, and animal abuse is a problem that has yet to be rectified. Whales continue to be ensnared in fishermen's nets; bear cubs are still caught in the wild and kept in captivity for the purposes of harvesting their bile (a digestive fluid used by some practitioners of traditional Chinese medicine); and rabbits, guinea pigs, hamsters, mice, and other animals are exposed to experimental drug and cosmetic tests. This is the context in which Bong's *Okja*, which follows a young country girl's frantic attempt to rescue her best friend—a genetically modified, hippo-size "super pig" that has been bred to feed hundreds of people—from the clutches of a multinational corporation, arrived. However, the film's global distribution, in addition to its international cast of characters and border-crossing narrative (which takes the female protagonist Mija [An Sŏ-hyŏn] and her pig, Okja. to New York City), means that it cannot be pinned to any one geopolitical setting. Moreover, the film is a tonally mixed amalgam of comedy and tragedy. Thus, it resists easy categorization and situates the eponymous animal in a liminal zone, where its fate rests in the hands of humans with opposing agendas. As the director stated in an interview following *Okja*'s release, "Films either show animals as soulmates or else we see them in documentaries being butchered. I wanted to merge those worlds."[43]

Larded with moments of comedic interplay between Korean- and non–Korean-speaking characters (played by Tilda Swinton, Paul Dano, Jake Gyllenhaal, and other actors whose performances are intentionally "hammy") as well as fantastical interludes in which the animal at the heart of this "creature feature" (which is no less a technological invention than the monster at the heart of Bong's earlier film *The Host* [*Koemul*, 2013]) barely escapes death at the hands of her pursuers, *Okja* brings together disparate genre elements and, like *An Omnivorous Family's Dilemma*, flirts with controversy in its conjuring up of past atrocities and conflation of human rights abuses and animal rights abuses. Culminating with a scene filled with concentration camp iconography that evokes the horrors of the Holocaust, the film gestures toward a history that is not only beyond its narrative scope but also arguably unrepresentable. Indeed, it would be easy to make the case that the staging of such a scene—like that of other, sillier moments in which representatives of the fictional Mirando Corporation and members of the nonfictional Animal Liberation Front are grossly caricatured as comic figures—undercuts what Yasco Horsman refers to as "the 'seriousness' of the debates about animal rights" and suggests that the prospect of speciesism ever disappearing from South Korea is as likely as a pig learning to fly.[44]

"Seriousness" (with its associations with calmness, earnestness, sincerity, and sobriety) is a term that frequently finds its way into contemporary discourses and histories of rights-based activism aimed at improving the lives of animals, an undertaking that is at once touted and questioned by commentators who view such activities with a mixture of admiration and skepticism. As Wesley Jamison notes in "A Profile of Animal Rights Activists," the stateside movement to end abuses and injustices suffered by nonhumans—which has its roots in the eighteenth-century philosophy of Immanuel Kant, Jean-Jacques Rousseau, Jeremy Bentham, and others, as well as the antivivisectionist efforts of British scientists and medical practitioners of the nineteenth century—has often been dismissed by members of the country's "political class" (by which he means legislators, lobbyists, policy experts, and the like) as "something less than serious."[45] Two philosophers who, in the words of Susan Finsen and Lawrence Finsen, "propelled animal issues into serious discussion," at least within academic circles, during the 1970s were Peter Singer and Tom Regan.[46] Notably, in the preface to his enormously influential book *Animal Liberation*, Singer informs the reader: "Five years ago I myself would have laughed at the statements . . . I have now written in complete seriousness."[47] This comment suggests a sudden about-face or coming into consciousness on Singer's part. It also hints at the urgency with which he, Regan, and other high-profile liberationists addressed the pressing need to change naysayers' minds about meat consumption and animal testing during the early years of the movement.

Today, laughter is not necessarily shunned by proponents of these philosophers' ideas, and indeed a few writers now suggest that one way to win over "potential converts" is to adopt a more lighthearted mode of public outreach and messaging. For example, John Kistler encourages animal rights activists "to lighten up [their] often-depressing stories and statistics" and to not take themselves too seriously.[48] While he admits that the continued exploitation and mistreatment of nonhuman creatures "are serious issues, and not a laughing matter," Kistler believes that "the over-seriousness of some activists may actually be detrimental to their persuasiveness (not to mention their own psychological well-being)." Superficial though this gloss on a complex issue might be, his words provide a framework with which to begin making sense of *Okja*'s tonal variances and generic elasticity—the film's "stretchable" accommodation of seemingly antagonistic modes of performance in addition to its director's willingness to combine sadness and tragedy with broad, comedy-based entertainment and fun (a mix that Kistler endorses). Tellingly, the juxtaposition of such extremes contributed to the film's mixed reception following its release on Netflix, especially among print journalists and online commentators who openly questioned its commitment to a serious issue.

For example, *Vulture* contributor Kevin Lincoln asks, "What's really going on here? Is this a high-pitched, mostly comedic caper with a dressing of animal-rights activism, or is it a serious movie about the abuses of capitalism and industrial farming, told through Bong's wacky and brutal villain?" The villain in question is not, as some readers might suspect, either of the two megalomaniacal characters played by Swinton over the course of the film's bifurcated narrative (twin sisters Lucy and Nancy Mirando, current and former CEOs, respectively, of the corporation that bears their family name). Instead, Lincoln is referring to Gyllenhaal's Dr. Johnny Wilcox, an eccentric zoologist-turned–TV personality who takes part in Lucy's nefarious plan to sell genetically modified super pigs to unsuspecting consumers around the world. "Squealing like an alcoholic teakettle [and] wearing a child's shorts and a car salesman's mustache," as Lincoln puts it, this intentionally cartoonish company mascot left many critics scratching their heads in disbelief or uncertainty about the actor's methods and the character's motivations. Indeed, Jordan Crucchiola found Dr. Johnny's "screeching voice and neurotic behavior to be physically repulsive," so much so that the blogger "wanted someone—anyone—to punch him until he died." In contrast, Lincoln struggles to come to terms with the actor's "*committed* performance." "If the commitment is to anything other than hyperbole," he states, "I'm not entirely sure what it is."[49]

Although they admit to liking Bong's high-flying, genre-defying film, these two pop culture commentators are not alone in feeling flummoxed by Gyllenhaal's peculiar turn as a shrieking, self-described animal lover who gradually shrinks to "a level of cruelty that's genuinely terrifying," in Crucchiola's words[50] (see figure 11.2). In searching for some way to navigate the shoals of this admittedly discombobulating film, several critics have resorted to comparisons to other cultural icons while adopting a flamboyant mode of discourse that mimics the actor's exhibitionist tendencies. Kevin Jagernauth compares Dr. Johnny to the

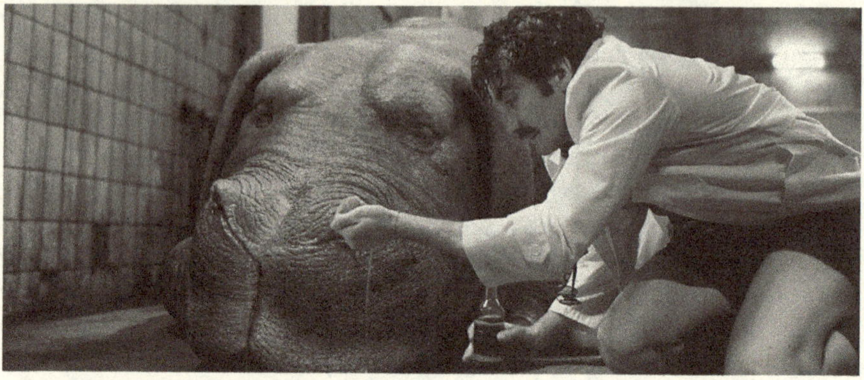

FIGURE 11.2 Jake Gyllenhaal gives a flamboyant performance as the eccentric zoologist-turned–TV personality Dr. Johnny Wilcox opposite the title creature (a genetically modified super pig) in Bong Joon-ho's *Okja* (2017), a film that foregrounds the theatrical nature of animal rights activism.

Australian television personality Steve Irwin after the world's most famous crocodile hunter has "consumed a couple of six-packs of Red Bull."[51] Reviewer Andrew Parker argues that Gyllenhaal's performance, which he labels "high camp," channels not one but several celebrities, including "Groucho Marx, Rip Taylor, and professional wrestler Dalton Castle."[52] E. Nina Rothe, a contributor to *Huffington Post*, likens Dr. Johnny to Captain Jack Sparrow, a Keith Richards–Pepé Le Pew mashup brought to life by Johnny Depp in the *Pirates of the Caribbean* swashbuckler franchise.[53] Other critics likely had another Depp performance in mind when they described Gyllenhaal's character as being "gonzo," a term that conjures up the drug-fueled, stream-of-consciousness writing style of Hunter S. Thompson (the inspiration for the director Terry Gilliam's cultish 1998 road movie, *Fear and Loathing in Las Vegas*, in which the chameleonic actor plays the journalist's wildly unhinged alter ego Raoul Duke).[54] Of course, the term "gonzo" has also been applied to other recent big-screen performances awash in gestural excess and scene-chewing theatricality, from James McAvoy's scheming, sociopathic detective in *Filth* (2013) to Matthew McConaughey's pot-bellied, snaggle-toothed prospector in *Gold* (2016). Multiple roles inhabited by the dependably outrageous Nicolas Cage have been described with that term (including Peter Loew in *Vampire's Kiss* [1989], Cameron Poe in *Con Air* [1997], Brent Ryan in *Mom and Dad* [2017], and Red Miller in *Mandy* [2018]), and the annals of exploitation cinema contain more than a few examples of big, showy performances by cult actors whose gestural articulations (of body and voice) are in excess of what is required by the narrative.

As Ernest Mathijs states in "From Being to Acting," the spectator's "expectations, appreciations and interpretations of acting explode in a carnival of signs" when confronted with the bizarre, ornamental, and hyperbolic performance styles on view in representative examples of cult cinema.[55] This sometimes results in a corresponding form of rhetorical insobriety or overindulgence on the part of critics who, flailing about for analogies and metaphors, ironically can be seen as "camping it up" when writing about "the perceived excessiveness of such performances."[56] Notably, Mathijs emphasizes "referentiality," one of the eight performative techniques introduced in James Naremore's earlier attempt to codify actorly dynamics (the others being "mimesis," "ostentation," "characterization," "polysemous expression," "expertise," "authority," and "received action"). Referential acting, according to Mathijs, is the "key feature of cult acting," and it depends in part on the audience's knowledge of a performer's roles in previous films as well as her or his relationship to "real-life templates" who serve as the basis for performative allusions.[57] If Gyllenhaal's acting in *Okja* can be called cultish, owing to his exaggerated mannerisms and gestural excesses, we might ask who (or what) is he "riffing on" or referring to? And how might his distracting performance create new circuits of intertextual meaning while opening up dialogic possibilities within the text that either conform to or oppose the filmmaker's intended message about animal rights and factory farming? The film's coscreenwriter, Jon Ronson—who, as the author *The Men Who Stare at Goats* [2004], was himself labeled a "gonzo" journalist before he turned his attention to Hollywood productions—has singled out one of the real-world inspirations for Dr. Johnny. In an interview, Ronson explains that the character is based loosely on the Welsh television presenter Johnny Morris, the jovial host of the BBC One program *Animal Magic* (1962–1983) whose anthropomorphizing of forest and zoo denizens distinguished it from other wildlife programs. However, Bong disputes this notion, contending that any similarities between the perpetually soused, apparently demented character played by the American actor and the "cuddly" star of *Animal Magic* are "minimal."[58]

Because referentiality gives us only a partial grip on those slippery, untamed performances that—like Gyllenhaal's in *Okja*—threaten to shatter the illusion of narrative representation, Mathijs offers another, more useful hermeneutic tool in his essay. Although it is "furthest removed from referential acting," the mode of performance that he calls "mad acting" (typified by Max Schreck in *Nosferatu* [1922], Divine in *Pink Flamingos* [1972], and Klaus Kinski in *Aguirre, the Wrath of God* [1972], among others) is in some ways complementary as both a codifier of onscreen signifiers and a source of spectatorial pleasure.[59] To this list of performers we would add such idiosyncratic screen icons as Timothy Carey, Crispen Glover, and Sid Haig, who practically stole the show from the ostensible lead, Richard Davalos, in the racing movie *Pit Stop* (1969), directed by Jack Hill. Playing a hotshot driver named Hawk Sidney, Haig imbued his role with a mixture of sadism and surrealism, "hamming it up" with such maniacal glee and in such a laughably distracting way that his brief but memorable appearances are like "pit stops" in the narrative's progression, fissuring the diegesis with moments of pure spectacle.

Like Mathijs, the theorist Paul McDonald is interested in the "tension" between representation and presentation, or story and show, in motion picture acting.[60] But he goes beyond this "basic contradiction" upon which narrative film rests to emphasize how "spectacular acting"—on view in mainstream productions with bankable stars like Jim Carrey (*Liar, Liar* [1997]), Julia Roberts (*Ocean's Eleven* [2001]), Brad Pitt (*The Curious Case of Benjamin Button* [2008]), and Will Smith (*Hancock* [2008])—becomes a kind of story-arresting cinematic exhibitionism when presented by way of signifying codes and amplifying technologies (editing, lighting, lensing, framing, staging, and so on) that highlight their exceptionalism and thus distinguish them "from the anonymous bodies of supporting actors." To varying degrees, these stars are granted considerable space in which to display their skills and virtuosity in a sometimes self-conscious, attention-grabbing way, and often at the expense of an otherwise seamless diegesis torn between story and spectacle. Along those lines, Gyllenhaal, the biggest star in *Okja*, crystallizes the contradictions of this transnational text, momentarily drawing attention away from the lesser-known Korean performers (including An Sŏ-hyŏn and Pyŏn Hŭi-bong, who play Mija and her grizzled grandfather, respectively) while personifying the film's wildly divergent tones and stylistic exuberance. Gyllenhaal is simultaneously integrated into and extricated from the film's globe-trotting plot, and this synthesis of the contained and the uncontained hints at the carceral dialectics at the heart of *Okja*, in which the pig shuttles between a caged and uncaged existence.

What we are proposing, then, is a counterreading of Gyllenhaal's performance, which has largely been described as a flashy accessory needed to ensure the film's commercial viability and as a textual distraction that steers audiences away from more serious concerns related to animal rights and the activist work required to ensure those rights. In doing so, we are following in the footsteps of the scholar Justin Smith, who locates in Vincent Price's portrayal of the eponymous character in Michael Reeves's *Witchfinder General* (1968) not only the film's "magnetic center" but also "an internalized commentary upon the action."[61] According to Smith, the "combination of explicit authority and implicit emotional register . . . renders Price's Hopkins a captivating creation, a mesmeric figure whose presence transcends the narrative action." Similarly, Gyllenhaal's Wilcox embodies the film's wildly swinging tonal registers, its pendulum-like to-and-fro between emotional extremes. Moreover, his performance, as an actorly distraction that ostensibly transcends the text, actually brings us more forcefully into contact with the increasingly theatrical nature of animal rights activism, especially that which adopts excessive, flamboyant, histrionic, and (yes) humorous rhetorical maneuvers to make a point that might otherwise fail to resonate in more serious discourse.

Tellingly, within weeks of *Okja*'s Netflix release, PETA posted a short video on its website that illustrated, through a combination of broad physical comedy and melodrama, how one audience member was affected by Bong's film. The first half of this twenty-second video ("Before *Okja*") shows a grocery store shopper nonchalantly placing packaged meat items into her basket. The second half ("After *Okja*") spotlights the same woman, only this time she is dressed in black rather than bright red and wears a frown that erupts into a burst of overflowing sorrow. She falls to her knees in the middle of the frozen food aisle, letting out a plaintive cry that catches the attention of other shoppers. As over-the-top as anything in *Okja*, this bit of acting—at once "referential" and "mad"—might just be proof that there is some method to Gyllenhaal's madness. At the very least, this PETA production, on a considerably smaller scale than the film that inspired it, reminds us that, as Thomas Vernon Reed wrote in *The Art of Protest*, "all politics involves a theatrical element" and, as David Schlossman wrote in *Actors and Activists*, "all protest constitutes a type of performance, whether or not participants recognize it as such."[62]

On April 30, 2015, three organizations advocating animal rights—the Green Party, KARA, and Lawyers for Animal Rights—held a joint press conference at the Korea Press Center in Seoul that condemned factory-style livestock farming and animal abuse. The press conference was preceded by a performance in which two animal rights activists separately caged in cramped stalls donned the masks of a hen and a pig. Behind these steel cages stood two other activists masked as a hen and a pig holding picket signs that read "allow the basic rights of a hen to be able to stretch her wings" and "allow the basic rights of a pig to turn her body and walk around." In this tactical, theatricalized call for interspecies empathy, the activist performers temporarily put themselves in the place of suffering animals that are deprived of basic levels of mobility and freedom. On May 30, 2013, these three organizations—along with 1,129 citizens—had filed a civil lawsuit arguing that the Livestock Law was unconstitutional and violated the Animal Protection Law, as well as ignoring governmental responsibility for safeguarding the environment by encouraging factory-style farming. The government responded in March 2014, insisting that the current law did not violate any basic rights of citizens and also reminding people that the reversal of scientific farming would infringe on the rights of livestock farmers.[63] The complainants held the April 30, 2015, press conference to publicize their counterargument, which was submitted to the Constitutional Court on the same day and asserts that "the Livestock Law endangers human health by allowing pig stalls and battery cages for egg-laying hens outlawed in the E.U. [European Union] and Canada, a farming method that is conducive to the spread of livestock epidemics."[64]

Activist performances are common practices of animal rights advocacy demonstrations on the streets of Korea. On August 18, 2017, for example, in the Kwanghwamun Square in downtown Seoul (a traditional gathering place for protesters in the capital), Coexistence of Animal Rights on Earth and eleven other animal welfare and environmental groups staged a performance of two caged activists wearing hen masks and being sprayed with pesticide in response to the recent discovery of eggs contaminated by fipronil (an insecticide) in the consumer market. Activists gathered in the square to hold a press conference condemning factory-style poultry farming that uses battery cages, which cram six egg-laying hens into one cage and thus give them no space for movement. Unlike free-range chickens capable of cleaning their own skins with mud to keep mites off, caged hens are unable to protect themselves from the attack of insects in the summer, necessitating the excessive use of fipronil. Surrounding the makeshift stage where activists gave a hammy performance depicting a sinister chemical attack on helpless caged hens by an uncaring human in a biohazard suit were pro–animal rights protesters displaying signs saying, for example, "Pesticide-polluted eggs are results of turning away from animal welfare," "Guarantee hens' freedom for mud bathing," and "Today's hens are living in a space smaller than an A4 paper sheet." The rhetoric of animal rights activism is as provocative as these pantomime performances that highlight human cruelty and animal suffering. For example, Pak Ch'ang-gil—a professor emeritus at Songkonghoe University who represented Voice4Animals at the performance and press conference—called factory-style farming "the most demonic system on earth," an eye-catching comment that was quoted in a newspaper headline.[65]

On July 5, 2017, spokespeople for KARA announced that, along with Bong Joon-ho, they were starting the *Okja* Liberation Project to ban pig stalls. The organization aimed to collect a hundred thousand citizen signatures in favor of the ban. In support of the movement, Bong posed for a photograph with a picket sign reading "I, Bong Joon-ho, sign [a petition] to support the banning of stalls, the symbol of factory-style farming." KARA circulated an elongated poster for the campaign that reprinted the film poster of *Okja* in the middle. Above that was a list of the campaign's sponsors (Bong and KARA) and slogans ("Farm over factory!" and "Animals are not meat-producing factories"). Below the reprinted poster was a picture of pigs in stalls with the following text:

> For Mija, Okja is [a] family [member] whom she has to save against the system that regards animals as meat-producing factories. However, 99 percent of [the] meat we consume is produced in factory-style farming that cage animals in crammed stalls where they are unable to move their bodies all their lives. Please participate in the 100,000-signature campaign that will liberate 10 million Okjas, who are raised only to become food with all their instincts suppressed, from stalls. Beginning with the E.U., stalls are banned in many other countries. With 100,000 signatures, we will request legislation that outlaws pig stalls and cages in South Korea.[66]

On July 28, after collecting more than ten thousand signatures, KARA held a special screening of *Okja* at Taehan Theater, followed by a postscreening conversation about factory-style farming with Bong and Im Sun-rye, KARA's president and a filmmaker herself.[67]

Significantly, filmmakers have been at the forefront of recent efforts to raise public consciousness and promote the South Korean government's newly enforced legislation designed to protect the well-being of animals. Chief among these filmmakers is Im Sun-rye, the director of such critically lauded Korean New Wave films as *Three Friends* (*Sech'ingu*, 1996) and *Waikiki Brothers* (*Waikiki pŭradŏsŭ*, 2001) and producer of the animal rights–themed omnibus film *Sorry, Thanks* (*Mihanhae, komawŏ*, 2011), which brings together the individual contributions of four filmmakers (including her own short, *Cat's Kiss*).[68] Despite its diverse range of cinematic styles (a common complaint leveled against multidirector omnibus films), *Sorry, Thanks* displays thematic consistency in its approach to the lives of canine and feline pets and is just one of the many independent productions to have been featured at the Animal Film Festival, an annual event launched in the southern city of Suncheon in 2013. *Sorry, Thanks* is also a film that, like Bong's *Okja*, has been adopted by nonprofit organizations and advocacy groups in the hopes of effecting change at the institutional level and in the hearts and minds of movie audiences at home and abroad. Significantly, Im has served as executive director of KARA for eleven years, illustrating the strong affinity between independent filmmakers and rights activists who share a commitment to ending animal testing, dog-meat consumption, factory farming, and other exploitative or cruel practices that have long colored the global perception of South Korea as a land where speciesism runs rampant.

Conclusion

In March 2018, President Moon Jae-in (Moon Chae-in), a well-known animal rights enthusiast and former human rights lawyer, proposed to amend the South Korean constitution to add Clause 3, Article 37: "The nation must implement a policy for the protection of animals." Although the proposed amendment was ultimately discarded in the National Assembly (Kokhoe), it drew wide public support that went beyond activist groups (a public opinion poll showed that 64.3 percent of respondents supported the amendment, and 200,000 people signed a petition in favor of the bill).[69] This attests to the maturation of animal rights advocacy in South Korea and the country's willingness to move beyond anthropocentric models of what a just society looks like in favor of a more inclusive environment where human and nonhuman rights are equally protected. Perhaps there is more potential value to this aborted bill than the prospect of South Korea's joining European nations in the constitutional protection of animals or becoming the first Asian nation to pursue such a progressive policy. As the political scientist Pak Wŏn-ho states, "the animal protection clause in the constitution is not just about animals but actually defines the boundary of pain that we can sympathize with as a community."[70]

Many of the ideas that we have broached in this chapter could be summed up by the renowned rights advocate Joan Dunayer, who states in *Animal Equality*,

"Nonhuman animals occupy oppression's deepest level."[71] Dunayer notes that derogatory metaphors in the English language, such as the use of "cow" to denote a dull, fat woman and "pig" to denote either a male chauvinist or someone who lives in filth, "rely on speciesism for their pejorative effect." Besides encouraging injustice toward humans ("especially those who belong to vulnerable groups"), such negative images work to maintain the hierarchical order of things, further subjugating animal groups whose typical behaviors are grossly distorted in the process (for example, pigs are actually not filthy creatures). Of course, hackneyed expressions circulate in the Korean language as well (such as, *ch'ŏng kaeguri* ["blue frog"], meaning a person who does things the opposite way he or she has been told to do; *yŏu* ["fox"], for a calculating female who gets what she wants; and *nŭkdae* ["wolf"], meaning a predatory male with a dirty mind). The idea that animals "fall below humans in a natural hierarchy" has been an entrenched part of the Western philosophical tradition since the time of Aristotle, who argued that animals lacked the faculties needed to reason and therefore could be appropriately used as "resources for human purposes."[72] This "subordination thesis"—introduced by the Greek philosopher and subsequently supported by theologians of the Middle Ages such as Augustine and Thomas Aquinas—has become the dominant strain of thinking, reinforced through Judeo-Christian teachings that maintain that "God created humans in his own image."[73] As David DeGrazia points out, philosophers such as René Descartes, Thomas Hobbes, and John Locke contributed to the entrenchment of the Aristotelian thesis that human beings can and should claim supremacy over lesser beings. But they went even further in arguing that animals lacked attributes that only humans had, including "a capacity for language and innovative behavior," which were outward signs of an interior state. Most cinematic representations of animals subscribe to this idea by repeatedly emphasizing animals' usefulness to humans and denying that animals have any deeper consciousness that might give the lie to several centuries' worth of received wisdom about these so-called lesser beings. In doing so, a majority of films—Korean ones in particular—privilege instrumentality over interiority and perpetuate a speciesist ideology that has only recently been challenged or deconstructed by activist cultural producers.

We could point to numerous examples of the problematic ways in which animals are reductively represented and harshly treated in South Korean cinema, including the slaughterhouse scenes in Yi Sŏng-gu's *The Sun and the Moon* (*Irwŏl*, 1967; a golden age film about a family of butchers), the emphasis on harvesting bear bile in the same director's *Where the Buckwheat Blooms* (*Memilkkotp'il muryŏp*, 1969; another classic adaptation, this time about a group of itinerant peddlers going from market to market with their ever-dependable horses and donkeys), and the casual violence directed against a dog in *The Quiet Family* (*Choyonghan kajok*, 1998; in which the canine is kicked brutally by the family's patriarch while they feast on food). The fact that this scene from a black comedy by the director Kim Ji-woon (Kim Chi-yun), which prompts laughter after the offscreen yelp of the abused dog, has largely been overlooked by critics provides further evidence that a different way of looking at Korean cinema is needed if animals are to be granted the respect or level of attention that we lavish on human characters. Thus, it is high time to embrace or seek out a new, nonhuman hermeneutics to account for the precarious place of animals in film, an "animanalysis" that—similar to theorist Anat Pick's notion of "creaturely poetics" (which emphasizes the "shared embodiedness of humans and animals")[74]—recognizes multiple forms of personhood in its pursuit of a more thorough assessment of textual and thematic material.

Coda

"I Am (Not) a Human Being"

The Question of Robot Rights in South Korean Cinema

> Perhaps here . . . I should answer the question of whether I'm a robot. No, I'm not, but some of my best friends are!
> —Rosi Braidotti, *Posthuman Knowledge*

In the previous chapters, we have endeavored to lay bare some of the reasons why South Korean filmmakers—be they independent documentarians like Kim Dong-won (Kim Tong-wŏn) and Yi Sŭng-jun or commercial artists working in the mainstream motion picture industry such as Chang Hun and Chang Chun-hwan—might be drawn to rights advocacy, not only as a topic of cinematic discourse but also as a personal commitment to creating social change beyond the camera lens. Through textual analysis of representative films as well as a contextual framing of those works, we have sought to limn the contours of a relatively new genre, one that nevertheless has roots in the nation's earlier cultural output. As alluded to in the introduction and chapter 1, underground nonfiction films of the 1980s, including *Blue Bird* (*P'arangsae*, 1986) and *Sanggye-dong Olympics* (1988)—not to mention the first large-scale narrative productions undertaken by the most recognizable directors of the *minjung* era, who would launch the Korean New Wave in the years that immediately followed (films such as *Chilsu and Mansu* [*Ch'ilsuwa Mansu*, 1988], by Park Kwang-su; *The Lovers of Woomook-baemi*

[*Umukbaemiŭi sarang*, 1990], by Jang Sun-woo [Chang Sŏn-u]; and *Song of Resurrection* [*Puhwalŭi norae*, 1990], by Yi Chŏng-guk—opened a space for cultural commentary about the working class and for the dissemination of political dissent that would expand exponentially during the decades that followed. These and other predecessors to the contemporary human rights film made it possible to imagine a progressive path out of the proverbial darkness (that of the authoritarian past) and toward an "enlightened" state. Today, it is not unusual to see a big-budget feature about the pursuit of social justice or the protection of civil liberties contending for the top spot at the box office. And with that cultural shift has come a diversification of film subjects, which range from temporary workers' rights to the sexual harassment experienced by women and the struggles of people with disabilities to gain inclusion in a society that has transformed significantly since winning democratic freedoms three decades ago.[1]

The rights claims that are made by the members of various communities (such as LGBTQ people, migrants, former prisoners, and North Korean defectors) and that are foregrounded in different minoritarian strains of South Korea's human rights cinema rest on a supposition that is central to the 1948 Universal Declaration of Human Rights (UDHR). Proclaimed by the U.N. General Assembly on December 10 of that year and held up as a kind of founding document that protects human rights symbolically (if not legally) as a universal "norm," the UDHR presents humans as beings "born free and equal in dignity." Indeed, the first word in the expression "human rights" is the starting point for a broader discussion of what the second word might mean. Thus, it follows that many of the social movements that have emerged in South Korea since the 1970s, including those of laborers and students who fought for better work and educational standards (such as health and safety measures as well as a living minimum wage), should assert their members' essential humanity as the basis for rights protections. In fact, if there is one thing that rhetorically links the social movements of the past to those that receive media attention today, it is the protest chant "We are not animals, we are human begins"—a variation on the most famous rallying cry of the 1970s, labor activist Chŏn T'ae-il's literally incendiary proclamation, shouted seconds before his self-immolation (on November 13, 1970, in front of the Peace Market [P'yŏnghwasijang]), "We are not machines!"

Underlying those two phrases ("we are not animals" and "we are not machines") is the unspoken recognition that to be a nonhuman is to be undeserving of the rights (including that of "life, liberty, and security of person") that were sacralized over seventy years ago in the UDHR. If the assorted safeguards that are brought together under the moral and philosophical category of human rights, such as the protection against cruel punishment, degrading treatment, and discrimination as well as certain guarantees or entitlements (for example, the freedom of movement and the right to own property), are reserved for people because of their humanity, then how are we to ensure that animals (the topic of chapter 11) are not persecuted or treated unfairly? Does the introduction of nonhuman rights into the already contested, cordoned-off territory of human rights protections undermine the latter through a distributive repopulation of the moral ground upon which a "person"—no longer strictly defined as a being capable of reason or consciousness—stands alongside other equally amorphous or fluidly situated entities? Complicating these questions is the tendency, discernible among even the most open-minded of rights advocates, to characterize one's progressive attitudes toward matters of social justice (especially those requiring an intersubjective feeling for the other) in evolutionary terms—as if the capacity for compassion, within and across species, comes from humankind's spiritual growth or transformative maturation (leaving barbarism behind for a more civilized, cosmopolitan worldview).

On a smaller scale, individuals themselves can be said to "evolve," shucking off the cool indifference of their youth in favor of a more mature understanding of other people's pain. This is something that leaped to mind when we watched a segment of the CBS news magazine series *60 Minutes* that aired on December 2, 2012. That episode of the U.S. television program featured an interview with the former North Korean prisoner Shin Dong-hyuk (Sin Tong-hyŏk). While recounting to Anderson Cooper his story of escaping from Camp 14, the young man explained that now, when he sees footage from the Holocaust, it "moves [him] to tears." "I think I am still evolving," Shin stated, "from an *animal* to a *human*." Ironically, evolutionary theory has been mobilized by activists who support the idea of "distributed" rights to emphasize the "continuity between the species," which—as Emily Patterson-Kane and Heather Piper note—"appears contrary to human moral disengagement from animals."[2] It is a theoretical approach, in other words, that points toward the similarity, not difference, "between human and animal mental life," thus establishing a broader basis for rights claims that are predicated on consciousness.[3] Moreover, the emerging study of "machine consciousness" (also known as "synthetic consciousness"), which is part of the larger field of artificial intelligence and cognitive robotics, might result in an even wider playing field on which to map a "distributed idea of humanity."[4] If, indeed, robots—as Darwinian devices (to paraphrase the biorobotics expert John Long)—represent yet another evolutionary stage in human development, then a similarly evolved conception of nonhuman rights will be required for humans to coexist peacefully in a posthuman world. This is something that several Korean writers, filmmakers, and even legislators have begun to think about.

In the spring of 2007, South Korea's Ministry of Commerce, Industry, and Energy (Sanŭp t'ongsang jawŏnbu) announced that a small task force of legal experts and scientists had drawn up the world's first government-backed set of guidelines for the ethical treatment of robots. Partly inspired by Isaac Asimov's "Three Laws of Robotics" (which the American author introduced in his 1942 short story "Runaround")[5] but going well beyond that and other classic works of speculative science fiction to propose actual, real-world codes of conduct for humans who might be inclined to misuse or abuse nonhuman machines, the "Robot Ethics Charter" thus put South Korea in the spotlight as a country willing—in theory, if not in practice—to extend protections and rights to all.[6] Over a decade later, in 2018, the European Union debated whether or not to grant "electronic personhood" to autonomous robots with artificial intelligence (AI). The idea originated in a January 27, 2017, report by the European Parliament's Commission on Legal Affairs, which recommended "creating a specific legal status for robots in the long run, so that at least the most sophisticated autonomous robots could be established as having the status of electronic persons responsible for making good any damage they may cause, and possibly applying electronic personality to cases where robots make autonomous decisions or otherwise interact with third parties independently."[7] Ultimately, 156 AI experts from fourteen European countries opposed the motion, which they deemed "'inappropriate' from a 'legal and ethical perspective.'"[8] As these experts maintained, the idea of "electronic personhood" was not put forth to guarantee human rights to AI but to transfer liability from manufacturers to individual robots. In July 2017, the South Korean lawmaker Pak Yŏng-sŏn (along with thirty-seven colleagues) proposed the Basic Robot Law, which likewise recognizes AI as "electronic persons" with rights and obligations. However, like the "Robot Ethics Charter" ten years earlier, the new bill put more emphasis on compliance with anthropocentric ethics and regulating liability for machine errors than on protecting nonhuman rights. Nevertheless, this unpassed bill has a positive clause: it urges the government to devise a policy that would enable the "socially disenfranchised to enjoy opportunities and benefits provided by robots and robot technology," thus envisioning an ideal society distinguished by alliances between human minorities and nonhumans.[9]

Since the early 2000s, the controversial concept of robot rights has gained currency in this heavily automated country, which has a higher level of robot density than any other (710 industrial units per ten thousand employees in the manufacturing sector as of 2017).[10] In 2020, Pibo (short for "personal interconnect robot") debuted as the nation's first so-called robot companion, aimed primarily at single professionals or young families (further strengthening parallels between pet animals and robots). Although the biggest obstacle to enacting rights-based laws in South Korea, as in neighboring Japan, is the "irreconcilable division between the supporters and opponents of human exceptionalism" (as Jennifer Robertson notes in *Robo Sapiens Japanicus*),[11] public opinion appears to have evolved in recent years, and it now favors a more open-minded approach to a subject that once was debated only by the most forward-thinking philosophers and techno-futurists. Contributing to that attitudinal shift is a host of internationally distributed cultural productions—from K-dramas such as *Borg Mom* (MBC, 2017), *I'm Not a Robot* (*Roboti aniya*; MBC, 2017–2018), and *My Absolute Boyfriend* (*Chŏldae kŭi*; SBS, 2019) to web series such as *Bong-soon: A Cyborg in Love* (*Saranghamyŏn chuknŭn yŏja Bong-suni*, 2016), *I Am . . .* (2017), and *109 Strange Things* (*Pyŏil taitnae*, 2017)—in which humanoid automatons are partnered (professionally and sometimes romantically) with flesh-and-blood characters who must overcome prejudices and preconceptions if they are to develop alongside their new caregiving and -receiving companions. Additionally, a few noteworthy motion pictures, including the science-fiction–themed omnibus film *Doomsday Book* (*Illyu myŏlmang pogosŏ*, 2012) and Ho-jae Lee's *Robot Sound* (*Robot, sori*, 2016), openly question the moral priority given to humans in social justice campaigns while pointing toward a not-too-distant future when sentient machines might achieve a level of spiritual transcendence or enlightenment that their nonrobotic brethren (including Buddhist monks) can only aspire to reach.

Such representations, however, are largely inconsistent with the nation's cinematic and television output of previous decades. From the 1976 animated film *Robot Taekwon V* (*Robot'ŭ t'aegwŏn pŭi*, 1976) to the *Blade Runner*–inspired science-fiction film *Natural City* (*Naech'urŏl sit'i*, 2003), humanoid machines designed to wreak havoc on human populations have loomed large in the Korean cultural imagination, corresponding to the general fear of robots as figures of methodical menace and rampaging destruction. This is especially true of the latter motion picture, a box-office flop at the time of its release whose commercial failure perhaps reflects audiences' dissatisfaction with worn-out tropes, including that of the unfeeling, combat-ready cyborg as a symbol of the security threats awaiting humans in the foreseeable future (an only slightly exaggerated version of previous generations' military state). Written and directed by Min Pyŏng-ch'ŏn, *Natural City* revolves around two police officers' efforts to track down rogue cyborgs, also known as "deviants," whose built-in obsolescence (as robots with three-year life spans) can be surreptitiously circumvented through the "parasitic transplantation of artificial intelligence into human bodies." In his overview of South Korean science fiction, Gord Sellar suggests that those narrative elements reflect anxieties about cultural "contamination," rendered in such a way that "(foreign) generic influence" (Ridley Scott's *Blade Runner*, about replicant-human entanglements and distinguished by its Japanese and neo-noir iconography) registers the uncertainty of the nation's "postcolonial identity."[12] As the nonliving embodiments of "technology run amok," cinema's androids and cyborgs have been harnessed as elicitors of fear and paranoia, frequently demonstrating their physical and computational superiority over living, breathing characters in narratives set in the near or distant future. But they have also been used as ways to allegorize various existential dilemmas faced by humans (whom they uncannily resemble), including the experiences of otherness, social isolation, and exploitation that affect millions of people around the world. All of this makes the robot a globally salient, ever-adaptable avatar of the posthuman condition in a neoliberal age.

As Louise LePage states, "robots are hybrid signifiers and subjects, and they resonate at multiple levels."[13] Cultural productions, including South Korean films, have contributed to that hybridized signification, often by sending contradictory messages that cancel each other out, paradoxically slowing scientific and technological progress even as they point toward a future of radically transformed social relations that is within reach. For instance, in his discussion of *Robot Taekwon V*, Joon Yang Kim notes that the "eponymous heroic mechanical giant" has been interpreted as "a national icon of the modernization and industrialization of the country under the military dictatorship in the 1960s and 1970s."[14] More interesting to Kim, though, is the character Mary, a blond-haired, blue-eyed undercover operative (working for the Red Empire) who "believes herself to be a human," only to discover (after an accident that severs her arm from her torso) that she is a machine. Ironically, as a robot initially distinguished from the film's main characters—the Korean taekwondo champion Hun and his girlfriend, Yŏng-hŭi—by her lack of human consciousness, Mary is thrust into sudden self-awareness once the accident occurs, leaving her both humiliated and angry (as well as jealous, another very human emotion, now that she knows that she will never gain Hun's love). "In this triangular affair," Kim notes, "the mechanical 'girl' is not socially equal with the human rival, since as an android she cannot be a member of the film's human family."[15] Nor is she anything more than an exploitable pawn of the mechanical empire, sent on a mission to steal the blueprint of the eponymous weapon that Hun will successfully commandeer against her in the film's climactic scene. As a liminal being, unfit to belong to either group, Mary ultimately must be destroyed, just as the deviant cyborgs in *Natural City* eventually are. But while both films culminate with "human victory over mechanical evil," they leave room for spectators to sympathize with self-sacrificing nonhuman characters, who, more than anything, simply long to be human (and can be, according to a line of dialogue spoken in *Robot Taekwon V*, but only if they have "good hearts").

Notably, Kim contextualizes this 1976 film in relation to sociopolitical developments specific to the Yushin [Yusin] era of the authoritarian regime of President Park Chung-hee [Pak Chŏng-hŭi]. Although Mary's hair and eye color as well as her "miniskirt and thigh-high boots" mark her as a decidedly Western figure of otherness relative to the country's "sartorial codes acceptable for women of the period," she can be seen as "an analogy for the female South Korean worker of the lowest class: invented, violently controlled, and eventually abandoned by the country's 1970s capitalism."[16] At this juncture in his analysis, Kim returns to Chŏn T'ae-il's famous declaration, "We are not machines"—a phrase (shouted by the young garment worker during a moment of martyrdom symbolizing that decade's fight for civil liberties and social justice) that could also be used to condemn systems of repression that threaten the rights of nonhumans. "This raises a new question," Kim concludes, asking, "What would the social and cultural consequences be if the conception of machines was such that they were no longer easily distinguished from humans, and vice versa?"

It is the "vice versa" of that question that appears to have motivated Park Chan-wook to make *I'm a Cyborg, But That's OK* (*Ssaibogŭjiman kwaench'ana*,

2006), a film in which a young factory worker, Yŏng-gun (Yim Su-jŏng), exhibits the outward characteristics of a robot and is institutionalized after cutting open her wrist in an attempt to recharge her battery and feed herself with transistor electricity. Park peppers this tragicomic story with flashbacks that reveal the familial roots of Yŏng-gun's mental instability or psychosis, which appears to have been inherited from her grandmother (who believed herself to be a mouse). But the writer-director also makes Yŏng-gun's ontological status unclear, forcing the audience to question whether her marked otherness is merely a delusional state or a more radical form of alterity requiring an intersubjective leap on the audience's part. Thankfully, the text "teaches" its audience how to do that, through embedded instances of human-machine interfacing that hint at the ethical and philosophical underpinnings of *I'm a Cyborg, But That's OK*.

Korean film scholar Steve Choe reveals this when discussing a pivotal scene near the end of the film, which shows another patient in the psychiatric ward—a kleptomaniac named Il-sun (Jung Ji-hoon [Chŏng Ch-hun], also known as Rain)—resigning himself to the "okay-ness" of Yŏng-gun's "cyborg-being." Having struggled to convince the emaciated woman to eat food for several days, Il-sun finally succeeds by fashioning a "rice megatron" with a keepsake locket that was given to him by his long-absent mother (who, it turns out, is the source of his own mental anguish). Claiming that the object "will convert human sustenance into electrical energy," the young man meets Yŏng-gun on her terms, not those of the asylum's staff members (whom she calls the "white ones"). As Choe argues, "by interacting on *her* level of belief, while not patronizing and eschewing premeditated deception, [Il-sun] gains [Yŏng-gun's] trust so that she can eat a spoonful of rice."[17] The young man also models for the audience what an empathetically oriented, intersubjective bond might look like, reversing the direction of his thieving tendencies and giving something unconditionally to the female protagonist.

In fact, that scene had been anticipated by several instances when Yŏng-gun demonstrated her own capacity for posthuman interconnectedness with machine-like things, including objects that are typically taken for granted by her fellow asylum patients. Those objects include a grandfather clock that makes a hiccupping sound, a buzzing fluorescent light, and a hospital vending machine, itself a kind of "robot" (not unlike an ATM or automated telephone response system).[18] Ostensibly presented as proof of her delusional state, magnified by her tendency to imagine herself as a killer robot capable of taking out the "white ones" with an automated spray of bullets from her fingertips (a clearly comical spoofing of the stereotypes mentioned above), those moments emphasize Yŏng-gun's ability to see the "person" in the machine. The fact that she is, biologically speaking, a human rather than a cyborg makes this machinic interfacing all the more extraordinary and suggests ways that we might allow for nonhuman consciousness and (by extension) nonhuman rights—something that is highlighted when Yŏng-gun asks the lighting fixture above her bed if he is aware of his identity as a lighting fixture. In this way, *I'm a Cyborg, But That's OK* gestures toward precisely the kind of relational ethics that the posthumanist scholar Rosi Braidotti has called for: a transversal bonding that is both "naturecultural" and "humanimal."[19]

For Braidotti and other theorists of what she calls the "posthuman condition," a "zoe-" rather than "bios-" centered justice, in which the lives of all living things (not just those of humans) are valued, would make it possible to do away with binaries like self versus other. Indeed, it would encourage us to see the lie of human exceptionalism, decentering the anthropocentric subject as a locus of being while gaining our balance atop "the shifting grounds on which new, diverse and even contradictory understandings" of becoming are generated. As Braidotti states, "Nowadays we can no longer start uncritically from the centrality of the human—as Man and as Anthropos—to uphold the old dualities."[20] Channeling Donna Haraway, Braidotti remarks that "'we,' the human heirs of Western postmodernity, are increasingly burnt out and fatigued, while 'they'—the technological artifacts that we have brought into being—are smarter and more alive than ever."[21] Acknowledging this does not mean fatalistically recognizing the specter of human obsolescence in the face of robotic superiority. Quite the opposite, as Min-Sun Kim and Eun-Joo Kim argue in their study of humanoid robots as cultural others, the ethical modality upon which posthumanism rests allows us to "glimpse the Infinite within our finite existence." Stated differently, the "self" can be the "fully human personality that it is [only] by assuming the moral responsibility demanded of it."[22]

According to Cary Wolfe, it has become increasingly difficult to ignore the fact that the human, through its imbrication within "technical, medical, informatic, and economic networks," has become decentered from its artificially "hallowed" place of privilege and dominion over nonhumans. As a response to that decentering, posthumanism becomes a way, paradoxically, to locate the human, to gain a bearing on its "embodiment and embeddedness . . . in not just its biological but also its technological world."[23] The latter, in Wolfe's Lyotardian phrasing, relates to "the prosthetic coevolution of the human animal with the technicity of tools and external archival mechanisms (such as language and culture)" that were the preconditions for the "human" to come into discursive existence in the first place (in the Foucauldian sense). But that technological world encompasses not just the archeologically excavated tools of the past but also the present and potential (or future) means through which "we" become part of "them," including cybernetics systems and nanotechnology. Here, "them" is taken to mean the "ultimate Other" that is the robot (designed to provide industrial, professional, or personal services).[24] For the media theorist R. L. Rutsky, such merging of human and nonhuman subjects can be likened to a "mutation," albeit an enabling one—not in the sense that it fortifies "the boundaries of the self" or "armors the body" against external threats. Instead, when human beings "let go of part of what it has meant to be human, to be a human subject, and to allow ourselves to change," we are better able to "acknowledge the otherness that is part of us."[25] Films such as *I'm a Cyborg, But That's OK* and *Doomsday Book* subscribe to this techno-utopian conception of a posthuman unconscious, either by "opening the boundaries of individual and collective identity" or by "changing the relations that have distinguished between subject and object, self and other, us and them."[26]

In the coming years, robots will fulfill a variety of basic yet increasingly complex functions in such fields as health care, transportation, and the military, and as ubiquitous labor-saving devices integrated into people's everyday domestic lives. As such, they will continue to be thought of as objects rather than as subjects, functionally subservient extensions of humans that satisfy the latter's wants and needs rather than individual selves pursuing their own desires. However, robots' foreseeable claims to personhood, which are highlighted in several Korean-language TV programs and feature-length films, might necessitate a broader definition of "functionality," given these cultural productions' emphasis on the inner lives of characters who, in some cases, do not look so different from humans on the outside. South Korea's remarkable if limited commitment to expanding the vocabulary of rights-based advocacy, discernible in ostensibly trivial yet significant forms of commercial entertainment (including K-dramas and web series that emphasize familial bonding, physical beauty, sexual attraction, commodity fetishism, and other familiar genre elements), augurs a new era in nonhuman representations. At once formulaic and unconventional, programs like MBC's tellingly titled *I'm Not a Robot,* though conservative in some respects, are contributing to the mainstreaming of a potentially radical idea and making it safe for legislators, philosophers, and social activists to make a more defensible case for AI rights. To quote Rosi Braidotti, "No, I'm not a robot, but that begs the question of what kind of human I am, or we are becoming, in this posthuman predicament."[27]

Acknowledgments

We wish to acknowledge the contributions of friends, colleagues, and inspirational figures in the field of Korean cinema studies, without whose support we would not have been able to complete this project, including: Jinsoo An, Ji-yoon An, Colette Balmain, Robert L. Cagle, Ji-Yeon O. Cho, Jun-hyoung Cho, Michelle Cho, Steve Choe, Youngmin Choe, Ellie Choi, Hyaeweol Choi, Jinhee Choi, JungBong Choi, Chung Chong-hwa, Steven Chung, Adam Hartzell, Joseph Jonghyun Jeon, Kelly Y. Jeong, Dal Yong Jin, Dong Hoon Kim, Kyu Hyun Kim, Christina Klein, Hyangjin Lee, Irene Lee, Nam Lee, Nikki J. Y. Lee, Sangjoon Lee, Roald Maliangkay, Daniel Martin, Kathleen McHugh, Darcy Paquet, Liora Sarfati, Chi-Yun Shin, Julian Stringer, and Travis Workman. We would particularly like to acknowledge our dear friend Andrew Jackson, the founder of the annual Korean Screen Culture Conference, where several of this book's chapters debuted as conference papers. Barbara Wall and Andrew Logie deserve special thanks, as they organized KSCC conferences in Hamburg (2017) and Helsinki (2018), where we gave keynote speeches that laid the foundation for chapters 10 and 11. We likewise owe a debt of gratitude to Hyun Seon Park, who organized the Century of Global Korean Cinema conference in Seoul, where an early draft of chapter 1 was presented in October 2019, exactly one hundred years after Korean cinema was born. We are also grateful to Kim Min-a, a section manager in charge of film production for the National Human Rights Commission of Korea, and Lego Hyun Park, director of the Seoul Human Rights Film Festival. Their contrasting perspectives and insights on human rights films, cited in chapter 1, were instrumental to our own conception of this institutional genre. Much appreciation also goes to Yi Sŭng-jun, the director of *Planet of Snail* (*Talp'aengiŭi pyŏl*, 2011), who not only met with us to share information about the production background of his film but generously gave us permission to use a film still on our book's cover.

A shorter version of chapter 2 ("*If You Were Me*: Transnational Crossings and South Korean Omnibus Films") was published in *Transnational Cinemas* 3, no. 1 (2012): 107–128. Chapter 5, "*Always*, *Blind*, and *Silenced*: Disability Discourses in Contemporary South Korean Cinema," previously appeared in a different form in the *Journal of Literary and Cultural Disability Studies* 11, no. 3 (2017): 249–269. We thank Elena Di Giovanni and Gian Maria Greco for their editorial assistance in preparing the earlier version of chapter 5. A considerably shorter version of chapter 8 ("Story as Freedom or Prison? Narrative Invention and Human Rights Interventions in *Camp 14: Total Control Zone*") was published in *The Palgrave Handbook of Incarceration in Popular Culture* (edited by Marcus Harmes, Meredith Harmes, and Barbara Harmes [London: Palgrave; 2020]) under the chapter title "Human Rights Documentary or Plot-Driven Prison Drama? Animation and Nonfiction 'Storytelling' in *Camp 14: Total Control Zone*." We owe a debt of gratitude to the editors of that volume for their efforts in helping us hone that piece.

Notes

Introduction

1 See Maeng Su-jin, "Movements on Screen," in *Movements on Screen: Understanding Korean Society through Independent Films*, ed. Korean Film Archive (Seoul: Korean Film Archive, 2018), 147–159. See also Jeong Seung-hoon, "The Seoul Film Collective: Leftist Strife, Open Cinema, and the Last Chapter of Korean Film Theory," *Quarterly Review of Film and Video* 34, no. 4 (2017): 348–360.

2 Ryu Chae-hyŏng, "Naesyŏnŏl sinemarosŏŭi *Pyŏnhoin, T'aeksi unjŏnsa*, and *1987* (*The Attorney* [2013], *A Taxi Driver* [2017], *1987: When the Day Comes* [2017] as National Cinemas)," *Manhwa Aenimeisyŏn yŏngu* (Cartoon and Animation Studies) 53 (December 2018): 277.

3 For more information on human rights as a sweeping "grand narrative," see Makau Mutua, *Human Rights: A Political and Cultural Critique* (Philadelphia: University of Pennsylvania Press, 2002).

4 Paul Y. Chang and Gi-Wook Shin, "Democratization and the Evolution of Social Movements in Korea: Institutionalization and Diffusion," in *South Korean Social Movements: From Democracy to Civil Society*, ed. Gi-Wook Shin and Paul Y. Chang (New York: Routledge, 2011), 3–18.

5 Gilles Deleuze and Félix Guattari, "What Is a Minor Literature?," *Mississippi Review* 11, no. 3 (Winter–Spring 1983): 13–33.

6 Julia Lesage, "Torture Documentaries," *Jump Cut: A Review of Contemporary Media* 51 (Spring 2009), https://www.ejumpcut.org/archive/jc51.2009/TortureDocumentaries/3.html.

7 Blaine Harden, *Escape from Camp 14: One Man's Remarkable Odyssey from North Korea to Freedom in the West*, 2nd ed. (New York: Penguin, 2015).

8 Gilles Deleuze, *Cinema 2: The Time-Image* (Minneapolis: University of Minnesota Press, 1989), 133.

9 Cary Wolfe, *Animal Rites: American Culture, the Discourse of Species, and Posthumanist Theory* (Chicago: University of Chicago Press, 2003), 1.

10 Akira Mizuta Lippit, *Electric Animal: Toward a Rhetoric of Wildlife* (Minneapolis: University of Minnesota Press, 2000), 165.

11 Michalinos Zembylas and Vivienne Bozalek, "A Critical Engagement with the Social and Political Consequences of Human Rights: The Contribution of the Affective Turn and Posthumanism," *Acta Academica* 46, no. 4 (2014): 34–35.

12 Zembylas and Bozalek, 32.

Chapter 1 The Rise of Rights-Advocacy Cinema in Postauthoritarian South Korea

1 Quoted in Cho Hyo-je, "Inkwŏn iranŭn malŭl yurae (The origins of the word 'human rights')," *Hankyoreh*, May 28, 2013, http://www.hani.co.kr/arti/opinion/column/589389.html.

2 Paul Chang, *Protest Dialectics: State Repression and South Korea's Democracy Movement, 1970–1979* (Stanford, CA: Stanford University Press, 2015), 160.

3 Chang, 160. The term "human rights" was explicitly adopted by activists such as Bishop Chi Haksun, who proclaimed the "Declaration of Conscience" in July 1974 and indicted the Park Chung-hee regime for crushing "people's basic human rights and basic human dignity by the will of a single person in power" (quoted in Chang, *Protest Dialectics*, 161).

4 Lee Jeong-gi and Chon Bum-soo, "A Study on the Effects of Human Rights Film Watching on Changes to the Perception of Human Rights," *Korean Political Communication Research* 27 (Winter 2012): 153; Ryoo Hoon, "The Trend of Korean Films on Human Rights," *Journal of Multiculture and Peace* 32, no.2 (December 2009): 179–180.

5 Nam Lee, "*The Night before the Strike* (1990): The Legendary Minjung Realist Film," in *Rediscovering Korean Cinema*, ed. Sangjoon Lee (Ann Arbor: University of Michigan Press, 2019), 256, 258n8.

6 Young-a Park, *Unexpected Alliances: Independent Filmmakers, the State, and the Film Industry in Postauthoritarian South Korea* (Stanford, CA: Stanford University Press, 2015), 13.

7 "The Nobel Peace Prize for 2000," Nobel Prize, October 13, 2000, https://www.nobelprize.org/prizes/peace/2000/press-release.

8 Park, *Unexpected Alliances*, 13.

9 Jeong-Woo Koo, Suk-Ki Kong, and Chisung Chung, "Measuring Human Rights: A Reflection on Korean Experiences," *Human Rights Quarterly* 34, no.4 (November 2012): 1014.

10 Michael Goodhart, "How Do Human Rights Matter?," in *Why Human Rights Still Matter in Contemporary Global Affairs*, ed. Mahmood Monshipouri (New York: Routledge, 2020), 28.

11 Chang, *Protest Dialectics*, 161. Literally translated as "revitalization reform," Yushin (or Yusin) refers to a full-fledged authoritarian constitutional amendment of 1972 that removed all limits on presidential terms and strengthened the executive branch's power to control other branches of the government.

12 Chang, *Protest Dialectics*, 164.

13 Michalinos Zembylas and Vivienne Bozalek, "A Critical Engagement with the Social and Political Consequences of Human Rights: The Contribution of the Affective Turn and Posthumanism," *Acta Academica* 46, no. 4 (2014): 30.

14 Michalinos Zembylas, "Emotions, Critical Pedagogy, and Human Rights Education," in *Human Rights Education: Theory, Research, Praxis*, ed. Monisha Bajaj (Philadelphia: University of Pennsylvania Press, 2017), 49–50.

15 Zembylas, "Emotions, Critical Pedagogy, and Human Rights Education," 50, 52.

16 Chang, *Protest Dialectics*, 161–165.
17 Paul Y. Chang and Gi-Wook Shin, "Democratization and the Evolution of Social Movements in Korea: Institutionalization and Diffusion," in *South Korean Social Movements: From Democracy to Civil Society*, ed. Gi-Wook Shin and Paul Y. Chang (New York: Routledge, 2011), 6.
18 Chang and Shin, 6.
19 Chang and Shin, 6.
20 Lee and Chon, "A Study on the Effects of Human Rights Film Watching on Changes to the Perception of Human Rights," 153; Ryoo, "The Trend of Korean Films on Human Rights," 181–182.
21 Office of the United Nations High Commissioner for Human Rights, "World Conference on Human Rights, Vienna, 1993," https://www.ohchr.org/EN/AboutUs/Pages/ViennaWC.aspx.
22 "Vienna Declaration and Programme of Action," June 25, 1993, https://www.ohchr.org/Documents/Events/OHCHR20/VDPA_booklet_English.pdf.
23 National Human Rights Commission of Korea, "Purpose," https://www.humanrights.go.kr/site/homepage/menu/viewMenu?menuid=002001001001.
24 Republic of Korea National Human Rights Commission, "National Human Rights Commission Act," May 24, 2001, 1, https://www.refworld.org/pdfid/3ddd1a634.pdf.
25 Republic of Korea National Human Rights Commission, "National Human Rights Commission Act," 2.
26 Paek Un-jo, "Taehanmin'guk Kukka ingwŏn wiwŏnhoeŭi ippŏpkwajŏngae kwanhan yŏngu (The study on the legislative process of the Law of National Human Rights Commission of the Republic of Korea)," PhD diss., Inha University, 2002, 7.
27 Authors' interview with Kim Min-a, NHRCK, Seoul, December 22, 2015.
28 National Human Rights Commission of Korea, *Dignity and Justice for All of Us* (English-language guidebook) (Seoul: NHRCK, 2010), 18.
29 Interview with Kim.
30 Cho Hyŏn-sŏk, "Yŏnghwa 'Kŭ namjaŭi sajŏng' sangyŏng ch'ungdol (Confrontation with the screening of 'The Man with an Affair')," *Seoul Sinmun*, November 14, 2003, http://www.seoul.co.kr/news/newsView.php?id=20031114010005.
31 Interview with Kim.
32 This law remained in existence, but starting in 2001, the government allowed the SHRFF to submit its films for rating classification after completing its screenings. In 2008, the law was changed, and this exemption was eliminated.
33 Authors' interview with Lego Hyun Park, SHRFF, Seoul, July 11, 2019.
34 Interview with Park.
35 Jürgen Habermas, "The Public Sphere," in *Media Studies: A Reader*, ed. Sue Thornham, Carole Bassett, and Paul Marris (New York: New York University Press, 2010), 45.
36 Rick Altman, "A Semantic/Syntactic Approach to Film Genre," *Cinema Journal* 23, no.3 (Spring 1984): 7.
37 Linda Williams, "Film Bodies: Gender, Genre, and Excess," *Film Quarterly* 44, no. 4 (Summer 1991): 2–13.
38 John Protevi, *Political Affect: Connecting the Social and the Somatic* (Minneapolis: University of Minnesota Press, 2009).
39 The entire speech of President Moon after the screening can be viewed on YouTube (albeit currently without a translation). See MediaVOP, "Mun Jae-in taet'ongnyŏngŭi

'1987' kamsang hugi (President Moon Jae-in's reflection on 1987)," https://www.youtube.com/watch?v=MuR-MMZpS30.

40 Protevi, *Political Affect*, 45.

41 Protevi, 45.

Chapter 2 *If You Were Me*

Epigraph: Sophia A. McClennen, and Joseph R. Slaughter, "Introducing Human Rights and Literary Forms; or, the Vehicles and Vocabularies of Human Rights," *Comparative Literature Studies* 46, no. 1 (2009): 7.

1 Sophia A. McClennen, and Joseph R. Slaughter, "Introducing Human Rights and Literary Forms; or, the Vehicles and Vocabularies of Human Rights," *Comparative Literature Studies* 46, no. 1 (2009): 9.

2 McClennen and Slaughter, 11, 12.

3 McClennen and Slaughter, 6.

4 Bryan S. Turner, *Vulnerability and Human Rights* (University Park: Pennsylvania State University Press, 2006), 32.

5 Brian Orend, *Human Rights: Concepts and Context* (Peterborough, ON: Broadview, 2002), 16.

6 Luc Boltanski, *Distant Suffering: Morality, Media and Politics* (Cambridge: Cambridge University Press, 1999), 6.

7 McClennen and Slaughter, "Introducing Human Rights and Literary Forms," 2.

8 Jiwei Ci, "Taking the Reasons for Human Rights Seriously," *Political Theory* 33, no. 2 (April 2005): 243.

9 Cindy Hing-Yuk Wong, *Film Festivals: Culture, People, and Power on the Global Screen* (New Brunswick, NJ: Rutgers University Press, 2011), 178.

10 Nancy Fraser, "Rethinking the Public Sphere," in *Habermas and the Public Sphere*, ed. Craig Calhoun (Cambridge, MA: MIT Press, 1992), 123.

11 Wong, *Film Festivals*, 173.

12 Elena Di Giovanni, "From Darkness to Light in Subtitling," in *Between Text and Image*, ed. Delia Chiaro, Christine Heiss, and Chiara Bucaria (Forlì, Italy: University of Bologna, 2008), 202.

13 Quoted in Jeremy Lehrer, "Bringing Abuses to Light," *Human Rights* 24, no. 3 (Summer 1997): 15.

14 Wong, *Film Festivals*, 175.

15 Drake Zimmerman and Ruth Cobb, eds., *Enduring the Darkness: A Story of Conscience, Hope, and Triumph: Letters from Kim Song-man, an Amnesty International Prisoner of Conscience in South Korea* (Normal, IL: Amnesty International Adoption Group #202, 2000); Namhee Lee, *The Making of Minjung: Democracy and the Politics of Representation in South Korea* (Ithaca, NY: Cornell University, 2007), 101.

16 Donald Kirk, *Korea Betrayed: Kim Dae Jung and Sunshine* (New York: Palgrave Macmillan, 2009).

17 David R. Black and Shona Bezanson, "The Olympic Games, Human Rights and Democratisation: Lessons from Seoul and Implications for Beijing," *Third World Quarterly* 25, no. 7 (2004): 1253

18 Republic of Korea National Human Rights Commission, "Article 1, National Human Rights Commission Act," May 24, 2001, 1, https://www.refworld.org/pdfid/3ddd1a634.pdf.

19 Republic of Korea National Human Rights Commission, "National Human Rights Commission Act," February 25, 2019, https://www.humanrights.go.kr/site/homepage/menu/viewMenu?menuid=002001001002.

20 Park Chan-wook's two trips to Nepal were not covered by the NHRCK and thus had to be paid for out of his own pocket.

21 Kim To-hun, "Ingwŏn yŏnghwa p'ŭrojekt'ŭ kihoek Nam Kyu-sŏn (Human right film project planner Nam Kyu-sŏn)," *Cine21*, July 21, 2004, http://www.cine21.com/news/view/?mag_id=25286.

22 Mette Hjort, "On the Plurality of Cinematic Transnationalism," in *World Cinemas, Transnational Perspectives*, ed. Natasa Durovicova and Kathleen Newman (New York: Routledge, 2010), 22–24.

23 Bérénice Reynaud, "Cutting Edge and Missed Encounters—Digital Short Films by Three Filmmakers," *Senses of Cinema*, May 2002, http://www.sensesofcinema.com/2002/20/tsai_digital.

24 Hjort, "On the Plurality of Cinematic Transnationalism," 24.

25 Kim Ŭn-hyŏng, "*Yŏsŏt kaeŭi sisŏn:* Kŭnyŏ ŭi mugae mandŭn Im Sun-rye kamdok (Director who made 'her weight' in *If You Were Me*)," *Cine 21*, November 10, 2003, http://m.cine21.com/news/view/?mag_id=21786.

26 Kevin Gray, "From Human to Workers' Rights: The Emergence of a Migrant Workers' Union Movement in Korea," *Global Society* 21, no. 2 (April 2007): 299.

27 Gray, 300.

28 Paul Close and David Askew, *Asia Pacific and Human Rights: A Global Political Economy Perspective* (Farnham, UK: Ashgate, 2004), 22.

29 Close and David Askew, 22.

30 Yi Yŏng-jin, "Yŏsŏt kamdokŭi ingwŏn yŏnghwa p'ŭrojekt'ŭ (Six directors' human rights film project)," *Cine 21*, November 22, 2002, http://www.cine21.com/news/view/?mag_id=15292.

31 Quoted in "Kŏmsadŭl naedal ilkwajung ingwŏn yŏnghwa kamsang (Public prosecutors will watch a human rights film during work hours next month)," *Cine 21*, November 27, 2003, http://m.cine21.com/news/view/?mag_id=22065.

32 Anon., "Hŭimangŭi inmunhak: T'albuk kwa iju (Humanities of hope: Defection and migration)," Daegu Human Rights Office of the National Human Rights Commission of Korea Blog, June 26, 2013, https://m.blog.naver.com/PostView.nhn?blogId=humandg&logNo=101711005 89&proxyReferer=https:%2F%2Fwww.google.com%2F.

33 Ko Pu-ŭng, "Uri anŭi tiasp'ora (Diaspora within us)," *Munhakmadang* (Literature yard), 19 (Summer 2007): 41–42.

34 Yun Il-su, "Ingwŏn chonjungsim hyangsangŭl wihan yŏnghwa ch'iryo (Cinema therapy to improve the respect for human rights)," *Hang'uk ŏnŏmunhak* (Korean language literature) 73 (June 2010): 277, 281, and 283.

35 The Korean title "Taeruk hoengdan" is more accurately translated as "Continental Crossing."

Chapter 3 Hell Is Other High Schoolers

1 Sung-ae Lee, "'How Can I Be the Protagonist of My Own Life?' Intimations of Hope for Teen Subjectivities in Korean Fiction and Film," in *Subjectivity in Asian Children's Literature and Film*, ed. John Stephens (New York: Routledge, 2013), 101.

2 Won Kim, "The Race to Appropriate 'Koreanness': National Restoration, Internal Development, and Traces of Popular Culture," in *Cultures of Yusin: South Korea in the 1970s*, ed. Youngju Ryu (Ann Arbor: University of Michigan Press, 2018), 40–43.

3 Kye Un-gyŏng, "Haksaeng ingwŏnmunjae wa sangjing p'oknyŏk (Students' rights and symbolic violence in their comments on *Once upon a Time in High School*)," *Munhak kwa yŏngsang* (Journal of literature and film) 12, no. 2 (Summer 2011): 337–338.

4 Jinhee Choi, *The South Korean Film Renaissance: Local Hitmakers, Global Provocateurs* (Middletown, CT: Wesleyan University Press, 2010), 120.

5 Jang Wan Ko, Sheena Choi, and Hyowon Park, "Republic of Korea," in *Handbook of Comparative Education Law: Selected Asian Nations*, ed. Charles Russo (Lanham, MD: Rowman and Littlefield, 2018), 95.

6 Trent Bax, *Bullying and Violence in South Korea: From Home to School and Beyond* (New York: Palgrave Macmillan, 2017), 85.

7 Danielle L. Chubb, *Contentious Activism and Inter-Korean Relations* (New York: Columbia University Press, 2014), 19.

8 "Act on the Prevention of and Countermeasures against Violence in Schools," Law Viewer, accessed December 23, 2020, http://elaw.klri.re.kr/eng_mobile/viewer.do?hseq=24031&type=new&key=.

9 Ko, Choi, and Park, "Republic of Korea," 96.

10 Quoted in "Act on the Prevention of and Countermeasures against Violence in Schools."

11 Special Reporting Team, "Schools' Committees for Countermeasures against Violence Criticized," *Korea JoongAng Daily*, August 7, 2019, http://koreajoongangdaily.joins.com/news/article/article.aspx?aid=3066474.

12 That thoroughfare, which was the site of a horse transportation depot during the Chosŏn Dynasty, became the home to Sangmun and Ŭngwang Girls' High Schools (real-life models for the Chungmun and Ŭnmyŏng High Schools in the film) after the development of Gangnam's coveted Eighth School District in the 1970s.

13 Lee, "'How Can I Be the Protagonist of My Own Life?,'" 97.

14 Lee, 97.

15 Lee, 97.

16 Choi, *The South Korean Film Renaissance*, 121.

17 Choi, 121.

18 Choi, 121.

19 Lee, "'How Can I Be the Protagonist of My Own Life?,'" 99.

20 Kye, "Haksaeng ingwŏnmunjae wa sangjing p'oknyŏk," 341–348 and 352–357.

21 Park Sung-woo, "Damages Ordered Paid in Milyang Assault Case," *Korea JoongAng Daily*, August 17, 2007, http://koreajoongangdaily.joins.com/news/article/article.aspx?aid=2879431.

22 Nicola Smith and Junho Lee, "South Korean Parents Hire Thugs to Stop School Bullies," *Telegraph*, January 22, 2019, https://www.telegraph.co.uk/news/2019/01/22/south-korean-parents-hire-thugs-stop-school-bullies.

23 Peter Y. Paik, "Stories of Cruel Youth: The South Korean Anti-Teenager Movie," in *Transgression in Korea: Beyond Resistance and Control*, ed. Juhn Y. Ahn (Ann Arbor: University of Michigan Press, 2018), 200.

24 Paik, 200.

25 Paik, 200 (emphasis added).

26 Oh Kyu-wook, "Korea Struggles to Save Students from Bullying," *Korea Herald*, March 20, 2013, http://www.koreaherald.com/view.php?ud=20130320000605. See also Smith and Lee, "South Korean Parents Hire Thugs."

27 Not surprisingly, those latter terms have been used by various nonprofits, nongovernmental organizations, and school organizations around the world to combat the spread of violence, as seen, for instance, in the online campaign "Don't Be a Monster" and the slogan of one West Virginia elementary school's antibullying club, "Be a Hero, Not a Villain."

28 Keumjoo Kwak and Seung-ha Lee, "The Korean Research Tradition on Wang-ta," in *School Bullying in Different Cultures: Eastern and Western Perspectives*, ed. Peter K. Smith, Keumjoo Kwak, and Yuichi Toda (Cambridge: Cambridge University Press, 2016), 94.

29 Jun-mo Kwon, "Conceptualization of Wangtta in Korea and Methodological Review of Wangtta Researchers," *Korean Journal of Psychology* 5, no. 2 (1999): 59–72.

30 Hee Jeong Yoo, "The Implications of Social Rejection and Peer Victimization: Beyond Social Phenomenon," *Journal of Korean Medical Science* 29, no. 9 (September 2014): 1186–1187, https://www.ncbi.nlm.nih.gov/pmc/articles/PMC4168169/.

31 Anthony A. Peguero and Lindsay Kahle, "Gender, Weight, and Inequality Associated with School Bullying," in *The Causes and Consequences of Group Violence: From Bullies to Terrorists*, ed. James Hawdon, John Ryan, and Marc Lucht (Lanham, MD: Lexington Books, 2014), 155.

32 Bax, *Bullying and Violence in South Korea*, 33.

33 David P. Farrington, "Understanding and Preventing Bullying," *Crime and Justice* 17 (1993): 383.

34 Kye Un-gyŏng, "*P'asukkun* kwa *Maljukgŏri chanhoksa* ŭi hakkyo konggangkwa sangjing p'oknyŏk ŭi chaesaengsan (Space of school and reproduction of symbolic violence in *Bleak Night* and *Once upon a Time in High School*)," *Munhakkwa yŏngsang* (Journal of literature and film) 13, no. 2 (Summer 2012): 194–195.

35 Kye, 194–195.

36 THR Staff, "*Bleak Night*: Film Review," *Hollywood Reporter*, February 15, 2011, https://www.hollywoodreporter.com/review/bleak-night-film-review-99747.

37 Anon., "Bleak Night," *Gay Asia Films*, May 26, 2014, https://gayasiafilms.wordpress.com/2014/05/26/bleak-night-2/.

38 Justin McCurry, "South Korea Must End Gay Solider 'Witch-Hunt,' Campaigners Say," *Guardian*, May 4, 2017, https://www.theguardian.com/world/2017/may/04/south-korea-must-end-gay-soldier-witch-hunt-campaigners-say; Elise Hu, "For South Korea's LGBT Community, an Uphill Battle for Rights," *NPR*, July 25, 2017, https://www.npr.org/sections/parallels/2017/07/25/538464851/for-south-koreas-lgbt-community-an-uphill-battle-for-rights.

39 National Human Rights Commission of Korea, *Sŏngjŏkchihyang sŏngbyŏlchŏngch'esŏnge ttarŭn ch'abyŏl shilt'aejosa* (The status of discrimination based on sexual orientation and gender identity) (Seoul: NHRCK, 2014), https://www.humanrights.go.kr/site/program/board/basicboard/view?currentpage=4&menuid=001003001004&pagesize=10&boardtypeid=16&boardid=611289. Forms of peer harassment were physical violence (experienced by 4.5 percent of the respondents), verbal abuse (47.5 percent), property damage or theft (8.0 percent), slandering (28.0 percent), forced outing (24.5 percent), threats of outing (13.0 percent), daily confrontation (16.0 percent), homophobic remarks (21.0 percent), sexual abuse or violence (10.0 percent), isolation or bullying (14.5 percent), internet slandering or bullying (17.0 percent), and other harassment (6.0 percent).

40 Si-u Chŏng, "Intŏbyu Yi-Song Hŭi-il (Interview with Lee-Song Hee-il)," *Ten Asia*, September 26, 2014, http://tenasia.hankyung.com/archives/328889.

41 Kabejja, "Sticks and Stones: School Violence in K-Dramas and Reality," *SeoulBeats*, September 13, 2017, https://seoulbeats.com/2017/09/sticks-and-stones-school-violence-in-k-dramas-and-reality.

42 The abuse that Kwŏn Sŭng-min experienced was reported widely following his suicide. It included being subjected to water torture, having his arm nearly set on fire, being forced to eat food off the floor, and being dragged around by an electrical cable (Kabejja, "Sticks and Stones"). See also Paula Hancocks, "South Korea Teenagers Bullied to Death," *CNN.com*, July 26, 2012, https://www.cnn.com/2012/07/25/world/asia/south-korea-school-bully/index.html.

43 The director Kang Hyo-jin's comedic fantasy *The Dude in Me* (*Naeanŭi kŭnom*, 2019) further illustrates the complementarity of the gangster and teenpic genres through a body-swap scenario in which a career criminal switches places with a bullied high schooler, using his wiles to turn the tables on the boy's abusers. Although its premise is ridiculous, this crowd-pleasing film gestures toward the painful experiences of individuals who are forced to do the bidding of others—which sometimes lead them to take their own lives (notably, it is the teenager's near-fatal, coma-inducing fall from a tall building's rooftop, mistakenly reported as a suicide attempt, that leads to the body swap after he lands on the gangster below).

44 Yi Hyŏn-su, "Pak Ki-hyŏng kamdok *P'ongnyŏk ssŏk'ŭl* ŭn siljae sagŏn i pat'ang (Park Ki-hyŏg's *Gangster High* is based on a real-life event)," *Star News*, October 17, 2006, http://star.mt.co.kr/stview.php?no=2006101720072366251.

45 For an elaboration on the educational reforms that have taken place in South Korea over the past several years, see Michael J. Seth, *Education Fever: Society, Politics, and the Pursuit of Schooling in South Korea* (Honolulu: University of Hawai'i Press, 2002).

46 For more information about the changing perceptions of juvenile delinquency in South Korea from the 1970s to the 2000s, see Hun-Soo Kim and Hyŏn-sil Kim, *Juvenile Delinquency and Youth Crime* (New York: Nova Science, 2008), 4–8.

Chapter 4 Indie Filmmaking and Queer Advocacy

1 There are contradictory reports on *D-War*'s production and marketing costs, and two different numbers—700 billion won and 300 billion won—have been cited in South Korean press reports and U.S. trade magazines. It is conjectured that the higher number includes the research and development expenses (including for special effects, computer-generated imagery, miniatures, and makeup) of Sim's production company, Younggu-Art, over the course of the six-year production process.

2 Leesong Hee-il, "Yisong Hŭi-il kamdokŭi Tiwŏe kwanhan kŭl chŏnmun (The entire text of Leesong Hee-il's blog about *D-War*)," *Max Movie*, August 4, 2007, https://news.maxmovie.com/13617.

3 Marco Grosoli, *Eric Rohmer's Film Theory (1948–1953): From "Ecole Scherer" to "Politique des Auteurs"* (Amsterdam: Amsterdam University Press, 2017), 15.

4 François Truffaut, "A Certain Tendency of the French Cinema," in *Movies and Methods*, ed. Bill Nichols (Berkeley: University of California Press, 1976), 224–237.

5 Phil Ho Kim and C. Collin Singer, "Three Periods of Korean Queer Cinema: Invisible, Camouflage, and Blockbuster," *Acta Koreana* 14, no. 1 (June 2011): 124.

6 Kang Sŏk-yun, "Nanŭn chŏnsaga anida (I am not a warrior)," *Tonip yŏnghwa* (Independent film magazine), August 2000, 55.

7 "Tonip yŏnghwanŭn muŏtinga? (What is independent film?)," Association for Korean Independent Film and Video, http://www.kifv.org/intro_kifv/overview_02.html.

8 Leesong Hee-il, "*Sosuja yŏngwha rŭl wihayŏ* (For minority cinema)," *Tonip yŏnghwa* (Independent film magazine), August 2000, 66.

9 Leesong, 68.

10 Leesong, 69.

11 Leesong, 70.

12 Leesong, 73.

13 Cristina Johnston, *French Minority Cinema* (New York: Rodopi, 2010), 16–17.

14 Nicole Anderson, "Deconstruction and Ethics": An (Ir)Responsibility," in *Jacques Derrida: Key Concepts*, ed. Claire Colebrook (London: Routledge, 2015), 51. See also Jacques Derrida, *Of Grammatology*, trans. Gayatri Chakravorty Spivak (Baltimore: Johns Hopkins University Press, 1976), and *Writing and Difference*, trans. Alan Bass (Chicago: University of Chicago Press, 1978).

15 Homi K. Bhabha, "DissemiNation: Time, Narrative, and the Margins of the Modern Nation," in *Nation and Narration*, ed. Homi K. Bhabha (London: Routledge, 1990), 307.

16 Yingjin Zhang, "From 'Minority Film' to 'Minority Discourse': Questions of Nationhood and Ethnicity in Chinese Cinema," *Cinema Journal* 36, no. 3 (Spring 1997): 83.

17 Gilles Deleuze and Félix Guattari, "What Is a Minor Literature?," *Mississippi Review* 11, no. 3 (Winter–Spring 1983): 16.

18 Deleuze and Guattari, 18.

19 Pak So-yŏng, "1970-nyŏndae hosŭt'isŭ yŏnghwahwa yŏngu (A study of the filmization of hostesses' memoirs in the 1970s)," *Hanminjok Ŏmunhwa* (Korean language studies) 81 (September 2018): 251.

20 Quoted in Yi Chin-haeng, Yi Chŏng-su, and Han Sŭng-sang, "Yisong Hŭ-il ŭl manada (We met Leesong Hee-il)," *Tonip yŏnghwa* (Independent film magazine), May 2007, 71.

21 Deleuze and Guattari, "What Is a Minor Literature?," 16.

22 Thomas Schatz, *Hollywood Genres: Formulas, Filmmaking, and the Studio System* (New York: McGraw-Hill, 1981), 225.

23 O Chŏng-hyŏn, "*Huhoe haji ana* kamdok Yisong Hŭi-il int'ŏbyu (Interview with Leesong Hee-il, director of *No Regret*)," *Cine 21*, November 14, 2006, http://www.cine21.com/news/view/?mag_id=42651.

24 Deleuze and Guattari, "What Is a Minor Literature?," 17.

25 Alexander Doty, *Making Things Perfectly Queer: Interpreting Mass Culture* (Minneapolis: University of Minnesota Press, 1993), xvi.

26 Unsang Kim, "Queer Korean Cinema, National Others, and Making of Queer Space in *Stateless Things* (2011)," *Journal of Japanese and Korean Cinema* 9, no. 1 (2017): 62.

27 Ryu Chi-wŏn, "Tongsŏngaeja taebyŏn (Representing homosexuals)," *Newsweek*, Korean edition, December 26, 2016–January 3, 2017, 66.

28 Deleuze and Guattari, "What Is a Minor Literature?," 17.

29 Kyungtae Kim, "Intimate Freedom: Queering Anarchism in Leesong Hee-il's Films," *Korea Journal* 58, no. 2 (Summer 2018): 62.

30 K. Kim, 62.

31 K. Kim, 61.

32 Leesong Hee-il, "Yŏnghwa, 'chŏngch'i ŭi pokwŏn (Film, the return of politics)," *Munhakkwa sahoe* (Literature and society) 110 (Summer 2015): 266–270 and 277–280.

33 Leesong, 284.
34 Leesong Hee-il, "Obŏ tŏ reinbou sagikkun (Over the rainbow, trickster)," *Tonip yŏnghwa* (Independent film magazine), Winter 2001, 103.
35 K. Kim, "Intimate Freedom," 62.
36 P. Kim and Singer, "Three Periods of Korean Queer Cinema," 117.
37 P. Kim and Singer, 122.
38 P. Kim and Singer, 127.
39 P. Kim and Singer, 129.
40 Unsang Kim, "The Critical Social Turn of Queer Korean Cinema: Hospitality and the Temporal Economy of Queer Kinship in *The Bacchus Lady* (2016)," *Korea Journal* 58, no.2 (Summer 2018): 91.
41 U. Kim, 91.
42 U. Kim, 90.
43 Authors' interview with Kim Min-a, NHRCK, Seoul, December 22, 2015.
44 Quoted in Park Da-hae and Kwon Ji-dam, "National Assembly Fails to Hold Debate on Comprehensive Anti-Discrimination Legislation," *Hankyoreh*, May 31, 2019, http://english.hani.co.kr/arti/english_edition/e_national/896150.html.
45 Seth Abramovitch, "Joe Biden Cites *Will & Grace* in Endorsement of Same-Sex Marriage," *Hollywood Reporter*, May 16, 2012, https://www.hollywoodreporter.com/live-feed/joe-biden-cites-will-grace-320724-0.
46 Ŏm tong-jin, "Tŭrama *Insaeng ŭn arŭmdawŏ* pogo nae adŭl keidoelkka? (Will my son become gay after watching the drama *Life Is Beautiful*?)," *JoongAng Ilbo* (JoonAng daily), October 4, 2010, https://news.joins.com/article/4495068.
47 Kang Hye-ran, "Tŭrama *Insaeng ŭn arŭmdawŏ* tongsŏngae k'ŏp'ŭl ŏnyaksik sakje (Cutting the same-sex couple's engagement in the drama *Life Is Beautiful*)," *JoongAng Ilbo* (JoonAng daily), October 25, 2010, https://news.joins.com/article/4565191.
48 Hŏ Hwan-ju, "*Insaengŭn arŭmdawŏ* Kim Su-hyŏn chakka Keiingwŏndanch'e mujigae ingwŏnsang susang (Kim Su-hyŏn of *Life Is Beautiful* receives the Rainbow Human Rights Award from a gay human rights organization)," *Pressian*, December 28, 2019, http://www.pressian.com/news/article/?no=102800.
49 Quoted in Kim A-ri, "Kimjo Gwangsu 'Narŭl injŏnghaettamyŏn 20-nyŏn tŏ haengbok'aessŭlt'ende' (Kimjo Gwangsu 'I would have been happier twenty more years had I recognized myself')," *Hankyoreh 21*, November 14, 2019, http://h21.hani.co.kr/arti/culture/culture_general/47849.html.

Chapter 5 *Always*, *Blind*, and *Silenced*

1 Kenneth L. Robey, Linda Beckley, and Matthew Kirschner, "Implicit Infantilizing Attitudes about Disability," *Journal of Developmental and Physical Disabilities* 18, no. 4 (2006): 441.
2 Janet E. Lord, "Persons with Disabilities in International Humanitarian Law—Paternalism, Protectionism or Rights?" in *Disability, Human Rights and the Limits of Humanitarianism*, ed. Cathy Schlund-Vials and Michael Gill (London: Routledge, 2014), 169.
3 Jane Erin, "Individual and Societal Responses to Diversity and Visual Impairment," in *Diversity and Visual Impairment: The Influence of Race, Gender, Religion, and Ethnicity on the Individual*, ed. Madeline Milian and Jane Erin (New York: American Foundation for the Blind Press, 2001), 10.

4 Wan Ho Kim, Yoon Ghil Park, Hyung-Ik Shin, and Sang Hee Im, "The World Report on Disability and Recent Developments in South Korea," *American Journal of Physical Medicine and Rehabilitation* 93, no. 1, supplement (2014): 58.

5 According to one estimate, approximately 650 million people in the world live with disabilities. See Katharina Heyer, *Rights Enabled: The Disability Revolution, from the US, to Germany and Japan, to the United Nations* (Ann Arbor: University of Michigan Press, 2015), 173. According to the World Bank, however, approximately one billion people in the world today "experience some form of disability." See World Bank, "Disability Inclusion," https://www.worldbank.org/en/topic/disability.

6 Chung Wan Woo, "'Seeing Another/Seeing Oneself': Nondisabled Audiences' Perspectives on Disability in Two South Korean Films, *Oasis* (2002) and *Malaton* (2005)," PhD diss., Syracuse University, 2012, 61.

7 United Nations, "The International Year of Disabled Persons 1981," https://www.un.org/development/desa/disabilities/the-international-year-of-disabled-persons-1981.html.

8 Dong Chul You and Se Kwang Hwang, "Achievements of and Challenges Facing the Korean Disabled People's Movement," *Disability and Society* 33, no. 8 (December 2018): 1262.

9 Yi In-yŏng, "Sinsahoe undongŭrosŏ ŭi changaeinundongae kwanhan koch'al (The disabled people's movement as a new social movement)," MA thesis, Chungang University, 2001, 41.

10 You and Hwang, "Achievements of and Challenges Facing the Korean Disabled People's Movement," 1264.

11 You and Hwang, 1265.

12 Heyer, *Rights Enabled*, 172.

13 Kim et al., "The World Report on Disability and Recent Developments in South Korea," 59.

14 Kim et al., 60.

15 Kim et al., 60.

16 National Commission of Human Rights of Korea, *Annual Report 2016*, 63, https://www.humanrights.go.kr/site/program/board/basicboard/view?menuid=002003003001&pagesize=10&boardtypeid=7017&boardid=7602641.

17 You and Hwang, "Achievements of and Challenges Facing the Korean Disabled People's Movement," 1272.

18 Woo, "'Seeing Another/Seeing Oneself,'" 61.

19 Woo, 62.

20 Shin Jeong Kim and Kyung Ah Kang, "Meaning of Life for Adolescents with a Physical Disability in Korea," *Journal of Advanced Nursing* 43, no. 2 (2003): 145.

21 Weol Soon Kim-Rupnow, "Disability and Korean Culture," in *Culture and Disability: Providing Culturally Competent Services*, ed. John H. Stone (Thousand Oaks, CA: SAGE Publications, 2004), 119–120.

22 Hyun-Kyung You and Lori A. McGraw, "The Intersection of Motherhood and Disability: Being a 'Good' Korean Mother to an 'Imperfect Child,'" *Journal of Comparative Family Studies* 42, no. 4 (2011): 581.

23 You and McGraw, 581.

24 David T. Mitchell and Sharon L. Snyder, "Introduction: Disability Studies and the Double Bind of Representation," in *The Body and Physical Difference: Discourses of Disability*, ed. David T. Mitchell and Sharon L. Snyder (Ann Arbor: University of Michigan Press, 1997), 2.

25 Mitchell and Snyder, 2.

26 G. N. Karna, *United Nations and the Rights of Disabled Persons: A Study in Indian Perspective* (New Delhi: APH Publishing, 1999), 52.

27 Mitchell and Snyder, "Introduction," 3. Somewhat controversially, Mitchell and Snyder suggest that discourses of prevention and recovery are what distinguish disability from disease. This is why we have opted not to discuss Korean films like *A Moment to Remember* (*Nae mŏrisokŭi chiugae*, 2004), which shows how a romantic relationship can be tested once one of the partners is diagnosed with Alzheimer's disease.

28 As Michael Bérubé states, the term "disability" is "the most labile and pliable of categories: it names thousands of human conditions and varieties of impairment, from the slight to the severe, from imperceptible physical incapacity to inexplicable developmental delay" (foreword to *Claiming Disability: Knowledge and Identity*, ed. Simi Linton [New York: New York University Press, 1998], xii).

29 Mitchell and Snyder, "Introduction," 17.

30 Mitchell and Snyder, 17.

31 Kirk Honeycutt, "*Always*: Busan Film Review," *Hollywood Reporter*, October 6, 2011, http://www.hollywoodreporter.com/review/film-review-245017.

32 Honeycutt, "*Always*." See also Amber Topping, "*Always* Film Review—*City Lights* Meets *An Affair to Remember* in This Hidden Romantic Gem," *Silver Petticoat Review*, November 18, 2016, https://www.silverpetticoatreview.com/2016/11/18/always-2011-film-review/; and Manfred Selzer, "Always," *Asian Movie Web*, http://www.asianmovieweb.com/en/reviews/always.htm.

33 Lennard J. Davis, *Enforcing Normalcy: Disability, Deafness, and the Body* (New York: Verso, 1995), 3–4.

34 Marja Evelyn Mogk, introduction to *Different Bodies: Essays on Disability in Film and Television*, ed. Marja Evelyn Mogk (Jefferson, NC: McFarland, 2013), 2.

35 Jan Grue, *Disability and Discourse Analysis* (Burlington, VT: Ashgate, 2015), 112 and 119.

36 Evan Ramstad and Soo-ah Shin, "South Korea Toughens Penalties for Abusers of Disabled," *Wall Street Journal*, October 28, 2011, http://www.wsj.com/articles/SB10001424052970203554104577003300408901364.

37 One of the educators received a twelve-year prison sentence in 2012, after the Dogani Law lifted legal restrictions that had blocked prosecution of sexual violence against minors and the disabled by abolishing the statute of limitation and reclassifying the crime (which had been categorized as "subject to complaint" [*ch'ingojoe*]) so that those who commit it could be brought to justice regardless of whether the victim had complained or settled with the perpetrator.

38 Gong Jiyoung, "The Crucible," trans. Bruce Fulton and Ju-Chan Fulton, *Azalea* 4 (2011): 41–69.

39 Gong, 41–69.

40 Launched in Seoul and other cities, this platform was initiated by the Korean Barrier Free Film Committee (founded by the rights activist Yi Ŭn-gyŏng). See Claire Lee, "'Barrier-Free' films Offer Universal Experience," *Korea Herald*, October 31, 2011, http://www.koreaherald.com/view.php?ud=20111031000792.

41 Cho Hŭp and O Sŭng-hyŏn, "Munhwajŏk kongronjang ŭrosŏ *Dogani* (*Silenced* as a culture public sphere: From cognitive to affective communication)," *Munhakkwa yŏngsang* (Journal of literature and film) 12, no. 4 (Winter 2012): 846.

42 Quoted in "Dogani sindŭrom chisangp'a nyusŭdo tarwŏ (The dogani syndrome, network news covers)," *Chosun Ilbo*, September 30, 2011, https://news.chosun.com/site/data/html_dir/2011/09/30/2011093000382.html.

43 Michael Robinson, "Contemporary Cultural Production in South Korea: Vanishing Meta-Narratives of Nation," in *New Korean Cinema*, ed. Chi-Yun Shin and Julian Stringer (New York: New York University Press, 2005), 27.

Chapter 6 Barrier-Free Cinema

1 Eunjung Kim, *Curative Violence: Rehabilitating Disability, Gender, and Sexuality in Modern Korea* (Durham, NC: Duke University Press, 2017), 1–2.
2 Kim, 1.
3 Kim, 1.
4 Kim, 2.
5 Kim, 5.
6 Kim, 3.
7 Kim, 3.
8 Bae Yu-yeon, "*Quit Your Life* and Park No-sik, an Action Star with a Spirit of Defiance," in *Masculinity on Screen: Understanding Korean Society and Masculinity through Films*, ed. Korean Film Archive (Sejong, Korea: Korean Film Archive, 2017), 90–91.
9 Catherine Kudlick, "Social History of Medicine and Disability History," in *The Oxford Handbook of Disability History*, ed. Michael Rembis, Catherine Kudlick, and Kim E. Nielsen (New York: Oxford University Press, 2018), 114.
10 Kudlick, 112.
11 Kim, *Curative Violence*, 6.
12 Kim, 24.
13 Authors' interview with Yi Sŭng-jun, Seoul, December 16, 2015.
14 As the film's coproducer, NHK retained the rights to a shorter TV version, which is fifty-two minutes long (as opposed to the ninety-minute feature version that premiered at the IDFA).
15 Kye Un-gyŏng, "*Talp'aengiŭi pyŏl* ŭi kŭkmihakjŏk changch'i rŭl t'onghan chagibanyŏngjŏk hyokwa (Self-reflexivity through dramatic aesthetics: *Planet of Snail*)," *Munhakkwa yŏngsang* (Journal of literature and film) 15, no. 4 (Winter 2014): 795.
16 Kye, 796.
17 Authors' interview with Yi Sŭng-jun, Seoul, December 16, 2015.
18 Katharina Heyer, *Rights Enabled: The Disability Revolution, from the US, to Germany and Japan, to the United Nations* (Ann Arbor: University of Michigan Press, 2015).
19 Dong Chul You and Se Kwang Hwang, "Achievements of and Challenges Facing the Korean Disabled People's Movement," *Disability and Society* 33, no. 8 (December 2018): 1265.
20 You and Hwang, 1268.
21 After the film's completion, Yŏng-ch'an began graduate studies in counseling, an ambitious endeavor supported by his wife, who often attends his classes as a study assistant (interview with Yi).
22 Janet E. Lord, "Persons with Disabilities in International Humanitarian Law—Paternalism, Protectionism or Rights?" in *Disability, Human Rights and the Limits of Humanitarianism*, ed. Cathy Schlund-Vials and Michael Gill (London: Routledge, 2014), 169.
23 Sarah D. Phillips, *Disability and Mobile Citizenship in Postsocialist Ukraine* (Bloomington: Indiana University Press, 2010), 8.

24 Phillips, 8.

25 Paul Darke, "Understanding Cinematic Representations of Disability," in *Disability Reader: Social Science Perspectives*, ed. Tom Shakespeare (New York: Continuum, 1998), 181. See also Ellen Ryan and Karen A. Bannister, *Ability Speaks: Talking with a Person with Disability* (Madrid: Editorial Aresta, 2009), 21–27.

26 Peter Knegt, "Seung-Jun Yi on His IDFA Award-Winning *Planet of Snail*," *IndieWire*, November 28, 2011, http://www.indiewire.com/article/seung-jun-yi-on-his-idfa-award-winning-planet-of-snail.

27 Mark Feeney, "*Planet of Snail* Offers Sweet but Flat Portrait of Two Lives," Boston.com, September 11, 2012, http://www.boston.com/ae/movies/2012/09/11/planet-snail-offers-sweet-but-flat-portrait-two-lives/uQqaw67HUVcoy62IwWk19L/story.html.

28 Christopher McQuain, "*Planet of Snail*," DVDTalk, February 12, 2013, http://www.dvdtalk.com/reviews/59256/ planet-of-snail/.

29 Authors' interview with Yi.

30 Nahzeem Oluwafemi Mimiko, "From Insularity to *Segyehwa*: The Political Economy of Globalization in Korea," in *Korea and Globalization: Politics, Economics and Culture*, ed. James B. Lewis and Amadu Sesay (London: Routledge, 2002), 68.

31 Dal Yong Jin, *Korea's Online Gaming Empire* (Cambridge, MA: MIT Press, 2010), 27.

32 Kyung Hyun Kim, *Virtual Hallyu: Korean Cinema of the Global Era* (Durham, NC: Duke University Press, 2011), 27.

33 Shin Jeong Kim and Kyung Ah Kang, "Meaning of Life for Adolescents with a Physical Disability in Korea," *Journal of Advanced Nursing* 43, no. 2 (2003): 146.

34 Kim and Kang, 146.

35 Ryan and Bannister, *Ability Speaks*, 23.

36 Sin Chin-a, "*Talp'aengiŭi pyŏl* Yi Sŭng-jun kamdok (*Planet of Snail* director Yi Sŭng-jun)," *No Cut News*, March 14, 2012, http://www.nocutnews.co.kr/news/922369.

37 International Labour Organization, *Equality at Work: Tackling the Challenges: Global Report under the Follow-up to the ILO Declaration on Fundamental Principles and Rights at Work* (Geneva: International Labour Office, 2008), 44.

38 David B. Wright, *Human Physiology and Health* (Portsmouth, NH: Heinemann, 2000), 82.

39 Michael D. Seidman and Marie Moneysmith, *Save Your Hearing Now: The Revolutionary Program That Can Prevent and May Even Reverse Hearing Loss* (New York: Grand Central Publishing, 2009), 17, 32.

40 Slavoj Žižek, *For They Know Not What They Do: Enjoyment as a Political Factor* (New York: Verso, 2002), xvii. Because Žižek makes a connection between snails and tortoises, two creatures that embody a combined sense of toughness and vulnerability, we are drawn to the uncanny parallels between this chapter's main case study and a Chinese film that was theatrically released a few months before *Planet of Snail*: a 2010 Mandarin-language production entitled *Ocean Heaven* (*Hai yang tian tang*), which foregrounds images of sea turtles as a metaphor for autism. Starring Jet Li in his first truly nonaction role, this sentimental drama would appear to be worlds away from the quotidian poetics of the quietly observational South Korean film, a documentary that lacks the trappings of most narrative-driven fictionalized or sensationalized motion pictures concerning disability rights. Yet side-by-side analyses reveal that the two films have much in common visually and

thematically, which demonstrates once again *Planet of Snail*'s transnational valences.

41 Žižek, xvii.

42 Carolyn S. Stevens, *Disability in Japan* (London: Routledge, 2013), 91.

43 "Anti-Discrimination against and Remedies for Persons with Disabilities Act" (Public Law No. 8431, First Enacted April 10, 2007), National Human Rights Commission of Korea, https://www.humanrights.go.kr/site/homepage/menu/viewMenu?menuid=002003001005.

44 Chŏng Chun-ho, "Changaein kwallamsŏkŭn maen apkusŏk . . . 'mŏna mŏn' yŏnghwagwallam (Disability seats are in the front corner . . . 'far far away' movie attendance)," *Hanguk Ilbo* (Korea times), May 6, 2015, https://www.hankookilbo.com/News/Read/201510061567184835.

45 Kim Hye-wŏn and Yi Chi-ŭn, "Sigakchangaeinŭl wihan paeriŏp'ŭri yŏnghwa-wŭi kuknae chejakhyŏnhwang mit p'yohyŏnyangsik yŏngu (A study on the production situation and expression-mode of barrier-free film for visually-impaired persons)," *Yŏngsangmunhaw k'ont'ench'ŭ yŏngu* (Screen culture content study) 6 (2013): 112.

46 Yi Sŭng-jun has acknowledged that he was given creative control of *Planet of Snail*'s barrier-free version and could come up with his own captions and audio descriptions for hearing- and visually-impaired audiences (deciding which narrative information to emphasize in each scene and which portions to leave out).

47 Kim and Yi, "Sigakchangaeinŭl wihan paeriŏp'ŭri yŏnghwa-wŭi kuknae chejakhyŏn hwang mit p'yohyŏnyangsik yŏngu," 119.

48 Yi Ŭn-gyŏng, "Perip'ŭri yŏnghwa (Barrier free films)," *Han'guk yŏnghwa* (Korean cinema) 33 (December 2012): 22.

49 "Anti-Discrimination against and Remedies for Persons with Disabilities Act," National Human Rights Commission of Korea.

Chapter 7 Beyond Torture Epistephilia

1 Marina Lazreg, "Doing Torture in Film: Confronting Ambiguity and Ambivalence," in *Screening Torture: Media Representations of State Terror and Political Domination*, ed. Michael Flynn and Fabiola F. Salek (New York: Columbia University Press, 2012), 270.

2 Jung Han-seok, *Kim Dong-won* (Seoul: Korean Film Council, 2007), 15.

3 Jung, 139.

4 Quoted in Kang Sŏng-yul, Maeng Su-jin, et. al., *Hang'uk tongniptak'yu ŭi taebu Kim Tong-wŏn* (The godfather of Korean independent documentary, Kim Dong-Won) (Seoul: Sŏhae Munjip, 2010), 251.

5 Quoted in Kang et al., 60.

6 Bill Nichols, *Introduction to Documentary*, 3rd ed. (Bloomington: Indiana University Press, 2017), 137.

7 Nichols, 139.

8 Nichols, 140.

9 Quoted in Kang et al., *Hang'uk tongniptak'yu ŭi taebu Kim Tong-wŏn*, 251–252.

10 Kang et al., 223. Kim originally intended to crosscut contemporary anticommunist posters in the subway and make the point that the Red Scare is well and alive in the twenty-first century, but he edited out those inserted images.

11 Quoted in Kang et al., 230.

12 Nam Lee, "*Repatriation* and the History of Korean Documentary Filmmaking," *Asian Cinema* 16, no. 1 (Spring–Summer 2005): 17.

13 Quoted in Kang et al., *Hang'uk tongniptak'yu ŭi taebu Kim Tong-wŏn*, 220.
14 Quoted in Young-a Park, *Unexpected Alliances: Independent Filmmakers, the State, and the Film Industry in Postauthoritarian South Korea* (Stanford, CA: Stanford University Press, 2015), 120.
15 Quoted in Park, 242.
16 Park, 258.
17 Park, 271.
18 Park, 14 and 119.
19 Quoted in Park, 249.
20 Quoted in Yi Chi-yŏn, "Ppongjjaki chinshiida (The fox-trot is truth)," *Toknip Yŏnghwa* (Independent film magazine) 20 (April 2004): 38–39.
21 Quoted in Yi, 40.
22 Jung, *Kim Dong-won*, 34.
23 Before showing the completed film to Kim Yŏng-sik and other former prisoners who remained in South Korea, Kim Dong-won worried that they would be disappointed upon learning about his negative attitude toward North Korea. The filmmaker was relieved that none of them explicitly criticized or opposed his documentary. Some liked it and praised his "humanistic approach." Others thought it boring or remained reserved. Kim estimated that he had received an overall B grade from his subjects. He sent videotape and DVD copies to North Korea through informal routes three times and heard that only one of the sixty-three repatriated prisoners (Kim Sŏn-myŏng) saw it. See Kang et al., *Hang'uk tongniptak'yu ŭi taebu Kim Tong-wŏn*, 219 and 253–254; Yi Chi-yŏn, "Kim Tong-wŏn, Hwang Chŏl-min taedam (Kim Dong-won, Hwang Chŏl-min conversation)," *Toknip Yŏnghwa* (Independent film magazine) 19 (December 2003): 57–58.
24 Nichols, *Introduction to Documentary*, 41.
25 The historical information presented in this paragraph is from Ch'oe Chŏng-gi, *Pijŏnhyang changgisu* (Unconverted long-term prisoners) (Seoul: Ch'eksesang, 2002), 22–27 and 42–46.
26 Lazreg, "Doing Torture in Film," 270.
27 Jung, *Kim Dong-won*, 34–35.
28 Yi, "Kim Tong-wŏn, Hwang Chŏl-min taedam," 61–62.
29 Elizabeth Cowie, "The Spectacle of Actuality," in *Collecting Visible Evidence*, ed. Jane Gaines and Michael Renov (Minneapolis: University of Minnesota Press, 1999), 32.
30 Thomas Austin, "*Standard Operating Procedure*, the Mystery of Photography and the Politics of Pity," *Screen* 52, no. 3 (Autumn 2011): 353.
31 Patricia R. Zimmermann, *States of Emergency: Documentaries, Wars, Democracy* (Minneapolis: University of Minnesota Press, 2000), 62.
32 Wŏn Hŭi-bok, "Tak'u kamdok Kim Tong-wŏn (Documentary filmmaker Kim Dong-won)," *Kyunghyang Shinmun*, October 28, 2017, http://news.khan.co.kr/kh_news/khan_art_view.html?artid=201710281516001&code=940100.
33 Yi, "Kim Tong-wŏn, Hwang Chŏl-min taedam," 60.
34 Julia Lesage, "Torture Documentaries," *Jump Cut: A Review of Contemporary Media* 51 (Spring 2009), https://www.ejumpcut.org/archive/jc51.2009/TortureDocumentaries/3.html.
35 Nicholas D. Kristof, "Free in Seoul after 44 Years, and Still Defiant," *New York Times* (August 20, 1995), https://www.nytimes.com/1995/08/20/world/free-in-seoul-after-44-years-and-still-defiant.html.
36 Yi, "Kim Tong-wŏn, Hwang Chŏl-min taedam," 61–62.

37 Quoted in "Kim Tong-wŏn kamdokron (Kim Dong-won auteurism)," *Toknip Yŏnghwa* (Independent film magazine) 20 (April 2004), 28.
38 Austin, "*Standard Operating Procedure*, the Mystery of Photography and the Politics of Pity," 357.

Chapter 8 Story as Freedom or Prison?

Epigraph: Blaine Harden, *Escape from Camp 14: One Man's Remarkable Odyssey from North Korea to Freedom in the West*, 2nd ed. (New York: Penguin, 2015), xxvii.

1 The North Korean penal system is primarily divided into two subsystems: the *kwalliso* labor camps for political prisoners, administered by the Ministry of State Security and the primary focus of this chapter; and the *kyohwaso* penitentiaries administered by the Ministry of People's Security ("ordinary" correctional facilities where "reeducation" of the "wayward" takes place). For more information, see Barbara Demick, *Nothing to Envy: Ordinary Lives in North Korea* (New York: Spiegel and Grau, 2010), 175; Do Kyung-ok, Kim Soo-Am, Han Dong-ho, Lee Keum-Soon, and Hong Min, *White Paper on Human Rights in North Korea* (Seoul: Korea Institute for National Unification, 2015), 84–87.
2 Camp 15 also operates a separate revolutionary zone where prisoners who can be released are housed.
3 David R. Hawk, *The Parallel Gulag: North Korea's "An-Jeon-Bu" Prison Camps* (Washington: Committee for Human Rights in North Korea, 2017), 4 and 7.
4 Established in 1958, Camp 18 initially housed purged political prisoners and South Korean prisoners of war. In 1975, most political prisoners were transferred to other camps, and the administration of Camp 18 was handed over to the Ministry of Social Security (currently, the Ministry of People's Security). Since then, the camp has primarily housed nonpolitical prisoners, and 80 percent of its prisoners were freed and settled as laborers between the early 1980s and mid-1990s. After the remaining five thousand political prisoners were transferred to Kaech'ŏn, the original camp in Pongch'ang closed in 2006 or 2007. Many commentators in South Korea conjecture that Shin Dong-hyuk was born to a nonpolitical prisoner father (who might have been freed when Shin was a toddler) and grew up in Camp 18 under conditions different from those described in Harden's *Escape from Camp 14*. See Chu Sŏng-ha, "Sin Tong-hyŏk-ŭi Chŭngŏn pŏnbong ŏttŏk'e pwayahana (How to view Shin Dong-hyuk's testimony change)," *Donga Ilbo*, January 27, 2015, http://www.donga.com/news/article/all/20150127/69297930/1.
5 Harden, *Escape from Camp 14*, xii–13.
6 Hŏ Chae-hyŏn, "Kŭnŭn ch'ŏŭmbut'ŏ 18ho suyongsoesŏ saratta (He lived in Camp 18 from the beginning)," *Hankyoreh*, April 3, 2016, https://news.v.daum.net/v/JFaLSTVq4w?f=p.
7 Shin acknowledged that the septuagenarian man in the first North Korean video released in October 2014 was his father but claimed that North Korea was holding him as a hostage and had forced him to lie. Shin denied knowing the other witnesses provided by North Korea and defectors in South Korea who disputed his claims. See Sin Sang-mi, "Puk'hani norinŭn Sin Tong-hyŏk ŭi misŭt'eri ch'ujŏk (Chasing Shin Dong-hyuk's mystery watched by North Korea)," *Ilyo Sisa* (Weekly issue), March 17, 2016, http://www.ilyosisa.co.kr/news/articleView.html?idxno=97645.
8 Chu, "Sin Tong-hyŏk-ŭi Chŭngŏn pŏnbong ŏttŏk'e pwayahana"

9 Kim Myŏng-sŏng, "T'abukja Sin Tong-hyŏk ŭl tullŏsan katjja nollan (Hoax controversy surrounding Shin Dong-hyuk)," *Chosun Ilbo*, November 21, 2014, https://m.chosun.com/svc/article.html?sname=premium&contid=2014112102579.
10 Harden, *Escape from Camp 14*, xv.
11 Chŏng Yong-su, "Han'guk saltŏn T'albukja 28-myŏng Puk'han ŭro chaeippuk (28 defectors who lived in South Korea reenter North Korea)," *JoongAng Ilbo* (JoongAng daily), September 30, 2019, https://news.joins.com/article/23590770; Pae Chae-sŏng, "T'abukja 10-myŏng chung 2-myŏng 'Puk'han toragago sipta' (2 out of 10 defectors say 'I want to go back to North Korea')," *JoongAng Ilbo* (JoonAng daily), January 31, 2018, https://news.joins.com/article/22335244.
12 Jiyoung Song, "Why Do North Korean Defector Testimonies So Often Fall Apart?," *Guardian*, October 13, 2015, https://www.theguardian.com/world/2015/oct/13/why-do-north-korean-defector-testimonies-so-often-fall-apart.
13 Jonathan Dawson, "Animation," *Encyclopedia of the Documentary Film*, ed. Ian Aitken (New York: Routledge, 2006), 42.
14 Hayden White, "Historical Emplotment and the Problem of Truth," in *The History and Narrative Reader*, ed. Geoffrey Roberts (New York: Routledge, 2001), 375.
15 Harden, *Escape from Camp 14*, xiii.
16 Hillary L. Chute, *Disaster Drawn: Visual Witness, Comics, and Documentary Form* (Cambridge, MA: Harvard University Press, 2016).
17 David R. Hawk, *The Hidden Gulag: The Lives and Voices of Those Who Are Sent to the Mountains: Exposing Crimes against Humanity in North Korea's Vast Prison System*, 2nd ed. (Washington: U.S. Committee for Human Rights in North Korea, 2012).
18 Yong Kim, *Long Road Home: Testimony of a North Korean Camp Survivor* (New York: Columbia University Press, 2009); Hyok Kang, *This is Paradise! My North Korean Childhood* (London: Little, Brown, 2005); Jin-sung Jang, *Dear Leader: Poet, Spy, Escapee—A Look inside North Korea* (New York: Atria, 2014).
19 Chol-hwan Kang and Pierre Rigoulot, *The Aquariums of Pyongyang: Ten Years in a North Korean Gulag*, trans. Yair Reiner (New York: Basic, 2001), 155–164.
20 Kang and Rigoulot, 155–164.
21 Kang and Rigoulot, 163.
22 Kang and Rigoulot, 163.
23 Our use of the expression "missing picture" was inspired by the title of the director Rithy Panh's 2013 documentary *The Missing Picture*, which combines news reporting and archival footage of Pol Pot's rise to power in the filmmaker's native Cambodia, along with stop-motion animation of clay figurines to dramatize that history of collective trauma and public memory.
24 Kang and Rigoulot, *The Aquariums of Pyongyang*, 162.
25 Kang and Rigoulot, 162.
26 Michel Foucault, *Discipline and Punish: The Birth of the Prison* (New York: Vintage, 1995), 195–229.
27 Foucault, 201–203.
28 Erving Goffman, *Asylums: Essays on the Social Situation of Mental Patients and Other Inmates* (New York: Anchor, 1961).
29 Wayne Gillespie, "The Context of Imprisonment," in *Living in Prison: A History of the Correctional System with an Insider's View*, ed. Stephen Stanko, Wayne Gillespie, and Gordon A. Crews (Westport, CT: Greenwood Press, 2004), 63–64.
30 Michelle Inderbitzin, Kristin A. Bates, and Randy R. Gainey, *Deviance and Social Control: A Sociological Perspective* (Thousand Oaks, CA: SAGE Publications, 2017), 459.
31 Goffman, *Asylums*, 14.

32 Kim, *Long Road Home*, 81. See also Harden, *Escape from Camp 14*, 72.
33 Harden, *Escape from Camp 14*, 73.
34 Norma Kang Muico, "Forced Labour in North Korean Prison Camps," Anti-Slavery International, 2007, 14–19, https://digitalcommons.ilr.cornell.edu/globaldocs/2884/; Daniel Tudor and James Pearson, *North Korea Confidential: Private Markets, Fashion Trends, Prison Camps, Dissenters and Defectors* (North Clarendon, VT: Tuttle, 2015), 124 and 126.
35 Kim Yong briefly alludes to a rebellion that occurred at Camp 14 in 1990, three years before his arrival. He heard that inmates had killed several guards during the uprising, and in retaliation "jailors crammed 1,500 prisoners into an empty mine shaft and massacred them with multiple explosives." "After this," Kim states, "the guards became even more iron-fisted, but at the same time, public executions decreased in number, replaced by secret murders" (*Long Road Home*, 80).
36 Stella Bruzzi, *New Documentary: A Critical Introduction* (New York: Routledge. 2000), 40.
37 Charles Wolfe, "Historicizing the 'Voice of God': The Place of Voice-Over Commentary in Classical Documentary," in *The Documentary Film Reader: History, Theory, Criticism*, ed. Jonathan Kahana (Oxford: Oxford University Press, 2016), 264.
38 Wolfe, 264–280.
39 Bruzzi, *New Documentary*, 43.
40 Bill Nichols, *Ideology and the Image: Social Representation in the Cinema* (Bloomington: Indiana University Press, 1981), 205.
41 Bruzzi, *New Documentary*, 40–41.
42 Kim, *Long Road Home*, 81.
43 Harden, *Escape from Camp 14*, 1.
44 Harden, 1.
45 *Camp 14: Total Control Zone* (press booklet) (Munich: Global Screen, 2012), https://ff.hrw.org/sites/default/files/Camp14PressKit_0.pdf.
46 Harden, *Escape from Camp 14*, 30.
47 Besides Sacco's drawings, one can also see "the will to record through the work of the line" in Palestinian cartoonist Naji al-Ali's more politically charged output, which so incensed some readers that he became the target of a rogue Mossad member (who killed the artist in an assassination attempt). See Chute, *Disaster Drawn*, 211–213.
48 Chute, 265.
49 Quoted in Joe Coscarelli, "The Appalling Sketches of What Happens in a North Korean Prison Camp," *New York*, February 18, 2014, http://nymag.com/intelligencer/2014/02/north-koren-prison-camp-drawings-un-report.html?gtm=bottom&gtm=top.
50 Chute, *Disaster Drawn*, 265.
51 Nicole Hahn Rafter, *Shots in the Mirror: Crime Films and Society* (Oxford: Oxford University Press, 2000); David Wilson and Sean O'Sullivan, *Images of Incarceration: Representations of Prison in Film and Television Drama* (Winchester, UK: Waterside, 2004); Paul Mason, "Relocating Hollywood's Prison Film Discourse," in *Captured by the Media: Prison Discourse in Popular Culture*, ed. Paul Mason (Portland, OR: Willan, 2006), 191–209; Michelle Brown, *The Culture of Punishment: Prison, Society, and Spectacle* (New York: New York University Press, 2009); Frances Pheasant-Kelly, *Abject Spaces in American Cinema: Institutional Settings, Identity, and Psychoanalysis in Film* (London: I. B. Tauris, 2013); Alison Griffiths, *Carceral Fantasies: Cinema and Prison in Early Twentieth-Century America* (New

York: Columbia University Press, 2016); Kevin Kehrwald, *Prison Movies: Cinema behind Bars* (New York: Columbia University Press, 2017).

52 Brown, *The Culture of Punishment*, 58.

53 Rafter, *Shots in the Mirror*, 118 and 121.

54 Mason, "Relocating Hollywood's Prison Film Discourse," 191.

55 Kristen Whissel, "The Spectacle of Punishment and the 'Melodramatic Imagination' in the Classical-Era Prison Film," in *Punishment in Popular Culture*, ed. Austin Sarat (New York: New York University Press, 2015), 79–116.

56 Rafter, *Shots in the Mirror*, 163.

57 Brown, *The Culture of Punishment*, 59.

58 Rafter, *Shots in the Mirror*, 120.

59 Park's drawing of the firing squad recalls Sacco's treatment of a similar event—the execution of several Muslims in Srebrenica during the Bosnian War—in his 2011 graphic novel *Safe Area Goražde* (an image that is featured on the cover of Chute's *Disaster Drawn*).

60 In recent years, a few stories of female refugees have provided insights into the particular struggles faced by women in North Korea. For example, see Yeonmi Park, *In Order to Live: A North Korean Girl's Journey to Freedom* (New York: Penguin, 2015); Eunsun Kim's *A Thousand Miles to Freedom: My Escape from North Korea* (New York: St. Martin's, 2015).

61 Rafter, *Shots in the Mirror*, 170–171.

62 Stephan Haggard and Marcus Noland, "Repression and Punishment in North Korea: Survey Evidence of Prison Camp Experiences," *East-West Center Working Papers* 20 (October 2009): 1–39.

63 Rafter, *Shots in the Mirror*, 121.

64 Paul Ward, *Documentary: The Margins of Reality* (New York: Columbia University Press, 2005), 82–99; David Saunders, *Documentary* (New York: Routledge, 2010), 167–185; Daniel Marcus and Selmin Kara, *Contemporary Documentary* (New York: Routledge, 2016).

65 Annabelle Honess Roe, *Animated Documentary* (New York: Palgrave Macmillan, 2013), 23–26.

66 Lucia Ricciardelli, *American Documentary Filmmaking in the Digital Age: Depictions of War in Burns, Moore, and Morris* (New York: Routledge, 2015), 58.

67 Chute, *Disaster Drawn*, 210.

68 Chute, 210.

69 Ricciardelli, *American Documentary Filmmaking in the Digital Age*, 59.

70 Roe, *Animated Documentary*, 25.

71 Inderbitzin, Bates, and Gainey, *Deviance and Social Control*, 459.

72 Do et al., *White Paper on Human Rights in North Korea*, 117.

73 Dawson, "Animation," 42.

74 Andrei Lankov, "After the Shin Dong-hyuk Affair: Separating Fact, Fiction," *NK News*, February 3, 2015, https://www.nknews.org/2015/02/after-the-shin-dong-hyuk-affair-separating-fact-fiction/.

Chapter 9 Between *Scenery* and Scenario

Epigraph: Roland Barthes, *Mythologies*, trans. Richard Howard (New York: Hill and Wang, 2013), 233.

1 Darcy Paquet, *New Korean Cinema: Breaking the Waves* (New York: Columbia University Press, 2012), 109.

2 See, for example, Marcia Landy, *Cinema and Counter-History* (Bloomington: Indiana University Press, 2015), 123–184. See also Sean Redmond, *Liquid Space: Science Fiction Film and Television in the Digital Age* (London: I. B. Tauris, 2017); Daniela Berghahn and Claudia Sternberg, "Locating Migrant and Diasporic Cinema in Contemporary Europe," in *European Cinema in Motion: Migrant and Diasporic Film in Contemporary Europe*, ed. Daniela Berghahn and Claudia Sternberg (New York: Palgrave Macmillan, 2010), 12–49.

3 Steven Denney, "The Sad Plight of South Korea's Migrant Workers," *Diplomat*, April 09, 2015, http://thediplomat.com/2015/04/the-sad-plight-of-south-koreas-migrant-workers/.

4 We have written about this development elsewhere. See Hye Seung Chung, "Where Is Ronny . . . ," *Journal of Korean Studies* 18, no. 1 (Spring 2013): 147–150, and "Multiculturalism as 'New Enlightenment': The Myth of Hypergamy and Social Integration in *Punch*," *Journal of Korean Studies* 23, no. 1 (2018): 135–152; Hye Seung Chung and David Scott Diffrient, *Movie Migrations: Transnational Genre Flows and South Korean Cinema* (New Brunswick, NJ: Rutgers University Press, 2015), 208–239.

5 Michael J. Seth, *A Concise History of Korea: From Antiquity to the Present*, 2nd ed. (Lanham, MD: Rowman and Littlefield, 2016), 234 and 278.

6 Hakjae Kim, "Migrant Workers in South Korean Society," in *Democratic Governance in Northeast Asia: A Human-Centered Approach to Evaluating Democracy*, ed. Brendan Howe (New York: Palgrave Macmillan, 2015), 51–70.

7 Amnesty International, "South Korea: 'Migrant Workers Are Also Human Beings,'" August 16, 2006, 16, https://lib.ohchr.org/HRBodies/UPR/Documents/Session2/KR/AI_KOR_UPR_S2_2008anx_Migrantworkersarealsohumanbeings.pdf.

8 Sayuri Umeda, "Guest Worker Programs: South Korea," February 2013, https://www.loc.gov/law/help/guestworker/southkorea.php. See also Elizabeth Hervey Stephen, *South Korea's Demographic Dividend: Echoes of the Past or Prologue to the Future?* (Lanham, MD: Rowman and Littlefield, 2019), 98.

9 Hye-Kyung Lee, "An Overview of International Migration to South Korea," in *Social Transformation and Migration: National and Local Experiences in South Korea, Turkey, Mexico and Australia*, ed. Stephen Castles, Derya Ozkul, and Magdalena Arias Cubas (New York: Palgrave Macmillan, 2015), 83.

10 Keiko Yamanaka, "Civil Society and Social Movements for Immigrant Rights in Japan and South Korea: Convergence and Divergence in Unskilled Immigration Policy," *Korea Observer* 41, no. 4 (Winter 2010): 637–638.

11 Woo-Seon Kim, "Church and Civil Society in Korea after Democratization: The NGOs' Activism for Migrant Workers," PhD diss., University of California, 2007, 2n4.

12 EuyRyung Jun, "Virtuous Citizens and Sentimental Society: Ethics and Politics in Neoliberal South Korean," PhD diss., University of North Carolina, 2011, 33.

13 EuyRyung Jun, "'The Frog That Has Forgotten Its Past': Advocating for Migrant Workers in South Korea," *positions* 24, no. 3 (August 2016): 673.

14 Yamanaka, "Civil Society and Social Movements for Immigrant Rights in Japan and South Korea," 637.

15 Yamanaka, 638.

16 Jun, "'The Frog That Has Forgotten Its Past,'" 675.

17 Kim, "Migrant Workers in South Korean Society," 63.

18 Timothy Lim, "South Korea as an 'Ordinary' Country: A Comparative Inquiry into the Prospects for 'Permanent' Immigration to Korea," *Journal of Ethnic and Migration Studies* 38, no. 3 (February 2012): 511–512. See also Ock Hyun-ju, "Only

the Beginning for Korea's Migrant Workers' Labor Movement," *Korea Herald*, July 21, 2015, http://www.koreaherald.com/view.php?ud=20150721000840.

19 EuyRyung Jun, "Migrant Workers amidst the Waves of Volunteers: Participation and Empowerment in South Korean Migrant Advocacy," *Anthropological Quarterly* 89, no. 3 (Summer 2016): 773.

20 Jun, "'The Frog That Has Forgotten Its Past,'" 686.

21 Hyun Mee Kim, "Are There 'Proper' Migrants? The Making of Affective Personhood through Films by Migrants in South Korea," in *Visuality, Emotions and Minority Culture: Feeling Ethnic*, ed. John Nyuyet Erni (Berlin: Springer-Verlag, 2016), 63. See also Koichi Iwabuchi, Hyun Mee Kim, and Hsiao-Chuan Hsia, "Rethinking Multiculturalism from a Trans-East-Asian Perspective," in *Multiculturalism in East Asia: A Transnational Exploration of Japan, South Korea, and Taiwan*, ed. Koichi Iwabuchi, Hyun Mee Kim, and Hsiao-Chuan Hsia (Lanham, MD: Rowman and Littlefield, 2016), 7; Robert Prey, "Different Takes: Migrant World Television and Multiculturalism in South Korea," *Global Media Journal* 4, no. 1 (January 2011): 115.

22 Prey, "Different Takes," 123.

23 Kim, "Are There 'Proper' Migrants?," 59.

24 Jun, "'The Frog That Has Forgotten Its Past,'" 676.

25 Claire Lee, "What Our Dreams Say about Us," *Korea Herald*, December 10, 2013, http://www.koreaherald.com/view.php?ud=20131210000850.

26 Seonyoung Seo and Tracey Skelton, "Regulatory Migration Regimes and the Production of Space: The Case of Nepalese Workers in South Korea," *Geoforum* 78 (January 2017): 159.

27 Seo and Skelton, 160.

28 Seo and Skelton, 159–168 (emphasis added).

29 Francis Leo Collins, "Transnational Mobilities and Urban Spatialities: Notes from the Asia-Pacific," *Progress in Human Geography* 36, no. 3 (June 2012): 321.

30 Choe Sang-Hun, "Migrants Expected Warm Welcome on Korean Resort Island. They Were Wrong," *New York Times*, September 12, 2018, https://www.nytimes.com/2018/09/12/world/asia/south-korea-jeju-yemen-refugees.html.

31 Chŏng Sŏng-il, "Angae sokŭi p'unggyŏng (Scenery in the fog)," *Cine 21*, December 19, 2013, http://www.cine21.com/news/view/?mag_id=75278.

32 Chŏng Han-sŏk, "P'unggyŏng, kkum, kŏri (Scenery, dream, street)," *Cine 21*, January 16, 2014, http://www.cine21.com/news/view/?mag_id=75632.

33 Angela Ndalianis, "Art Cinema," in *The Cinema Book*, ed. Pam Cook (London: British Film Institute, 2007), 83–87.

34 Paul Shepard, *Man in the Landscape: A Historic View of the Esthetics of Nature* (Athens: University of Georgia Press, 2010), 119.

35 We wish to thank Yvonne Schulz Zinda for drawing our attention to this Beijing-based artist's work.

36 Barthes, *Mythologies*, 233.

37 Shepard, *Man in the Landscape*, 119; Larry W. Riggs, *Molière and Modernity: Absent Mothers and Masculine Births* (Charlottesville, VA: Rookwood, 2005), 14.

38 Quoted in David R. Castillo, "Monumental Landscapes in the Society of the Spectacle," in *Spectacle and Topophilia: Reading Early Modern and Postmodern Hispanic Cultures*, ed. David R. Castillo and Bradley J. Nelson (Nashville, TN: Vanderbilt University Press, 2012), 15n1 (emphasis added).

39 Shepard, *Man in the Landscape*, 119.

40 Eunsun Cho, "The Female Body and Enunciation in *Adada* and *Surrogate Mother*," in *Im Kwon-taek: The Making of a Korean National Cinema*,

ed. David E. James and Kyun Hyun Kim (Detroit, MI: Wayne State University Press, 2002), 86 and 90.

41 Cho, 90.

42 Adam Hartzell, "*Adada*," May 25, 2019, https://koreanfilm.org/kfilm80s.html.

43 Cho, "The Female Body and Enunciation in *Adada* and *Surrogate Mother*," 91.

44 Cho Hae Joang, "*Sopyonje*: Its Cultural and Historical Meaning," in *Im Kwon-taek: The Making of a Korean National Cinema*, ed. David E. James and Kyun Hyun Kim (Detroit, MI: Wayne State University Press, 2002), 148.

45 Hyangjin Lee, *Contemporary Korean Cinema: Identity, Culture and Politics* (Manchester: Manchester University Press, 2000), 122.

46 Cho Jun-hyoung, "Making Familiar Things Unfamiliar," Lee Man-hee Collection DVD liner notes (Seoul: Korean Film Archive, 2010), 52–53.

47 The Bangladeshi carpenter is reminiscent of a fictional character in another of Zhang's films, *Iri* (2008)—namely, the undocumented woodworker Mohammed Jano (played by an Iraqi-born cinematographer of the same name), who is arrested and detained by the police.

Chapter 10 "Powers of the False" and "Real Fiction"

1 Bill Nichols, *Representing Reality: Issues and Concepts in Documentary* (Bloomington: Indiana University Press, 1991), 3.

2 Nichols, 4.

3 Michael Renov, "Introduction: The Truth about Non-Fiction," in *Theorizing Documentary*, ed. Michael Renov (New York: Routledge, 1993), 2.

4 Bill Nichols, *Blurred Boundaries: Questions of Meaning in Contemporary Culture* (Bloomington: Indiana University Press, 1994), 1.

5 Jane Roscoe and Craig Hight, *Faking It: Mock-Documentary and the Subversion of Factuality* (Manchester, UK: Manchester University Press, 2001), 6.

6 Roscoe and Hight, 7.

7 Ohad Landesman, "In and out of This World: Digital Video and the Aesthetics of Realism in the New Hybrid Documentary," *Studies in Documentary Film* 2, no. 1 (2008): 36.

8 The other films in the series include *The Trip* (*Yŏhaeng*, 2009; about Jeju), *Seoul* (2009), *Lost and Found* (*Myŏl tto kŭrŏtgae kkaji*, 2009; Ch'unch'ŏn), and *To Her* (*Kŭnyŏaegae*, 2010; Busan). The series generated sequels collectively called Korea through Movies Season 2 (consisting of *Second Half* [*Matitnŭn insaeng*, 2010; Kangnŭng], *Dr. Jump* [*Toyak sŏnsaeng*, 2011; Daegu] and *Yeosu* [2011]) and Season 3 (consisting of *City of Blossom* [*Tosi ŭi p'ungnyŏn*, 2012; Puch'ŏn], *Maehwa Gwangju* [2012], and *Barbie* [2012; P'ohang]).

9 The station, Kyŏngin Pangsong, existed from 1997 to 2004.

10 Gilles Deleuze, *Cinema 2: The Time-Image* (Minneapolis: University of Minnesota Press, 1989), 133.

11 Peter X. Feng, "Becoming Chinese American, Becoming Asian American: *Chan Is Missing*," in *Screening Asian Americans*, ed. Peter Feng (New Brunswick, NJ: Rutgers University Press, 2002), 209–210.

12 Hight and Roscoe, *Faking It*, 8.

13 Gilles Deleuze, *Nietzsche and Philosophy*, trans. Hugh Tomlinson (London: Continuum, 1983), 184.

14 Daniel W. Smith, *Essays on Deleuze* (Edinburgh: Edinburgh University Press, 2012), 139.

15 Deleuze, *Cinema 2*, 137–138.

16 Before helming *The City of Cranes*, Mun directed the Polish-Korean coproduction *Taekwondo* (*Ibangin*, 1988), the dystopian science fiction *The Butterfly* (*Nabi*, 2001), and the love triangle story *The Romance* (*Romangsŭ*, 2006).

17 Mahbub Alam, *Na nŭn chiguinida* (I am an Earthian) (Seoul: Text, 2010), 136.

18 Nichols, *Representing Reality*, 39 and 43.

19 Another recent Korean film, director Chang Chin's comedy-drama *We Are Brothers* (*Urinŭn hyŏngjeimnida*, 2014), likewise foregrounds the constructedness of documentary images by showing a TV news cameraman explaining how he will record footage of the eponymous characters returning home. The young man tells the two reunited brothers (whose story of a thirty-year separation and recent reconciliation will be featured as part of a forthcoming feel-good program) that he first has to film them outside the house and then go inside the building to record them entering through the front door—an aesthetic choice, he says, that will make the documentary more dramatic, like a "narrative."

20 Landesman, "In and out of This World," 36.

21 Yi Yŏng-jin, "Rodŭmubi ija p'eik'ŭ tak'ument'ari sit'i obŭ k'ŭrein (Road movie and fake documentary *The City of Cranes*)," *Cine 21*, May 5, 2010, http://www.cine21.com/news/view/mag_id/60697.

22 The idea of a menial migrant worker turning out to be a local celebrity is also present in the first episode of *If You Were Me 3* (*Sebŏnjje sisŏn*, 2006). Titled "Muhammad the Hermit King," the episode, directed by Chŏng Yun-chŏl, focuses on a Thai chemical factory worker who is mocked for his dark skin and chastised for not wearing a security mask in the Korean workplace. One day, to escape an immigration raid, Muhammad is forced to take a day off and hide in a public bathhouse. From a bathtub, he watches a TV program in which reporters visit a Thai sea village in search of a legendary diver (the eponymous king) who is rumored to be able to stay underwater from morning to night. The king's mother tells the Korean reporters that her son has gone abroad for work and shows his picture (proving that he is none other than Muhammad).

23 Ipek A. Celik, "'I Wanted You to Be Present': Guilt and the History of Violence in Michael Haneke's *Caché*," *Cinema Journal* 50, no. 1 (Fall 2010): 71.

24 Celik, 70.

25 Yi Hŭi-yong, "Han'gukŭi Mongolindŭl (Mongolians in Korea)," *Yonhap News*, July 10, 2016, https://www.yna.co.kr/view/AKR20160706121400371.

26 Migrant workers are granted an initial work visa for a maximum of three years, after which employers can apply on behalf of workers for an extension of another year and ten months. Since 2009, employers have been allowed to renew workers' contracts and apply for an additional four years and ten months. Each term is limited to four years and ten months, and after two full terms, work visas are no longer renewable. The terms are defined in that way instead of as two consecutive five-year periods to prevent workers from being eligible for permanent residency and naturalization. See Kim Ki-don, "Ijunodongja koyonghŏgaje 10-nyŏn (10 years of the Employment Permit System)," *Pressian*, August 17, 2014, http://www.pressian.com/news/article.html?no=119539.

27 The former system was in place from 1991 to 2004 and resulted in abuse and exploitation of migrant trainees, who were forced to provide labor for nominal wages in exchange of skills training. Although the South Korean government improved working conditions under the Employment Permit System (extending basic rights such as minimum wages and industrial safety and health protection to migrant laborers), this government-run migrant labor program remains

employer-centered and did little to allow migrant workers to claim rights equal to those of their Korean counterparts. Viewers of Zhang Lu's *Ode to the Goose* (*Kunsan: Kŏwirŭl nolaehada*, 2018) are given a sense of laborers' dissatisfaction with the Employment Permit System during a scene in which a Chinese Korean protest leader expresses a common complaint during an outdoor rally, telling the small group of men and women gathered before him (some of whom are carrying cardboard signs reading "Protect Foreign Workers' Human Rights!") that it is a "ridiculous" system that "has nothing to do with us." He then explains that "the 'Employment' Permit System for Foreign Workers grants *businesses* the right to employ foreign workers, but a 'Work' Permit System for Foreign Workers is what's really important to *us* . . . This is the system that grants *us* the right to work in companies."

28 Chung Ah-young, "Illegal Foreign Workers Face Tougher Rules," *Korea Times*, March 16, 2016, http://www.koreatimes.co.kr/www/news/nation/2016/04/116_200526.html.

29 Ch'a T'ae-un, "Oegukin pulbyŏpch'eyuja 208,000 (Illegal foreigners 208,000)," *Yonhap News*, January 27, 2015, https://www.yna.co.kr/view/AKR20150127069500372.

30 "Kukkabyŏl pulbŏoch'eryu oegugin hyŏnhwang (Illegal foreign migrant status by country)," Population Statistics, Korean Statistical Information Service, October 16, 2020, http://kosis.kr/statisticsList/statisticsListIndex.do?menuId=M_01_01&vwcd=MT_ZTITLE&parmTabId=M_01_01&parentId=A.1;A_9.2;#A_9.2.

31 Kim Bo-eun, "Foreign Workers Fall Victim to Discriminatory Rules," *Korea Times*, March 21, 2016, http://www.koreatimes.co.kr/www/news/nation/2016/04/116_200833.html.

32 Simon Phillips, "A Mongolian Migrant Worker's Story," *Korea Times*, June 19, 2007, http://www.koreatimes.co.kr/www/news/special/2007/06/177_5055.html.

33 Kim, "Foreign Workers Fall Victim to Discriminatory Rules."

34 Phillips, "A Mongolian Migrant Worker's Story."

35 Mahbub, *Na nŭn chiguinida*, 155.

36 Sissy Helff, "Scapes of Refuge in Multicultural Britain: Representing Refugees in Digital Docudrama and Mockumentary," in *Multi-ethnic Britain 2000+: New Perspectives in Literature, Film and the Arts*, ed. Lars Eckstein, Barbara Korte, Eva Ulrike Pirker, and Christoph Reinfandt (New York: Rodopi, 2008), 289.

Chapter 11 Animal Rights Advocacy, Holocaustal Imagery, and Interspecies Empathy in *An Omnivorous Family's Dilemma* and *Okja*

1 Karen Joy Fowler, *We Are All Completely beside Ourselves* (New York: Plume, 2014); Melanie Joy, *Why We Love Dogs, Eat Pigs, and Wear Cows* (San Francisco: Conari, 2010).

2 Quoted in Eric Kohn, "*Okja*: How One Visit to a Slaughterhouse Turned Bong Joon Ho into a Vegan," *IndieWire*, June 7, 2017, https://www.indiewire.com/2017/06/okja-bong-joon-ho-vegan-1201839076/.

3 Han Kang, *The Vegetarian*, trans. Deborah Smith (London: Hogarth, 2015).

4 This information is derived from the Food and Agriculture Organization of the United Nations, FAOSTAT online statistical service, quoted in "List of Countries by Meat Consumption," https://data.oecd.org/agroutput/meat-consumption.htm.

5 Tom Philip, "The People Who Saw *Okja* and Became Vegetarians" *GQ*, January 26, 2018, https://www.gq.com/story/the-people-who-saw-okja-and-became-vegetarians.

6 Jacob Oller, "*Okja* Made My Carnivore Girlfriend Go Vegetarian," *Film School Rejects*, June 6, 2017, https://filmschoolrejects.com/okja-made-carnivore-girlfriend-go-vegetarian/.

7 Oller, "*Okja* Made My Carnivore Girlfriend Go Vegetarian."

8 Chris Fuhrmeister, "Will *Okja* Really Turn the World Vegan?," *Eater*, July 14, 2017, https://www.eater.com/2017/7/14/15967500/okja-netflix-movie-reaction-vegan-meat-industry.

9 Alanna Ramsier, "11 Things That Happened When People Watched *Okja*," PETA, June 30, 2017, https://www.peta.org/blog/okja-turning-people-vegan/.

10 Simon Ward, *Okja: The Art and Making of the Film* (London: Titan, 2018), 3.

11 Elmer Veldkamp, "To All That Fly or Crawl: A Recent History of Mourning for Animals in Korea," in *Mourning Animals: Rituals and Practices Surrounding Animal Death*, ed. Margo DeMello (East Lansing: Michigan State University, 2016), 55.

12 James H. Grayson, "How Folktales Contributed to the Confucianisation of Korea: Mother Green Tree Frog and Her Children," November 13, 2014, Gresham College, https://www.gresham.ac.uk/lectures-and-events/how-folktales-contributed-to-the-confucianisation-of-korea-mother-green-tree-fro.

13 Kichung Kim, *An Introduction to Classical Korean Literature: From Hyangga to P'ansori* (New York: Routledge, 2015), 204.

14 Kichung Kim, 205.

15 Kim Hŭng-gyu, *Understanding Korean Literature* (New York: Routledge, 2015), 95.

16 James H. Grayson, *Myths and Legends from Korea* (New York: Routledge, 2001), 276 (emphasis added).

17 Hwang Sun-mi, *The Hen Who Dreamed She Could Fly*, trans. Chi-Young Kim (New York: Penguin, 2013), and *The Dog Who Dared to Dream*, trans. Chi-Young Kim (New York: Penguin, 2016).

18 Hwang, *The Hen Who Dreamed She Could Fly*, 5–6.

19 Hwang, 7.

20 Hwang, *The Dog Who Dared to Dream*, 5–6.

21 Kathryn Gillespie and Rosemary-Claire Collard, introduction to *Critical Animal Geographies: Politics, Intersections and Hierarchies in a Multispecies World*, ed. Kathryn Gillespie and Rosemary-Claire Collard (New York: Routledge, 2015), 6.

22 Catherine Elick, *Talking Animals in Children's Fiction: A Critical Study* (Jefferson, NC: McFarland and Company, 2015), 53 and 103.

23 Jonathan Balcombe, *Pleasurable Kingdom: Animals and the Nature of Feeling Good* (New York: Macmillan, 2006), and "Pleasure and Animal Welfare," in *Encyclopedia of Animal Rights and Animal Welfare*, 2nd ed., ed. Marc Bekoff (Santa Barbara, CA: ABC-CLIO, 2010), 412–416.

24 Clive Phillips, *The Welfare of Animals: The Silent Majority* (Springer, 2008), 47, 49; Julien Dugnoille, "From Plate to Pet: Promotion of Trans-species Companionship by Korean Animal Activists," *Anthropology Today* 30, no. 6 (December 2014): 3–7.

25 Angi Buettner, *Holocaust Images and Picturing Catastrophe: The Cultural Politics of Seeing* (New York: Routledge, 2016), 117.

26 Wesley J. Smith, *A Rat Is a Pig Is a Dog Is a Boy: The Human Cost of the Animal Rights Movement* (New York: Encounter, 2012), 37–39.

27 Smith, 39.

28 Smith, 37.

29 Quoted in Undine Sellbach, "The Lives of Animals: Wittgenstein, Coetzee, and the Extent of the Sympathetic Imagination," in *Animals and the Human Imagination:*

A Companion to Animal Studies, ed. Aaron Gross and Anne Vallely (New York: Columbia University Press, 2012), 315.

30 Smith, *A Rat Is a Pig Is a Dog Is a Boy*, 37.

31 Charles Patterson, *Eternal Treblinka: Our Treatment of Animals and the Holocaust* (New York: Lantern Books, 2002), vii.

32 Brett Lunceford, "PETA and the Rhetoric of Nude Protest," in *Arguments about Animal Ethics*, ed. Greg Goodale and Jason Edward Black (Lanham, MD: Lexington, 2010), 100.

33 Lunceford, 101.

34 Dugnoille, "From Plate to Pet," 3–7.

35 Cass R. Sunstein, "Introduction: What Are Animal Rights?," in *Animal Rights: Current Debates and New Directions*, ed. Cass R. Sunstein and Martha C. Nussbaum (New York: Oxford University Press, 2004), 4.

36 Stephen R. L. Clark, *Animals and Their Moral Standing* (New York: Routledge, 1997), 143.

37 Frank R. Ascione, *Children and Animals: Exploring the Roots of Kindness and Cruelty* (West Lafayette, IN: Purdue University Press, 2005), 10–11.

38 In an interview, Hwang alluded to her bonding with a female pig, saying, "Although we are different species, a mother's love is the same. If the director had been male, it would have become a totally different film." Quoted in Chŏng Yong-in, "Taejidapke saŭnkosŭl poyŏjuryŏ haetta (I wanted to show pigs live like pigs)," *Chugan Kyŏnghyang* (Weekly Kyunghyang) 1126 (May 19, 2015): 19.

39 In a 2015 interview, Hwang elaborated on this point, saying: "People may love their dogs and cats or perhaps wild animals. I was the same. I separated pets from animals raised to become food. This film is my own confession." By sharing her personal journey of recognizing and accepting pigs as individual living beings with names and personalities rather than as the source of factory-processed meat, Hwang encourages viewers to draw their own ethical conclusion but hopes that some audience members will "stop eating meat altogether" while others "might support small organic farms where animal welfare is observed." Quoted in Yi Sŏn-mi, "Riŭl toejirŭl ponjŏk itnayo (Have you seen 'real pig'?)," *Salimiyagi* (Salim story) 36 (May 2015): 6–7.

40 Peter H. Lee, *An Anthology of Traditional Korean Literature* (Honolulu: University of Hawai'i Press, 2017), 605–606.

41 For an extended discussion of *A Pig's Dream*, see David Scott Diffrient, "Animals in Korean Cinema: From Absent Referent to Present-Day Predicament," *Cine-Files*, no. 14 (Spring 2019), http://www.thecine-files.com/diffrient.

42 Laura McMahon, "Screening Pigs: Visibility, Materiality and the Production of Species," in *Animal Life and the Moving Image*, ed. Michael Lawrence and Laura McMahon (London: British Film Institute, 2015), 203–218.

43 Quoted in Ryan Gilby, "*Okja* Director Bong Joon-ho: 'In Films, Animals Are Either Soulmates or Butchered,'" *Guardian*, June 16, 2017, https://www.theguardian.com/film/2017/jun/16/okja-director-bong-joon-ho-in-films-animals-are-either-soulmates-or-butchered.

44 Yasco Horsman, "Braying, Howling, Growling for Justice: Animal Personhood in Law, Literature, and Cinema," *Law and Literature* 28, no. 3 (2016): 319–334.

45 Wesley Jamison, "A Profile of Rights Activists," in *Animal Rights: History and Scope of a Radical Social Movement*, ed. Harold D. Guither (Carbondale: Southern Illinois University Press, 1998), 60.

46 Susan Finsen and Lawrence Finsen, "Animal Rights Movement," in *Encyclopedia of Animal Rights and Welfare*, ed. Marc Bekoff (Westport, CT: Greenwood Press, 1998), 51.

47 Peter Singer, *Animal Liberation* (New York: HarperCollins, 2009); see also Peter Singer, *Writings on an Ethical Life* (New York: HarperCollins, 2000), 21.

48 John M. Kistler, *People Promoting and People Opposing Animal Rights: In Their Own Words* (Westport, CT: Greenwood, 2002), 10.

49 Jordan Crucchiola and Kevin Lincoln, "Is Jake Gyllenhaal's *Okja* Performance Brilliant or Awful?," *Vulture*, June 29, 2017, https://www.vulture.com/2017/06/jake-gyllenhaal-in-okja-brilliant-or-awful.html.

50 Crucchiola and Lincoln, "Is Jake Gyllenhaal's *Okja* Performance Brilliant or Awful?"

51 Kevin Jagernauth, "Jake Gyllenhaal Talks Reactions to *Okja* Performance," *The Playlist*, August 3, 2017, https://theplaylist.net/jake-gyllenhaal-talks-reactions-ojka-performance-people-just-think-genuinely-bad-20170803/. This echoes a sentiment expressed by Jake Coyle, Writing for the *Associated Press* three days after the film's May 18, 2017, premiere at the Cannes Film Festival, Coyle calls Gyllenhaal's character "a high-strung cocktail of neuroses in cargo shorts" ("With Bong Leading the Way, Gyllenhaal Goes Big in *Okja*," *Seattle Times*, May 21, 2017, https://www.seattletimes.com/nation-world/with-bong-leading-the-way-gyllenhaal-goes-big-in-okja.

52 Andrew Parker, "*Okja*, Starring Tilda Swinton and Jake Gyllenhaal," *Gate*, June 23, 2017, https://www.thegate.ca/film/029181/review-okja-starring-tilda-swinton-jake-gyllenhaal.

53 E. Nina Rothe, "Cinematic Activism: Tilda Swinton, Jake Gyllenhaal, Bong Joon Ho, Paul Dano and the Cast of *Okja* in Cannes," *Huffington Post*, May 29, 2017, https://www.huffpost.com/entry/cinematic-activism-tilda-swinton-jake-gyllenhaal_b_592be5c2e4b08861edoccae1.

54 Peter Debruge, "Film Review: *Okja*," *Variety*, May 19, 2017, https://variety.com/2017/film/reviews/okja-review-1202434900/.

55 Ernest Mathijs, "From Being to Acting: Performance in Cult Cinema," in *Theorizing Film Acting*, ed. Aaron Taylor (New York: Routledge, 2012), 135.

56 Mathijs, 136.

57 Mathijs, 137.

58 Quoted in James Mottram, "Jake Gyllenhaal on *Okja*: The World's First Vegetarian Action Movie," *iNews*, June 22, 2017, https://inews.co.uk/essentials/jake-gyllenhaal-okja-worlds-first-vegetarian-action-movie-523702.

59 Mathijs, "From Being to Acting," 148.

60 Paul McDonald, "Spectacular Acting: On the Exhibitionist Dynamics of Film Star Performance," in *Theorizing Film Acting*, ed. Aaron Taylor (New York: Routledge, 2012), 170.

61 Justin Smith, "Vincent Price and Cult Performance: The Case of *Witchfinder General*," in *Cult Film Stardom: Offbeat Attractions and Processes of Cultification*, ed. Kate Egan and Sarah Thomas (New York: Palgrave Macmillan, 2013), 118.

62 Thomas Vernon Reed, *The Art of Protest: Culture and Activism from the Civil Rights Movement to the Streets of Seattle* (Minneapolis: University of Minnesota Press, 2005), 42; David A. Schlossman, *Actors and Activists: Politics, Performance, and Exchange among Social Worlds* (New York: Routledge, 2002), 87.

63 Chŏng Yong-bin, "'Tongmulgongjang' poda 'tongmullongjang'i tŏ natchi anŭlkka? (Isn't 'animal farm' better than 'animal factory'?)," *Chugan Kyŏnghyang* (Weekly Kyunghyang) 1126 (May 19, 2015): 16.

64 Quoted in Kim Hyŏn-ji, "Tongmul haktae, kukkaga chojanghago puch'ugyŏtta (Animal abuse engineered and encouraged by the government)," *OhMyNews*,

May 4, 2015, http://www.ohmynews.com/NWS_Web/View/at_pg.aspx?CNTN_CD=A0002104376&PAGE_CD=N0001&CMPT_CD=M0019.

65 Quoted in Hong Sang-ji, "'Kongjangsik ch'uksan, chigusangesŏ kajang angmajŏgin sisŭt'em' ('Factory-style livestock farming, the most demonic system on earth')," *JoongAng Ilbo* (JoongAng daily), August 18, 2017, http://news.joins.com/article/21855016.

66 Ko Han-sol, "Tongmulbohodanch'e K'ara, 'Okja haebang p'ŭrojekt'ŭ' shijang (Animal protection group KARA begins 'Okja Liberation Project')," *Hankyoreh*, July 15, 2017, http://www.hani.co.kr/arti/society/society_general/801523.html.

67 Yi Pyŏng-uk, "'Okja haebang p'ŭrojekt'ŭ' K'ara, yŏnghwa 'Okja' t'ŭkpyŏlsangyŏnghoe kaech'oe ('Okja Liberation Project,' KARA holds a special screening of *Okja*)," *News 1*, July 28, 2017, http://news1.kr/articles/?3060963.

68 Besides Im's contribution, *Sorry, Thanks* includes short films directed by Pak Hŏng-sik (*My Younger Brother*), O Chŏm-gyun (*Chu Chu*), and Song Il-gon (*Thank You, I'm Sorry*).

69 "South Korean Animal Groups Unite in Supporting the Inclusion of Animal Protection in a Revised Constitution," Humane Society International, April 17, 2018, https://www.hsi.org/news-media/korea-constitution-animals-041718.

70 Pak Wŏn-ho, "Why Animal Rights Matter," *Korea JoongAng Daily*, July 29, 2018, https://koreajoongangdaily.joins.com/2018/07/29/columns/Why-animal-rights-matter/3051231.html.

71 Joan Dunayer, *Animal Equality: Language and Liberation* (Derwood, MD: Ryce, 2001), 157.

72 David DeGrazia, *Animal Rights: A Very Short Introduction* (New York: Oxford University Press, 2002), 3.

73 DeGrazia, 4.

74 Anat Pick, *Creaturely Poetics: Animality and Vulnerability in Literature and Film* (New York: Columbia University Press, 2011).

Coda

Epigraph: Rosi Braidotti, *Posthuman Knowledge* (Cambridge: Polity Press, 2019), 5.

1 Today, it is not unusual to see several different rights-related topics jostling against one another in a single motion picture. For instance, the director Ch'oe Chin-sŏng's *Steel Cold Winter* (*Sonyŏ*, 2013), whose title is more accurately translated as "Girl," brings together a host of hot-button issues such as school bullying, teen suicide, sexual assault, mental disability, and even animal rights (notably, the same video footage of pigs being dumped into a pit that was shown in *An Omnivorous Family's Dilemma* [*Chapsik kajokŭi tilema*, 2014] appears in this film, during a crucial scene revolving around a dead man's past dealings with Taeyang Food Industry representatives).

2 Emily Patterson-Kane and Heather Piper, "Animal Abuse and Cruelty," in *The Oxford Handbook of Evolutionary Perspectives on Violence, Homicide, and War*, ed. Todd K. Shackelford and Viviana A. Weekes-Shackelford (New York: Oxford University Press, 2012), 261.

3 Tom Regan, *The Case for Animal Rights* (Berkeley: University of California Press, 1985), 18.

4 Braidotti, *Posthuman Knowledge*, 7.

5 Isaac Asimov, *I, Robot* (New York: Bantam Dell, 2004), 25–45.

6 Quoted in "South Korea Creates Ethical Code for Righteous Robots," *New Scientist*, March 8, 2007, https://www.newscientist.com/article/dn11334-south-korea-creates-ethical-code-for-righteous-robots/.

7 Mady Delvaux, "Report with Recommendations to the Commission on Civil Law Rules on Robots," European Parliament Committee on Legal Affairs, January 27, 2017, https://www.europarl.europa.eu/doceo/document/A-8-2017-0005_EN.html?redirect.

8 Janosch Delcker, "Europe Divided over Robot 'Personhood,'" *Politico*, April 11, 2018, https://www.politico.eu/article/europe-divided-over-robot-ai-artificial-intelligence-personhood.

9 Chang Min-sŏn, *Ingongjinŭng sidaeŭi pomjŏk chaengjŏme taehan yŏngu* (A study on legal issues in the artificial intelligence age) (Seoul: Korea Legislation Research Institute, 2018), 175.

10 Niall McCarthy, "These Countries Have the Most Robot Workers," World Economic Forum, May 1, 2019, https://www.weforum.org/agenda/2019/05/infographic-the-countries-with-the-highest-density-of-robot-workers.

11 Jennifer Robertson, *Robo Sapiens Japanicus: Robots, Gender, Family, and the Japanese Nation* (Berkeley: University of California Press, 2018), 145.

12 Gord Sellar, "Another Undiscovered Country: Culture, Reception and the Adoption of the Science Fiction Genre in South Korea," *Acta Koreana* 14, no. 1 (June 2011): 13–14.

13 Louise LePage, "'Thinking Something Makes It So': Performing Robots, the Workings of Mimesis and the Importance of Character," in *Twenty-First Century Drama: What Happens Now*, ed. Siân Adiseshiah and Louise LePage (London: Palgrave Macmillan, 2016), 284.

14 Joon Yang Kim, "The East Asian Post-Human Prometheus," in *Pervasive Animation*, ed. Suzanne Buchan (New York: Routledge, 2013), 182–183.

15 Kim, 180.

16 Kim, 182.

17 Steve Choe, "The Invention of Romance: Park Chan-wook's *I'm a Cyborg, but That's OK*," in *Simultaneous Worlds: Global Science Fiction Cinema*, ed. Jennifer L. Feeley and Sarah Ann Wells (Minneapolis: University of Minnesota Press, 2015), 210–222.

18 Min-Sun Kim and Eun-Joo Kim, "Humanoid Robots as 'The Cultural Other,'" *AI and Sociology* 28, no. 3 (August 2013): 320.

19 Braidotti, *Posthuman Knowledge*, 12.

20 Braidotti, 8.

21 Braidotti, 15.

22 Kim and Kim, "Humanoid Robots as 'The Cultural Other,'" 310–311.

23 Cary Wolfe, *What Is Posthumanism?* (Minneapolis: University of Minnesota Press, 2010), xv.

24 Kim and Kim, "Humanoid Robots as 'The Cultural Other,'" 310–311.

25 R. L. Rutsky, *High Technē: Art and Technology from the Machine Aesthetic to the Posthuman* (Minneapolis: University of Minnesota Press, 1999), 21.

26 Rutsky, 21–22.

27 Braidotti, *Posthuman Knowledge*, 11.

Index

About the Authors

HYE SEUNG CHUNG is a professor of film and media studies at Colorado State University and the author of *Hollywood Asian: Philip Ahn and the Politics of Cross-Ethnic Performance*, *Kim Ki-duk*, and *Hollywood Diplomacy: Film Regulation, Foreign Relations, and East Asian Representations* (Rutgers University Press). She is the coauthor of *Movie Migrations: Transnational Genre Flows and South Korean Cinema* (Rutgers University Press).

DAVID SCOTT DIFFRIENT is a professor of film and media studies at Colorado State University and the author of *M*A*S*H* and *Omnibus Films: Theorizing Transauthorial Cinema*. He is the coauthor of *Movie Migrations: Transnational Genre Flows and South Korean Cinema* (Rutgers University Press).